D0613043

THE AUTUMN GARDEN
Hellman's brilliant Chekhovian drama of lost loves and dreams among people gathered at a Gulf of Mexico resort.

CAMINO REAL
Williams's theatrical fantasy with its sense of carnival, features masque characters such as Lord Byron, Kilroy, and Don Quixote.

TEA AND SYMPATHY
Anderson's sensitive and honest portrait of an adolescent's sexuality and the compassion of an older woman.

A HATFUL OF RAIN
Gazzo's powerful play of drug addiction and the failings of modern American life.

THE ZOO STORY
Albee's shocking, absurdist drama of sudden violence during a chance encounter in Central Park.

OTHER LAUREL AMERICAN DRAMA SERIES EDITIONS:

Famous American Plays of the 1920s
Selected and introduced by Kenneth Macgowan

Famous American Plays of the 1940s
Selected and introduced by Henry Hewes

Famous American Plays of the 1960s
Selected and introduced by Harold Clurman

Famous American Plays of the 1970s
Selected and introduced by Ted Hoffman

Famous American Plays of the 1980s
Selected and introduced by Robert Marx

QUANTITY SALES

Most Dell books are available at special quantity discounts when purchased in bulk by corporations, organizations, and special-interest groups. Custom imprinting or excerpting can also be done to fit special needs. For details write: Dell Publishing, 666 Fifth Avenue, New York, NY 10103. Attn.: Special Sales Department.

INDIVIDUAL SALES

Are there any Dell books you want but cannot find in your local stores? If so, you can order them directly from us. You can get any Dell book in print. Simply include the book's title, author, and ISBN number if you have it, along with a check or money order (no cash can be accepted) for the full retail price plus $1.50 to cover shipping and handling. Mail to: Dell Readers Service, P.O. Box 5057, Des Plaines, IL 60017.

Selected and introduced by
LEE STRASBERG

FAMOUS
AMERICAN PLAYS
OF THE

1950s

Foreword by Gordon Davidson

PROPERTY of ST. JOHNS COUNTY PUBLIC LIBRARY

LAUREL

ST. AUGUSTINE
FLORIDA
32084

A LAUREL BOOK
Published by
Dell Publishing
a division of
The Bantam Doubleday Dell Publishing Group, Inc.
666 Fifth Avenue
New York, New York 10103

Copyright © 1962 by Lee Strasberg
Foreword © 1988 by Gordon Davidson

All rights reserved. No part of this book may be reproduced or
transmitted in any form or by any means, electronic or
mechanical, including photocopying, recording, or by any
information storage and retrieval system, without the written
permission of the Publisher, except where permitted by law.

The trademark Laurel® is registered in the U.S. Patent and
Trademark Office.

ISBN: 0-440-32491-2

Printed in the United States of America
Published simultaneously in Canada

New Dell Edition

September 1988

10 9 8 7 6 5 4 3 2 1

KRI

Contents

Foreword   ix

INTRODUCTION   13

BENITO CERENO / *Robert Lowell* 23

HOGAN'S GOAT / *William Alfred* 79

WE BOMBED IN NEW HAVEN / *Joseph Heller*   175

THE INDIAN WANTS THE BRONX / *Israel Horovitz* 275

THE BOYS IN THE BAND / *Mark Crowley* 311

Foreword

When I first scanned the Famous American Plays series, I felt somewhat awed by the task of composing a foreword to all the volumes. The idiosyncratic nature of the series—an attribute I find quite appealing—dictates that each volume not only embody the temperament of a decade but also reflect the spirit of the editor selecting the plays. These editors, an assortment of distinguished critics and theater practitioners including Kenneth Macgowan, Harold Clurman, Henry Hewes, Lee Strasberg, Ted Hoffman, and Robert Marx, define "the best" differently with each decade, each volume, even from play to play.

Yet somehow, despite the bent of the individual editor and with all the regrettable omissions—many choices shaped by the limitation of plays available for publication at the time where, for example, is arguably the most famous and continuously developing twentieth-century American playwright Neil Simon?)—I still believe that the series comprises a living document to a crucial aspect of this century's American theater: the evolution and shifting emphasis in theme, approach, and even location. American theater has been on the move from Broadway to off-Broadway, from off-Broadway to off-off-Broadway, and finally from the singular concentration in and among the streets of New York to what has become the most exciting transformation of this century— the decentralization of American professional theater to include virtually every state in the union. The plays in these volumes reveal this journey and reflect the incredible changes not only in the theater but in our culture. The process of decentralization has affected and will continue to affect the very nature of the plays being written and the audiences attending them.

In the volumes covering the 1920s through the 1950s, all the plays—except for Eugene O'Neill's *The Moon of the Caribbees*—were Broadway plays. In the 1960s, only two plays included made it to Broadway from off-Broadway and from a regional theater. In the 1970s, only one did, although two others later moved to or reappeared briefly on Broadway. In the 1980s, *all* the plays started either off-Broadway, off-off-Broadway, or in regional theaters around the country, and three of them subsequently have appeared on Broadway.

The shifting emphasis in theme can be seen through the eyes of those who introduce each volume. In the 1920s the theater was considered a scene of "curious conflict" between realism and a freer form of theatricality. In the next decade, attention to the socioeconomic details of an individual's psychological condition became what Harold Clurman called "the most significant difference" between the theater of the twenties and the thirties. What informs many of the plays in that collection is a sense of political alertness married to an almost naive inexperience with actual events. Many of these plays, from *Idiot's Delight* to *End of Summer*, show what Clurman described as *interest* in subject matter rather than any authentic familiarity with it.

In the forties, we find a drama that reveals a new sense of history and a new relationship to it. As the editor of that volume reflects, "History is no longer regarded as a clear and orderly process of cause and effect, but rather as a series of traffic snarls and collisions of many people and forces moving in different directions." Plays written prior to the tragedy at Pearl Harbor give none-too-buried warnings of the imminence of danger, yet all the while they continued to reassure audiences that all would be well as long as everybody maintained faith in American hope and glory. But the theater, like the country, was trying to learn some very hard lessons by sidestepping the mistakes of past generations, on and off-stage. *Home of the Brave* and *All My Sons* were both cautionary tales as much as they were realistic studies of the cost and consequences of war. The end of the conflict overseas brought renewed optimism on the boards, a response to victory that led to enthusiastic, if slightly ill-informed, ideas about theatrical innovation. But the audience for early ex-

erimental theater turned out to be far smaller than antici-
ated, although directors like Elia Kazan were making great
nd subtle strides in discerning authorial personality—what
ditor Henry Hewes calls "subconscious searchings"—in the
ork of newly discovered playwrights like Tennessee
Villiams.

Lee Strasberg found "numerous important playwrights
but] fewer important plays in the 1950s." Yet Strasberg,
imself an innovator in modern acting technique, discerns a
niquely modern thematic perspective in these plays in the
using of present, past, and future time and in the revelation
f psychological insight. Strasberg anticipates the founding
f a "new theater" that would "broaden the vision of man on
he stage" by its "awareness and perception of drama in
haracters to which drama had never been previously at-
ributed, more subtle and more varied sense of relationship
etween people, and a deeper penetration of their motiva-
on." It was an exciting time for the actor, the first genera-
on to be influenced by Strasberg's ideas. Unfortunately, too
ew of the plays chosen for that volume proved of lasting
mportance. Even Strasberg seems to have suspected this—
e ends his introduction, written in 1962, with a poignantly
ptimistic look to the impending creation of a repertory
eater at Lincoln Center, under the guiding spirit of then-
resident and Mrs. Kennedy.

Thus, as illustrated by the impressive list of plays collected
these volumes, the plays of the twenties, thirties, forties,
d fifties embody the evolution of the theater on many
vels. In the sixties, however, was *revolution*. A remarkable
ansformation had its true beginning in the early 1960s.

With the help of the Ford Foundation and the vision of W.
acNeill Lowry, Vice President for the Arts, the theater and
eater professionals began to venture out from New York
ity—not as they used to, tied to a rubber band that snapped
em back at the end of a tour or summer stock engagement
time for the "new season on Broadway"—but as pioneers
d adventurers to new lands, eager to set down roots and
eate some sense of permanence in cities all across the
nited States, and to explore and reflect those communities
stage. In 1963 the Tyrone Guthrie Theater opened its

doors in Minneapolis, in 1965 the Long Wharf in Ne
Haven, Connecticut. In 1965 ACT traveled from Pittsburg
to Chicago and finally set up a permanent home in Sa
Francisco. In 1964 the Actors Theatre of Louisville opene
its doors. In 1963 the Seattle Repertory Theatre began, an
in April 1967 the Mark Taper Forum in Los Angeles we
comed audiences for the first time. All in all, since that tim
309 theaters have been established in 43 states and 150 citie
They were founded by individual artists, by partners, and b
collectives. Some have inherited the structure of not-for
profit corporate entities with boards of directors, some hav
built buildings, some have established local, regional, an
national profiles, and all have together produced an eno
mous body of work in less than thirty years. The Theatr
Communications Group was formed in New York City as
service organization to bind this far-flung community to
gether through meetings, publications, and advocacy.

I felt the excitement of this revolution firsthand; in fac
my career echoes the movement of the times. While when
first began looking for work in the theater in 1958 (I was sti
in the army), I thought about the possibility of finding wor
outside of New York, it was *in* New York that my life i
theater had really begun: seeing Laurence Olivier in tha
famous double bill *Oedipus the Critic* (that memorable offstag
howl); seeing the Lunts, Laurette Taylor, Gertrude Law
rence, Lee J. Cobb, Ray Bolger, John Gielgud, Judith Ande
son, Melvyn Douglas, Paul Muni, Ralph Richardson. Wha
performers! But, at that time, my options outside New Yor
were limited. There was summer stock; there was colleg
theater (my dad taught and directed at Brooklyn College
There was Nina Vance and the Alley Theatre in Housto
Margo Jones in Dallas; Zelda Fichandler at the Arena Stag
in Washington, D.C.; the Cleveland Playhouse under F
Elmo Lowe; and a couple of theaters in San Francisco, in
cluding The Theatre of the Golden Hind and Herbert Bla
and Jules Irving's Actors Workshop. And that was about it

I felt compelled to start in New York. I chose a position a
an apprentice stage manager at the American Shakespea
Festival. I worked with and under the mentorship of Joh
Houseman, Jack Landau, Jean Rosenthal, Bernard Gerste

Marc Blitzstein, David Hays, Dorothy Jeakins. It was as an assistant to Houseman that, finally, in 1964, I made my way to Los Angeles, where John was directing a production of *King Lear* starring Morris Carnovsky for The Theatre Group, a professional theater on the campus of UCLA. Three years later I opened the Mark Taper Forum, a 750-seat thrust stage in the Los Angeles Music Center. In April 1987 we celebrated the twentieth anniversary of our continuous production of plays: world and American premieres, classic revivals, young people's theater, and a host of developmental programs. The Taper is one of a network of theaters, a *family* of theaters that, though situated differently, still have many similarities: in structure, in attempts at creating subscription audiences, in nurturing artists, in revealing the life of the community they serve.

The regional theater movement began as an alternative to the commercial pressures of Broadway and as an alternative to living in New York City. It therefore initially concerned itself with the presentation of classics, modern and ancient, that were done commercially only sporadically. Dedicated to the development of companies of actors, designers, directors, these theaters preserved and reinterpreted the living library: Shakespeare, Shaw, Molière, Ibsen, Pirandello, the Greeks, as well as the American giants of the thirties, forties, and fifties. In fact, many of the plays reproduced in this series were and are the staples of regional theater programming. Audiences were willing to go to a theater with a recognizable, and to some extent familiar, list of plays performed and produced well. Actors and directors and designers searched for ways to make these plays come alive for contemporary audiences. These same audiences tended to shy away from new plays or unknown authors, unless they had the imprimatur, the stamp of approval, of a Broadway success (or at least a decent enough run on Broadway). Work on the "great plays" gave actors and directors a chance to stretch themselves and refine their skills (voice, movement, diction).

Then, to borrow from a book popular in the sixties, something happened. Concurrent with the social and cultural revolution with which we are all so familiar, Broadway really began to decline. (The "fabulous invalid," as it was known, began to look terminal.) Simultaneously, New York became a less hospitable or even challenging environment for artistic creativity. The reasons for this have been documented; they include soaring production costs, escalating ticket prices, urban blight, urban flight, expense account theatergoing and the loss of the regular audience; competition for attention and talent from TV and movies; and, to varying degrees, the usurpation by other media (including popular music) of the content, subject matter, and even form that was previously the territory and province of the theater.

And in the sixties the artists took to the streets, lofts, basements, churches, and parks to write the plays that began to speak of their horror, outrage, and pain over war, assassination, and the gradual corruption of the spirit exemplified by Saran Wrap and defense budgets. As Edward Parone wrote in his introduction to a collection of plays entitled *Collision Course*, these plays were "written on impulse in short bursts that seem to want to impinge directly upon their audiences without the barrier of intellect or manners or preconceptions." And in turn the regional theater began to turn its attention to the presentation of new plays (note: some, like the Mark Taper Forum and the New York Public Theater, did this from the beginning), and with this came the creation of a system for developing new theater pieces through commissions, readings, laboratories, workshops, festivals, conferences, and the use of small venues (second spaces) as homes for venturesome work.

Like many revolutions, these changes grew of necessity; only in retrospect do we see their far-reaching effects. Not only did these developments allow audiences throughout the United States to participate in the adventure and excitement of creating and discovering new works of art, but they changed or reversed the flow of material and talent (plays, playwrights, actors, directors, and designers) both out of New York and back. Broadway is no longer the generator of material and the source of personnel for the theater. It is a grand and heady as well as pain-inducing receiver of the fruits of theater from elsewhere—traditionally London and now more and more the rest of the United States.

The decentralization of the American theater is the most

challenging and enduring transformation of the last three decades. It's both the best and worst thing that could have happened, because it also makes it that much more difficult to see, taste, judge, be influenced by, and know one another's work, and it puts an extra pressure on the need to share and find some ground upon which artists and audience have common experiences. The lack of a center or single pulse makes the gift of a collection like this one, a compilation of all our work, that much more valuable.

The decentralization also has brought to the surface a whole new set of problems, questions, esthetics, and challenges for the theater of the future. First and foremost is the need for a belief in the theater as an art form rather than as a business that produces a product which is either a success (a hit that makes money) or a failure (a flop and a financial disaster). The theater searches for survival as an institution, with all of the responsibilities an institution has to itself and its community. It serves a community and must be aware of the cultural, ethnic, and social diversity of its artists and its audience. It can speak to the specifics of a city, state, region, and to a nation. It can give voice to the needs of the community as well as reflect the hopes and aspirations of a wide cross-section of its population. It can be a place that nurtures, trains, and develops talent. It can nurture the soul.

Some challenges are immediate, even practical. These resident regional theaters are housed in buildings as diverse in size and shape as their location. We have birthed in this same time period thrust stages, arena stages, small theaters, black boxes, *and very few* conventional proscenium theaters. Our writers are therefore exploring ways to create new forms of realism, naturalism, expressionism, and theatricality that let us know we are in a theater and not in front of a movie or television screen.

Other challenges are intellectual or spiritual. The "death of Freud" and the journey through the Jungian jungle may lead us to a more mythic search to satisfy our spiritual hunger and needs. The desire to better come to grips with our political and social realities can lead writers to explorations and insights unattainable on *Nightline*, but possible also because of the new access to information that even Johnny

Carson's nightly monologue provides.

Language and metaphor, technology in the service of (revealing, not dehumanizing) the individual, and acting that examines both the truth of human behavior and the extraordinary capacity of humans to perform with style, skill, and bravery—these are the possibilities that challenge the leadership of this network of theaters today in the United States.

Finally, the theater has to face its relationship and responsibility to the changing multicultural essence of this country. The challenges of nontraditional casting, of cross-cultural writing and nonhomogeneous audiences are the big questions for the future. These volumes of famous American plays, impressive and important as they are, still reflect a harsh reality: in over seven decades, the collection contains only two black playwrights, no Hispanic or Asian-American writers, and only three women. These plays therefore reflect a theater in desperate need to get in touch with its own heart and the heartbeat of the society in which it dwells. One can only imagine what future volumes will contain and what extraordinary leaps of imagination, heart, and mind they will reveal. One hopes the series will continue long into the twenty-first century as a tribute to a theater that reflects a diversity of ideas, a wealth of voices, and a fervent belief in the centrality of the art to all our lives.

—Gordon Davidson

Introduction

We no longer look for a clear line of progress and development; we are used to the idea that life is a constant flux and struggle. We recognize that the life of the theatre doesn't conveniently fall into decades, so we do not expect the drama of the fifties to show such logic of development that there is a definite sequence of progress, or of decay. Yet, looking back at the fifties, what are we to make of a theatre which inspires the feeling of having hit bottom, yet produces the greatest American play of our time—O'Neill's *Long Day's Journey Into Night*? The public in the Broadway theatre is satiated and bored, and the public off Broadway is growing; the audience in the large city centers is decreasing and the college and community theatres are hungry for good plays. We have numerous important playwrights, yet fewer important plays. (In what other country would playwrights of the caliber of Odets and Saroyan be permitted to remain idle?) The plays that we do have are vilified as decadent, morbid, sadistic, and perverse, because of the characters they deal with.

This criticism has become so widespread and outspoken in the last decade that it actually influenced an author of the caliber of Tennessee Williams to write a different type of play. While I would like to see a world that offers more hope than the present period of crisis, cold war, and personal frustration, I cannot share the feeling of those who practically make our playwrights responsible for the presence of these difficulties. I remember the first time I came in contact with this feeling; it was in the twenties, when I had just witnessed what has remained one of the memorable performances of my life—Pauline Lord in O'Neill's *Anna Christie*. I attended a lecture by a vice-president of the Drama League of America summarizing the season, and you can imagine the shock to my youthful susceptibilities to hear his displeasure at the type of characters O'Neill was describing. "Now in all honesty," he asked, "would you invite a person of that sort to your home to eat at your table?" This implication that dramatic characters were to be judged as dinner partners was something new to me. I had never considered whether Oedipus, Lear, Othello, or Macbeth would make good dinner companions. I imagine they would be rather frightening. I was almost equally taken aback recently when, in talking to a highly intelligent theatre visitor from abroad, I found it necessary to explain that, of course, Tennessee Williams was not in favor of the kind of world he wrote about. If there is despair and horror in his plays, it is a result of the pain he suffers at the sight of it around him.

Yet somehow these critics seem able to divorce themselves completely from the characters in the play. A playwright friend of mine told me of an evening at Lindy's where some people were complaining about his plays. "There are no people like that," they said. "Why not write about people like us?" One of the men at the table had recently flown South to threaten his wife with a revolver, another had claustrophobia and couldn't be left alone in a room, a third had constant change of moods which drove him to despair. . . .

We should, by now, be properly forewarned against the malicious error that if a playwright holds up the world's evils, this means he upholds them. We should remember that the Elizabethan theatre—and this, of course, consists largely of the works of Shakespeare—has been characterized as little more than dramas of "obscure unendurable realities, revolting images of sexual appetites and activities" with "a fillip of the excessive, the devious, the perverse." There is even a contemporary parallel in the possibility that Shakespeare left the theatre out of the feeling that the time for his great tragedies had passed, and that the audience now demanded the new romantic comedies of Beaumont and Fletcher. In Restoration times, Shakespeare was castigated in such terms as "there is not a monkey but understands Nature better, nor a Pug in Barbary that has not a truer taste of things." Do not imagine that the beauty of Shakespeare's writing mitigated this attitude. Of Desdemona's language it was said, "No woman bred out of a pigsty could talk so meanly." And, finally, the critic Thomas Rymer, from whom the above stems, caps his criticism by his patriotic complaint of "how could Shakespeare treat the character of Iago, the soldier, as a villain instead of the open-hearted, frank, plain dealing character confidently worn by them for some thousands of years?" Professor Marvin Rosenberg, from whose excellent book *The Masks of Othello* the above material is taken, remarks: "English drama for two centuries was to suffer from this critical typing." It seems we have not finished with it yet. (And remember, the French are just passing out of the stage of talking about Shakespeare as a barbarian.)

There is a more respectable attitude of criticism, one that does not stoop to the social tea party approach. It speaks in the name of the beliefs of the dignity of man. It wishes to see less of the hopelessness and impotence of man, less of negativism and defeatism. It questions whether we should be compelled to face the horrid truth that man is a failure and the universe he inhabits meaningless. Surely, one cannot disagree with these demands. Especially not when they are couched in even more seemingly moderate terms, along with the willingness to accept the premise that the duty of the artist is to state the truth as he sees it and that duty comes before any supposed duty to cheer up his readers. He is simply asked to see the whole truth rather than that part of it which it has become the fashion to dwell upon exclusively. "Is, in other words, his own condition and that of his acquaintance as bad as his works suggest?" And it is here that the artist of the past is brought as witness. After all, he did see the seamy side of things . . . but with what beauty and glory.

We sentimentalize the past as we tend to sentimentalize our own youth, looking back on it from the difficulties of the present. We forget that the laughter of Molière brought him to an unhallowed grave because the Church would not permit him to be buried in Christian ceremony, that the beauty of Caravaggio brought him to the halls of the Inquisition, that an artist of the spiritual power and beauty of Rembrandt was criticized as an artist of the gutter who painted with colors of dirt, that the beautiful and magnificent works of many musicians were received with outcries of rage and disdain. We forget that the themes and ideas of Ibsen and Shaw caused such vituperative criticism that it was even difficult to appreciate the craftsmanship and brilliance which now seem so evident. We fail to realize that the plays of the great dramatists of the past in their own time must have made upon their contemporary audience the same frightening and "abrasive" impression that we complain of in our own playwrights.

The reason for the development of the Aristotelian theory of catharsis may derive precisely from the need to explain to an audience why they should be subjected to the spectacle of these horrors. The catalogue of crimes committed in Aeschylus's play *Agamemnon* to show that sin begets sin, the sequence of events in Sophocles's *Oedipus*, would automatically create censorship problems in many cities of America if these were new plays. Maybe Matthew Arnold was right when he wrote of Sophocles that he "saw life steadily, and saw it whole." But even Sophocles himself could write at the end of his life that, "Not to be born is, past all praying, best," and he summarized the basic uncertainty of life by the line, "Human life, even in its utmost splendor and struggle, hangs on the edge of an abyss."

We look at these plays through the gauze of memory. The meanings are now diffused, the actuality of their words now become symbolic images, the events on the stage impersonal and artistic . . . appreciated without feeling that it means you, except in the abstract. It may be true that there is a difference in what our playwrights feel today. Perhaps they feel that we are not just on the edge of an abyss, but are finally being pushed over, that man's inhumanity to man has reached a peak from which our idealistic beliefs have not saved us, that man's ability to destroy himself is not any more in the hands of Fate or the Gods, but in his own fallible hands. So they turn our eyes to this dreadful spectacle in various ways, personal, impersonal, subjective, political, or otherwise. But are they to be blamed for what they see? Are they to be blamed for what they describe? "Be it life or death, we crave only reality," wrote Thoreau. Perhaps many of these terrifying, perverted, morbid visions of reality will, like the visions of Bosch, look equally beautiful to the distant future. The cry will be muted, the pain dulled, the significance and meaning become bolder and more transparent. Our playwrights should be encouraged to look even more deeply, more intensely, to shed the fear of stating their visions. Only then can their art fulfill its function to hold, as it were, the mirror up to nature. The aesthetic criticism of our creative artists can be even more harmful and dangerous than was the political restraint in the fifties.

There exists another criticism of our contemporary playwrights, coming mainly from literary critics and

academic students of drama. Accustomed to the study
and analysis of texts, they find the literary quality of
our modern drama lamentably poor and unpoetic, and
the intellectual content on an equally low plane. This
might be well enough if it were merely a demand for
more intense dramatic forms of expression, but it
leads to strange conclusions. Since they recognize that
the language is the result of the character and since
they realize that characters today do speak differently,
express themselves haltingly, then away with modern
characters. Back to characters of the past, back to spectacle, back to symbols—lively symbols to clothe what
is otherwise too bitter. These critics now study Shakespeare, but in Elizabethan times they would have criticized him as a popular dramatist who was lowering the
standard of classical drama as exemplified by Ben Jon-
son, and perhaps have gone even farther, as did the
French and the Restoration in considering him tasteless
and "barbarian." In Greek times, they would have
criticized Euripides for "his realism, his interest in
abnormal psychology, his portraits of women in love,
his new and emotional music, his unorthodoxy, his
argumentativeness." They might even have been responsible for his exile.

This problem cannot be dismissed quite so sum-
marily as I seem to be doing. But on the other hand, I
am old enough to remember the shock and excitement
of the language of many of the modern plays. I remember the actual physical reaction to the language of
What Price Glory? I remember the thrill to the language of Clifford Odets which literally came from the
stage like bullets from a machine-gun. Perhaps it is
now old hat, and we are so accustomed to it that we
fail to evaluate it correctly. Maybe it needs the film of
memory to bring proper perspective to it, to see it as a
summary of an age. But what can be said for an intellectual critic for whom *Long Day's Journey Into
Night* is made up of "a mother who takes dope, a tuber-

cular son, a suicidal other son, a jack-of-all-noise father
. . . mutual hatred, morbid love, hysterical weeping,
soul-clawing"? And lesser plays such as Jack Gelber's
The Connection and Michael Gazzo's *A Hatful of
Rain* . . . just plays about dope addiction?

One can only assume that by the same standard
Othello is only a play about a handkerchief. Inherent
in this attitude is ignorant sentimentalization of the
past and snobbish condescension to the present. But
more fundamental is ignorance of the basic development of drama and theatre away from the word toward
a picturing of an event on the stage by the characters
who participate in it. I have read many plays before
production and I continue to be surprised and startled
by what happens to these words on the stage. I remember reading Odets's *Awake and Sing*. It was one of the
best first scripts by a dramatist that I have ever read.
The language seemed a little odd. Yet, I was unprepared for a moment of poetic creation which everyone
who saw the Group Theatre production must surely
remember.

The grandfather is left alone on the stage with Moe
Axelrod, the war veteran embittered by life. Everyone
has gone. Moe wanders around, looks for an orange.
"No oranges, huh?—what a dump!" They sit down to
play cards. The grandfather goes to his room, puts on a
record, and through the half-open door of the bedroom, one hears the strains of Caruso singing, "O Para-
diso." They play. The grandfather explains, "From
'L'Africana,' a big explorer comes to a new land.
Caruso stands on the ship and looks on a Utopia. You
hear? 'Oh Paradise! Oh paradise on earth! Oh blue
sky, oh fragrant air. . . .'" "Ask him does he see any
oranges?" remarks Moe.

This was one of the great moments on the stage—
poetic, strangely dramatic and theatrical. There are
few words, little plot, conflict, or the kind of categories
dear to dramatic analysts. This is playwriting. This is

theatre. This is what the modern dramatist creates, without words, without plot.

I remember another moment in Odets's *Country Girl*. The actor who is being given his chance for a comeback is rehearsing with his young director. It is late at night. They are tired. The actor tells the story of his difficulties with his wife (which later turn out to be fictitious). Suddenly she appears. She has come to walk him home. There is a moment of embarrassment. Then suddenly she turns towards the audience, walks down to the footlights and, looking at the darkened auditorium, says, "Nothing is quite so mysterious and silent as a dark theatre. . . . A night without a star . . ."

Each performance, at this moment, you could feel a shiver of experience run through the audience. Maybe it was the dual sense of being there and yet not being there. Whatever it was, it was a moment of poetry, of theatre, of drama, without the words a Shakespeare or any classic dramatist would have used.

One can have varying opinions of Tennessee Williams's *The Glass Menagerie*, but on the stage something is created which was never previously created in drama—a sense of remembering. Not flashbacks—but somehow what is transpiring on the stage is actually being remembered. I do not know how this is achieved. I can only testify to its presence. When you miss this, you miss the basic core of the play, and no bandying with words and literary categories can make up for it.

Arthur Miller's *Death of a Salesman* has posed tough problems for the literary fraternity. Is it really a tragedy, or is the audience confusing pathos with tragedy? Is it possible for Willy Loman, its protagonist, to be a tragic figure without fulfilling the requisites for such a figure? One critic said, "Willy's suburban little man's ambitions and his problems as a superannuated employee do not qualify him for a role in classic tragedy." In the meantime, one of the greatest achievements in playwriting is left unrecognized. This is the ability to fuse present, past, and future into one unified moment, a typically modern recognition based on modern psychology fused with modern theatrical vision. It is not mechanical flashbacks swinging back and forth as a storytelling device as commonly used in the movies and in television. But the present suddenly ignites the past and returns to the present to create the future. Never before or since has this been done on the stage. Yet it is almost unrecognized and remains unappreciated for the epoch-making achievement that it is. This is modern drama . . . this is modern theatre . . . this is the broadening of the vision of man on the stage, the awareness and perception of drama in characters to which drama had never been previously attributed, new uses of time and space on the stage, more subtle and more varied sense of relationships between people, and a deeper penetration of their motivation. To read plays as a succession of words intended for literary analysis is to miss the nature of drama and of theatre.

The theatre generation after the first World War felt itself to be part of a new dream which it hoped would lead to a new theatre. It was not to be words, scenery, and acting as separate elements uniting into a somewhat mechanical entity. It was to be the word transfigured from its purely logical and literary meaning on a page by the living presence of the actor whose creation of the moment, the event, the situation, brought out or added dramatic meaning to the word. The actor was not to be simply a reciter with illustrative gestures, as described by the acting manuals, but the creator of the character visioned by the dramatist, able to create thought, behavior, sensation and emotion. The actor's presence and behavior was to be changed and affected by the scenery, which was no longer a static background, or an interior decorator's design, or a picturesque tableau, but was the world upon which and within which the actor lived, and which helped or hindered the development of the dramatic logic. The lighting on the stage was to be a living, moving "actor" which contributed not simply the time of day but the atmosphere and inner pulsation of the scene . . . all these elements and more leading to what we proudly proclaimed in the words of Edward Gordon Craig to be "the art of the theatre."

This dream was shattered not by the development of the realistic drama (that beloved bugaboo for everything wrong with the theatre today) but by the fact that the central element for the creation of the art of the theatre—a coherent unified company of actors with artistic leadership to express its vision of the dramatist's intention—was missing. All modern efforts in the theatre have recognized the importance of this relation between theatre and drama. When Antoine created the Thèâtre Libre, he pointed out that plays representing his point of view already existed but that these plays were not appreciated because they were produced in an old-fashioned way. Scenes that demanded intimacy and reality were played artificially with the actors seated in a formal manner derived from conventional classic procedure. Otto Brahm announced his effort to parallel Antoine with an essay on modern acting. The Moscow Art Theatre set out to reform the methods of staging, and by successfully producing Chekhov's *The Seagull*, which had been a failure in a previous production, proved the importance of the relation between drama and theatre.

Here in America, the ideas of the modern movement were superficially accepted. They especially influenced the scene designer who created more imaginative images on the stage but often left the actor far behind, as in R. E. Jones's settings for *Macbeth* and in the visions dreamed and designed by Norman Bel Geddes for *The Divine Comedy* (unproduced). The Group Theatre was probably the only organization in America that recognized the importance of the whole and the role of the actor. Although the Group foundered after ten years, it left a heritage of intentions which still smolders. But essentially the vision of the modern movement in the theatre has become a mirage much too easily confused with pictorially set and abstractly and conventionally composed university productions, which nowadays seem to pass for art. The expected deeper understanding of drama as a part of a theatre art has not materialized. We are still unaware of the extent to which our ideas of plays are dependent on the type of production to which we are accustomed.

When Edmund Kean first appeared in London in 1814 in the role of Shylock, he was enthusiastically welcomed by the critic William Hazlitt as "the first gleam of genius breaking athwart the gloom of the stage." But Hazlitt also thought that Kean's interpretation did not agree with the essentially gloomy character of Shylock. Two years later, when he reprinted his review, Hazlitt admitted that his idea of Shylock had been gained "more from seeing other players perform it than from the text of Shakespeare," and that Kean's manner was "much nearer the mark."

When Tennessee Williams's *Summer and Smoke* was first produced, it was generally received as an "affecting failure," a play of "rich texture" but "dependent on a too novelistic or sprawling structure." The acting and the production were considered excellent. Yet, in the early fifties, when the play was revived by the Circle-in-the-Square, directed by José Quintero, with the memorable performance of Geraldine Page, the play was suddenly completely logical and moving. It had lost its sprawling quality. Was it the original production which, despite its technical excellence, was responsible for the early impression? The set, by its somewhat abstract theatricality, simply did not permit the play to breathe or the characters to behave in a logical fashion. When O'Neill's *The Iceman Cometh*, first produced in 1946, was received as an overlong work that needed judicious cutting, one critic, John Gassner, did think it might be improved by a less lumbering style of production. He turned out to be right. For, when the play was revived in the fifties, again by the Circle-in-the-Square, in a production that first brought Jason Robards, Jr. to attention, the play's intrinsic power, rugged strength, sardonic humor, somehow appeared in its true significance as an imposing "picture of failure in the case of denizens of a beachfront saloon who sustain themselves with desperate illusions," and the boredom of the original production was replaced by a "raffish" aliveness.

The plays in the present volume were not deliberately picked to prove a point. The exigencies of copyright had a good deal to do with the choice. Yet the plays illustrate some of the tendencies we have discussed. Miss Lillian Hellman's play, *The Autumn Garden,* produced in the spring of 1950–1951 season, was generally recognized as containing "some of the most incisive and revealing dialogue of which this vigorous playwright was capable," but the play itself seemed diffused and rambling, and the characters, though excellently drawn, somehow left hanging in the air. Still these characteristics seemed to me to stem more from the production than from the play itself. Miss Hellman's previous plays had all possessed a tightly knit structure, a sense of overt conflict. This play did not lack these qualities. It seemed to me to be a deliberately different effort to widen the horizon. Its seeming indirectness was intended to place the emphasis on the characters, on their inner conflicts and relationships rather than the outward drama. The retelling of their stories was not meant to further the plot, but to relive their experiences in the present. The play was well done, but in a style more suited to the earlier plays. The characters ceased to exist when they left the stage. When they returned, their reappearance seemed unmotivated. The characters described their experiences rather than re-creating them. They seemed to "act" rather than to live. An almost "Chekhovian" environment was needed to be created, one that would permit a sense of continuous action with the characters continuing to live and behave after their dialogue stopped. The setting would have had to be more open to permit action to go on while other people were speaking, and thus to create a kind of symphonic orchestration of the behavior and the attitudes of the people. A production visualized along these lines would have served to bring out the inherent humaneness of the characters (it has been pointed out that, rare for a Hellman play, there were no downright villains in the piece) and their inability to act would have been dramatized on the stage.

Tennessee Williams's *Camino Real* is peculiarly suited to illustrate the relations between theatre and drama. Many of us in the theatre have a special fondness for this play. Yet neither of the two productions have been able to create for the audience what we see in it. In the first place, I am not sure that Mr. Williams's additions to his original version are really necessary. Mr. Williams has a tendency to rewrite his plays, in a desire to clarify. Thus, for instance, *Orpheus Descending* is a revised version of the play *Battle of Angels,* which was originally produced by the Theatre Guild in 1941 and was a total failure. It never reached New York. I am sure that the play needed revision and correction, but the fact remains that almost everything about that production was wrong, so that the values of the play could not possibly show. Yet, on the basis of this production, Mr. Williams rewrote the play, making it clearer and more symbolic, but less human and believable.

To test my reaction, I encouraged a group of young performers at The Actors' Studio to work on the first part of the original version. The result was surprising. It came through as one of Mr. Williams's finest efforts, suffused with the kind of poetic melody and sympathy for people which *The Glass Menagerie* represents. In the same way, when Mr. Williams rewrote *Camino Real*, he added characters and scenes which only destroy the original fable and the sense of a folk legend which is inherent in the play. If someone ever captures in a production a circus quality, a sense of the show-booth and the color of a county fair, a vision of primitive orgiastic rites which carnival time suggests, it would help us to appreciate this effort of Mr. Williams as he originally imagined it—a sort of "American Blues," a sort of jazz symphony.

Robert Anderson's *Tea and Sympathy* is a beautifully direct, sensitive, and honest piece of playwriting. Enhanced by wonderful casting and equally sensitive and dynamic staging by Elia Kazan, and a luminous environment provided by Jo Mielziner, it created an atmosphere of warm humanity. The promise of this first play has not been fulfilled in the later work of Mr. Anderson. The sense of personal involvement and sympathy for the characters is missing.

Michael Gazzo's *Hatful of Rain* grew out of a project started at the Actors' Studio. It is not a play about dope addiction. In fact, this was missing in the original version. The ideas of the play are in no way representative of the Studio, but the process by which the play was helped into being is. The close interrelation between playwright, director, and actors served to define characters and events and to give each moment the character of life. This was especially useful in creating a vividness of dialogue and a relation between word, gesture, and behavior which contributed enormously to the success of the play and was its distinguishing characteristic. But for a playwright to develop, he must have a deep core of experience and of meaning which he desires to transmit. The second play of Mr. Gazzo got nowhere. In its original version, it contained some excellent scenes, but even more original was its effort to capture the sound, smell and rhythm of a jazz world. Somehow, this was lost in the final version. The ear for fresh and colorful dialogue remained, but separated from an environment which could give it life, it seemed overblown and forced.

It is fortunate that we are able to include at least one example of the work of the young American playwright. Mr. Albee's work seems eminently suitable for that purpose. There is a tendency to see our contemporary plays too much as representative of the avant-garde, the theatre of the absurd, the theatre-for-the-sake-of-theatre. This misses the point.

The work of Brecht is not to be lumped together with other efforts to break the realistic form (Brecht himself called his own theatre "realistic") and the looser shape and forms of some of our recent plays are not always simply a search for the theatrical. The best work derives from some essentially personal experience behind which the author tries to find some larger significance. The work of Mr. Albee possesses the ability to convey some strangely suggestive meaning and event; the scene has tension and dramatic excitement. But behind this there hovers the sense of life, of a real experience between human beings. It is this combination which makes one look forward to Mr. Albee's future work with great expectations.

I cannot leave these remarks without an additional personal postscript. As I write, the plans for the Lincoln Center Repertory Theatre become more imminent, and the Actors' Studio has just announced its intention to create a producing unit based on a new principle of a flexible "floating" company. The atmosphere for the artist is changing decisively, thanks to the action of the President and Mrs. Kennedy. It has for some time now seemed to me that we are ready for a theatre that should represent our time. The country is hungry for it—not for the leavings of Broadway or for accidentally organized or amateurish efforts. The talent for it now exists in many areas. I am a pessimistic optimist. Knowing the nature of life, I expect and am prepared for the worst, but knowing the nature of man, I hope for the best. The time is ripe for it. I hope the audience is.

LEE STRASBERG

THE AUTUMN
GARDEN

A PLAY IN THREE ACTS

by Lillian Hellman

for Dash

Copyright 1951, by Lillian Hellman
Reprinted by permission of Little, Brown & Co.
All rights reserved.

*All amateur and stock rights are controlled by the author
without whose permission in writing no performance of
this play may be given.*

First production, March 7, 1951,
at the Coronet Theater, New York,
with the following cast:

ROSE GRIGGS, *Florence Eldridge*
MRS. MARY ELLIS, *Ethel Griffies*
GENERAL BENJAMIN GRIGGS, *Colin Keith-Johnston*
EDWARD CROSSMAN, *Kent Smith*
FREDERICK ELLIS, *James Lipton*
CARRIE ELLIS, *Margaret Barker*
SOPHIE TUCKERMAN, *Joan Lorring*
LEON, *Maxwell Glanville*
CONSTANCE TUCKERMAN, *Carol Goodner*
NICHOLAS DENERY, *Fredric March*
NINA DENERY, *Jane Wyatt*
HILDA, *Lois Holmes*

The time is September 1949. The place
is the Tuckerman house in a summer
resort on the Gulf of Mexico, about
one hundred miles from New Orleans.

ACT ONE / *Monday night after dinner.*

ACT TWO / SCENE I: *The following Sunday morning.*
           SCENE II: *That night.*

ACT THREE / *Early the next morning.*

Act one

SCENE: *The living room of the Tuckerman house in a town on the Gulf of Mexico, a hundred miles from New Orleans. A September evening, 1949, after dinner. To the right of the living room is a side porch, separated from the room by a glass door. Upstage left is a door leading into the entrance hall of the house: through this door we can see the hall and staircase. On the porch are chairs and tables. The furniture of the living room is handsome but a little shabby. It is all inherited from another day. (Right and left are the audience's right and left.)*

ON STAGE AT RISE OF CURTAIN

GENERAL GRIGGS, *a good-looking man of fifty-three, is seated at one side of the room reading a newspaper. His wife—*

ROSE GRIGGS, *ex-pretty, soft-looking and about forty-three, is seated at a table wearing an evening dress that is much too young for her. She is chatting across the room with—*

CARRIE ELLIS, *a distinguished-looking woman of about forty-five, who is sitting on a side chair, near her son, Frederick, and her mother-in-law—*

MRS. MARY ELLIS, *in her seventies, sprightly in manner and movement when she wishes to be, broken and senile when she wishes to be broken and senile. She has piled cushions on her chair so she can read a manuscript over the shoulder of her grandson—*

FREDERICK ELLIS, *a pleasant-looking young man of around twenty-five. Occasionally he makes a correction in the manuscript, looks up amused and annoyed at his grandmother. On the right porch—*

EDWARD CROSSMAN, *about forty-six, tired and worn-looking as if he is not in good health, is sitting alone, his back to those in the room. There is a second of silence after the curtain goes up.*

ROSE [*gets up from her chair. She finds silence uncomfortable and breaks into song "We Stroll the Lane Together"*]. Now where is it? Everything's been so topsy-turvy all evening. If I can't have it immediately after dinner then I just about don't want it. At home you can bet it's right waiting for us when we leave the dining room, isn't it, Ben? Too bad it's Thursday. I'd almost rather go and see him than go to the party. [*To* MRS. ELLIS.] I think it's what keeps you awake, Mrs. Ellis. I mean a little is good for your heart, the doctor told me always to have a little, but my goodness the amount you have every night.

MRS. ELLIS [*pleasantly*]. Would you mind telling me what you're talking about, Mrs. Griggs? You said if it wasn't for the party you'd go and see *him,* but you thought *I* drank too much on a Thursday?

ROSE [*giggles*]. Coffee. I mean you drink too much coffee.

MRS. ELLIS. Then it is coffee you wish to go and see?

ROSE. Now, now. You're teasing. You know very well I mean Robert Taylor in that thing.

MRS. ELLIS. Believe me, I did *not* know you meant Robert Taylor in that thing. You know, General Griggs, after seven summers I have come to the conclusion that your wife considers it vulgar to mention anything by name. There's nothing particularly genteel about pronouns, my dear. Coffee is coffee and not it, Robert Taylor is Robert Taylor and not him, I suppose, and a fool is a fool and not her.

ROSE [*pleasantly*]. I know. It's a naughty habit. Ben has been telling me for years. [*She is close to* BEN.] Do you like my dress, Ben?

GRIGGS. It's nice.

ROSE. Have I too much rouge? [*To others.*] Know what she used to say? [*Quickly.*] Ben's mother, I mean. She used to say it before she died. [*To* CROSSMAN.] Come and join us. [*To others.*] She used to say that Southern women painted a triangle of rouge on their faces as if they were going out to square the hypotenuse. Ben came from Boston, and his mother was sometimes a little sharp about Southerners.

MRS. ELLIS. Who could have blamed her?

ROSE [*calling out to* CROSSMAN]. Know what she told me last winter when I met her at the Club?

CROSSMAN [*turns, smiles*]. Ben's mother?

ROSE. No. Your sister, of course. She said we see more of you here on your summer vacation than she sees all year round in New Orleans. She says you're getting to be a regular old hermit. You have to watch that as you get older. You might get to like being alone—and that's dangerous.

MRS. ELLIS. I used to like being alone. When you get old, of course, then you don't any more. But somewhere in the middle years, it's fine to be alone. A room of one's own isn't nearly enough. A house, or, best, an island of one's own. Don't you agree, General Griggs? [*Very quickly.*] Happiest year of my life was when my husband died. Every month was springtime and every day I seemed to be tipsy, as if my blood had turned a lovely *vin rosé.*

CARRIE. You're lyrical, Mother.

MRS. ELLIS [*to* FREDERICK]. Do you know I almost divorced your grandfather, Frederick? During the racing season in 1901.

FREDERICK [*looks up, laughs*]. You don't feel it's a little late to talk about it?

[*The phone rings.*]

MRS. ELLIS. I thought you might like to write my biography—when you're finished with regional poetry.

[*As the phone rings again,* SOPHIE *comes into the hall to answer it.*]

SOPHIE [*into the phone*]. No, sir. We do not take transient guests. No, never, sir. Only permanent guests. You might telephone to Mrs. Prescott in the village. Thank you, sir.

ROSE [*calls into hall*]. Dear Sophie, where *is* coffee?

[SOPHIE *comes to the hall door. She is a plain-looking, shy girl of about seventeen. She has a hesitant, over-polite manner and speaks with a slight accent. She has on a party dress, covered by a kitchen apron.*]

SOPHIE. Aunt Constance is most sorry for the delay. We bring it immediately. [*She disappears.*]

ROSE. Frederick, do you know I've been giving Sophie dancing lessons, or trying to? She's a charming child, your intended, but she's never going to be a dancer.

FREDERICK [*pleasantly*]. Terrible expression, Mrs. Griggs: my intended. Sounds like my indentured. Did you tell Mrs. Griggs, Mother? I thought we agreed that since there were no definite plans as yet—

CARRIE [*a little uncomfortable*]. It's natural that I should speak about my son's marriage, isn't it?

ROSE. Why, goodness, yes indeed it is. I'd have felt hurt—

GRIGGS. Don't you know that women have no honor, Frederick, when it comes to keeping secrets about marriage or cancer?

FREDERICK [*looks at his mother*]. No, sir. I didn't know. I'm too young for my age.

MRS. ELLIS [*who has been busy reading the manuscript*]. I know I'm too young to be reading Payson's book. Full of the most confused sex. I can't tell who is what. And all out of doors. Is that new, so much sex out of doors? Is it, General?

GRIGGS. I don't think it's a question of "new." I think it's a question of climate.

MRS. ELLIS [*points to book*]. But aren't sexual relations the way they used to be: between *men and women?* It's so twitched about in Mr. Payson's book. You know, I think the whole country is changing.

GRIGGS [*as if he wished to help* FREDERICK]. Has Payson written a good book, Fred?

FREDERICK. It's a wonderful book. I think he's going to be the most important young writer—

CARRIE. You said the first two books were wonderful, Frederick. And they didn't sell very well.

MRS. ELLIS. I don't know why they didn't—I always thought houses of prostitution had a big lending-library trade.

[FREDERICK *gets up, as if he were angry.*]

CARRIE. Will this new book sell, Frederick?

FREDERICK. I don't know, Mother.

CARRIE. I hope it sells. Any man is better off supporting himself.

FREDERICK [*smiles*]. Mother, sometimes I think no people are quite so moral about money as those who clip coupons for a living.

MRS. ELLIS. And why not? Particularly your mother who is given the coupons already clipped by me who has the hardship of clipping them. That leaves her more time to grow moral. And then, of course, you who don't even have that much trouble are left at leisure to be moral about those who have to go to the trouble of living on unearned money.

CARRIE [*to* GENERAL GRIGGS]. You mustn't look uncomfortable, General. You should know by this time that my mother-in-law enjoys discussing family matters in public. And the more uncomfortable you look, the longer she will continue.

GRIGGS. Do I look uncomfortable? I was thinking how hard it is to be young.

ROSE [*to* BEN]. Won't you come to the party? [*To others.*] Ben has never gone to the Carter party. I am sure they're just as insulted every year—

GRIGGS. I don't think so.

ROSE. But what will you do with yourself? Why don't you go to see Robert Taylor? It's that war picture where he does so well and you'll want to see if it's accurate.

GRIGGS. No. I don't want to see if it's accurate.

ROSE. Do you like my dress?

GRIGGS. It's nice.

MRS. ELLIS. You are a patient man. [*To* ROSE.] Do you know you've asked him that five times since rising from dinner?

ROSE. Well, I feel young and gay, and I'm going to a party. I wish the Denerys would come before we leave. I like meeting new people and they sound so interesting. I thought they were supposed to arrive in time for dinner. [*To* CARRIE.] Is he absolutely fascinating?

CARRIE. I don't know, Mrs. Griggs. I haven't seen him in twenty years or more.

ROSE [*calling to* CROSSMAN]. Is he fascinating, Mr. Crossman?

CROSSMAN [*pleasantly*]. You're making it a little harder than usual. Is who fascinating?

ROSE. Nicholas Denery, of course.

CROSSMAN. Of course. I don't know.

ROSE. But, goodness. Didn't you all grow up together? I mean you and Constance and Mrs. Ellis and—

CROSSMAN. I don't remember any of us as fascinating. Do you, Carrie?

[CARRIE *shakes her head, laughs.*]

[SOPHIE, *carrying a tray with brandy and brandy glasses, comes into the room. She is followed by* LEON, *a young, colored butler, carrying coffee and coffee cups.* FREDERICK *rises and takes the tray from* SOPHIE. *She looks at him and smiles.*]

ROSE. Let's see your dress, Sophie.

[SOPHIE *smiles shyly, begins to take off her apron as* LEON *pours coffee.*]

Oh. It's right nice. But you should wear tighter things, dear. [*Comes in back of her, begins to fool with her hair.*] I'd like to try your hair again. [SOPHIE *moves to help* LEON *but is cornered by* ROSE.] Now you just sit down. How's this?

[CROSSMAN *comes into the room.*]

CROSSMAN. Makes her look like everybody else. That's desirable, isn't it?

ROSE. What does Frederick think? We're out to please Frederick, after all, aren't we, dear?

FREDERICK [*turns to look*]. I like Sophie her own way.

SOPHIE [*smiles*]. I have no "way."

ROSE. But most European girls have such chic—

[GENERAL GRIGGS *gets up, as if he were annoyed.*]
They have, Ben. You said it yourself when you came back from the Pacific, and I was jealous.

MRS. ELLIS. Pacific? I thought you fought in Europe.

GRIGGS. I did. Robert Taylor fought in the Pacific. [*He rises, wanders off to the porch.*]

ROSE [*holding Sophie's hair another way*]. Or is *this* better?

FREDERICK [*smiles to* SOPHIE]. Don't you mind being pulled about?

SOPHIE. No. Well. [*Gently pulls away.*] I am grateful for the trouble that Mrs. Griggs— Thank you.

CROSSMAN. Sophie doesn't mind anything. All she has said all summer is thank you.

[*Through his speech the phone rings.* FREDERICK *starts for the phone. At the same time,* CONSTANCE TUCKERMAN *comes through the hall. She is a handsome woman of forty-three or forty-four. She is carrying two flower vases. She puts down one of the vases in order to answer the phone.*]

CONSTANCE. Yes. Just a minute. Frederick. Mr. Payson would like to speak to you. [*She picks up the other vase, comes into the door, as if she were in a hurry.* FREDERICK *immediately moves to the phone.*] Sorry coffee was late. You all want more just ring. And do, Carrie, explain to the Carters why I can't come to their party this year—

ROSE. Any news from them, Constance?

CONSTANCE [*carefully*]. News from whom?

ROSE [*laughs*]. Oh, come now. Stop pretending. When do the Denerys arrive?

CONSTANCE. Don't wait up for them, Rose. You'll see them at breakfast. [*She turns, goes out and goes up the stairs.*]

ROSE. My, Constance is nervous. Well, I suppose I should be if I were seeing an old beau for the first time in— But I don't believe in old beaux. Beaux should be brand-new, or just friends, don't you think?

[CROSSMAN *starts out to porch, carrying his coffee and the brandy bottle.* ROSE *points outside, meaning* GENERAL GRIGGS *and* CROSSMAN.]

Now are you boys just going to sit here and share the bottle—

CROSSMAN. General Griggs is only being kind when he says he shares the bottle with me.

[*He goes off.* FREDERICK *comes in, starts to speak, changes his mind.*]

CARRIE [*carefully*]. Was that Mr. Payson on the phone? Is he coming to the party?

FREDERICK. How many generations do you have to summer in this joint before you're invited to the Carters'?

MRS. ELLIS. Oh, that's not true. They're very liberal lately. [*Points to* ROSE.] After all, the last few years they've always included Mrs. Griggs. [*To* ROSE.] And nobody can be more *nouveau riche* than your family, can they? I mean your brother during the war and all that.

ROSE [*giggles*]. My. Everybody is so jealous of Henry.

MRS. ELLIS. Well, of course we are. I wish we were *nouveau riche* again.

FREDERICK [*sharply*]. All right, Grandma.

ROSE. Oh, I don't mind. I enjoy your grandmother.

FREDERICK [*to his mother*]. I'm sorry I'm not going to be able to take you to the party. I hope you'll excuse me, Sophie. Mother. Grandma.

CARRIE [*carefully*]. What has happened, Frederick?

FREDERICK. Payson had a wire from his publishers. They want the manuscript in the mail tomorrow morning. [*He goes to take the manuscript from the table.*] So I'll have to proofread it with him tonight. It's a nasty job alone, almost impossible—

CARRIE [*slowly*]. I don't understand.

ROSE [*hurriedly*]. I must fix my face. As you get older your face needs arranging more often. [*She goes off*].

CARRIE. We're ready to leave, Frederick.

FREDERICK. Mother, I'm not going to the party. I wasn't making a joke—

CARRIE. Oh. I hoped you were. You have no obligation to us, or Sophie? An appointment broken, because Payson summons you?

FREDERICK. I am sorry, Sophie. Maybe I can pick you up later. [*Haltingly.*] I *am* sorry.

SOPHIE. I do not mind, really. It is better this way.

CARRIE. Don't you? Why not? [*No answer.*] Why don't you mind, Sophie?

SOPHIE [*smiles*]. I do not like parties. I did not want to go. Now Frederick has some important business and must leave quickly—

CARRIE. Perhaps you are going to make *too* good a wife.

FREDERICK. Suppose you let me decide that, Mother. Good night. Have a good time. See you in the morning—

CARRIE. I want to talk to you, Frederick.

FREDERICK [*stops, smiles*]. When you use that tone of voice you need two hours. Let's make it in the morning, Mother.

[*SOPHIE has turned away, gone upstage, as if she wanted to be as far away as possible.*]

CARRIE. I ask you to break your appointment with Payson. As a favor to me.

FREDERICK. There's nothing important about my being at the party and it is important to him. He wants to consult me—

CARRIE [*sharply*]. He is always consulting you. You talk like a public accountant or a landscape gardener. Why should he want to consult *you* about his work?

FREDERICK [*hurt*]. Maybe because I try to write and maybe because he thinks I know a little. I realize that's hard for you to believe—

CARRIE. I didn't mean that.

FREDERICK. I think you did. Good night.

CARRIE. You have no sense of obligation to me. [*Looks around for* SOPHIE *who is trying at this minute to leave the room.*] And none to Sophie. Who evidently won't speak for herself. Do stay here, Sophie, it's your business as well as mine— [SOPHIE *stands still.*] I am getting tired of Mr. Payson, Frederick, and with good reason. When he came to stay with us in town last winter, I fully understood that he was a brilliant and gifted man and I was glad for you to have such a friend. But when he followed you down here this summer—

FREDERICK [*slowly, angrily*]. He did not follow me down here and I wouldn't like you to put it that way again. He came here for the summer and is that your business, Mother?

CARRIE. There is just too much of Mr. Payson. Every day or every evening— How often do you take Sophie with you? [*Sharply.*] How often have you seen Mr. Payson this summer, Sophie? [*There is no answer.*] Please answer me.

FREDERICK. And please stop using that tone to Sophie. Say what you have to say to me.

CARRIE [*turning to* MRS. ELLIS, *who has been watching them*]. Mother—

MRS. ELLIS. I've been dozing. How many hours have passed?

CARRIE [*slowly*]. You are always dozing when there is something unpleasant to face out with Frederick.

MRS. ELLIS. What better time? You all want to know something's been worrying me all day? Nobody in the South has tapeworm any more. In my day that was all you ever heard. Tapeworm, tapeworm, tapeworm. [*Gets up.*] Now kiss your mother good night, boy. Otherwise she'll be most unhappy. And say you forgive her.

FREDERICK. I have nothing to forgive her for, Grandma.

MRS. ELLIS. Of course not. But even when your mother starts out being right she talks and talks until she gets around to being wrong. [*She exits. There is silence.*]

CARRIE [*softly*]. I'm sorry if I spoke unfairly, or at the wrong time—

FREDERICK [*comes to her, smiling*]. You didn't, you didn't. Now don't feel bad. Nothing's happened. And don't let Grandma tease you.

CARRIE. I know. [*She turns to go.*] You go ahead, dear. Try to join us later.

[*He kisses her. She smiles, pleased, and goes out.* FREDERICK *turns to* SOPHIE.]

FREDERICK. Sophie, Mother didn't mean to be sharp with you. But when she is, you mustn't let her. She's a little bossy from time to time, but no harm in it. You look so worried.

SOPHIE [*very puzzled*]. Your mother is not angry now?

FREDERICK. Of course not. You mustn't take these things too seriously. Mother is like that.

SOPHIE [*smiles*]. You know it is most difficult in another language. Everything in English sounds so important. I get a headache from the strain of listening.

FREDERICK [*laughs*]. Don't. It's not worth it. [*Looks at her, then slowly:*] Mother is right: I have been rude and neglectful. But I haven't meant to be, Sophie.

SOPHIE. No, no. You have not been.

FREDERICK. And in two weeks Mother and I will be going off to Europe. I hope you don't mind about the European trip. It was all arranged long before you and I— [*Stares at her, smiles.*] got engaged.

[SOPHIE *smiles at him as if she were embarrassed, then she coughs and clears her throat.*]

We're an awkward pair. I like you, Sophie.

SOPHIE [*warmly*]. I like you, Frederick.

FREDERICK. Sophie, I think we'll have to sit down soon and talk about ourselves. I don't think we even know how we got engaged. We haven't said much of anything—

SOPHIE. Sometimes it is better not to say things. There is time and things will come as they come.

FREDERICK. The day we got engaged, we tried to speak as honestly as we both knew how but we didn't say very much—

SOPHIE. And I think we should not try so hard to talk. Sometimes it is wise to let things grow more roots before one blows them away with many words— [*Shyly touches his hand.*] It will come better if we give it time.

FREDERICK. We will give it time. And you'll make no decisions and set no dates until you are sure about what you think and feel.

SOPHIE. Oh, I have made the decision for myself. And I am pleased.

FREDERICK [*pleased*]. And you are quite sure of your decision?

SOPHIE. You know, sometimes I have thought that with rich people— [*Very quickly.*] with educated people, I mean, decisions are made only in order to speak about changing them. It happens often with Aunt Constance and with your mother, also, I think. And the others.

FREDERICK. Yes. [*Takes her hand.*] We'll get along fine. I want you to know that I feel very lucky—

SOPHIE. Lucky? You will have to be patient with me. I am not a good success here.

FREDERICK. Now, you stop that. I don't want you a good success. And you're to stop thinking it. You're to stop a lot of things: letting Mother boss you about, letting Mrs. Griggs tell you what to wear, or pull your hair—

SOPHIE. Oh, I do not mind. Because I look so bad makes Mrs. Griggs think she looks so good.

FREDERICK [*smiles*]. Good night, my dear.

SOPHIE [*smiles*]. Good night.

[*He exits.* SOPHIE *begins to pick up the coffee cups, brandy glasses, etc. After a minute* ROSE GRIGGS *comes down the steps carrying a light summer wrap. She comes in the room.*]

ROSE. Where are the Ellises?

SOPHIE. They went to the party, Mrs. Griggs.

ROSE. No! Without me? I *must* say that's very rude. They can't have done that, Sophie— [*She hurries to the hall, looks out. Then she comes back in, goes to the porch.*] Ben. [*He looks up.*] The Ellises left without me, Ben!

GRIGGS. Yes?

ROSE. You'll have to walk me over. I just won't go in, alone.

GRIGGS. It's across the street, Rose. Not a very dangerous journey.

ROSE [*gently*]. Ben. [*He rises, comes in.*] You know, I think it's shocking. In front of other people. God knows what they know or guess this summer. [*Suddenly notices* SOPHIE *who is collecting cups.*] Sophie. Don't wait here listening.

[SOPHIE *turns, surprised, but before she can speak . . .*]

GRIGGS [*sharply*]. Rose!

ROSE [*who is always charming at this point. To* SOPHIE].

I am sorry, my dear. Please most earnestly I ask your pardon—

SOPHIE. Yes, ma'am.

ROSE [*tries to catch her at door*]. I'm just a nervous old silly these days. Now say you forgive me—

[SOPHIE *disappears.*]

GRIGGS [*smiles, as if he has seen this before*]. All right, Rose. You're charming.

ROSE. You won't even walk over with me, just to the door?

GRIGGS. Certainly I will.

ROSE [*smiles*]. No, you don't have to. I just wanted to see if you would. Will you call for me, at twelve, say?

GRIGGS. No.

ROSE. Then will you meet me at twelve, at the tavern?

GRIGGS. No. What mischief is this, Rose?

ROSE. Is it mischief to want to talk with you?

GRIGGS. Again? Tonight? And every night and every day? The same things over and over? We're worn out, Rose, both of us. [*Kindly.*] There is no more to say.

ROSE [*softly*]. No more to say. Do people get divorces, after twenty-five years, by just saying they want them and that's all and walking off?

GRIGGS. I suppose some men do. But I haven't walked off and I have said all I know how to say.

ROSE. But you haven't really explained anything to me. You tell me that you want a divorce— And I ask why, why, why. We've been happy together.

GRIGGS [*looks at her*]. You don't believe that.

ROSE. When people get our age, well, the worst is over —and what else can one do? [*Exasperated.*] I never really heard of such a thing. I'm just not taking you seriously and I do wish you'd stop talking about it. [*After a pause.*] You've never given me a good reason. I ask you ten times a day if there's another woman. I could understand that. Of course you say no, naturally—

GRIGGS. There is no other woman.

ROSE [*giggles*]. You know what I think? I think it's that little blonde at the drugstore, and the minute my back is turned—

GRIGGS. Please, Rose. Please stop that.

ROSE. Never at any time, during this divorce talk, have you mentioned them. You'd think we didn't have sons, and the awful effect on them. Did you write them today?

GRIGGS. I did not write them because you begged me not to.

ROSE. Oh, yes, I forgot. It will break their hearts.

GRIGGS. Their hearts won't be broken. They won't even bother to finish the letter.

ROSE [*softly, shocked*]. You can't love them, to speak that way.

GRIGGS. I don't love them. I did love them but I don't now. They're hard men to love.

ROSE. Oh, I don't believe a word you say. You've always enjoyed shocking me. You've been a wonderful father and you're just as devoted to them as they are to you.

GRIGGS. They aren't the least devoted to me—when they think about me it is to find my name useful and when it isn't useful they disapprove of me.

ROSE [*moving to door*]. Look, Ben. I just can't stay and talk all night. I'm late now. There's no use our saying the same things over and over again— [*He laughs.*] If you won't come to the party what are you going to do?

GRIGGS. I am going down by the water, sit on a bench and study from a Chinese grammar.

ROSE. You'll be lonely.

GRIGGS. Yes, but not for parties.

ROSE. It's very hard to take seriously a man who spends

the evening with a Chinese grammar. I'll never forget that winter with the Hebrew phonograph records. [*Pats his arm.*] Now, good night, darling. And don't worry about me: I am going to try to have a good time. We'll talk about all this another day. [*She starts out.*]

GRIGGS [*sharply*]. No. No, we're not going to do that. You're turning it into a pleasure, Rose, something to chatter about on a dull winter night in the years to come. I've told you it isn't going to be that way. [*She is in the hall.*] It isn't going to be that way. When you go back to town next week I'm not going with you. [*He turns to see that she has gone.*]

ROSE'S VOICE [*from the hall*]. Good night, darling.

GRIGGS [*he stands still for a minute. Then he turns, sees his book on the porch table. Goes out to the porch, realizes the doors have been open. To* CROSSMAN]. I guess we thought the doors were closed. I am sorry.

CROSSMAN. Don't be.

GRIGGS. There are so many things I want to do that I don't know which to do first. Have you ever thought about starting a new life?

CROSSMAN [*smiles*]. I've often thought that if I started all over again, I'd go right back to where I started and start from there. Othewise, it wouldn't prove anything.

GRIGGS [*laughs*]. Where'd you start from?

CROSSMAN [*laughs*]. Nowhere. That's the trouble.

GRIGGS. I started with mathematics. Seems strange now, but that's why I went to West Point—wonderful mathematics department. So I got myself two wars instead. I want to go somewhere now and study for a few years, or— [*Smiles.*] Anyway, sit down by myself and think.

CROSSMAN. Europe?

GRIGGS. I don't think so. Europe seemed like a tourist joint the last time. With all the aimless, dead bitterness of—tourist joints. I don't want sentimental journeys to old battlefields. I'll start tame enough: I've written my sister that I'd like to stay with her for a month or two.

CROSSMAN. Isn't that a sentimental journey?

GRIGGS. I suppose it is. I really want to see her because she looks like my mother. The last six months I've thought a lot about my mother. If I could just go back to her for a day. Crazy at my age—

CROSSMAN. I know. We all do at times. Age has nothing to do with it. It's when we're in trouble.

GRIGGS. I don't know why I want to say this but, well, don't think too badly of my wife.

CROSSMAN. Why should I think badly of anybody?

GRIGGS [*as he turns to go*]. All professional soldiers marry Rose. It's in the Army Manual. She is as she always was. It is my fault, not hers.

CROSSMAN. Haven't you lived in the South long enough to know that nothing is ever anybody's fault?

[GENERAL GRIGGS *laughs, starts out as* CONSTANCE *comes down stairs.* CONSTANCE *has on a different dress and is buttoning the belt as she comes into the room.* GENERAL GRIGGS *crosses the room and exits by the stage left windows.* CONSTANCE *looks around, finds the room is neat, goes out to the porch, talking as she goes.*]

CONSTANCE. I *think* everything is ready. I've put Nick in Sophie's room— Sophie says she doesn't mind sleeping down here. Anyway it happens every summer. And I've given Mrs. Denery the yellow room. They wanted *two* rooms, Nick said on the phone.

CROSSMAN. Fashionable people don't sleep together, don't you know that? It's not sanitary.

CONSTANCE [*sits down*]. I'm tired, Ned.

CROSSMAN. Have a brandy.

CONSTANCE. No. It would make me nervous.

CROSSMAN. Remarkable the things that make people

nervous: coffee, brandy, relatives, running water, too much sun, too little sun. Never anything in themselves, eh, Constance?

CONSTANCE. They have a maid and a chauffeur. I'll have to put them in the boathouse. It's all so much work at the end of the season. Sophie's been cleaning all day, and I've been cooking— Why did I say they could come?

CROSSMAN [*smiles*]. I wonder why.

CONSTANCE. Well, of course, I want to see Nick again. But I am nervous about meeting her. [*Points to his glass.*] Do you think perhaps a sip?

CROSSMAN. Only drunkards borrow other people's drinks. Have one of your own. [*Through her next speech he pours her a drink and hands it to her. When she finishes it, he will take back the glass and pour himself a drink.*]

CONSTANCE. I got out Mama's good, old linen sheets. I don't care how rich the Denerys are, or where they've been, they never could have had finer linen. And I've stuffed some crabs and there's white wine— Remember how Nick loved stuffed crabs?

CROSSMAN [*smiles*]. No. I don't remember.

CONSTANCE. It was twenty-three years ago, the eighteenth of next month. I mean the night he decided to go to Paris to study. Not so many young men from New Orleans went to Paris in those days.

CROSSMAN. Just as many young men met rich young ladies on boats.

CONSTANCE [*sharply*]. *He fell in love.* People can't be blamed for changing their hearts—it just happens. They've had a fine marriage, and *that's* given me happiness all these years.

CROSSMAN. How do you know they've had a "fine" marriage?

CONSTANCE [*smiles*]. I know.

CROSSMAN. The rest of us don't know anything about any marriage—but you know all about one you've never seen. You're very wise, Constance. It must come from not thinking.

CONSTANCE. Is this dress all right?

CROSSMAN. You've changed your dress three times since dinner.

CONSTANCE. My dresses are all so sort of— She'll think they're cheap. [*Smiles.*] Well, and so they are. [*There is silence. Then:*] Have we changed much, Ned?

CROSSMAN. Yes, my dear. You've changed, I've changed. But you're still handsome, if that's what you mean.

CONSTANCE. Ned, you don't look so well this summer. [*He is pouring himself another brandy. She points to bottle.*] I wanted to tell you— Don't you think—

CROSSMAN [*very pleasantly*]. Don't I think you should mind your business? Yes, I do.

[SOPHIE *comes into living room carrying sheets, a quilt, a pillow, puts them down and moves to porch.*]

CONSTANCE. Isn't what happens to you my business?

SOPHIE. You look pretty, Aunt Constance.

CONSTANCE [*to* CROSSMAN]. Sophie made this dress for me. Last winter. What could the girls at school have thought? Sophie sitting sewing for an old country aunt when she could have been out dancing—

SOPHIE. I sew better than I dance.

CONSTANCE [*to* CROSSMAN]. Sophie's mother taught her to sew. You know that Ann-Marie is a modiste?

SOPHIE [*laughs*]. Oh, she is not. She is what you call here a home-seamstress, or sometimes a factory worker.

CONSTANCE. But she *designs*. She wrote me and you told me—

SOPHIE [*laughs*]. Oh no. You did not understand. She does—

[*Outside the house there is the noise of a car coming to a stop.* CONSTANCE *turns toward the room, then steps back, moves around the table and suddenly runs into the house.* CROSSMAN *turns to stare at her.*]

SOPHIE [*timidly, pointing out toward living room*]. Should I— Should I stay, Mr. Ned?

CROSSMAN. I don't know the etiquette of such meetings.

SOPHIE. Why is Aunt Constance so nervous about the visit of this lady and gentleman?

CROSSMAN. Because she was once in love with Nicholas Denery, this gentleman.

SOPHIE. Oh. Such a long, long time to stay nervous. [*Sententious.*] Great love in tender natures. And things of such kind. [*As he turns to stare at her.*] It always happens that way with ladies. For them it is once and not again: it is their good breeding that makes it so.

CROSSMAN. What is the matter with you?

SOPHIE [*laughs*]. I try very hard to sound nice. I try too hard, perhaps? [*She begins to move out into the room; then, as she hears voices, she runs out of the room, exits off porch.*]

NICK'S VOICE [*offstage*]. Constance!

[NICK *appears in the hall and comes into the room. He is about forty-five, handsome, a little soft-looking and in a few years will be too heavy. He is followed by* NINA DENERY, *who is a woman of about forty, good-looking, chic, tired and delicate. She stops and stands in the doorway.*]

NICK [*calling*]. Constance!

[NICK *and* NINA *are followed by a maid,* HILDA, *who stands waiting in the hall. She is carrying a jewelry case, an overnight bag, two coats.* CROSSMAN *starts to come forward, changes his mind, draws back.*]

HILDA [*in German*]. Shall I take the bags upstairs, madame?

NINA [*in German*]. We don't know where upstairs is.

NICK. Oh, I know where upstairs is. I know every foot of this house. [*Examining the room.*] It was *the* great summer mansion and as kids we were here more than we were at home— [*Softly.*] The great summer mansion! Did the house change, or me? [*Sees* NINA *in doorway.*] Come on in.

NINA. Perhaps it would be pleasanter for you to see old friends without me. In any case, I am very tired—

NICK. Oh, now don't get tired. We've just come. What have you got to be tired about? Do you realize how often these days you're tired?

NINA. I realize it very well. And I know it bores you.

NICK. It *worries* me. [*By this time,* NICK, *wandering around the room, has reached the porch.* CROSSMAN *turns and, realizing that he has been seen, now comes forward.*] Could you tell me where we could find Miss Tuckerman?

CROSSMAN. Hello, Nick. Good to see you.

NICK [*after a second*]. My God, Willy. How many years, how many years? [*He puts his arm around* CROSSMAN, *embraces him.*] Nina, this may be my oldest and best friend in the world. Nina, tell Willy how often I've talked about him and what I said.

CROSSMAN [*who is shaking hands with* NINA, *amused*]. Then I hope he told you that my name is Edward, not Willy.

NINA [*amused*]. I hope so—but I am not sure.

NICK. Your mother always called you Willy. Don't you remember?

CROSSMAN [*goes out into the hall*]. No. I thought it was my brother's name. [*Calls out, loudly.*] Constance, Nick is here.

NICK [*coming to* CROSSMAN]. Tell me before I see her. What has happened here? I don't know anything.

CROSSMAN. There's very little to know. Old man Tuckerman surprised everybody by dying broke. Constance sold the New Orleans house and managed to hang on to this by turning it into what is called a summer guest house. That's about all, Nick.

NICK. Where is Mrs. Tuckerman? I was crazy about her, Nina: she had style.

CROSSMAN. I don't know where she is, although I've asked myself often enough. She died shortly after Mr. Tuckerman—just to show him anybody could do it.

NICK [*laughs, pats* CROSSMAN]. Good to see you, boy. You know, if anybody had asked me, I would have said this room was as large as an eighteenth-century ballroom and as elegant. I think it shrank. All the fine things were sold?

CROSSMAN. The size hasn't changed. And nothing was sold.

NICK. Could I have been so wrong all these years? Seems so shabby now and—

NINA [*quickly*]. I think it is a pleasant room.

NICK. Does Sam live here?

CROSSMAN. Sam died during the war. He went to Europe, oh, in the thirties, married there and never came back. You'll meet his daughter. Constance imported her five years ago.

NICK. Well, Sam was always the devoted brother until it came to being devoted. And Constance sacrificed her life for him.

CROSSMAN [*to* NINA]. Nick is still a Southerner. With us every well-born lady sacrifices her life for something: a man, a house, sometimes a gardenia bush. Is it the same where you come from?

NINA [*smiles*]. New York is too cold for gardenias.

[*Through* CROSSMAN'S *speech,* CONSTANCE *appears in the hall. As she moves into the room, she trips, recovers herself, smiles nervously and waits for* NICK *to come to her. He takes her face in his hands and kisses her. Then he stands back to look at her.*]

NICK. This is a good hour of my life, Constance.

CONSTANCE [*softly*]. And of mine.

NICK [*holds her face*]. You've changed and you've changed well. Do you still have the portrait, Constance?

CONSTANCE [*smiles*]. *Still* have the portrait! It's the only important thing I have got— [*Then she remembers* NINA, *becomes confused, moves away from him and comes to* NINA.] Forgive me, Mrs. Denery.

NINA [*puts out her hand, warmly*]. Hello.

CONSTANCE [*flossy*]. I should have been here to make you as welcome as you truly are. I was reading when you arrived, reading a book, and I didn't hear the car. [*She sees* CROSSMAN *is staring at her and she looks nervously away from him.*]

NICK. I had expected you standing in the driveway with the sun in your face, in the kind of lovely pink thing you used to wear—

NINA. The sun is not usually out at night—even for you.

NICK [*to* CONSTANCE]. Instead, you are reading. As if you were waiting for the groceries to come.

CONSTANCE [*quickly*]. I wasn't reading. It was a silly lie. I was just pretending— [*Embarrassed.*] Well, I'm even forgetting my manners. You must be hungry, Mrs. Denery, and I've got—

NICK [*laughs, takes her hands, pulls her to the couch*]. No, no. Stop your manners, girl. There's a great deal I want to know. [*They sit down.*] Now. Is the portrait as good as I remember it? I want Nina to see it. Nina knows a great deal about painting. Sometimes I think she knows more than I.

CONSTANCE [*smiles to* NINA, *nods. Then to* NICK]. You know, Nick, I subscribe to the New York Sunday *Times*. Because of the art section. I wanted to follow your career.

NICK [*carefully*]. You haven't often found me in the *Times*. I've only exhibited in Europe.

CONSTANCE [*relieved*]. Oh. That explains it. [*There is a slight, awkward pause.*] I like painting. I like Renoir best. The summer ladies in the gardens, so very, very pretty.

NICK [*bored*]. Yes, very pretty. This is the same wonderful place— My God, we had happy summers here, all of us. We loved each other so very much. Remember, Ned?

CROSSMAN. I don't remember that much love.

NINA [*laughs*]. I like you, Mr. Crossman.

NICK. Of course you like him. These are my oldest friends. I think as one grows older it is more and more necessary to reach out your hand for the sturdy old vines you knew when you were young and let them lead you back to the roots of things that matter. [NINA *coughs*. CROSSMAN *moves away, smiling. Even* CONSTANCE *is a little overwhelmed*.] Isn't that true, Ned? Now what have you been up to all these years?

CROSSMAN. I still work in the bank and come here for my vacation. That's about all.

NICK. I bumped into Louis Prescott in Paris a couple of years ago and he told me you and Constance had never married— [*Pats* CONSTANCE'S *hand;* CONSTANCE *looks embarrassed*.] Couldn't understand it. No wonder you drink too much, Ned.

CROSSMAN. Louis Prescott go all the way to Paris to tell you that?

NICK [*anxious, gets up*]. Oh, look old boy. I didn't mean anything—I drink too much myself. I only want to know about you and have you know about me. I hope you didn't mind, Ned.

CROSSMAN. Not a bit. I want to know about you, too. Ever had syphilis, Nick? Kind of thing one has to know right off, if you understand me.

CONSTANCE [*gets up, very disturbed*]. Ned, how can you speak that way?

NICK [*smiles*]. You've grown edgy. I didn't remember you that way.

CROSSMAN [*pleasantly*]. Oh, I don't think I've changed. See you in the morning.

NICK. Hope you'll take me around, show me all the old places—

CROSSMAN. Of course I will. Good night, Mrs. Denery. [*He exits up staircase.*]

NICK [*to* CONSTANCE, *meaning* CROSSMAN]. I'm sorry if I said anything—

CONSTANCE. You know, for years I've been meeting you and Mrs. Denery—in my mind, I mean—and I've played all kinds of roles. Sometimes I was the dignified old friend, and sometimes I was a very, very old lady welcoming you to a gracious table. It was so important to me—our first meeting— [*Sadly.*] And now when it happens—

NICK [*heartily*]. Nonsense. My home-coming is just as it should be. It's as if I had gone away yesterday. We took up right where we left off: even Ned and I. Let us be as we were, my dear, with no years between us, and no pretending.

CONSTANCE [*delighted with him, warmly*]. Thank you. [*Goes to* NINA.] All these years I wanted to write you. I did write but I never sent the letters. It seemed so intrusive of me. I could see you getting the letter and just not knowing who I was.

NICK. I told Nina about you the first night I met her and through the years she has done quite a little teasing— You are too modest, Constance. [*Suddenly.*] Now are you going to let me do another portrait of you?

CONSTANCE [*laughs*]. Another portrait? No, no, indeed. I want to remember myself as I was in the picture upstairs.

NICK. Go and get it for me. I want to look at it with you. [*She smiles, exits. There is silence.*] You haven't been too warm or gracious, Nina.

NINA. What can I do when I don't even know the plot?

NICK. What are you talking about?

NINA. You told me about Constance Tuckerman the first night we met? And about dear Willy or Ned, and I've done quite a little teasing about her all these years?

NICK. I did tell you about her immediately—

NINA. You mentioned her very casually, last week, years after the night you met me and you said that you could hardly remember anything more about her than a rather silly—

NICK [*quickly*]. Are you going to be bad-tempered for our whole visit here? For years I've looked forward to coming back—

[NINA *laughs*.]

NINA. So you came to do her portrait?

NICK. No, I didn't "come to do her portrait." I thought about it driving down here. If the one I did is as good as I remember, it would be wonderful for the show. The young girl, the woman at forty-five. She's aged. Have we changed that much? I don't think you've changed, darling.

NINA. I've changed a great deal. And I wouldn't want it pointed out to me in a portrait to be hung side by side with a picture of what I used to be. [*He doesn't answer her.*] That isn't a nice reason for being here and if I had known it—

NICK. We have no "reason" for being here. I just wanted to come back. Nothing mysterious about it—

NINA. You're simply looking for a new area in which to exercise yourself. It has happened many, many times before. But it *always* happens when we return from Europe and spend a month in New York. It's been too important to you, for many years, that you cannot manage to charm my family. And so, when our visit is finished there, you inevitably look around for— Well, you know. You know what's been and the trouble.

NICK [*cheerfully*]. I don't know what the hell you're talking about.

NINA. I'm tired of such troubles, Nick—

NICK. Do you know that these sharp moods of yours grow more sharp with time? Now I would like to have a happy visit here. But if something is disturbing you and you'd prefer not to stay, I'll arrange immediately—

NINA [*as if she were a little frightened*]. I'd only prefer to go to bed. Sorry if I've been churly about your— home-coming. [*She starts out, meets* CONSTANCE *who comes in carrying portrait.*] Will you excuse me, Constance? The long drive gave me a headache.

CONSTANCE. I am sorry. Will I bring you a tray upstairs?

NINA. No, thank you.

[CONSTANCE *moves as if to show her the way.*]

NICK. Come, I want to see the picture. Nina will find her way. [*He takes the picture from* CONSTANCE.]

CONSTANCE. The yellow room on the left. Your maid is unpacking. I peeked in. What lovely clothes. Can I come and see them tomorrow?

NINA [*going up the stairs*]. Yes, of course. Thank you and good night.

[CONSTANCE *watches her and then comes into room.*]

NICK [*who is looking at the picture*]. I was nervous about seeing it. Damn good work for a boy eighteen.

CONSTANCE. You were twenty-two, Nick.

NICK. No, I wasn't. I—

CONSTANCE. You finished it the morning of your birthday. [*She points to windows.*] And when you put down your brushes you said damn good work for a boy of twenty-two, and then you asked me to marry you. Don't you remember— [*She stops, embarrassed.*] Why should you remember? And I don't want to talk that way.

NICK [*who is preoccupied with the picture*]. Oh, nonsense. Talk any way you like. We were in love, very much in love, and why shouldn't we speak of it?

CONSTANCE [*hastily, very embarrassed*]. After I die, the picture will go to the Delgado Museum.

NICK [*laughs*]. I want to borrow it first. I'm having a retrospective show this winter, in London. I've done a lot of fancy people in Europe, you know that, but

I'll be more proud of this— And I want to do another portrait of you as you are now. [*Moves toward window, excited.*] You standing there. As before. Wonderful idea; young girl, woman at— Be a sensation. Constance, it's fascinating how faces change, mold firm or loose, have lines that start in youth and—

CONSTANCE [*amazed*]. Oh, Nick. I don't want to see myself now. I don't want to see all the changes. And I don't want other people to stand and talk about them. I don't want people to laugh at me or pity me. [*Hurt.*] Oh, Nick.

NICK. I see. [*Turns.*] Well, it would have meant a lot to me. But that's that. I'll be off to bed now—

CONSTANCE [*coming after him*]. But we haven't had a minute. And I have supper all ready for you—

NICK. Good night, my dear.

CONSTANCE [*slowly*]. You think I'm being selfish and vain? I mean, am I the only woman who wouldn't like—

NICK. No, I think most women would feel the same way. [*He starts out.*]

CONSTANCE. Do you prefer breakfast in bed? And what shall I make for your dinner? Pompano—

[*He is at the door as* CARRIE *and* ROSE *come into the hall.* CARRIE *is holding* ROSE'S *arm.*]

CARRIE. Hello, Nick.

NICK [*takes her hands*]. My God, Carrie. I didn't know you were here. How come? It's wonderful—

CARRIE. We come every summer.

NICK. You're handsome, Carrie. But you always were.

CARRIE [*smiles*]. And you always remembered to say so. [ROSE *coughs delicately.*] This is Mrs. Griggs. [*To* CONSTANCE.] Mrs. Griggs didn't feel well, so I brought her home. She became a little dizzy, dancing.

ROSE [*to* NICK, *who is shaking hands with her*]. You're a famous gentleman in this town, sir, and I've been

looking forward so to seeing you. We lead dull lives
here, you know—

NICK [*laughs*]. *You* don't look as if you do.

ROSE. Oh, thank you. But I don't look well tonight. I
became suddenly a little ill—

CARRIE [*tartly*]. Yes. Well, come along. If you still feel
ill.

NICK. Can I help you, Mrs. Griggs?

ROSE [*delighted*]. Oh, thank you. That would be nice.
I haven't been well this summer—

[NICK *starts into hall.*]

CONSTANCE. Nick—

[*He pays no attention.* CARRIE *moves quickly ahead of
him, takes* ROSE's *arm.*]

CARRIE. Come. Good night, Nick. I look forward to seeing you in the morning. Hope you're staying for a
while.

NICK. I think we'll have to leave tomorrow.

ROSE. Oh, don't do that. [*Then:*] Constance, if Ben
comes in would you tell him I was taken ill?

[CARRIE *impatiently pushes her ahead and up the steps.*]

NICK [*meaning* ROSE]. Pretty woman, or was. [*Looks at*
CONSTANCE.] What is it, Con?

CONSTANCE. How can you talk of leaving tomorrow?
[*He doesn't answer.*] Don't be mad with me, Nick.

NICK. I don't get mad, darling.

CONSTANCE [*catches him as he is almost out the door*].
Please, Nick, please let me change my mind. You are
welcome to take this picture and I am flattered you
wish to do another. But I'll have to pose early, before they're all down for breakfast—

NICK [*turns casually*]. Good. We'll start in the morning.
Do you make a living out of this place, darling?

CONSTANCE [*gaily*]. Not much of one. The last few
years have been a little hard. I brought Sam's daughter from Europe—she and her mother went through
the occupation and were very poor—and I've tried to

send her to the best school and then she was to make her debut only now she wants to get married, I think, and—

NICK. The girl expected all that from you?

CONSTANCE. Oh, no. Her mother didn't want to come and Sophie didn't want to leave her mother. I finally had really to *demand* that Sam's daughter was not to grow up— Well, I just can't describe it. At thirteen she was working in a fish store or whatever you call it over there. I just *made* her come over—

NICK. Why didn't you ever marry Ned?

CONSTANCE. I can't answer such questions, Nick. Even for you.

NICK. Why not? I'd tell you about myself or Nina.

CONSTANCE. Oh, it's one thing to talk about lives that have been good and full and happy and quite another— Well, I don't know. We just never did marry.

NICK [*bored*]. Well, then, tomorrow morning. I'll do a good portrait of you because it's the face of a good woman—

[*He stops as* SOPHIE *comes in. She sees* NICK *and* CONSTANCE *and draws back a little.*]

CONSTANCE. Sophie. [SOPHIE *comes into the room.*] This is Sam's daughter.

NICK [*very warmly to* SOPHIE]. I've been looking forward to meeting you for many years.

[CONSTANCE *turns, puzzled.*]

SOPHIE. How do you do, sir?

NICK. You follow in the great tradition of Tuckerman good looks.

SOPHIE. Er. Er.

CONSTANCE [*smiles*]. Don't er, dear. Say thank you. [GRIGGS *enters from left porch.*] Do come in. [GRIGGS *comes in.*] This is General Griggs. My very old friend, Nicholas Denery.

NICK. Are you General Benjamin Griggs? I've read about you in Raymond's book and Powell's.

GRIGGS [*as they shake hands*]. I hear they disagree about me.

NICK. We almost met before this. When your boys marched into Paris. I was in France during the German occupation.

[SOPHIE *turns sharply*.]

GRIGGS. That must have been unpleasant for you.

NICK. Yes, it was. But in the end, one has to be just; the Germans were damn smart about the French. They acted like gentlemen.

GRIGGS [*pleasantly*]. That's a side of them I didn't see. [*Looks over at* SOPHIE.] You didn't either, Sophie?

[*During his speech* HILDA, *the maid, appears in the doorway*.]

HILDA [*in German*]. Excuse me, Mr. Denery. Mrs. Denery would like you to come for a minute before you retire. She has a little surprise gift she bought for you in New Orleans.

NICK [*in German*]. No. Tell Mrs. Denery I will see her in the morning. Tell her to take a sleeping pill.

HILDA [*in German*]. Thank you, sir.

CONSTANCE [*who hasn't understood the German but who is puzzled because* SOPHIE *is frowning and* GRIGGS *has turned away*]. Can I— Does Nina want something?

NICK. No, no. She's fine.

[SOPHIE *begins to make up the couch.* NICK *turns to her*.] That means one of us must have put you out of your room. I'm sorry and I thank you.

SOPHIE. Not at all, sir. It is nothing.

NICK [*comes to her*]. You're a sweet child and I look forward to knowing you. Good night. [*To* GRIGGS.] Good night, sir. A great pleasure. [GRIGGS *bows.* NICK *kisses* CONSTANCE.] Wonderful to be here, darling.

[*He goes out.* CONSTANCE *moves to help* SOPHIE *make up the couch. There is silence for a minute while they arrange the bedclothes.* GRIGGS *watches them*.]

CONSTANCE. I suppose I shouldn't ask but what did the German maid want? Something from the kitchen or— [*No answer.*] Sophie. [*No answer.*] Sophie.

SOPHIE [*slowly*]. Mrs. Denery wanted to say good night to Mr. Denery.

GRIGGS. Mrs. Denery had bought a little gift for him in New Orleans and wanted to give it to him.

CONSTANCE. After all these years. To have a little gift for him. Isn't that nice? [*She looks at* GRIGGS *and* SOPHIE. *Neither answers her. She becomes conscious of something strained.*] What did Nick say?

SOPHIE. He said she should take a sleeping pill and go to sleep.

CONSTANCE. Just like that?

SOPHIE. Down at the beach there is the frankfurter concession. I think I will get the sleeping-pill concession and grow very rich.

CONSTANCE. Why, Sophie. Are you disturbed about something, dear? [*Looks at her dress.*] You didn't go to the party! I've been so busy, I didn't realize— Why, where's Fred and—

SOPHIE. I did not wish to go to the party, Aunt Constance. And Frederick had a most important appointment.

CONSTANCE. More important than being with you? Young people get engaged and act toward each other with such— I don't know. [*To* GRIGGS.] In our day we made marriage more romantic and I must say I think we had more fun. If you can't have fine dreams now, then when can you have them? [*Pats* SOPHIE.] Never mind. I guess the new way is more sensible. But I liked our way better. [*To* GRIGGS.] Didn't you? Oh, what's the matter with me? I forgot. Rose came back from the party. She said she was ill. I mean, I think she just didn't feel well— Carrie is upstairs with her. [*He doesn't move.*] I think Carrie probably wants to go back to the party and is waiting for you to come.

GRIGGS. Yes. Of course. Thank you. Good night. [*He exits.*]

CONSTANCE [*she kisses* SOPHIE]. You'll be comfortable? See you in the morning, dear.

[*She exits through the hall.* SOPHIE *finishes with the couch, goes out. After a second,* CROSSMAN *comes down the stairs. He sticks his head in the door, sees nobody, crosses the room, goes out to the porch, takes the bottle of brandy and a glass, moves back into the room and crosses it as* SOPHIE *returns carrying pajamas and a robe.*]

CROSSMAN [*his voice and his manner are slightly different now*]. I needed another book and another bottle. Royalty gone to bed? Does anybody improve with age? Just tell me that, Sophie, and I'll have something to lie awake and think about.

SOPHIE. I do not know, Mr. Ned.

CROSSMAN. For God's sake, Sophie, have an opinion about *something*. Try it, and see what comes out.

SOPHIE [*laughs*]. Some people improve with age, some do not.

CROSSMAN [*nods, amused*]. Wonderful, Sophie, wonderful. Some improve with age, some do not. Medical statistics show that 61 per cent of those who improve have bought our book on Dianetics and smoke Iglewitz cigarettes. You're beginning to talk like an advertisement, which is the very highest form of American talk. [*Sharply.*] It's not *your* language, nor your native land. You don't have to care about it. You shouldn't even understand it.

SOPHIE. Sometimes I understand.

CROSSMAN. That's dangerous to admit, Sophie. You've been so busy cultivating a pseudo-stupidity. Not that you'd ever be a brilliant girl, but at least you used to be normal. Another five years and you won't be *pseudo*-stupid.

SOPHIE [*smiles*]. I will not mind. It will be easier. [*Carefully.*] You notice me too much, Mr. Ned.

Please do not feel sorry or notice me so much.

CROSSMAN. You came here a nice little girl who had seen a lot of war and trouble. You had spirit, in a quiet way, and you were gay, in a quiet way, which is the only way women should be gay since they are never really gay at all. Only serious people are ever gay and women are very seldom serious people. They are earnest instead. But earnestness has nothing to do with seriousness. So. [*Suddenly*.] What the hell is this marriage business between you and Fred Ellis?

SOPHIE [*softly*]. It is the marriage business between me and Fred Ellis.

CROSSMAN. But what's the matter with you? Haven't you got sense enough to know—

SOPHIE [*quickly*]. I do the best I can. I do the best I can. And I thank you for worrying about me, but you are an educated man with ideas in English that I am not qualified to understand.

CROSSMAN. Listen to me, Sophie. Sometimes when I've had enough to drink—just exactly enough—I feel as if I were given to understand that which I may not understand again. And sometimes then—but rarely—I have an urge to speak out. Fewer drinks, more drinks, and I'm less certain that I see the truth, or I get bored, and none of my opinions and none of the people and issues involved seem worth the trouble. Right now, I've had just enough: so listen to me, Sophie. I say turn yourself around, girl, and go home. Beat it quick.

SOPHIE. You take many words to say simple things. All of you. And you make the simple things—like going to sleep—so hard, and the hard things—like staying awake—so easy. Go home, shall I? Just like that, you say it. Aunt Constance has used up all her money on me, wasted it, and for why and what? How can I go home?

CROSSMAN. If that's all it is I'll find you the money to go home.

SOPHIE [*wearily*]. Oh, Mr. Ned. We owe money in our village, my mother and I. In my kind of Europe you can't live where you owe money. Go home. Did I ever want to come? I have no place here and I am lost and homesick. I like my mother, I— Every night I plan to go. But it is five years now and there is no plan and no chance to find one. Therefore I will do the best I can. [*Very sharply.*] And I will not cry about it and I will not speak of it again.

CROSSMAN [*softly, as if he were moved*]. The best you can?

SOPHIE. I think so. [*Sweetly.*] Maybe you've never tried to do that, Mr. Ned. Maybe none of you have tried.

CROSSMAN. Sophie, lonely people talking to each other can make each other lonelier. They should be careful because maybe lonely people are the only people who can't afford to cry. I'm sorry. [*He exits through the hall, goes up the stairs as the curtain falls.*]

CURTAIN

Act two

SCENE I

SCENE: *The same as Act one. A week later, eight-thirty Sunday morning.*

AT RISE: CONSTANCE *is standing against the outside edge of the porch, leaning on the railing.* NICK *is standing in front of an easel.* CONSTANCE *has on a most unbecoming house dress and her hair is drawn back tight. She looks ten years older. In the living room,* SOPHIE *has finished folding her bedclothes and is hurrying around the room with a carpet sweeper. After a second,* LEON *appears from the direction of the dining room with a tray and dishes and moves out to the porch. He puts down the tray, moves the table, begins to place the dishes.* CONSTANCE *tries desperately to ask him if everything is all right in the kitchen. She does this by moving her lips and trying not to move her head.* LEON *sees her motions but doesn't understand what she is trying to say. The noise of the rattling dishes, and the carpet sweeper, becomes sharp.*

NICK. Constance, please ask them to stop that noise. [*Waves his hand to* LEON *and* SOPHIE.] Go away, both of you.

CONSTANCE. They can't, Nick. I explain it to you every morning! We simply have to get ready for breakfast. [*Quietly.*] Sophie, is everything all right in the kitchen?

SOPHIE. Yes, ma'am. Everything is fine.

NICK [*to* CONSTANCE, *sharply*]. Please keep the pose. Just a few minutes more.

CONSTANCE [*to* LEON]. Tell Sadie not to cook the liver until everybody is downstairs, like she always does. Did she remember about the grits this Sunday? [*To* NICK, *sees his face.*] All right. I'm sorry. But really, I can't run a boardinghouse and pose for—

[*She sighs, settles back.* SOPHIE *picks up her bedclothes and exits through the hall.* LEON *finishes with the porch table and comes back into the living room as* MRS. ELLIS *comes down the steps.*]

MRS. ELLIS [*to* LEON]. My breakfast ready?

LEON. No, ma'am. We'll ring the bell.

MRS. ELLIS. What's the matter with my breakfast?

LEON. Nothing the matter with it. It will be like always.

MRS. ELLIS. It gets later and later every day.

LEON. No, ma'am. That's just you. Want it in the dining room or on the porch?

MRS. ELLIS. Too damp on the porch. Whole house is damp. I haven't slept all summer, Leon.

LEON. Just as well not to sleep in summer.

MRS. ELLIS [*as* LEON *exits*]. You're going to have to explain that to me sometime. [*She turns, goes toward porch, comes around in front of* CONSTANCE.] Constance, he's made you look right mean and ten years older. Why have you done that, Nicholas?

[SOPHIE *comes back into living room with a large urn of coffee and small cups. She puts the tray on a table.*]

NICK [*to* MRS. ELLIS]. Shoo, shoo. This is forbidden ground.

MRS. ELLIS [*calls*]. Sophie, give me a cup. I have to stay awake for church. [*To* CONSTANCE.] Ten years older. When you pay an artist to paint your portrait he makes you ten years younger. I had my portrait done when I was twenty-one, holding my first baby. And the baby looked older than I did. Was rather a scandal or like those people in Tennessee.

NICK. You know if you wouldn't interrupt me every morning, I think I'd fall in love with you.

MRS. ELLIS [*she goes toward* SOPHIE *to get her coffee. During her speech,* SOPHIE *puts three spoons of sugar in the small cup*]. I wouldn't like that. Even if I was the right age I wouldn't like it. Although I realize it would make me dangerously different from every other woman in the world. You would never have been my dish of tea, and isn't that a silly way of saying it? [*To* SOPHIE: *she is now in the living room.*] You're the only one who ever remembers about my sugar. Sophie, will you come up to town [CROSSMAN *comes down the steps and into the room.*] and stay with me for a few weeks while Carrie and Frederick are in Europe?

SOPHIE. I would like that.

MRS. ELLIS. Ned, what shall I give Sophie for her wedding present? My pearls or my mother's diamonds?

CROSSMAN [*to* SOPHIE]. The rich always give something old and precious to their new brides. Something that doesn't cost them new money. Same thing true in your country?

SOPHIE [*smiles*]. I do not know the rich in my country.

MRS. ELLIS. He's quite right, Sophie. Not only something old but something so old that we're sick of it.

CROSSMAN. Why don't you give her a nice new check?

MRS. ELLIS. Only if I have to.

CONSTANCE [*on porch*]. Nick, my neck is breaking—

NICK. All right. All finished for this morning.

[*Turns the picture around so that* CONSTANCE *cannot see it.* SOPHIE *brings two cups of coffee to the porch.*]

CONSTANCE [*collapsing in a chair*]. Whew.

[*Takes the coffee from* SOPHIE, *pats her arm.* SOPHIE *takes the other cup to* NICK.]

NICK. You're the girl I want to paint. Change your mind and we'll start today. Why not, Sophie? [*He is holding her hand.*]

SOPHIE. I am not pretty, Mr. Nicholas.

NICK. You are better than pretty.

[CROSSMAN *comes out to the porch.* SOPHIE *disengages her hand, moves off.*]

CROSSMAN [*staring at* CONSTANCE]. My God, you look awful, Constance. What did you get done up like that for? You're poor enough not to have to pretend you are poor.

NICK [*laughing*]. Go way, Ned. You've got a hangover. I know I have.

[NINA *comes down the steps, comes into the room, says good morning to* MRS. ELLIS *who says good morning to her. She pours herself a cup of coffee. She is close enough to the porch to hear what is said.*]

CONSTANCE. You know, I waited up until twelve o'clock for you both—

NICK. We were late. We had a good get-together last

night. Like old times, wasn't it, Ned? [*To* CONSTANCE.] If you have the normal vanity you'd be pleased at the amount of time we spent on you. Ned loosened up and talked—

CROSSMAN. I did? I thought that was you.

NICK [*laughs*]. I knew you wouldn't remember what you'd said— Don't regret it: did you good to speak your heart out—for once.

CROSSMAN. My heart, eh?

NICK. In a juke-box song called Constance.

CONSTANCE. What? I don't understand.

CROSSMAN [*who has turned sharply, then decided to laugh*]. Neither do I. The stage of not remembering, or speaking out my heart, will come in time, I am sorry to say. But I hope it hasn't come yet.

[*As he turns to go out,* LEON *appears in the hall with a bell and begins to ring the bell.*]

NINA [*a little timidly*]. Good morning, Mr. Crossman.

CROSSMAN. Good morning, Mrs. Denery. I'm sorry you didn't join us last night—to hear me pour my heart out.

NINA. I'm never invited to the pouring of a heart.

CROSSMAN. I looked for you, but Nick said you had a headache.

NINA. Nick always says I have a headache when he doesn't want me to come along, or sees to it that I do have one.

MRS. ELLIS [*gets up quickly*]. All right, Leon. I'm ready. I haven't eaten since four this morning. [*Goes out. As she passes stairs, she shouts up.*] Carrie! Frederick! I simply won't wait breakfast any longer.

[CROSSMAN *follows her out.*]

CONSTANCE [*gets up*]. Well, they seemed to have managed in the kitchen without me. I reckon I better change now. Where'd you get this dress, Nick?

NICK. Place on Dreyenen Street.

CONSTANCE. In a Negro store! You bought this dress in a Negro store! [*He looks at her and laughs.*] I don't mean that. I mean Ned's right. You must have wanted to make me look just about as awful as— For some reason I don't understand. Nick, what *are* you doing? And why won't you let me see the portrait?

NICK. Haven't you yet figured out that Ned is jealous?

CONSTANCE. Jealous of what?

NICK. He's in love with you, girl. As much as he was when we were kids. You're all he talked about last night. How lonely he's been, how much he's wanted you, how often he asked you to marry him—

CONSTANCE. I just don't believe you. Ned never talks about himself. I just don't believe he said such things—

NICK. You know damn well he loves you and you know he's rotting away for you. He said last night—

CONSTANCE [*prissy*]. Nick, if he did talk, and it's most out of character, I don't think I should hear what he said in confidence just to you.

NICK. Oh, run along, honey. You're pleased as punch. When you're not pretending to be genteel.

CONSTANCE [*laughs*]. Genteel? How awful of me. Mama used to say gentility was the opposite of breeding and— [*She has started to move out of the room.*] Did Ned say—er—

[NICK *laughs, she laughs, and exits.* NICK *begins to put away portrait and to fold easel as* NINA *puts down her coffee and comes out to the porch.*]

NICK [*kisses her*]. Morning, darling. [NINA *sits down, watches him.*] What's the matter?

[LEON *appears with breakfast dishes. He serves* NICK *and* NINA *during the next few speeches.*]

NINA. Why have you done that? To Constance?

NICK. Done what? Tell her the truth?

NINA. How could you know it to be the truth? I don't believe Crossman talked to you—

NICK. Look, it makes her happy—and if I can get a little sense into her head it will make him happy. I don't have to have an affidavit to know what's going on in the human heart. [*He leans over, kisses her, sits down to eat his breakfast.*]

NINA [*laughs*]. Oh, you are enjoying yourself so much here. I've seldom seen it this hog-wild. [LEON *exits.*] You're on a rampage of good will. Makes me nervous for even the trees outside. But there's something impertinent about warning an oak tree. How should I do it?

NICK [*laughs*]. First tell me how to understand what you're talking about. [*They eat in silence for a minute.*]

NINA. Are we staying much longer, Nick?

NICK. A few more days. The house officially closes this week, Constance says. The Ellises go tomorrow and the Griggses on Tuesday, I think. Just till I finish.

NINA. Finish what?

NICK [*carefully*]. The portrait, Nina.

[ROSE GRIGGS *comes down the stairs, carrying a small overnight case. She is done up in a pretty, too fussy, hat and a pretty, too fussy, dress. She looks in the room, puts the case down, comes hurrying out to the porch.*]

ROSE. Oh, good morning. Sorry to interrupt. You look so handsome together. [*Makes a gesture to* NICK *meaning "Could you come here?"*] Nick—

NICK [*hospitable*]. Come on out.

ROSE. I'd rather. Could you—

NICK. Come and join us.

ROSE [*hesitantly*]. Well, I wanted to tell *you* but I don't want to worry Nina. You see—

NINA. I'd go away, Mrs. Griggs, but I've been dismissed from so many meals lately that I'm getting hungry.

ROSE [*smiles to* NINA. *Speaks to* NICK]. I called him last night. Just like you advised. And I'm driving right over now. He's the executor of my trust fund, you know. He's very wise: I've got gilt-edged securities.

NICK. Who is this?

ROSE. My brother, of course. Henry, like I told you. [*To*

NINA.] It sounds so mysterious, but it isn't. He's much older. You know he builds ships, I mean during our wars. I'll tell him the whole story, Nick, and he'll know what to do.

NICK [*amused*]. Of course he will.

ROSE. I'm going to drive over to my doctor's. He's going to wait for me on a hot Sunday. It'll be expensive— [*To* NINA.] I had a heart murmur. They had to take me out of school for a year.

NINA. Recently?

[NICK *chokes back a laugh*.]

ROSE [*giggles*]. That's charming—"recently." [*To* NICK.] There's so much I wanted to consult you about. I waited up for you last night, but—well. Should I do *just* as you told me yesterday?

NICK [*who doesn't remember what he told her*]. Sure.

ROSE. Everything?

NICK. Well—

NINA. I think, Mrs. Griggs, you'll have to remind Nick what he told you. Yesterday is a long time ago when you have so many ladies to attend to—

ROSE [*as* NICK *laughs*]. I shouldn't have brought it up like this. Oh, Mrs. Denery, you might as well know: it's about a divorce, and Nick has been most kind.

NINA. I am sure of it.

ROSE. Just one more thing. What should I do about our boys? Should I telephone them or let Henry? One of our sons works on the atom bomb, you know. He's the religious one and it will be traumatic for him. What do you think, Nick?

NINA [*gets up quickly, trying not to laugh, moves away*]. Goodness.

NICK. I think you should go and have your breakfast. It's my firm belief that women only look well in hats after they've eaten.

ROSE [*to* NICK, *softly, secretly*]. And I'm going to just *make* Henry commission the portrait—and for the very good price that he can afford to pay. You remember though that I told you she can't take the braces off her teeth for another six months.

NICK [*laughs*]. Go along now, my dear.

ROSE [*pleased*]. Thank you for all you've done. And forgive me, Nina. I'll be back tonight, Nick, before you go to bed because you'll want to know how everything turns out.

[*She exits through room.* NINA *stands without speaking.*]

NICK [*looks up at her*]. There was a day when we would have laughed together about this. Don't you have fun any more?

NINA. I don't think so.

NICK. She's quite nice, really. And very funny.

NINA. I suppose it's all right to flirt with, or to charm, women and men and children and animals but nowadays it seems to me you include books-in-vellum and sirloin steaks, red squirrels and lamp shades.

NICK [*smiles*]. Are you crazy? Flirt with that silly woman? Come and eat your breakfast, Nina. I've had enough seriousness where none is due.

[*Through this speech,* CARRIE *has come down the steps. She meets* SOPHIE *who is going through the hall to the dining room.* SOPHIE *is carrying a tray.*]

CARRIE. Good morning, dear. Is Frederick in the dining room?

SOPHIE. No. He has not come down as yet.

[*She goes on past.* CARRIE *comes into the room, continues on to the porch.*]

CARRIE [*to* NICK *and* NINA]. Good morning. Your maid said you wanted to see me, Nick.

NICK [*hesitantly*]. Carrie, I hesitated all day yesterday. I told myself perhaps you knew, but maybe, just maybe, you didn't.

NINA [*laughs*]. Oh, it sounds so serious.

CARRIE [*smiles*]. It does indeed.

NICK [*carefully*]. Don't you know that man's reputation, Carrie? You can't travel around Europe with him.

CARRIE. Travel around Europe with *him?* I'm going to Europe with Frederick. [*Then sharply, as she sees his face.*] What do you mean, Nick?

NICK. I—

[SOPHIE *comes into room, goes out to porch. During next speeches, she pours coffee.*]

CARRIE. Please tell me.

NICK. I saw Frederick in the travel agency yesterday with a man I once met in Europe. Not the sort of man you'd expect to see Frederick with.

CARRIE. Are you talking about Mr. Payson?

NICK. Yes, I am. Well, I waited until they left the travel place and then I went in.

NINA. Why did you go in?

NICK. Luther hadn't seen me since we were kids and we got to talking. He said he had booked your passage on the *Elizabeth* and now he had another for Mr. Payson and Fred had just paid for it— [CARRIE *gets up, turns sharply, does not speak.*] I didn't know whether you knew, Carrie, or if I should tell you—

CARRIE. I didn't know. I thank you for telling me. [*After a second, she turns.*] What did you mean, Nick, when you asked me if I knew Payson's reputation? I don't like to press you for gossip, but—

NINA. He didn't mean anything, Mrs. Ellis—

NICK. Oh, look here, Nina, you know he's part of Count Denna's set, and on the nasty fringe of that.

[SOPHIE, *very quietly, leaves the porch.*]

CARRIE. What does that mean: Count Denna's set and the nasty fringe of that?

NINA [*quickly*]. It means very little. The Count is a foolish old man who gives large parties—

NICK [*to* NINA]. Would you want your young son with such people at such parties?

NINA [*angrily*]. I have no son. And I don't know: perhaps I would have wanted only to leave him alone—

CARRIE [*gently*]. All people who have no children think that, Mrs. Denery. But it just isn't true. [*To* NICK.] I don't know much about Mr. Payson but I've been worried for a long time that he's taken Frederick in. Frederick admires his writing, and— Yet I know so little about him. He stayed with us a few weeks in town last winter. He'd just come back from Europe then—

NICK. He'd just come back from a filthy little scandal in Rome. It was all over the papers.

NINA. You don't know it was true.

CARRIE. What kind of scandal? [*No answer. Softly.*] Please help me. I don't understand.

NICK [*gets up*]. Look, Carrie, there's nothing to understand. The guy is just no good. That's all you need to know. He's nobody to travel around Europe with.

CARRIE. How could Fred have— [*She hesitates for a minute.*] It was kind and friendly of you to tell me. I am grateful to you both.

[*She goes slowly across the room and into the hall toward the dining room. There is a long pause:* NICK *takes a sip of coffee, looks around at* NINA.]

NICK. What would you have done?

NINA [*idly*]. I don't know. Have you ever tried leaving things alone?

NICK. I like Carrie. She doesn't know what the hell it's all about—and the chances are the boy doesn't either. I'm sorry for them. Aren't you? [*When she doesn't answer.*] What's the matter, Nina?

NINA. I can smell it: it's all around us. The flowerlike odor right before it becomes troublesome and heavy. It travels ahead of you, Nick, whenever you get most helpful, most loving and most lovable. Down through the years it runs ahead of us—I smell it—and I want to leave.

NICK [*pleasantly*]. I think maybe you're one of the few neurotics in the world who didn't marry a neurotic. I wonder how that happened?

NINA. *I want to leave.*

NICK [*sharply*]. Then leave.

NINA [*after a second*]. You won't come?

NICK. I told you: we'll go Friday. If you want to go before then, then go. But stop talking about it, Nina. Or we'll be in for one of your long farewells—and long returns. I don't think I can stand another. Spare yourself, darling. You pay so heavy, inside. [*Comes to her, puts his arms around her.*] Friday, then. And in the meantime, gentle down to the pretty lady you truly are. [*He kisses her. Exits.*]

[NINA *stands quietly for a minute.* SOPHIE *comes onto the porch, begins to gather the dishes.*]

SOPHIE [*gently*]. Would you like something, Mrs. Denery?

NINA [*softly*]. No, thank you.

[*She moves off, through the room and toward the staircase. As she starts up the stairs,* FREDERICK *comes down.*]

FREDERICK. Good morning.

NINA. Good morning, Mr. Ellis. [*Stops as if she wanted to tell him something.*] I—er. Good morning.

[*She goes up as* SOPHIE, *who has heard their voices, leaves the dishes and comes quickly into the room.*]

SOPHIE [*calling into the hall*]. Fred. Fred. [*He comes in. Shyly.*] Would you like to have your breakfast on the kitchen porch?

FREDERICK. Sure. Why?

SOPHIE. Your mother is—er— [*Points toward dining room.*] She has found out that— Come.

FREDERICK. Denery told her he saw me in the travel agency. I was sure he would. There's nothing to worry about. I intended to tell her this morning.

SOPHIE. But perhaps it would be more wise—

FREDERICK [*smiles to her*]. We'll be leaving here tomorrow and for Europe on the sixteenth. You and I won't see each other for six months. Sophie, you're sure you feel all right about my going?

SOPHIE [*quickly*]. Oh, I do.

FREDERICK. We will visit your mother. And—

SOPHIE [*very quickly*]. No, no, please do not do that. I have not written to her about us—

FREDERICK. Oh.

SOPHIE. You see, we have as yet no date of time, or—

FREDERICK [*smiles*]. I don't think you want a date of time, Sophie. And you don't have to be ashamed of wishing you could find another way. But if there isn't any other way for you, then I'll be just as good to you as I know how. And I know you will be to me.

SOPHIE. You are a kind man. And I will also be kind, I hope.

FREDERICK. It isn't any deal for you. You are a girl who should love, and will one day, of course.

SOPHIE [*puts her hand up to her mouth*]. Shssh. Such things should not be said. [*Cheerfully.*] It will be nice in your house with you, and I will be grateful for it.

FREDERICK. I have no house, Sophie. People like me never have their own house, so-to-speak.

SOPHIE. Never mind. Whatever house. It will be nice. We will make it so.

[*He smiles, pats her arm.*]

FREDERICK. Everybody in the dining room? [*She nods. He starts for hall.*] Might as well face it out.

SOPHIE. I would not. No, I would not. All of you face out too much. Every act of life should not be of such importance—

FREDERICK [*calling into dining room*]. Mother. [SOPHIE *shrugs, smiles, shakes her head, and exits.* FREDERICK *comes back into room, pours himself a cup of coffee. After a minute,* CARRIE *appears. She comes into the room obviously very disturbed. But she does not speak.*] There's nothing to be so upset about.

CARRIE [*after a pause*]. You think that, really?

[MRS. ELLIS *appears in the hall.*]

FREDERICK. We're going to have a companion. That's

all. We know nothing of traveling and Payson knows all of Europe.

MRS. ELLIS. Of course. You're lucky to get Mr. Payson to come along. [*Both of them turn to look at her.*]

FREDERICK [*after a second, to* CARRIE]. What is it, Mother?

CARRIE. I can't say it. It's shocking of you to take along a guest without consulting me. You and I have planned this trip for three years and—

FREDERICK. I didn't consult you because the idea came up quickly and Payson had to get his ticket before the travel office closed for the week end—

CARRIE. *Payson* had to get *his* ticket?

FREDERICK. I thought you'd given up going through my checkbooks.

CARRIE. *Please don't speak that way to me.* [*Pause, quietly, delicately.*] We are not going to Europe.

FREDERICK [*after a second, quietly*]. I am.

CARRIE. We are not going, Fred. We are not going.

MRS. ELLIS. Your mother's feelings are hurt. She had looked forward to being alone with you. Of course.

FREDERICK [*uncomfortably*]. We'll still be together.

CARRIE [*to* MRS. ELLIS]. I don't wish to be interpreted, Mother. [*To* FREDERICK.] There's no sense talking about it: we'll go another time.

FREDERICK [*laughs, unpleasantly*]. Will you stop acting as if you're taking me back to school? I will be disappointed if you don't wish to come with me but I am sailing on the sixteenth. [*Then, quietly:*] I've never had much fun. Never seen the things I wished to see, never met the people I wanted to meet or been the places where I could. There are wonderful things to see and to learn about and to try to understand. We're lucky to have somebody who knows about them and who is willing to have *us* tag along. *I'm* not much to drag around— [*Softly.*] I'll come back, and you can take up my life again. Six months isn't much to ask.

MRS. ELLIS. Six months? Sad to ask so little.

CARRIE [*as if she recognized a tone of voice*]. Mother, please. I—

MRS. ELLIS. Perhaps you won't want to come back at all? I wouldn't blame you.

CARRIE [*nervously*]. Fred, don't make a decision now. Promise me you'll think about it until tomorrow and then we'll talk quietly and—

MRS. ELLIS [*to* FREDERICK]. Don't make bargains with your mother. Everything always ends that way between you. I advise you to go now, or stay.

FREDERICK. I am going. There is nothing to think about. I'm going. [*He turns and exits, goes up staircase. There is a pause.*]

CARRIE [*angry*]. You always do that, Mother. You always arrange to come out his friend and make me his enemy. You've been amusing yourself that way all his life.

MRS. ELLIS. There's no time for all that, Carrie. I warned you to say and do nothing. I told you to make the best of it and go along with them.

CARRIE [*softly*]. How could I do that? That man is a scoundrel and Fred doesn't know it, and won't believe it. What am I to do now?

MRS. ELLIS. You're to go upstairs and say that you are reconciled to his leaving without you but that Frederick is to make clear to his guest that his ten thousand a year ends today and will not begin again. Tell him you've decided young people have a happier time in Europe without American money—

CARRIE [*sharply*]. I couldn't do that. He'd hate me for it. Maybe we'd better let him go, and perhaps I can join him later. Time will— [*Sees* MRS. ELLIS's *face.*] I will not cut off his allowance.

MRS. ELLIS. I didn't know it was you who wrote the check.

CARRIE [*with dignity*]. Are you quite sure you wish to speak this way?

MRS. ELLIS. Relatively sure.

CARRIE. Then I will say as sharply that the money is his father's money, and not yours to threaten him, or deprive him, in any proper sense.

MRS. ELLIS. In any *proper* sense. There is no morality to money, Carrie, and very immoral of you to think so.

CARRIE. If you stop his allowance, Mother, I will simply send him mine.

MRS. ELLIS. Then I won't give you yours. [CARRIE *turns sharply, as if she were deeply shocked.* MRS. ELLIS *now speaks, gently.*] Yes, old people are often harsh, Carrie, when they control the purse. You'll see, when your day comes. And then, too, one comes to be bored with those who fool themselves. I say to myself —one should have power, or give it over. But if one keeps it, it might as well be used, with as little mealymouthness as possible. Go up now, and press him hard, and do it straight. [CARRIE *turns slowly to exit.*] Tell yourself you're doing it for his own good.

CARRIE [*softly*]. I wouldn't be doing it otherwise.

MRS. ELLIS. Perhaps. Perhaps not. Doesn't really matter. [*Laughs, amused.*] I'm off to church now. You can skip church today, Carrie.

CARRIE. Thank you for the dispensation.

[*She begins to move off toward hall and toward stairs as* ROSE *comes from the direction of the dining room and into the room.*]

MRS. ELLIS [*to* CARRIE, *as* CARRIE *moves off*]. Quite all right. You have God's work to do. [*She turns to watch* ROSE *who is elaborately settling herself in a chair as if she were arranging for a scene—which is what she is doing.*] What are you doing, Mrs. Griggs? [ROSE *nervously points to left window.* MRS. ELLIS *looks toward it, watches* ROSE *fix her face.*] Is it Robert Taylor you're expecting or Vice-President Barkley? [GRIGGS *comes in from the left windows. He has on riding pants and an old shirt.*] Oh.

GRIGGS [*to them both*]. Good morning.

MRS. ELLIS. Your wife's getting ready to flirt. You'd be safer in church with me.

[*She exits as* GRIGGS *laughs. He goes to coffee urn.*]

ROSE [*meaning* MRS. ELLIS]. Nasty old thing. [*Then:*] I'm driving over to see him. I'm sorry I had to make such a decision, but I felt it was necessary now.

GRIGGS. Are you talking about your brother?

ROSE. Yes, of course. Now, I know it will be bad for you, Ben, but since *you're* being so stubborn, I didn't know what else to do.

GRIGGS. I think you should see Henry.

ROSE. But he's going to be very, very angry, Ben. And you know how much influence he has in Washington.

GRIGGS [*turns, carefully*]. Tell him to use his influence. And tell him to go to hell.

ROSE [*giggles*]. On a Sunday?

GRIGGS [*gently*]. Rose, no years will make you serious.

ROSE. You used to like me that way.

GRIGGS. So you always wanted to believe.

ROSE. How can I just walk into Henry's happy house and say Ben wants a divorce, and I don't even know the reason. I *ask* him and I *ask* him but he says there is no reason—

GRIGGS. I never said there was no reason. But it isn't the reason that you like, or will accept. If I were in love with another woman you'd rather enjoy that. And certainly Henry would.

ROSE. It would at least be human. And I am not convinced it isn't so. I've done a good deal of thinking about it, and I've just about decided it's why you stayed in Europe so long.

GRIGGS. I didn't arrange World War II and don't listen to the rumors that I did.

ROSE. He said it at the time. He said he had known a good many professional soldiers but nobody had managed to make so much fuss about the war as you did, or to stay away so long. Henry said that.

GRIGGS. I guessed it was Henry who said that.

ROSE [*laughs*]. But you didn't guess that it was Henry who got you the last promotion.

GRIGGS. Rose, stop that. You're lying. You always do it about now. [*Turns to her.*] Give Henry this reason: tell him my wife's too young for me. For Henry's simple mind, a simple reason.

ROSE. I've wanted to stay young, I've—

GRIGGS. You've done more than stay young: you've stayed a child.

ROSE. What about your mother, Ben, have you thought of her? It would kill her—

GRIGGS. She's been dead sixteen years. Do you think this will kill her?

ROSE. You know what I mean. She loved me and she was happy for our marriage.

GRIGGS. No, she didn't. She warned me not to marry— [*With feeling.*] I began my life with a serious woman. I doubt if any man gets over that, or ever really wants any other kind of woman.

ROSE. *Your mother loved me.* You have no right to malign the dead. I say she loved me, I know she did.

GRIGGS [*wearily*]. What difference does it make?

ROSE. You never think anybody loves me. Quite a few men have found me attractive—

GRIGGS [*quickly*]. And many more will, my dear.

ROSE. I always knew in the end I would have to tell you although I haven't seen him since you came home. That I promise you. I told him you were a war hero with a glorious record and he said he wouldn't either any longer—

GRIGGS [*who is at the left window*]. Henry's chauffeur is outside, Rose.

ROSE. He was very, very, very, very much in love with me while he was at the Pentagon.

GRIGGS. Good place to be in love. The car is outside, Rose.

ROSE. Even after we both knew it, he kept on saying

that you didn't make love to a friend, more than a friend's wife.

GRIGGS [*gently*]. Rose, don't let's talk this way.

ROSE. Does it hurt you? Well, you've hurt me enough. The third time you went to Europe was when it really began, maybe the second. Because I, too, wanted affection.

GRIGGS [*gently*]. I can understand that.

ROSE. Ask me who it was. Ask me, Ben, and I will tell you. [*No answer.*] Just ask me.

GRIGGS. No. I won't do that, Rose.

ROSE. Remember when the roses came from Teheran, I mean wired from Teheran, last birthday? That's who sent them. You didn't even like Teheran. You said it was filthy and the people downtrodden. But he sent roses.

GRIGGS. He sounds like the right man. Go to him, Rose, the flying time is nothing now.

ROSE [*angrily*]. You just stop being nasty. [*Then:*] And now I am going to tell you who it is.

GRIGGS [*begins to move toward door, as if he were backing away from her*]. Please, Rose. We have had so many years of this— Please. [*As she is closer to him.*] Do I have to tell you that I don't care who it is?

ROSE [*she begins to move on him*]. I'd like to whisper it. I knew if I ever told you I'd have to whisper it. [*He begins now really to back away.*] Ben, you come right here. Ben stand still. [*He starts to laugh.*] Stop that laughing. [*Very loudly, very close to him.*] It was your cousin, Ralph Sommers. There. [*She turns away.*] There. You won't ever speak with him about it?

GRIGGS. You can be sure of that.

ROSE [*outside an automobile horn is sounded*]. Oh, I'm late. I can't talk any more now, Ben. [*She starts for door, stops.*] What am I going to tell Henry? Anyway, you know Henry isn't going to allow me to give you a divorce. You know that, Ben. [*Carefully.*] And therefore I won't be able to do what you want, and the whole day is just wasted. Please tell me not to go, Ben.

GRIGGS [*as if he has held on to himself long enough*]. Tell Henry that I want a divorce. But in any case I am going away. I am leaving. That is all that matters to me or need matter to you or him. I would prefer a divorce. But I am going, whatever you and Henry decide. Understand that, Rose, the time has come to understand it.

ROSE [*gently, smiling*]. I am going to try, dear. Really I am. It's evidently important to you.

[*She exits through hall. GRIGGS sits down as if he were very tired. A minute later, CROSSMAN comes from the direction of the dining room, carrying the Sunday papers. He looks at Ben, goes to him, hands him the front page. BEN takes it, nods, sits holding it. CROSSMAN crosses to a chair, sits down, begins to read the comic section. A second later, NINA comes down the stairs, comes into the room, starts to speak to BEN and CROSSMAN, changes her mind and sits down. Then CONSTANCE, in an old-fashioned flowered hat and carrying a large palmetto fan, comes through the hall and into the room.*]

CONSTANCE. I'm off to church. Anybody want anything just ring for Leon or Sophie. [*Bravely.*] Want to come to church with me, Ned? [*He peers over his paper, amazed.*] All right. I just thought— Well, Nick told us that you told him last night—

CROSSMAN [*laughs*]. I think perhaps I shall never again go out at night.

CONSTANCE. Oh, it's good for all of us to confide in somebody— [*She becomes conscious of NINA and GRIGGS, smiles awkwardly and then with great determination leans over and kisses CROSSMAN.*] Good-by, darling.

[*Surprised, he gets up, stands watching her leave the room. Then he sits down, staring ahead.*]

NINA [*after a minute, hesitantly*]. I've got a car and a full picnic basket and a cold bottle of wine. Would you— [*Turning to* CROSSMAN *and then to* GRIGGS.] like to come along? I don't know where to go, but—

CROSSMAN. Got enough in your picnic basket for lunch *and* dinner?

NINA [*smiles*]. I think so.

CROSSMAN. Got a mandolin?

NINA [*smiles*]. No. Does that rule me out?

CROSSMAN. Almost. But we'll make do. The General whistles very well.

GRIGGS [*smiles, gets up*]. Is one bottle of wine enough on a Sunday?

NINA [*laughs as she goes toward hall*]. Not for the pure in heart. I'll get five or six more.

[GRIGGS *follows her out through hall.* CROSSMAN *gets up, folds the comic section, puts it under his arm, exits through hall. As he exits,* SOPHIE *comes on the porch. She begins to pile the breakfast dishes on a tray. She sees a half-used roll and a piece of bacon, fixes it for herself, goes out carrying the tray and chewing on the roll as the curtain falls.*]

CURTAIN

SCENE II

SCENE: *The same. Nine-thirty that evening.*

AT RISE: NICK *is lying on the couch. Next to him, on the floor, is an empty champagne glass. On the table, in a silver cooler, is a bottle of champagne.* CONSTANCE *is sitting at the table playing solitaire and humming to the record on the phonograph. On the porch,* SOPHIE *is reading to* MRS. MARY ELLIS.

NICK [*looks up from couch to* CONSTANCE, *irritably*]. Please don't hum.

CONSTANCE. Sorry. I always like that so much, I—

NICK. And please don't talk. Mozart doesn't need it.

CONSTANCE. Haydn.

NICK. Mozart.

CONSTANCE [*tartly*]. I'm sorry but it's Hadyn.

NICK. You know damn well I know what I'm talking about.

CONSTANCE. You don't know what you're talking about. Go look.

NICK [*gets up, picks up his glass, goes to phonograph, shuts it off, looks down, turns away annoyed, picks up a champagne bottle, pours himself a drink, then brings the bottle to* CONSTANCE]. Ready for another?

CONSTANCE. I haven't finished this.

[NICK *carries the bottle out to the porch.*]

MRS. ELLIS [*looks up at him*]. For the fourth time, we don't want any. Please go away. We're having a nice time. We're in the part I like best.

NICK. A nice time? Will I think such a time is a nice time when I am your age? I suppose so.

MRS. ELLIS. No, Mr. Denery. If you haven't learned to read at your age, you won't learn at mine.

NICK [*laughs, pats her shoulder*]. Never mind, I like you.

MRS. ELLIS. You must be damn hard up. People seldom like those who don't like them.

NICK [*pleased*]. You haven't forgotten how to flirt. Come on inside and talk to me. My wife disappears, everybody disappears— [*Stretches.*] I'm bored, I'm bored.

MRS. ELLIS. And that's a state of sin, isn't it?

NICK. Unfortunately, it isn't. I've always said I can stand any pain, any trouble—but not boredom.

MRS. ELLIS. My advice is to try something intellectual for a change. Sit down with your champagne—on which you've been chewing since early afternoon—and try to make a paper hat out of the newspaper or get yourself a nice long piece of string.

NICK [*goes to* SOPHIE]. Sophie, come in and dance with me.

MRS. ELLIS [*calls in*]. Constance, whistle for Mr. Denery, please.

NICK [*to* SOPHIE]. You don't want to sit here and read to Mrs. Ellis.

SOPHIE. Yes, sir, I do. I enjoy the adventures of Odysseus. And the dollar an hour Mrs. Ellis pays me for reading to her.

NICK [*laughs, as* MRS. ELLIS *laughs*]. Give you two dollars an hour to dance with me.

MRS. ELLIS. It's not nearly enough, Sophie.

NICK [*pats* MRS. ELLIS]. You're a corrupter of youth—you steal the best hours.

MRS. ELLIS [*shakes his hand off her shoulder*]. And you're a toucher: you constantly touch people or lean on them. Little moments of sensuality. One should have sensuality whole or not at all. Don't you find pecking at it ungratifying? There are many of you: the touchers and the leaners. All since the depression, is my theory.

NICK [*laughs, pats her again*]. You must have been quite a girl in your day.

MRS. ELLIS. I wasn't. I wasn't at all. [NICK *wanders into the room.* MRS. ELLIS *speaks to* SOPHIE.] I was too good for those who wanted me and not good enough for those I wanted. Like Frederick, Sophie. Life can be hard for such people and they seldom understand why and end bitter and confused.

SOPHIE. I know.

MRS. ELLIS. Do you? Frederick is a nice boy, Sophie—and that is all. But that's more than most, and precious in a small way.

SOPHIE. Yes, I think so.

[MRS. ELLIS *smiles, pats her hand;* SOPHIE *begins again to read.*]

NICK [*near the phonograph, to* CONSTANCE]. Dance with me?

CONSTANCE. I don't know how any more.

NICK [*turns away from the phonograph*]. Has it been wise, Constance, to lose all the graces in the service of this house?

CONSTANCE. Do you think I wanted it that way?

NICK. I'm not sure you didn't. You could have married Ned, instead of dangling him around, the way you've done.

CONSTANCE. Ned has come here each summer because, well, because I guess this is about the only home he has. I loved Ned and honored him, but—I just wasn't in love with him when we were young. You know that, and you'd have been the first to tell me that you can't marry unless you're in love— [*He begins to laugh.*] What are you laughing at?

NICK. "Can't marry unless you're in love." What do you think the rest of us did? I was in love with you. I've never been in love again.

CONSTANCE [*very sharply*]. *I don't want you to talk to me that way.* And I don't believe you. You fell in love with Nina and that's why you didn't come back— [*Desperately.*] You're *very* much in love with Nina. Then and now. Then—

NICK. Have it your way. What are you so angry about? Want to know something: I've never been angry in my life. [*Turns to her, smiles.*] In the end, we wouldn't have worked out. You're a good woman and I am not a good man.

CONSTANCE. Well, whatever the reason, things turned out for the best. [*Carefully.*] About Ned. What did he say last night? I mean did he really talk about me?

NICK [*expansively*]. He said he loved you and wanted you and had wasted his life loving you and wanting you. And that he wasn't coming here any more. This is his last summer in this house.

CONSTANCE [*she turns, pained, startled*]. His last summer? He said that? He really said it was his last summer—

[CARRIE *comes quickly into the room.*]

CARRIE. Has Fred come back?

NICK [*to her*]. Well, where have *you* been? Come and have a drink and talk to me. [*He moves to pour her a drink as she crosses to the porch.*]

CARRIE [*softly, to* MRS. ELLIS]. I've been everywhere. Everywhere possible. I even forced myself to call on Mr. Payson.

MRS. ELLIS. And what did he say?

CARRIE. That Fred came in to see him after he left here this morning, stayed a few minutes, no more, and he hasn't seen him since.

MRS. ELLIS. Ah, that's good.

CARRIE. What's good about it? It means we don't know where he's been since ten this morning. [*Softly, as she sits down.*] I don't know what else to do or where else to look. What should I do? Shall I call the police, what else is there to do?

MRS. ELLIS. Nothing.

CARRIE. How can I do nothing? You shouldn't have made me threaten him. We were wrong. It wasn't important that he wanted to go to Europe with a man his own age. What harm was there in it?

MRS. ELLIS. All his life you've been plucking him this way and plucking him that. Do what you like. Call the police.

NICK [*who has come to the door carrying a glass for* CARRIE. *He hears the last few speeches; gently*]. Can I do anything, Carrie?

CARRIE. I don't know, Nick. I only found one person who had seen him, down by the water—

NICK. Is he—would he have—is that what you're thinking, Carrie?

CARRIE. I'm afraid, I'm afraid.

NICK [*quickly, the kind of efficiency that comes with liquor and boredom*]. Then come on, Carrie. You must go to the police right away. I'll get a boat. Tell the police to follow along. Right away.

[CARRIE *gets up. Starts toward* NICK. SOPHIE *gets up.*]

SOPHIE [*angrily, in French, to* NICK]. Do not enjoy the excitement so much. Stop being a fool.

NICK [*amazed*]. What?

SOPHIE [*in German*]. I said don't enjoy yourself so much. Mind your business.

CARRIE. What? What is it, Sophie?

SOPHIE [*to* CARRIE]. Frederick is in the cove down by the dock. He has been there all day.

NICK [*to* SOPHIE]. You said I was a fool. I don't like such words, Sophie. I don't.

CARRIE [*carefully, to* SOPHIE]. You've let me go running about all day, frantic with terror—

SOPHIE. He wanted to be alone, Mrs. Ellis. That is not so terrible a thing to want.

CARRIE. How dare you take this on yourself? How dare you—

MRS. ELLIS. I hope this is not a sample of you as a mother-in-law.

SOPHIE [*gently, to* CARRIE]. He will return, Mrs. Ellis. Leave him alone.

NICK [*softly*]. Sophie, I think you owe me an apology. You are by way of being a rather sharp little girl underneath all that shyness, aren't you? I'm waiting. [*No answer.*] I'm waiting.

MRS. ELLIS. Well, wait outside, will you?

[*He stares at her, turns, goes in the room.*]

NICK [*very hurt, to* CONSTANCE]. I don't think I like it around here, Constance. No, I don't like it. [*He goes out left windows as* CONSTANCE *stares at him.*]

CARRIE. Since Frederick has confided in you, Sophie, perhaps you should go to him.

SOPHIE. He has not confided in me. Sometimes his troubles are his own.

[*She gets up, walks through room, sits down near* CONSTANCE, *who looks at her curiously. On the porch,* MRS. ELLIS *leans over and whispers to* CARRIE.]

CARRIE. Not tonight.

MRS. ELLIS. Why not tonight? We'll be leaving in the morning.

CARRIE. Because I've changed my mind. I think it best now that we let him go to Europe.

MRS. ELLIS [*gets up*]. He will not want to go to Europe. Haven't you understood that much?

CARRIE [*hesitantly*]. How do you know what he wants or feels—

MRS. ELLIS. I know. [*She comes into room, sits near* CONSTANCE *and* SOPHIE. *After a second* CARRIE *follows her in, stands near them.*] Sophie, I think a decision had best be made now. There should be no further postponement.

CARRIE [*very nervous*]. This isn't the time. Fred will be angry—

MRS. ELLIS [*to* SOPHIE]. I don't want to push you, child, but nothing will change, nothing. I know you've wanted to wait, and so did Frederick, both of you hoping that maybe— But it will all be the same a year from now. Miracles don't happen. I'm telling you the truth, Sophie.

SOPHIE. Yes, Mrs. Ellis, and I agree with you. Nothing will change. If Frederick is willing for an early marriage then I am also willing.

CONSTANCE. Is this the way it's been? *Willing* to marry, *willing* to marry—

SOPHIE [*looks at her*]. I do not use the correct word?

CONSTANCE [*to* MRS. ELLIS *and* CARRIE]. If that's the way it is, then I am not willing. I thought it was two young people who—who—who loved each other. I didn't ever understand it, and I didn't ask questions, but— Willing to get married. What have you been thinking of, why— [*Sharply, hurt.*] What kind of unpleasant thing has this been?

CARRIE. I—I know. I can't—

MRS. ELLIS [*to* CONSTANCE *and* CARRIE]. Why don't you take each other by the hand and go outside and gather in the dew?

SOPHIE. I think Aunt Constance is sad that we do not speak of it in the romantic words of love.

CONSTANCE. Yes, I am. And shocked. When Carrie first talked to me about the marriage, I asked you immediately and you told me you were in love—

SOPHIE. I never told you that, Aunt Constance.

CONSTANCE. I don't remember your exact words but of course I understood— You mean you and Frederick have never been in love? Why? Then why have you—

SOPHIE. Aunt Constance, I do not wish to go on with my life as it has been. I have not been happy, and I cannot continue here. I cannot be what you have wished me to be, and I do not want the world you want for me. It is too late—

CONSTANCE [*softly*]. Too late? You were thirteen years old when you came here. I've tried to give you everything—

SOPHIE. I came from another world and in that world thirteen is not young. I know what you have tried to give me, and I am grateful. But it has been a foolish waste for us both.

CONSTANCE [*softly*]. Were you happy at home, Sophie?

SOPHIE. I did not think in such words.

CONSTANCE. Please tell me.

SOPHIE. I was comfortable with myself, if that is what you mean, and I am no longer.

CONSTANCE [*gently, takes her hand*]. I have been so wrong. And so careless in not seeing it. Do you want to go home now?

SOPHIE. No. My mother cannot— Well, it is not that

easy. I do not— [*As if it were painful.*] I do not wish to go home now.

CONSTANCE [*puzzled*]. It's perfectly simple for you to go home. Why, why isn't it?

SOPHIE. I do not want to say, Aunt Constance. I do not want to. [*With feeling.*] Please do not talk of it any more. Please allow me to do what I wish to do, and know is best for me. [*Smiles.*] And don't look such a way. Frederick and I will have a nice life, we will make it so. [*Goes out.*]

CARRIE [*sharply*]. Don't be too disturbed, Constance. I have decided that Frederick should go to Europe and this time I am not going to allow any interference of any kind.

[FREDERICK *appears in the hall, comes into the room.*]

FREDERICK. I'm not going to Europe, Mother.

CARRIE [*turns to him*]. I have had a bad day. And I have thought of many things. I was mistaken and you were right. You must go wherever you want— however you want to go.

FREDERICK. I am not going, Mother. Payson made that very clear to me this morning.

MRS. ELLIS. Don't, Frederick. It's not necessary. I know.

FREDERICK. But evidently Mother doesn't. . . . Payson made it clear to me that I was not wanted and never had been unless I supplied the money.

[CONSTANCE *gets up, moves off to the porch.*]

CARRIE [*after a second*]. I— Er— I don't believe he meant that. You just tell him that it's all been a mistake and there will certainly be money for the trip. Just go right back and say that, Frederick—

FREDERICK [*very sharply*]. Mother! I don't want to see him again! Ever.

CARRIE. You often imagine people don't like you for yourself. *I'll* go and tell Mr. Payson that it's all fixed now—

MRS. ELLIS. Carrie, you're an ass. [*To* FREDERICK.] But

I hope you haven't wasted today feeling bitter about Mr. Payson. You have no right to bitterness. No right at all. Why shouldn't Mr. Payson have wanted your money, though I must say he seems to have been rather boorish about not getting it. People like us should pay for the interest of people like him. Why should they want us otherwise? I don't believe he ever pretended to feel anything else about you.

FREDERICK [*softly*]. No, he never pretended.

MRS. ELLIS. Then understand that you've been the fool, and not he the villain. Take next week to be sad: a week's long enough to be sad in, if it's true sadness. Plenty long enough.

FREDERICK [*smiles*]. All right, Grandma. I'll take a week.

[SOPHIE *appears at the hall door.*]

SOPHIE [*to* FREDERICK]. You have had no dinner? [*Puts out her hand.*] Then come. I have made a tray for you.

[*He turns, goes to her, takes her hand, goes out.*]

MRS. ELLIS [*gets up, looks at* CARRIE]. Are you going to interfere this time, Carrie? [*No answer. Gently.*] I hope not.

[*She goes out.* CARRIE *stands for a minute near the porch. Then she goes out to* CONSTANCE.]

CARRIE. I don't like it either.

CONSTANCE [*wearily*]. Whole thing sounds like the sale of a shore-front property. I don't know. Seems to me I've been so mixed up about so much. Well, maybe you all know what you're doing.

CARRIE. I don't know what I'm doing.

CONSTANCE. Why did you want the marriage, Carrie? I mean a month ago when you spoke to me—

CARRIE. I don't even know that.

CONSTANCE. You always seem so clear about everything. And so strong. Even when we were girls. I envied you that, Carrie, and wanted to be like you.

CARRIE [*laughs*]. Clear and strong? I wish I could tell

you what I've missed and what I've wanted. Don't envy me, Con.

[*She exits toward hall and staircase. As she does,* NICK *comes in. He is now a little more drunk than when he went out.*]

NICK. Come on out, Carrie. It's wonderful night. Take you for a sail.

CARRIE [*laughs*]. Good night, Nick.

NICK [*as she goes up steps*]. I'm lonely, Carrie. I wouldn't leave you if you were lonely. [*When she doesn't answer, he goes into room, looks around, sees* CONSTANCE *sitting on the porch, goes over, stands in the door looking out. After a second.*] I wish I wanted to go to bed with you, Con. I just can't want to. I don't know why. I just don't want it.

CONSTANCE [*very sharply*]. Stop talking that way. You've had too much to drink. [*She gets up, comes into room. He grabs her arm.*]

NICK. Now you're angry again. [*Puts his arms around her.*] I'll sing you a lullaby. Will you like that?

CONSTANCE. Look, Nick, you've been rather a trial tonight. Do go to bed.

NICK. I'm not going to bed. I'm lonely. I'm—

[*The phone rings.* CONSTANCE *goes to it.* NICK *pours himself a glass of champagne.*]

CONSTANCE. Yes? General Griggs isn't in, Rose. Oh. Yes. Just a minute. [*To* NICK.] Rose Griggs wants to talk to *you*.

NICK. What's the matter, she got some new trouble?

CONSTANCE [*annoyed*]. Do you want the call or don't you?

NICK. Tell her I'm busy.

CONSTANCE [*in phone*]. He's busy drinking, Rose. Shall I leave a message for General Griggs— Oh. [*She puts the phone down, annoyed.*] She says it's absolutely and positively urgent that she speak with *you*. Not her husband. Absolutely and positively.

[*She exits through hall.* NICK *rises and goes to phone.*]

NICK. Look here, my dear, don't be telling people you want to speak to me and not to your husband. Sounds awful. [*Laughs.*] Oh. A most agreeable doctor. Must get to know him. Look, you don't have to convince me. Save it for your husband. Oh, come on. You're getting like those people who believe their own press agents. Anyway, I once knew a woman with heart trouble and it gave her a nice color. You didn't go to the doctor to believe him— [*Sighs, listens.*] All right, of course I'm sorry. It sounds jolly nice and serious and I apologize. [*Listens.*] Oh. Well, that is kind of you. Yes, tell your brother I'd like to stay with him. Oh, by Friday, certainly. How old is your niece? Is she the one with the braces on her teeth? [NINA *appears from the hall entrance. She is followed by* GRIGGS *who is carrying the picnic basket.*] No, I won't paint anything out. That big a hack I'm not. Yes, we'll have plenty of time together. You're a good friend. [*To* NINA *and* GRIGGS.] Had a nice day? [*Into phone.*] No, I'm talking to your husband. Oh. Good-by. Take care of yourself. [*He hangs up.* [*To* GRIGGS.] That was Rose. [*Gaily, to* NINA.] I've had a dull day, darling. [CROSSMAN *comes in.*] Where'd you skip to?

NINA. We drove over to Pass Christian.

NICK. Did you put the car in the garage?

CROSSMAN [*gives* NINA *the keys*]. Yes, all safe.

NICK. Did you drive, Ned? That heavy Isotta? [*To* NINA.] Nobody who drinks as much as Ned should be driving that car. Or any car belonging to me.

NINA. And nobody as tight as you are should talk that way.

NICK [*laughs*]. Have a drink, Ned. [*He brings* CROSSMAN *a glass.*]

CROSSMAN. Thank you, no.

[NICK *turns, hands glass to* GRIGGS.]

GRIGGS. No, thank you.

NICK. What the hell is this? Refusing to have a drink

with me— [*To* CROSSMAN.] I'm trying to apologize to
you. Now take the drink—

NINA. Nick, please—

NICK. Stay out of it, Nina. Women don't know anything about the etiquette of drinking.

CROSSMAN [*laughs*]. Has it got etiquette now? [*As* NICK
again hands him glass. Shakes his head.] Thank you.

NICK [*drunk, hurt*]. Look here, old boy, I say in the
light of what's happened, you've just got to take this.
It's my way of apologizing and I shouldn't have to
explain that to a gentleman. [*He grabs* CROSSMAN'S
arm, playfully presses the glass to CROSSMAN'S *lips.*]

CROSSMAN [*quietly*]. Don't do that.

NICK. Come on, old boy. If I have to pour it down you—

CROSSMAN. Don't do that.

[NICK, *laughing, presses the glass hard against* CROSS-
MAN'S *mouth.* CROSSMAN *pushes the glass and it falls
to the floor.*]

NINA [*sits down*]. Well, we got rid of that glass. But
there are plenty more, Nick.

NICK [*sad, but firm to* CROSSMAN]. Now *you've* put
yourself on the defensive, my friend. That's always
tactically unwise, isn't it, General Griggs?

GRIGGS. I know nothing of tactics, Mr. Denery. Certainly not of yours.

NICK. Then what the hell are you doing as a general?

GRIGGS. Masquerading. They had a costume left over
and they lent it to me.

NICK [*to* CROSSMAN]. I'm waiting, Ned. Pour yourself a
drink, and make *your* apologies.

CROSSMAN. You are exactly the way I remember you.
And that I wouldn't have believed of any man. [*He
turns, goes out.*]

NICK [*like a hurt child*]. What the hell does that mean?
[*Calling.*] Hey, Ned. Come on back and have it your
way. [*Gets no answer, turns, hearty again.*] Come on,
General. Have a bottle with me.

NINA. Are we going to start again?

NICK. General, got something to tell you: your wife telephoned but she didn't want to speak to you.

GRIGGS. That's most understandable. Good night, Mrs. Denery, and thank you for a pleasant day.

NICK. But she'll want to speak to you in the morning. Better stick around in the morning.

GRIGGS [*stares at him*]. Thank you. Good night.

NICK [*following him*]. I think you're doing the wrong thing, wanting to leave Rose. You're going to be lonely at your age without—

GRIGGS. If my wife wishes to consult you, Mr. Denery, that's her business. But I don't wish to consult you. [*He exits.*]

NICK. Sorry. Forget it. [NICK *turns, takes his drink to the couch, lies down.*]

NINA [*after a pause*]. You know, it's a nasty business hating yourself.

NICK. Who's silly enough to do that?

NINA. Me.

NICK [*warmly*]. Come on over here, darling, and tell me about yourself. I've missed you.

NINA. To hate yourself, all the time.

NICK. I love you, Nina.

NINA [*gets up*]. Here we go with that routine. Now you'll bait me until I tell you that you've never loved any woman, or any man, nor ever will. [*Wearily.*] I'll be glad to get out of this house before Constance finds you out. She can go back to sleeping with her dreams. [*After a second.*] You still think you can wind up everybody's affairs by Friday?

NICK. Oh, sure. Friday. Then we're going up to spend a month with Rose's brother, Henry something or other. In New Orleans.

NINA [*carefully*]. What are you talking about?

NICK. Rose fixed it for me. I'm going to do a portrait of her niece, the heiress to the fortune. The girl is balding and has braces. [*Looks at her.*] Five thousand dollars.

NINA. Are you crazy?

NICK. Not a bit.

NINA. It's all right to kid around here—

NICK [*gets up*]. I *don't* know what you mean.

NINA [*violently*]. Please don't let's talk this way. Just tell Mrs. Griggs that you've changed your mind—

NICK. I demand that you tell me what you mean.

NINA [*angrily*]. How many years have we avoided saying it? Why must you walk into it now? [*Pauses, looks at him.*] All right. Maybe it's time: you haven't finished a portrait in twelve years. And money isn't your reason for wanting to do this portrait. You're setting up a silly flirtation with Mrs. Griggs. I'm not going to New Orleans, Nick. I am not going to watch it all again. I can't go on this way with myself— [*Then softly:*] Don't go. Call it off. You know how it will end. Please let's don't this time— We're not young any more, Nick. Somewhere we must have learned something.

NICK [*softly, carefully*]. If I haven't finished every picture I started it's because I'm good enough to know they weren't good enough. All these years you never understood that? I think I will never forgive you for talking that way.

NINA. Your trouble is that you're an amateur, a gifted amateur. And like all amateurs you have very handsome reasons for what you do not finish—between trains and boats.

NICK. You have thought that about me, all these years?

NINA. Yes.

NICK. Then it was good of you and loyal to pretend you believed in me.

NINA. Good? Loyal? What do they mean? I loved you.

NICK. Yes, good and loyal. But I, too, have a little vanity— [*She laughs; he comes to her.*] And no man can bear to live with a woman who feels that way about his work. I think you ought to leave tomorrow, Nina. For good and forever.

NINA [*softly*]. Yes. [*She turns.*] Yes, of course. [*She starts to exit. He follows behind her, talking.*]

NICK. But it must be different this time. Remember I said years ago— "Ten times of threatening is out, Nina," I said—the tenth time you stay gone.

NINA. All right. Ten times is out. [*Quietly, desperately.*] I promise for good and forever.

NICK [*she is climbing the staircase*]. This time, spare yourself the return. And the begging and the self-humiliation and the self-hate. And the disgusting self-contempt. This time they won't do any good. [*He is following her but we cannot see him.*] Let's write it down, darling. And have a drink to seal it.

[*On the words "disgusting self-contempt,"* CONSTANCE *comes into the hall. She hears the words, recognizes* NICK'S *voice and stands, frowning, and thoughtful. Then she turns out the lights on the porch, puts on all lights except one lamp, comes back into the living room and begins to empty the ashtrays, etc.* SOPHIE *comes into the room carrying pillow, sheets, quilts, a glass of milk, and crosses to couch. Without speaking,* CONSTANCE *moves to help her and together they begin to make the couch for the night.*]

SOPHIE [*after a minute, smiles*]. Do not worry for me, Aunt Constance.

CONSTANCE. I can't help it.

SOPHIE. I think perhaps you worry sometimes in order that you should not think.

CONSTANCE [*smiles*]. Yes, maybe. I won't say any more. I'll be lonely without you, Sophie. I don't like being alone, any more. It's not a good way to live. And with you married, I'll be alone forever, unless— Well, Ned's loved me and it's been such a waste, such a waste. I know it now but—well—I don't know. [*Shyly, as a young girl would say it.*] I wanted you to understand. You understand, Sophie? [SOPHIE *stares at her, frowning. Then* CONSTANCE *speaks happily.*] Sleep well, dear.

[*She comes to* SOPHIE, *kisses her, exits, closing door.* SOPHIE *finishes with the bed, brings her milk to the bed table, takes off her robe, puts it around her shoulders, gets into bed, and lies quietly, thinking. Then she turns as she hears footsteps in the hall and she is staring at the door as* NICK *opens it. He trips over a chair, recovers himself, turns on a lamp.*]

NICK [*sharply*]. Constance! What is this—a boys' school with lights out at eleven! [*He sees* SOPHIE.] Where's your aunt? I want to talk to her. What are you doing?

SOPHIE. I think I am asleep, Mr. Denery.

NICK. You're cute. Maybe too cute. [*He pours himself a drink.*] I'm going down to the tavern and see if I can get up a beach party. Tell your aunt. Just tell her that. [*Going toward door.*] Want to come? You couldn't be more welcome. [*She shakes her head.*] Oh, come on. Throw on a coat. I'm not mad at you any more. [*He comes back toward her, looks down at her.*] I couldn't paint you, Sophie. You're too thin. Damn shame you're so thin. [*Suddenly sits down on bed.*] I'm sick of trouble. Aren't you? Like to drive away with me for a few days? [*Smiles at her.*] Nobody would care. And we could be happy. I hate people not being happy. [*He lies down. His head is now on her knees.*] Move your knees, baby, they're bony. And get me a drink.

SOPHIE. Take the bottle upstairs, Mr. Denery.

NICK. Get me a drink. And make it poison. [*Slowly, wearily, she gets up, takes his glass, goes to bottle, pours drink. He begins to sing. She brings glass back to him. He reaches up to take the glass, decides to pull her toward him, and spills the liquid on the bed.*] Clumsy, honey, clumsy. But I'll forgive you. [*He is holding her, and laughing.*]

SOPHIE [*calmly*]. Please go somewhere else, Mr. Denery.

NICK [*springs up, drunk-angry*]. People aren't usually

rude to me, Sophie. Poor little girls always turn rude
when they're about to marry rich little boys. What a
life you're going to have. That boy doesn't even
know what's the matter with him—

SOPHIE [*very sharply*]. Please, Mr. Denery, go away.

NICK [*laughs*]. Oh, you know what's the matter with
him? No European would be as innocent of the
world as you pretend. [*Delighted.*] I tricked you into
telling me. Know that?

SOPHIE. You are drunk and I am tired. Please go away.

NICK [*sits down across the room*]. Go to sleep, child.
I'm not disturbing you. [*She stares at him, decides
she can't move him, gets into bed, picks up a book,
begins to read.*] I won't say a word. Ssh. Sophie's
reading. Do you like to read? Know the best way to
read? With someone you love. Out loud. Ever try it
that way, honey? [*He gets up, comes to bed, stands
near her, speaking over her shoulder.*] I used to
know a lot of poetry. Brought up on Millay. My
candle and all that. "I had to be a liar. My mother
was a leprechaun, my father was a friar." Crazy for
the girl. [*Leans over and kisses her hair. She pulls
her head away.*] Ever wash your hair in champagne,
darling? I knew a woman once. [*Tips the glass over
her head.*] Let's try it.

SOPHIE [*sharply*]. Let us not try it again.

NICK [*sits down beside her*]. Now for God's sake don't
get angry. [*Takes her shoulders and shakes her.*]
I'm sick of angry women. All men are sick of angry
women, if angry women knew the truth. Sophie,
we can always go away and starve. I'll manage to
fall in love with you.

SOPHIE [*he is holding her*]. Mr. Denery, I am sick of
you.

NICK [*softly*]. Tell me you don't like me and I will go
away and not come back.

SOPHIE. No, sir. I do not like you.

NICK. People have hated me. But nobody's ever not liked me. If I thought you weren't flirting, I'd be hurt. Is there any aspirin downstairs? If you kiss me, Sophie, be kind to me for just a minute, I'll go away. I may come back another day, but I'll go all by myself— [*Desperately.*] Please, Sophie, please.

SOPHIE [*sighs, holds up her side face to him*]. All right. Then you will go, remember. [*He takes her in his arms, pulls her down on the bed. She struggles to get away from him. She speaks angrily.*] Do not make yourself such a clown. [*When she cannot get away from him.*] I will call your wife, Mr. Denery.

NICK [*delighted*]. That would be fun, go ahead. We're getting a divorce. Sophie, let's make this night our night. God, Julie, if you only knew what I've been through—

SOPHIE [*violently*]. Oh shut up. [*She pulls away from him with great effort. He catches her robe and rolls over on it.*]

NICK [*giggles as he settles down comfortably*]. Come on back. It's nice and warm here and I love you very much. But we've got to get some sleep, darling. Really we have to. [*Then he turns over and lies still. She stands looking at him.*]

SOPHIE [*after a minute*]. Get up, Mr. Denery. I will help you upstairs. [*No answer.*] Please, please get up.

NICK [*gently, half passed-out*]. It's raining out. Just tell the concierge I'm your brother. She'll understa— [*The words fade off.* SOPHIE *waits a second and then leans over and with great strength begins to shake him.*] Stop that. [*He passes out, begins to breathe heavily. She turns, goes to hall, stands at the foot of the steps. Then she changes her mind and comes back into the room. She goes to the couch, stands, looking at him, decides to pull him by the legs. Softly.*] I'll go away in a few minutes. Don't be so young. Have a little pity. I am old and sick.

[SOPHIE *draws back, moves slowly to the other side of the room as the curtain falls.*]

CURTAIN

Act three

SCENE: *Seven o'clock the next morning.* NICK *is asleep on the couch.* SOPHIE *is sitting in a chair, drinking a cup of coffee. A minute after the rise of the curtain,* MRS. ELLIS *comes down the steps, comes into the room.*

MRS. ELLIS. I heard you bumping around in the kitchen, Sophie. The older you get the less you sleep, and the more you look forward to meals. Particularly breakfast, because you've been alone all night, and the nights are the hardest— [*She sees* NICK, *stares, moves over to look at him.*] What is this?

SOPHIE. It is Mr. Denery.

MRS. ELLIS [*turns to stare at her*]. What's he doing down here?

SOPHIE. He became drunk and went to sleep.

MRS. ELLIS. He has been here all night? [SOPHIE *nods.*] What's the matter with you? Get him out of here immediately.

SOPHIE. I cannot move him. I tried. Shall I get you some coffee?

MRS. ELLIS [*staring at her*]. Are you being silly, Sophie? Sometimes it is very hard to tell with you. Why didn't you call Constance or Mrs. Denery?

SOPHIE. I did not know what to do. Mr. and Mrs. Denery had some trouble between them, or so he said, and I thought it might be worse for her if— [*Smiles.*]

Is it so much? He was just a little foolish and sleepy. [*Goes toward door.*] I will get Leon and Sadie and we will take him upstairs.

MRS. ELLIS [*crosses to door*]. You will not get Leon and Sadie. Rose Griggs may be President of the gossip club for summer Anglo-Saxons, but Leon is certainly President of the Negro chapter. You will get this, er, out of here before anybody else sees him. [*She crosses back to bed, pulls blanket off* NICK.] At least he's dressed. Bring me that cup of coffee. [SO-PHIE *brings cup.*] Mr. Denery! Sit up! [NICK *moves his head slightly.* To SOPHIE.] Hold his head up.

[SOPHIE *holds* NICK's *head;* MRS. ELLIS *tries to make him drink.*]

NICK [*very softly*]. Please leave me alone.

MRS. ELLIS [*shouting in his ear*]. Mr. Denery, listen to me. *You are to get up and get out of here immediately.*

NICK [*giving a bewildered look around the room; then he closes his eyes*]. Julie.

SOPHIE. He has been speaking of Julie most of the night.

MRS. ELLIS [*very sharply*]. Shall I wake your wife and see if she can locate Julie for you, or would you rather be cremated here? Get up, Mr. Denery.

[*He opens his eyes, shuts them again.*]

SOPHIE. You see how it is? [*She tries to pull her robe from under him.*] Would you get off my robe, Mr. Denery?

MRS. ELLIS [*stares at her*]. Sophie, you're a damned little ninny. [*Very loudly, to* NICK.] Now get up. You have no right to be here. You must get up immediately. I say *you*, you get up. [*Shouting.*] Get to your room. Get out of here.

NICK [*turns, opens his eyes, half sits up, speaks gently*]. Don't scream at me, Mrs. Ellis. [*Sees* SOPHIE, *begins to realize where he is, groans deeply.*] I passed out?

SOPHIE. Yes, sir. Most deeply.

MRS. ELLIS. I'm sure after this he won't mind if you don't call him "sir."

NICK. Champagne's always been a lousy drink for me. How did I get down here? [*He turns over.*] I'm sorry, child. What happened?

SOPHIE. You fell asleep.

NICK [*hesitantly*]. Did I— God, I'm a fool. What did I— Did I do anything or say anything? Tell me, Sophie.

MRS. ELLIS. Please get up and get out of here.

NICK. I'm thirsty. I want a quart of water. Or a bottle of beer. Get me a bottle of cold beer, Sophie, will you? [*Looks around the bed.*] Where'd you sleep? Get me the beer, will you?

MRS. ELLIS [*carefully*]. Mr. Denery, you are in Sophie's bed, in the living room of a house in a small Southern town where for a hundred and fifty years it has been impossible to take a daily bath without everybody in town advising you not to dry out your skin. You know that as well as I do. Now get up and go out by the side lawn to the boathouse. Put your head under water, or however you usually treat these matters, and come back through the front door for breakfast.

NICK [*laughs*]. I couldn't eat breakfast.

MRS. ELLIS. I don't find you cute. I find only that you can harm a young girl. Do please understand that.

NICK. Yes, I do. And I'm sorry. [*He sits up, untangling himself from the robe.*] What's this? Oh, Sophie, child, I must have been a nuisance. I am *so* sorry.

MRS. ELLIS [*very loudly*]. Get up and get the hell out of here.

[*The door opens and* ROSE, *carrying her overnight handbag, sticks her head in.*]

ROSE [*to* MRS. ELLIS, *who is directly on a line with the door*]. You frightened me. I could hear you outside on the lawn, so early. Oh, Nick. How nice you're downstairs. I never expected it— [*Her voice trails*

off as she sees SOPHIE *and realizes* NICK *is on the bed.*]
Oh. [*Giggles, hesitantly.*] You look like you just
woke up, Nick. I mean, just woke up where you are.

MRS. ELLIS [*to* NICK]. Well, that's that. Perhaps you
wanted it this way, Mr. Denery.

[*She starts out as* LEON *appears carrying the coffee urn.*
ROSE *stands staring at* NICK.]

LEON [*very curious, but very hesitant in doorway*].
Should I put it here this morning, like every day,
or—

MRS. ELLIS. Who told you, Leon?

LEON. Told me what, Mrs. Ellis? Sadie says take on in
the urn—

MRS. ELLIS. I'm not talking about the urn. Who told
you about Mr. Denery being here?

LEON. Told me? Why Miss Sophie came in for coffee
for them.

MRS. ELLIS [*after a second, shrugs, points to coffee urn*].
Take it into the dining room.

LEON. You want me come back and straighten up,
Miss Sophie?

MRS. ELLIS [*waves him out*]. Mrs. Griggs will be glad to
straighten up. [*She exits.*]

ROSE [*softly to* NICK]. You were here all night? I come
back needing your help and advice as I've never before needed anything. And I find you—

NICK. Rose, please stop moving about. You're making
me seasick. And would you go outside? I'd like to
speak to Sophie.

ROSE. I am waiting for you to explain, Nick. I don't
understand.

NICK. There is no need for you to understand.

ROSE. I'm not judging you. I know that there's probably a good explanation— But please tell me, Nick,
what happened and then I won't be angry.

NICK. What the hell are you talking about? What's it
your business? Now go upstairs, Rose.

ROSE [*softly, indignant*]. "Go upstairs, Rose." "What's

it your business?" After I work my head off getting the commission of the portrait for you and after I go to the doctor's on your advice, although I never would have gone if I had known, and I come back here and find you this way. [*Sits down.*] You've hurt me and you picked a mighty bad day to do it.

[*The door opens and* CONSTANCE *comes in. She goes to* NICK, *stands looking at him.*]

CONSTANCE. Nick, I want you to go to that window and look across the street. [*He stares at her. Then he gets up slowly and slowly moves to the window.*] The Carters have three extra guests on their breakfast porch, the Gable sisters are unexpectedly entertaining— [*With feeling.*] This house was not built to be stared at.

NICK [*gently*]. It can't be that bad, Constance.

CONSTANCE. It is just that bad.

NICK. I'm sorry. I was silly and drunk but there's no sense making more out of it than that.

CONSTANCE. I am not making anything out of it. But I know what is being made out of it. In your elegant way of life, I daresay this is an ordinary occurrence. But not in our village. [*The telephone rings.* CONSTANCE *picks up phone, says "Hello," pauses, "Hello, Mrs. Sims." Then her face becomes angry and she hangs up. She stands looking at the phone, and then takes it off the hook. Turns to* NICK.] Please explain to me what happened. [*Points to telephone and then across the street.*] I only know what they know.

SOPHIE. Mr. Denery came down looking for someone to talk to. He saw me, recited a little poetry, spoke to me of his troubles, tried to embrace me in a most mild fashion. He was uncertain of my name and continued throughout the night to call me Julie although twice he called for Cecile. And fell into so deep a sleep that I could not move him. Alcohol. It is the same in my country, every country.

CONSTANCE [*softly, as if it pained her*]. You are taking a very light tone about it, Sophie.

SOPHIE [*turns away, goes toward couch, and through the next speeches will strip the bed and pile the clothes*]. I will speak whichever way you think most fits the drama, Aunt Constance.

CONSTANCE. Will you tell me why you stayed in the room? Why didn't you come and call me, or—

NICK. Oh, look here. It's obvious. The kid didn't want to make any fuss and thought I'd wake up and go any minute. Damn nice of you, Sophie, and I'm grateful.

CONSTANCE. It was the most dangerous "niceness" I've ever heard of.

[SOPHIE *looks up, stares at* CONSTANCE.]

NICK. I know it's hard for you, Constance, but it's not all that much.

CONSTANCE. Isn't it? You've looked out of the window. Now go down to the drugstore and listen to them and I think you'll change your mind.

NICK. Look. A foolish guy drinks, passes out—

ROSE [*amazed as she turns to look at* SOPHIE]. Why look at Sophie. Just as calm as can be. Making the bed. Like it happened to her every night.

CONSTANCE [*turns, realizes* ROSE *is in the room*]. What are you doing here, Rose?

ROSE. Sitting here thinking that no man sleeps in girl's bed unless she gives him to understand— [CONSTANCE *stares at her.*] You can blame Nick all you like. But you know very well that a nice girl would have screamed.

CONSTANCE. How dare you talk this way? Whatever gave you the right— I hope it will be convenient for you to leave today. I will apologize to the General.

ROSE [*softly*]. That's all right, Constance. I must leave today, in any case. You see, I have to— [*Sighs, sincerely.*] You won't be mad at me for long when you know the story. Oh, I'm very tired now. Could I have my breakfast in bed? Doctor's orders. [*She goes out, passes* CROSSMAN *who is coming in. In sepulchral tones.*] Good morning, dear Ned. [*Then in a sudden burst:*] Have you heard—?

CROSSMAN [*cheerful.*] Good morning. Yes, I've heard. I'm not the one deaf man in town.

[*Passes her. She stares at his back, reluctantly exits.*]

CONSTANCE [*turns*]. Ned, what should we do?

CROSSMAN. Is there always something that can be done, remedied, patched, pulled apart and put together again? There is nothing to "do," Con. [*Smiles to* SOPHIE, *amused.*] How are you, Sophie?

SOPHIE. I am all right, Mr. Ned.

NICK. Ned, is it as bad as [*Gestures toward window and* CONSTANCE.] Constance thinks?

CONSTANCE. What's the difference to you? You're just sitting there telling yourself what provincial people we are and how you wish you were in the Ritz bar with people who would find it amusing with their lunch. [*Very angrily.*] You came here as my friend and in our small life—in our terms—you have dishonored my house. It has taken me too many years to find out that you—

CROSSMAN. All right, Con, maybe that's the truth; but what's the good of discussing Nick's character and habits now?

NICK [*sincerely, to* CONSTANCE]. Whatever you think of me, I didn't want this. I know what it will mean to Sophie and I'll stay here and face anything that will help you. Anything I can say or do—

SOPHIE [*she finishes folding the clothes*]. What will it "mean" to me, Mr. Ned?

CONSTANCE [*softly*]. You're old enough to know. And I believe you do know.

SOPHIE. I want to know from Mr. Ned what he thinks.

CROSSMAN [*to* SOPHIE]. I know what you want to know: the Ellis name is a powerful name. They won't be gossiped about out loud. They won't gossip about you and they won't listen to gossip about you. In their own way they'll take care of things. [*Carefully.*] You can be quite sure of that. Quite sure.

SOPHIE [*after a second*]. And that is all?

CROSSMAN. That is all.

SOPHIE [*softly, carefully*]. Thank you, Mr. Ned.

CONSTANCE. Take care of things? She hasn't done anything. Except be stupid. The Tuckerman name is as good as the Ellis name—

CROSSMAN. Yes, yes. Sure enough.

[SOPHIE *looks at* CROSSMAN, *exits. She passes* LEON *in the hall. He is carrying his hat.*]

LEON. Mrs. Ellis is cutting up about her breakfast. And Sadie's waiting for orders. We're messed this morning, for good.

CONSTANCE. Not at all. Tell Sadie I'm coming. [*She goes toward door.*] What's your hat for, Leon?

LEON. Well, kind of a hot sun today.

CONSTANCE. Not in here. Rest your hat: you'll have plenty of time to gossip when the sun goes down. [*She goes out.*]

NICK [*miserably*]. Ned. Ned, you understand I never thought it would make all this— Is Constance being— I mean, is she being old-maid fussy or is it really unpleasant—

CROSSMAN. It is unpleasant. She loves the girl, and she's worried for her.

NICK [*groans*]. If I could do something—

CROSSMAN. You did; but don't make too much of it.

NICK [*the first kind word he's heard*]. Thank you, boy.

CROSSMAN. Or too little. [NICK *groans.*] Nobody will blame you too much. The girl's a foreigner and they don't understand her and therefore don't like her. You're a home-town boy and as such you didn't do anything they wouldn't do. Boys will be boys and in the South there's no age limit on boyishness. Therefore, she led you on, or whatever is this morning's phrase. You'll come off all right. But then I imagine you always do.

NICK. You think this is coming off all right?

CROSSMAN. No, I don't.

NICK. I didn't even want her. Never thought of her that way.

CROSSMAN [*too sympathetic*]. That *is* too bad. Better luck next time. You're young—in spirit.

[*He exits into hall toward dining room as* HILDA, *carrying a jewel case, and hat box, comes down the steps. She has on her hat and gloves.*]

NICK [*who is sitting on a line with the door and sees her, speaks in German*]. Where are you going?

HILDA [*in German*]. Good morning, sir. I am taking madame's luggage to the nine-thirty train.

[*She moves off as* NINA *appears.* NINA *has on a hat and gloves. On her heels is* ROSE *in a fluffy negligee.* ROSE *is talking as she follows* NINA *down the steps.*]

ROSE. I'm not trying to excuse him. Of course it was indiscreet but you're a woman of the world, Nina, and you know what young girls are with a tipsy man. Nina, do believe that I saw them this morning and he didn't have the slightest interest in her. Nina—

NINA [*turns to her, very pleasantly*]. I know it's eccentric of me, Mrs. Griggs, but I dislike being called by my first name before midnight.

ROSE [*hurt, softly*]. You shouldn't allow yourself such a nasty snub. I'm only trying to help Nick. I know him well enough to know that he didn't do a thing— [NINA *laughs.*] He's been my good friend. I'm trying to be a friend to him.

NINA. You will have every opportunity.

NICK [*very angry*]. Will you please not stand there in the hall discussing me?

ROSE. Oh! [*Looks at* NICK, *then at* NINA, *steps back into hall, calls toward kitchen.*] Leon! Could I have my tray upstairs? [*As she goes past room and upstairs.*] Anybody seen my husband this morning? [*Exits.*]

NICK. Nina. [*She comes in.*] I just want to say before you go that they're making an awful row about nothing—

NINA. You don't owe me an explanation, Nick.

NICK. Nothing happened, Nina, I swear. Nothing happened.

NINA. Try out phrases like "nothing happened" on women like Mrs. Griggs.

NICK [*smiles*]. I'm sorry as all hell but they sure are cutting up—

NINA. Well, it is a tasty little story. Particularly for a girl who is going to be married.

NICK. My God, I'd forgotten about the boy. I must say he's an easy boy to forget about. Now I'll have to take *him* out and explain—

NINA. Don't do that, Nick. He isn't a fool.

NICK [*looks around, thinking of anything to keep her in the room*]. Shall I get you a cup of coffee, darling?

NINA. No. Darling will have it on the train. [*She turns.*]

NICK. Nina, I swear I didn't sleep with her.

NINA. I believe you. The girl doesn't like you.

NICK. Doesn't she? She's been very kind to me. She could have raised hell. That doesn't sound as if she doesn't like me. [NINA *laughs.*] Don't laugh at me this morning. [*After a second.*] What can I do for her, Nina?

NINA. You used to send wicker hampers of white roses. With a card saying "White for purity and sad parting."

NICK. Stop being nasty to me. [*Then he smiles and comes toward her.*] Or maybe it's a good sign.

NINA. It isn't. I just say these things by rote. [*Turns.*] I don't know how long I'll be in New York, but you can call Horace and he'll take care of the legal stuff for us.

NICK [*close to her*]. I told you last night that I would agree to the separation because I knew with what justice you wanted to leave me.

NINA [*coldly*]. That's not at all what you said.

NICK. I was tight. It was what I meant to say—

NINA [*very angry*]. You're lying. You said just what you meant to say: I was to leave. And not make you sick with my usual begging to come back—

NICK. Stop, Nina. Take any kind of revenge you want, but—please—some other day. [*Leans down, puts his face against her face.*] Don't leave me. Don't ever leave me. We've had good times, wild times. They made up for what was bad and they always will. Most people don't get that much. We've only had one trouble; you hate yourself for loving me. Because you have contempt for me.

NINA. For myself. I have no right—

NICK. No, nobody has. No right at all.

NINA. I wouldn't have married you, Nick, if I had known—

NICK. You would have married me. Or somebody like me. You've needed to look down on me, darling. You've needed to make fun of me. And to be ashamed of yourself for doing it.

NINA [*softly*]. Am I that sick?

NICK. I don't know about such words. You found the man you deserved. That's all. I am no better and no worse than what you really wanted. You like to—to demean yourself. And so you chose me. You must say I haven't minded much. Because I've always loved you and known we'd last it out. Come back to me, Nina, without shame in wanting to. [*He leans down, kisses her neck.*] Put up with me a little longer, kid. I'm getting older and I'll soon wear down.

NINA [*she smiles, touched*]. I've never heard you speak of getting old.

NICK [*quickly*]. Yes. [*Then:*] The *Ile* sails next week. Let's get on. We'll have fun. Tell me we're together again and you're happy. Say it, Nina, quick.

NINA. I'm happy.

[*He takes her in his arms, kisses her. Then he stands away, looks at her, and smiles shyly.*]

NICK. There'll be no more of what you call my "home-comings." Old friends and all that. They are damn bores, with empty lives.

NINA. Is that so different from us?

NICK. If we could only do something for the kid. Take her with us, get her out of here until they get tired of the gossip—

NINA [*laughs*]. I don't think we will take her with us.

NICK [*laughs*]. Now, now. You know what I mean.

NINA. I know what you mean—and we're not taking her with us.

NICK. I suppose there isn't anything to do. [*Softly, his hand to his head.*] I feel sick, Nina.

NINA. You've got a hangover.

NICK. It's more than that. I've got a sore throat and my back aches. Come on, darling, let's get on the train.

NINA. You go. I'll stay and see if there's anything I can do. That's what you really want. Go on, Nicky. Maybe it's best.

NICK. I couldn't do that.

NINA. Don't waste time, darling. You'll miss the train. I'll bring your clothes with me.

NICK [*laughs, ruefully*]. If you didn't see through me so fast, you wouldn't dislike yourself so much. [*Comes to her.*] You're a wonderful girl. It's wonderful of you to take all this on—

NINA. I've had practice.—

NICK [*hurt*]. That's not true. You know this never happened before.

NINA [*smiles*]. Nicky, it always confuses you that the fifth time something happens it varies slightly from the second and fourth. No, it never happened in this house before. Cora had a husband and Sylvia wanted one. And this isn't a hotel in Antibes, and Sophie is not a rich Egyptian. And this time you didn't break your arm on a boat deck and it isn't 1928—

NICK. This is your day, Nina. But pass up the chance to play it too hard, will you? Take me or leave me now but don't—

NINA. You're right. Please go, darling. Your staying won't do any good. Neither will mine, but maybe—

NICK. When will you come? I tell you what: you take the car and drive to Mobile. I'll get off there and wait at the Battle House. Then we can drive the rest of the way together. Must be somewhere in Mobile I can waste time for a few hours—

NINA [*gaily*]. I'm sure. But let's have a week's rest. Now go on.

NICK [*takes her in his arms*]. I love you, Nina. And we'll have the best time of our lives. Good luck, darling. And thank you. [*He kisses her.*] They won't rag you, nobody ever does. We'll get the bridal suite on the *Ile* and have all our meals in bed. [*He moves away.*] If you possibly can, bring the new portrait with you. I can finish it now. And try to get me the old portrait, darling. Maybe Constance will sell it to you— [NINA *laughs.*] All right. Think what you want and I'll be what I am. I love you and you love me and that's that and always will be. [*He exits. She stands quietly.*]

NINA. You love me and I love you and that's that and always will be. [*Then she turns, goes to the bell cord, pulls it. After a second,* CONSTANCE *appears in the hall.* NINA *does not turn.*] Leon, could I have breakfast on the porch?

CONSTANCE [*in the doorway. She is carrying a tray*]. Yes, of course. I'll tell Leon to bring it.

[NINA *turns, stares at her.*]

NINA. I am very sorry, Constance.

CONSTANCE. I am sorry, too, my dear.

NINA. I don't know what else to say. I wish—

CONSTANCE. There's nothing for us to say. [*There is an awkward pause.*] Well. I'll tell Leon. Old lady Ellis is having her second breakfast. She always does on her last day. I don't know why. [*She starts out as* CARRIE, *followed by* FREDERICK, *comes down the steps.* CARRIE *has on her hat, etc., as if she were ready for traveling.* FREDERICK *is carrying two valises.*] Shall I send breakfast up to Nick?

NINA [*very quickly*]. No, no. I'll just have mine and—

FREDERICK [*calling to* CONSTANCE]. Where's Sophie?

CONSTANCE. I'll send her in.

FREDERICK [*smiles*]. Don't sound so solemn, Miss Constance.

CONSTANCE [*sharply*]. I didn't mean to.

[*She disappears in the direction of the dining room.* FREDERICK *and* CARRIE *come into the room.*]

NINA. Mr. Ellis, I should be carrying a sign that says my husband is deeply sorry and so am I.

[*He smiles at her. She turns, goes out on the porch, closes the door behind her.*]

CARRIE [*hesitantly*]. She's a nice woman, I think. Must be a hard life for her.

FREDERICK [*laughs*]. I don't think so. [*Turns as he hears* SOPHIE *in the hall.*] Now remember, Mother. [SOPHIE *appears in the door.* FREDERICK *goes to her, takes her chin in his hand, kisses her.*] I want to tell you something fast. I don't know how to explain it but I'm kind of glad this foolishness happened. It makes you seem closer to me, some silly way. You must believe that, although I can't make it clear. Now there are two things to do right away. Your choice.

SOPHIE. I have made bad gossip for you, Frederick. We must speak about that. Right away.

FREDERICK. There's no need to speak about it again. It's a comic story and that's all. And you must begin to laugh about it.

SOPHIE [*smiles*]. I did laugh but nobody would laugh with me. And nobody will laugh in New Orleans, either. Is that not so, Mrs. Ellis?

CARRIE. I think you should travel up with us, Sophie. Right now. Whatever is to be faced, we will do much better if we face it all together and do it quickly.

FREDERICK [*looks at her, as if they had had previous talk*]. You're putting it much too importantly. There's nothing to be faced.

CARRIE. I didn't mean to make it too important. Of course, it isn't—

SOPHIE [*puts her hand on his arm*]. It is important to you and you must not be kind and pretend that—

FREDERICK [*firmly*]. I'm not being kind. I told you the truth. I've been in trouble, now you've been in a little. That's all, now or ever. [*Shyly.*] As far as I'm concerned, it makes us seem less like strangers. I'd hope you'd feel the same way—

CARRIE [*quickly*]. Run and pack a bag, Sophie. It's a lovely day for driving and we'll be in town for lunch. I think you and I will have it at the club— Now let's not talk about it any more—

SOPHIE. No. It would be most mistaken of me to come now. My leaving here would seem as if I must be ashamed and you shamed for me. I must not come with you today. I must stay here. [*Smiles.*] It must be faced.

FREDERICK. All right. That makes sense. Mother and Grandma will drive up and I'll stay here—

SOPHIE [*very quickly*]. No, no. You must not stay here. [*Points to window, meaning town.*] They knew you had made plans to leave today as usual. And so you must leave. We must act as if nothing had happened, and if we do that, and are not worried, it will all end more quickly. [*Goes to* FREDERICK.] Believe me, Frederick. You know what I say is true. All must seem to be as it has been. [*To* MRS. ELLIS.] You tell him that, please, Mrs. Ellis.

CARRIE. I don't know. You belong with us now, Sophie. We don't want to leave you, or Constance. I think she should come along and—

SOPHIE. Oh, she would not do that. You know she

would not. [*Smiles, very cheerful.*] Now. You are both very kind. But you know what I say is best for us all, and of no importance whether I come one week or the next. [*Takes* FREDERICK'S *arm.*] You have said I must laugh about it. I do laugh, and so it will be nothing for me to stay.

[MRS. ELLIS *comes to the door from the direction of the dining room.*]

CARRIE. *Good-by, Sophie.* We will be waiting for you. [*She exits, passing* MRS. ELLIS *without speaking.*]

FREDERICK [*unhappily*]. You all seem to know what's right, what's best, so much faster than I do. I—

SOPHIE [*smiles, puts her hand over his mouth*]. This is best. Please.

FREDERICK. Then let us come back this week end. Can I do that?

SOPHIE [*she touches his face*]. I think so. You are a nice man, Frederick.

FREDERICK [*kisses her*]. And you're a nice girl to think so. See you in a few days. [*Turns to go out, passes* MRS. ELLIS.] I feel happy, Grandma.

[MRS. ELLIS *nods, waits for him to exit.* SOPHIE *sits down.*]

MRS. ELLIS [*after a second*]. Sophie.

SOPHIE [*smiles as if she knew what was coming*]. Yes.

MRS. ELLIS. Did *Carrie* ask you to leave with us? [SO-PHIE *nods.*] Ah. That's not good. When Carrie gets smart she gets very smart. Sophie, Frederick meant what he said to you. But I know them both and I would guess that in a week, or two or three, he will agree to go to Europe with his mother and he will tell you that it is only a postponement. And he will believe what he says. Time and decisions melt and merge for him and ten years from now he will be convinced that you refused to marry him. And he will always be a little sad about what could have been.

SOPHIE. Yes. Of course.

MRS. ELLIS. Carrie never will want him to marry. And she will never know it. Well, she, too, got cheated a long time ago. There is very little I can do—perhaps very little I want to do any more. Don't judge him too harshly, child.

SOPHIE [*smiles*]. No, I will not judge. I will write a letter to him.

MRS. ELLIS. That's my girl. Don't take from us what you don't have to take, or waste yourself on defeat. [*She gets up.*] Oh, Sophie, feel sorry for Frederick. He is nice and he is nothing. And his father before him and my other sons. And myself. Another way. Well. If there is ever a chance, come and see me.

[*She moves out.* SOPHIE *remains seated. After a second* CONSTANCE *comes in from the hall. She looks at* SOPHIE.]

CONSTANCE [*hesitantly*]. Carrie tells me you'll be going up to town in a few weeks to stay with them. I'm glad. [*No answer.*] Er. Why don't you go up to my room, dear, and lie down for a while? [*Points to porch.*] She's on the porch. I'm going to ask the Denerys to leave today. I am sure they will want to, anyway. And the Griggses will be going and then just you and I—

SOPHIE. I will not be going to New Orleans, Aunt Constance, and there will be no marriage between Frederick and me.

CONSTANCE [*stares at her*]. But Carrie told me—

SOPHIE. Now she believes that she wants me. But it will not be so.

CONSTANCE [*after a second*]. I wish I could say I was surprised or angry. But I'm not sorry. No marriage without love—

SOPHIE [*pleasantly*]. Yes. Yes.

CONSTANCE [*gently*]. You're not to feel bad or hurt.

SOPHIE. I do not.

CONSTANCE. I'm—I'm glad. Mighty glad. Everything

will work out for the best. You'll see. After everybody goes, we'll get the house and the accounts
cleaned up and straightened out as usual. [*Gaily.*]
And then I think you and I will take a little trip. I
haven't seen Memphis in years and maybe in a few
months— [*Gently.*] You know what? We can even
sell, rent, the place, if we want to. We can pick up
and go anywhere we want. You'll see, dear. We'll
have a nice time.

SOPHIE [*almost as if she were speaking to a child*]. Yes,
Aunt Constance.

[CONSTANCE *goes out.* SOPHIE *turns to watch* LEON *who,
during* CONSTANCE'S *speech, has come out on the
porch and is serving breakfast to* NINA. SOPHIE *rises
and goes out to the porch. She takes the coffee pot
from* LEON—*he has finished placing the other dishes—
nods to him, and pours* NINA'S *coffee.* LEON *exits.*
NINA *turns, sees* SOPHIE, *turns back.*]
You are a pretty woman, Mrs. Denery, when your
face is happy.

NINA. And you think my face is happy *this* morning?

SOPHIE. Oh, yes. You and Mr. Denery have had a nice
reconciliation.

NINA [*stares at her*]. Er. Yes, I suppose so.

SOPHIE. I am glad for you. That is as it has been and
will always be. [*She sits down.*] Now could I speak
with you and Mr. Denery?

NINA [*uncomfortably*]. Sophie, if there was anything I
can do— Er. Nick isn't here. I thought it best for us
all—

SOPHIE [*softly*]. Ah. Ah, my aunt will be most sad.

NINA. Sophie, there's no good my telling you how sorry,
how— What can I do?

SOPHIE. You can give me five thousand dollars, Mrs.
Denery. American dollars, of course. [*Demurely; her
accent from now on grows more pronounced.*] I have
been subjected to the most degrading experience

from which no young girl easily recovers. [*In French.*] A most degrading experience from which no young girl easily recovers—

NINA [*stares at her*]. It sounds exactly the same in French.

SOPHIE. Somehow sex and money are simpler in French. Well. In English, then, I have lost or will lose my most beloved fiancé; I cannot return to school and the comrades with whom my life has been so happy; my aunt is uncomfortable and unhappy in the only life she knows and is now burdened with me for many years to come. I am utterly, utterly miserable, Mrs. Denery. I am ruined. [NINA *bursts out laughing.* SOPHIE *smiles.*] Please do not laugh at me.

NINA. I suppose I should be grateful to you for making a joke of it.

SOPHIE. You make a mistake. I am most serious.

NINA [*stops laughing*]. Are you? Sophie, it is an unpleasant and foolish incident and I don't wish to minimize it. But don't you feel you're adding considerable drama to it?

SOPHIE. No, ma'am. I did not say that is the way I thought of it. But that is the way it will be considered in this place, in this life. Little is made into very much here.

NINA. It's just the same in your country.

SOPHIE. No, Mrs. Denery. You mean it is the same in Brussels or Strasbourg or Paris, with those whom you would meet. In my class, in my town, it is not so. In a poor house if a man falls asleep drunk—and certainly it happens with us each Saturday night—he is not alone with an innocent young girl because the young girl, at my age, is not so innocent and because her family is in the same room, not having any other place to go. It arranges itself differently; you have more rooms and therefore more troubles.

NINA. Yes. I understand the lecture. [*Pauses.*] Why do you want five thousand dollars, Sophie?

SOPHIE. I wish to go home.

NINA [*gently*]. Then I will be happy to give it to you. Happier than you know to think we can do something.

SOPHIE. Yes. I am sure. But I will not accept it as largesse—to make you happy. We will call it a loan, come by through blackmail. One does not have to be grateful for blackmail money, nor think of oneself as a charity girl.

NINA [*after a second*]. Blackmail money?

SOPHIE. Yes ma'am. You will give me five thousand dollars because if you do not I will say that Mr. Denery seduced me last night. [NINA *stares at her, laughs.*] You are gay this morning, madame.

NINA [*shocked*]. Sophie, Sophie. What a child you are. It's not necessary to talk this way.

SOPHIE. I wish to prevent you from giving favors to me.

NINA. I intended no favors. And I don't like this kind of talk. Nick did not seduce you and I want no more jokes about it. [*Pleasantly.*] Suppose we try to be friends—

SOPHIE. I am not joking, Mrs. Denery. And I do not wish us to be friends.

NINA [*gets up*]. I would like to give you the money. And I will give it to you for that reason and no other.

SOPHIE. It does not matter to me what you would like. You will give it to me for my reason—or I will not take it.

[*Angrily,* NINA *goes toward door, goes into the room, then turns and smiles at* SOPHIE.]

NINA. You are serious? Just for a word, a way of calling something, you would hurt my husband and me?

SOPHIE. For me it is more than a way of calling something.

NINA. You're a tough little girl.

SOPHIE. Don't you think people often say other people are tough when they do not know how to cheat them?

NINA [*angrily*]. I was not trying to cheat you of anything—

SOPHIE. Yes, you were. You wish to be the kind lady who most honorably stays to discharge—within reason—her obligations. And who goes off, as she has gone off many other times, to make the reconciliation with her husband. How would you and Mr. Denery go on living without such incidents as me? I have been able to give you a second, or a twentieth, honeymoon.

NINA [*angrily*]. Is that speech made before you raise your price?

SOPHIE [*smiles*]. No. A blackmail bargain is still a bargain.

[CROSSMAN *appears in the hall,* SOPHIE *sees him.*]

NINA. How would— How shall we make the arrangements?

SOPHIE [*calling*]. Mr. Ned. [*Pleasantly, to* NINA.] Mr. Ned will know what to do.

NINA [*after a second to* CROSSMAN.] I'd like to get a check cashed. It's rather a large check. Could you vouch for me at the bank?

CROSSMAN. Sure. That's easy enough. The bank's just around the corner.

SOPHIE. Would you like me to come with you, Mrs. Denery?

NINA [*smiles*]. You know, I think perhaps it's wisest for you to stay right here. You and I in a bank, cashing a check, this morning, could well be interpreted as a pay-off, or blackmail. [*She goes out.*]

SOPHIE. I will be going home, Mr. Ned.

CROSSMAN [*smiles*]. Good. [*Looks at her, turns to stare at* NINA, *as she passes him and goes into hall.*] At least I hope it's good.

SOPHIE. I think it is more good than it is not good. [*He goes out.*]

[ROSE *comes down the steps. Her manner is hurried, nervous. She goes immediately to windows. She looks out as if she saw somebody coming. Then she turns and sees* SOPHIE.]

ROSE [*very nervous*]. Oh. Good morning, Sophie.

SOPHIE. We have seen each other earlier this morning, Mrs. Griggs.

ROSE. Oh. It's like a nightmare to me, as if a year had gone by. I've asked for my breakfast tray twice and nobody pays any attention. And the doctor says that's the way it *must* be.

SOPHIE [*exiting*]. I will get it for you.

ROSE [*back at the window, speaks to* SOPHIE *who has left the room*]. Not you, Sophie. You have your own troubles, God knows. I don't know how any of us can eat anything today. [GRIGGS, *in riding pants and old shirt, comes in through the windows. Because she is upstage of the windows, he does not see her until she speaks.*] I've been looking everywhere for you, Ben.

GRIGGS [*turns*]. Rose. You knew where I was.

ROSE. That was all we needed here today: a telephone call to the stables. Oh, Ben, it was I who found them. But you don't know about it—

GRIGGS. I've heard all about it.

ROSE. Terrible, isn't it?

GRIGGS. Not very.

ROSE. He's been a disappointment to me. I've been lying on the bed thinking about it. Nick Denery, I mean.

GRIGGS. I'm sorry.

ROSE. You know, Ben, I've just about come to the conclusion that I'm often wrong about people, mostly men.

GRIGGS. And what did you and Henry—ah—put together, Rose?

ROSE. It was so hot in town. Henry's got that wonderful air conditioning, of course, but it's never like your own air. I think Sunday's the hottest day of the year, anyway. Athalia's braces cost twenty-five hundred dollars at that Greek dentist's and believe me they don't make anybody look prettier—

GRIGGS. What point did you come to about my decision?

ROSE. Decision? Your decision—

GRIGGS [*tensely*]. Please stop playing the fool. I'm afraid of you when you start playing that game.

ROSE. *You* afraid of *me*?

GRIGGS. Yes, me afraid of you. This very minute. Be kind, Rose, and tell me what has been decided for me.

ROSE [*softly, very nervous*]. It wasn't like that. Before I saw Henry I went to see Dr. Wills. You know he won't ever see patients on Sunday.

GRIGGS. Not unless the fee is over a hundred.

ROSE. I've always been sorry you didn't like Howard Wills. He's known as the best man in the South, Ben. He gave up a beach picnic with that woman, you know. Only that famous a man could buck having an open mistress—

GRIGGS. I don't want to hear about Wills. Come to the point. What did you and Henry—

ROSE [*grows sober, recognizing the tone*]. I've been uneasy. I've sometimes been in pain, all summer. But I guess I knew because I guess I've known since that army doctor in 1934— I didn't want to talk about it— [*Moves toward him, frightened.*] I have bad heart trouble, Ben.

GRIGGS [*after a second, as if he were sick*]. Don't play that trick, Rose. It's just too ugly.

ROSE. I am not playing a trick. Wills wrote you a letter about it. [*She reaches in the pocket of her robe, hands him a folded paper. He takes it from her, reads it.*]

GRIGGS [*violently*]. How much did Henry pay Wills for this?

ROSE [*gently, seriously*]. It wasn't bought. Even Henry couldn't buy it. [*She turns, goes toward door, as if she were a dignified woman.*]

GRIGGS [*softly*]. Tell me about it.

ROSE. There isn't much to tell. I've known some of it for years, and so have you. I just didn't know it was this bad, or didn't want to. Wills says I must lead a —well, a very different life. I'll have to go to the country somewhere and rest most of the day—not climb steps or go to parties or even see people much. I like people, I— Well, I just don't understand what I can do, except sit in the sun, and I hate sun— Oh, I don't know. He said worse than I am saying— I can't say it—

GRIGGS. Yes. [*After a second.*] I'm sorry.

ROSE. I know you are. You've been my good friend. I'm frightened, Ben. I play the fool, but I'm not so big a fool that I don't know I haven't got anybody to help me. I pretend about the boys and what they're like but I know just as well as you do that they're not very kind men and won't want me and won't come to help me. [*With feeling.*] And of course I know about Henry—I always have. I've got nobody and I'm not young and I'm scared. Awful scared.

GRIGGS. You don't have to be.

ROSE [*who is crying, very quietly*]. Wills says that if I take good care I might be, probably will be, in fine shape at the end of the year. Please stay with me this year, just this year. I will swear a solemn oath—believe me I'm telling the truth now—I will give you a divorce at the end of the year without another word. I'll go and do it without any fuss, any talk. But please help me now. I'm so scared. Help me, please. One year's a lot to ask, I know, but—

[GRIGGS *comes to her, presses her arm.*]

GRIGGS. Of course. Of course. Now don't let's speak of it again and we'll do what has to be done.

[*She turns, goes out. He stands where he is. A minute later,* CROSSMAN *comes in, stares at* GRIGGS *as if he knew something was wrong. Then he speaks casually.*]

CROSSMAN. Seen Sophie?

GRIGGS [*as if it were an effort, idly*]. In the kitchen, I guess. Tough break for the kid, isn't it?

CROSSMAN. Perhaps it isn't. I don't know.

[*He watches as* GRIGGS *takes out a cigarette and lights it.* GRIGGS's *hands are shaking and as he puts out the match, he stares at them.*]

GRIGGS [*smiles*]. My hands are shaking.

CROSSMAN. What's the matter?

GRIGGS. Worst disease of all. I'm all gone. I've just looked and there's no Benjamin Griggs.

CROSSMAN [*after a second*]. Oh, that. And you've just found that out?

GRIGGS. Just today. Just now.

CROSSMAN. My God, you're young.

GRIGGS [*laughs*]. I guess I was. [*Slowly, carefully.*] So at any given moment you're only the sum of your life up to then. There are no big moments you can reach unless you've a pile of smaller moments to stand on. That big hour of decision, the turning point in your life, the someday you've counted on when you'd suddenly wipe out your past mistakes, do the work you'd never done, think the way you'd never thought, have what you'd never had—it just doesn't come suddenly. You've trained yourself for it while you waited—or you've let it all run past you and frittered yourself away. [*Shakes his head.*] I've frittered myself away, Crossman.

CROSSMAN. Most people like us.

GRIGGS. That's no good to me. Most people like us haven't done anything to themselves; they've let it be done to them. I had no right to let it be done to me, but I let it be done. What consolation can I find in not having made myself any more useless than an Ellis, a Denery, a Tuckerman, a—

CROSSMAN. Say it. I won't mind. Or a Crossman.

GRIGGS. The difference is you've meant to fritter yourself away.

CROSSMAN. And does that make it better?

GRIGGS. Better? Worse? All I know is it makes it different. Rose is a sick woman. But you know I'm not talking only about Rose and me, don't you?

CROSSMAN. I know.

GRIGGS [*very slowly*]. I am not any too sure I didn't partly welcome the medical opinion that made it easier for me to give up. [*Then in a low voice as if to himself.*] And I don't like Rose. And I'll live to like her less.

[*He starts toward door.* CONSTANCE *appears in the hall carrying a tray. She is followed by* SOPHIE *who is carrying a carpet sweeper and a basket filled with cleaning rags, etc.* CONSTANCE *comes to the door. She speaks wearily.*]

CONSTANCE [*to* GRIGGS]. Sorry about Rose's breakfast. I forgot it. Sophie is going to help Rose to get packed. I don't mean to sound inhospitable but since you were going tomorrow, anyway— [*Gently.*] I'm just tired and it would be easier for us. Please forgive me but you're an old friend and you will understand.

GRIGGS [*smiles, pats her arm*]. I'll take the tray.

[*He takes it from her, goes up the steps.* CONSTANCE *comes in the room, sighs, sits down.*]

CROSSMAN. Sophie. [SOPHIE *comes to him.*] I was asked to give you this. [*He hands her an envelope.*]

SOPHIE. Thank you, Mr. Ned.

CONSTANCE [*idly, without much interest*]. Secrets?

CROSSMAN. That's right. Secrets. Old love letters or something.

[SOPHIE *laughs, goes out.*]

CONSTANCE [*after a silence*]. I hate this house today.

CROSSMAN. Well, they'll all be gone soon.

CONSTANCE. You won't go? Please.

CROSSMAN. I'll stay for a few days if you'd like me to.

CONSTANCE. Oh, yes. I need you to stay.

CROSSMAN [*points out of window*]. Don't worry about what the town thinks. Just act as if nothing had happened and they'll soon stop talking.

CONSTANCE. Oh, I'm not worrying about that. [*Pauses.*] I feel so lost, Ned. As if I distrusted myself, didn't have anything to stand on. I mean, right now, if you asked me, I just wouldn't know what I thought or believed, or ever had, or— [*Shyly.*] Well, what *have* I built my life on? Do you know what I mean?

CROSSMAN. Sure. I know.

CONSTANCE [*as if she had trouble with the words*]. It's— it's so painful. [*Then as if she wished to change the subject quickly.*] Sophie will be going back to Europe. She just told me. She *wants* to go. Did you know that?

CROSSMAN. Is that so?

CONSTANCE. I was so sure I was doing the right thing, bringing her here. You see? That's part of what I mean by not knowing the things I thought I knew. Well. She wants me to come with her and live with them, but I told her I'd be no happier in a new life than she was. [*Pauses as if she were coming to something that frightens her.*] Nick said you wouldn't be coming here next summer. Did you say anything like that, or was it one of Nick's lies? [*He does not answer her. She stares at him.*] Why, Ned?

CROSSMAN. Hasn't anything to do with you, Con. Just think I'd be better off. You know, it's kind of foolish—two weeks a year—coming back here and living a life that isn't me anymore. [*Laughs.*] It's too respectable for me, Con. I ain't up to it anymore.

CONSTANCE. Oh. It's what I look forward to every summer. What will I— [*Very quickly.*] Where is Nick? I haven't seen him. I wish they'd leave—

CROSSMAN. They've gone.

CONSTANCE [*stares at him*]. Without a word to me? Exactly the way he left years ago. I didn't ever tell you that, did I? We had a date for dinner. He didn't come. He just got on the boat. I didn't ever tell anybody before. [*Violently.*] What a fool. All these years of making a shabby man into the kind of hero who would come back some day all happy and shining—

CROSSMAN. Oh, don't do that. He never asked you to make him what he wasn't. Or to wait twenty years to find him out.

CONSTANCE. No, he didn't. That's true. [*She rises, goes to the portrait and stands staring at it.*] Do I look like this?

CROSSMAN. You look nice.

CONSTANCE. Come and look at it.

CROSSMAN. No. I don't want to.

CONSTANCE. Much older than I thought or— And I don't look very bright. [*Puts the picture away from her.*] Well, I haven't been very bright. I want to say something to you. I can't wait any longer. Would you forgive me?

CROSSMAN. Forgive you? For what?

CONSTANCE. For wasting all these years. For not knowing what I felt about you, or not wanting to. Ned, would you have me now?

CROSSMAN [*after a second*]. What did you say?

CONSTANCE. Would you marry me? [*There is a pause. Then* SOPHIE *comes from the direction of the dining room carrying a carpet sweeper and a cleaning basket. As she goes up the steps she is singing a cheerful French song.* CONSTANCE *smiles.*] She's happy. That's good. I think she'll come out all right, always.

CROSSMAN [*stares at* CONSTANCE, *then slowly, carefully*]. I live in a room and I go to work and I play a game called getting through the day while you wait for night. The night's for me—just me—and I can do anything with it I want. There used to be a lot of things to do with it, good things, but now there's a bar and another bar and the same people in each bar. When I've had enough I go back to my room— or somebody else's room—and that never means much one way or the other. A few years ago I'd have weeks of reading—night after night—just me. But I don't do that much anymore. Just read, all night long. You can feel good that way.

CONSTANCE. I never did that. I'm not a reader.

CROSSMAN [*as if he hadn't heard her*]. And a few years ago I'd go on the wagon twice a year. Now I don't do that anymore. And I don't care. [*Smiles.*] And all these years I told myself that if you'd loved me everything would have been different. I'd have had a good life, been worth something to myself. I wanted to tell myself that. I wanted to believe it. Griggs was right. I not only wasted myself, but I wanted it that way. All my life, I guess, I wanted it that way.

CONSTANCE. And you're not in love with me, Ned?

CROSSMAN. No, Con. Not now.

CONSTANCE [*gets up, goes to him*]. Let's have a nice dinner together, just you and me, and go to the movies. Could we do that?

CROSSMAN. I've kept myself busy looking into other people's hearts so I wouldn't have to look into my own. [*Softly.*] If I made you think I was still in love, I'm sorry. Sorry I fooled you and sorry I fooled myself. And I've never liked liars—least of all those who lie to themselves.

CONSTANCE. Never mind. Most of us lie to ourselves, darling, most of us.

CURTAIN

CAMINO REAL

by *Tennessee Williams*
for *Elia Kazan*

"In the middle of the journey of our life I came to myself in a dark wood where the straight way was lost."

CANTO I, DANTE's Inferno

© Copyright 1953 by Tennessee Williams.
Reprinted by permission of New Directions.

All Rights Reserved, including the right of reproduction in whole or in part in any form.

CAUTION: *Professionals and amateurs are hereby warned that Camino Real, being fully protected under the copyright laws of the United States, the British Empire including the Dominion of Canada, and all other countries of the Copyright Union, and other countries, is subject to royalty. All rights, including professional, amateur, motion-picture, recitation, lecturing, public reading, radio and television broadcasting, and the rights of translation into foreign languages, are strictly reserved. Particular emphasis is laid on the question of readings, permission for which must be obtained in writing from the author's agents. All enquiries should be addressed to the author's agents: Miss Audrey Wood, MCA Artists Ltd., 598 Madison Avenue, New York City.*

The amateur acting rights of Camino Real are controlled exclusively by the Dramatists Play Service, Inc., 14 East 38th Street, New York 16, N. Y., without whose permission in writing no amateur performances of it may be made.

A line spoken by La Madrecita in Block 15 is a quotation from Four Quartets by T. S. Eliot, copyright 1936, by Harcourt, Brace & Co., and reprinted with their permission.

The "Foreword," which appeared in slightly different form in the New York Times on March 15, 1953, copyright 1953 by the New York Times, is reprinted with its permission.

*First production, March 19, 1953,
at the Martin Beck Theatre, New York,
with the following cast:*

GUTMAN, *Frank Silvera*
SURVIVOR, *Guy Thomajan*
ROSITA, *Aza Bard*
FIRST OFFICER, *Henry Silva*
JACQUES CASANOVA, *Joseph Anthony*
LA MADRECITA DE LOS PERDIDOS, *Vivian Nathan*
HER SON, *Rolando Valdez*
KILROY, *Eli Wallach*
FIRST STREET CLEANER, *Nehemiah Persoff*
SECOND STREET CLEANER, *Fred Sadoff*
ABDULLAH, *Ernesto Gonzalez*
A BUM IN A WINDOW, *Martin Balsam*
A. RATT, *Mike Gazzo*
THE LOAN SHARK, *Salem Ludwig*
BARON DE CHARLUS, *David J. Stewart*
LOBO, *Ronne Aul*
SECOND OFFICER, *William Lennard*
A GROTESQUE MUMMER, *Cluck Sandor*
MARGUERITE GAUTIER, *Jo Van Fleet*
LADY MULLIGAN, *Lucille Patton*
WAITER, *Page Johnson*
LORD BYRON, *Hurd Hatfield*
NAVIGATOR OF THE FUGITIVO, *Antony Vorno*
PILOT OF THE FUGITIVO, *Martin Balsam*
MARKET WOMAN, *Charlotte Jones*
SECOND MARKET WOMAN, *Joanna Vischer*
STREET VENDOR, *Ruth Volner*
LORD MULLIGAN, *Parker Wilson*
THE GYPSY, *Jennie Goldstein*
HER DAUGHTER, ESMERALDA, *Barbara Baxley*
NURSIE, *Salem Ludwig*
EVA, *Mary Grey*
THE INSTRUCTOR, *David J. Stewart*
ASSISTANT INSTRUCTOR, *Parker Wilson*

MEDICAL STUDENT, *Page Johnson*

DON QUIXOTE, *Hurd Hatfield*

SANCHO PANZA, *(Not in production)*

PRUDENCE DUVERNOY, *(Not in production)*

OLYMPE, *(Not in production)*

STREET VENDORS: *Aza Bard, Ernesto Gonzalez, Charlotte Jones, Gluck Sandor, Joanna Vischer, Ruth Volner, Antony Vorno.*

GUESTS: *Martin Balsam, Mary Grey, Lucille Patton, Joanna Vischer, Parker Wilson.*

PASSENGERS: *Mike Gazzo, Mary Grey, Page Johnson, Charlotte Jones, William Lennard, Salem Ludwig, Joanna Vischer, Ruth Volner.*

AT THE FIESTA: *Ronne Aul, Martin Balsam, Aza Bard, Mike Gazzo, Ernesto Gonzalez, Mary Grey, Charlotte Jones, William Lennard, Nehemiah Persoff, Fred Sadoff, Gluck Sandor, Joanna Vischer, Antony Vorno, Parker Wilson.*

EDITOR'S NOTE: The version of *Camino Real* here published is considerably revised over the one presented on Broadway. Following the opening there, Mr. Williams went to his home at Key West and continued to work on this play. When he left six weeks later to direct Donald Windham's *Starless Night* in Houston, Texas, he took the playing version with him and reworked it whenever time allowed. It was with him when he drove in leisurely fashion back to New York. As delivered to the publisher, the manuscript of *Camino Real* was typed on three different typewriters and on stationery of hotels across the country.

Three characters, a prologue and several scenes that were not in the Broadway production have been added, or reinstated from earlier, preproduction versions, while other scenes have been deleted.

Camino Real is divided into a Prologue and Sixteen "Blocks," scenes with no perceptible time lapse between them for the most part. There are intermissions indicated after Block Six and Block Eleven.

The action takes place in an unspecified Latin-American country.

Prologue

*As the curtain rises, on an almost lightless stage, there
is a loud singing of wind, accompanied by distant,
measured reverberations like pounding surf or distant
shellfire. Above the ancient wall that backs the set and
the perimeter of mountains visible above the wall, are
flickers of a white radiance as though daybreak were
a white bird caught in a net and struggling to rise.*

*The plaza is seen fitfully by this light. It belongs to
a tropical seaport that bears a confusing, but somehow
harmonious, resemblance to such widely scattered
ports as Tangiers, Havana, Vera Cruz, Casablanca,
Shanghai, New Orleans.*

*On stage left is the luxury side of the street, con-
taining the façade of the Siete Mares hotel and its low
terrace on which are a number of glass-topped white
iron tables and chairs. In the downstairs there is a
great bay window in which are seen a pair of elegant
"dummies," one seated, one standing behind, looking
out into the plaza with painted smiles. Upstairs is a
small balcony and behind it a large window exposing a
wall on which is hung a phoenix painted on silk: this
should be softly lighted now and then in the play, since
resurrections are so much a part of its meaning.*

*Opposite the hotel is Skid Row which contains the
Gypsy's gaudy stall, the Loan Shark's establishment
with a window containing a variety of pawned articles,
and the "Ritz Men Only" which is a flea-bag hotel or
flophouse and which has a practical window above its*

downstairs entrance, in which a bum will appear from time to time to deliver appropriate or contrapuntal song titles.

Upstage is a great flight of stairs that mount the ancient wall to a sort of archway that leads out into "Terra Incognita," as it is called in the play, a wasteland between the walled town and the distant perimeter of snow-topped mountains.

Downstage right and left are a pair of arches which give entrance to dead-end streets.

Immediately after the curtain rises a shaft of blue light is thrown down a central aisle of the theatre, and in this light, advancing from the back of the house, appears DON QUIXOTE DE LA MANCHA, *dressed like an old "desert rat." As he enters the aisle he shouts, "Hola!", in a cracked old voice which is still full of energy and is answered by another voice which is impatient and tired, that of his squire,* SANCHO PANZA. *Stumbling with a fatigue which is only physical, the old knight comes down the aisle, and* SANCHO *follows a couple of yards behind him, loaded down with equipment that ranges from a medieval shield to a military canteen or Thermos bottle. Shouts are exchanged between them.*

QUIXOTE [*ranting above the wind in a voice which is nearly as old*]. Blue is the color of distance!

SANCHO [*wearily behind him*]. Yes, distance is blue.

QUIXOTE. Blue is also the color of nobility.

SANCHO. Yes, nobility's blue.

QUIXOTE. Blue is the color of distance and nobility, and that's why an old knight should always have somewhere about him a bit of blue ribbon ... [*He jostles the elbow of an aisle-sitter as he staggers with fatigue; he mumbles an apology.*]

SANCHO. Yes, a bit of blue ribbon.

QUIXOTE. A bit of faded blue ribbon, tucked away in whatever remains of his armor, or borne on the tip of his lance, his—unconquerable lance! It serves to

remind an old knight of distance that he has gone
and distance he has yet to go . . .

[SANCHO *mutters the Spanish word for excrement as
several pieces of rusty armor fall into the aisle.*]

[QUIXOTE *has now arrived at the foot of the steps onto
the forestage. He pauses there as if wandering out of
or into a dream.* SANCHO *draws up clanking behind
him.*]

[MR. GUTMAN, *a lordly fat man wearing a linen suit and
a pith helmet, appears dimly on the balcony of the
Siete Mares, a white cockatoo on his wrist. The bird
cries out harshly.*]

GUTMAN. Hush, Aurora.

QUIXOTE. It also reminds an old knight of that green
country he lived in which was the youth of his heart,
before such singing words as *Truth!*

SANCHO [*panting*]. —Truth.

QUIXOTE. *Valor!*

SANCHO. —Valor.

QUIXOTE [*elevating his lance*]. *Devoir!*

SANCHO. —Devoir . . .

QUIXOTE. —turned into the meaningless mumble of
some old monk hunched over cold mutton at supper!

[GUTMAN *alerts a pair of* GUARDS *in the plaza, who cross
with red lanterns to either side of the proscenium
where they lower black and white striped barrier
gates as if the proscenium marked a frontier. One
of them, with a hand on his holster, advances toward
the pair on the steps.*]

GUARD. Vien aquí. [SANCHO *hangs back but* QUIXOTE
stalks up to the barrier gate. The GUARD *turns a
flashlight on his long and exceedingly grave red face,
"frisks" him casually for concealed weapons, examines a rusty old knife and tosses it contemptuously away.*] Sus papeles! Sus documentos!

[QUIXOTE *fumblingly produces some tattered old papers from the lining of his hat.*]

GUTMAN [*impatiently*]. Who is it?

GUARD. An old desert rat name Quixote.

GUTMAN. Oh!— Expected!— Let him in.

[*The* GUARDS *raise the barrier gate and one sits down to smoke on the terrace.* SANCHO *hangs back still. A dispute takes place on the forestage and steps into the aisle.*]

QUIXOTE. Forward!

SANCHO. Aw, naw. I know this place. [*He produces a crumpled parchment.*] Here it is on the chart. Look, it says here: "Continue until you come to the square of a walled town which is the end of the Camino *Real* and the beginning of the *Camino Real*. Halt there," it says, "and turn back, Traveler, for the spring of humanity has gone dry in this place and—"

QUIXOTE [*he snatches the chart from him and reads the rest of the inscription*]. "—there are no birds in the country except wild birds that are tamed and kept in—" [*He holds the chart close to his nose.*] —Cages!

SANCHO [*urgently*]. Let's go back to La Mancha!

QUIXOTE. Forward!

SANCHO. The time has come for retreat!

QUIXOTE. The time for retreat never comes!

SANCHO. *I'm* going back to *La Mancha!* [*He dumps the knightly equipment into the orchestra pit.*]

QUIXOTE. *Without me?*

SANCHO [*bustling up the aisle*]. With you or without you, old tireless and tiresome master!

QUIXOTE [*imploringly*]. Saaaaaan-chooooooooo!

SANCHO [*near the top of the aisle*]. I'm going back to La Maaaaaaaaan-chaaaaaaa . . .

[*He disappears as the blue light in the aisle dims out. The* GUARD *puts out his cigarette and wanders out of the plaza. The wind moans and* GUTMAN *laughs softly as the* ANCIENT KNIGHT *enters the plaza with such a desolate air.*]

QUIXOTE [*looking about the plaza*]. —Lonely . . . [*To his surprise the word is echoed softly by almost un-*

seen figures huddled below the stairs and against the wall of the town. QUIXOTE *leans upon his lance and observes with a wry smile—*] —When so many are lonely as seem to be lonely, it would be inexcusably selfish to be lonely alone. [*He shakes out a dusty blanket. Shadowy arms extend toward him and voices murmur.*]

VOICE. Sleep. Sleep. Sleep.

QUIXOTE [*arranging his blanket*]. Yes, I'll sleep for a while, I'll sleep and dream for a while against the wall of this town . . . [*A mandolin or guitar plays "The Nightingale of France."*] —And my dream will be a pageant, a masque in which old meanings will be remembered and possibly new ones discovered, and when I wake from this sleep and this disturbing pageant of a dream, I'll choose one among its shadows to take along with me in the place of Sancho . . . [*He blows his nose between his fingers and wipes them on his shirttail.*] —For new companions are not as familiar as old ones but all the same—they're old ones with only slight differences of face and figure, which may or may not be improvements, and it would be selfish of me to be lonely alone . . . [*He stumbles down the incline into the Pit below the stairs where most of the* STREET PEOPLE *huddle beneath awnings of open stalls.*]

[*The white cockatoo squawks.*]

GUTMAN. Hush, Aurora.

QUIXOTE. And tomorrow at this same hour, which we call madrugada, the loveliest of all words, except the word alba, and that word also means daybreak—

—Yes, at daybreak tomorrow I will go on from here with a new companion and this old bit of blue ribbon to keep me in mind of distance that I have gone and distance I have yet to go, and also to keep me in mind of—

[*The cockatoo cries wildly.*]

[QUIXOTE *nods as if in agreement with the outcry and*

folds himself into his blanket below the great stairs.]

GUTMAN [*stroking the cockatoo's crest*]. Be still, Aurora. I know it's morning, Aurora. [*Daylight turns the plaza silver and slowly gold.* VENDORS *rise beneath white awnings of stalls. The* GYPSY'S *stall opens. A tall, courtly figure, in his late middle years (* JACQUES CASANOVA) *crosses from the Siete Mares to the* LOAN SHARK'S, *removing a silver snuff box from his pocket as* GUTMAN *speaks. His costume, like that of all the legendary characters in the play (except perhaps* QUIXOTE) *is generally "modern" but with vestigial touches of the period to which he was actually related. The cane and the snuff box and perhaps a brocaded vest may be sufficient to give this historical suggestion in* CASANOVA'S *case. He bears his hawk-like head with a sort of anxious pride on most occasions, a pride maintained under a steadily mounting pressure.*] —It's morning and after morning. It's afternoon, ha ha! And now I must go downstairs to announce the beginning of that old wanderer's dream ...

[*He withdraws from the balcony as old* PRUDENCE DUVERNOY *stumbles out of the hotel, as if not yet quite awake from an afternoon siesta. Chattering with beads and bracelets, she wanders vaguely down into the plaza, raising a faded green silk parasol, damp henna-streaked hair slipping under a monstrous hat of faded silk roses; she is searching for a lost poodle.*]

PRUDENCE. Trique? Trique?

[JACQUES *comes out of the* LOAN SHARK'S *replacing his case angrily in his pocket.*]

JACQUES. Why, I'd rather give it to a street beggar! This case is a Boucheron, I won it at faro at the summer palace, at Tsarskoe Selo in the winter of—

[*The* LOAN SHARK *slams the door.* JACQUES *glares, then shrugs and starts across the plaza. Old* PRUDENCE *is crouched over the filthy gray bundle of a dying mongrel by the fountain.*]

PRUDENCE. Trique, oh, Trique!

[*The* GYPSY'S *son,* ABDULLAH, *watches, giggling.*]

JACQUES [*reproving*]. It is a terrible thing for an old woman to outlive her dogs. [*He crosses to* PRUDENCE *and gently disengages the animal from her grasp.*] Madam, that is not Trique.

PRUDENCE. —When I woke up she wasn't in her basket ...

JACQUES. Sometimes we sleep too long in the afternoon and when we wake we find things changed, Signora.

PRUDENCE. Oh, you're Italian!

JACQUES. I am from Venice, Signora.

PRUDENCE. Ah, Venice, city of pearls! I saw you last night on the terrace dining with— Oh, I'm so worried about her! I'm an old friend of hers, perhaps she's mentioned me to you. Prudence Duvernoy? I was her best friend in the old days in Paris, but now she's forgotten so much ...

I hope you have influence with her! *A waltz of Camille's time in Paris is heard.*]

I want you to give her a message from a certain wealthy old gentleman that she met at one of those watering places she used to go to for her health. She resembled his daughter who died of consumption and so he adored Camille, lavished everything on her! What did she do? Took a young lover who hadn't a couple of pennies to rub together, disinherited by his father because of *her!* Oh, you can't do that, not now, not any more, you've got to be realistic on the Camino Real!

[GUTMAN *has come out on the terrace: he announces quietly—*]

GUTMAN. Block One on the Camino Real.

Block one

PRUDENCE [*continuing*]. Yes, you've got to be practical on it! Well, give her this message, please, Sir. He wants her back on any terms whatsoever! [*Her speech gathers furious momentum.*] Her evenings will be free. He wants only her mornings, mornings are hard on old men because their hearts beat slowly, and he wants only her mornings! Well, that's how it should be! A sensible arrangement! Elderly gentlemen have to content themselves with a lady's spare time before supper! Isn't that so? Of course so! And so I told him! I told him, Camille isn't well! She requires delicate care! Has many debts, creditors storm her door! "How much does she owe?" he asked me, and, oh, did I do some lightning mathematics! Jewels in pawn, I told him, pearls, rings, necklaces, bracelets, diamond ear-drops are in pawn! Horses put up for sale at a public auction!

JACQUES [*appalled by this torrent*]. Signora, Signora, all of these things are—

PRUDENCE. —What?

JACQUES. *Dreams!*

[GUTMAN *laughs. A woman sings at a distance.*]

PRUDENCE [*continuing with less assurance*]. —You're not so young as I thought when I saw you last night on the terrace by candlelight on the— Oh, but— Ho ho!— I bet there is *one* old fountain in this plaza that hasn't gone dry!

[*She pokes him obscenely.* He recoils. GUTMAN *laughs.* JACQUES *starts away but she seizes his arm again, and the torrent of speech continues.*]

PRUDENCE. Wait, wait, listen! Her candle is burning low. But how can you tell? She might have a lingering end, and charity hospitals? Why, you might as well take a flying leap into the Streetcleaners' barrel. Oh, I've told her and told her not to live in a dream! A dream is nothing to live in, why, it's gone like a— Don't let her elegance fool you! That girl has done the Camino in carriages but she has also done it on foot! She knows every stone the Camino is paved with! So tell her this. You tell her, she won't listen to me!— Times and conditions have undergone certain changes since we were friends in Paris, and now we dismiss young lovers with skins of silk and eyes like a child's first prayer, we put them away as lightly as we put away white gloves meant only for summer, and pick up a pair of black ones, suitable for winter . . .

[*The singing voice rises: then subsides.*]

JACQUES. Excuse me, Madam. [*He tears himself from her grasp and rushes into the Siete Mares.*]

PRUDENCE [*dazed, to* GUTMAN]. —What block is this?

GUTMAN. Block One.

PRUDENCE. I didn't hear the announcement . . .

GUTMAN [*coldly*]. Well, now you do.

[OLYMPE *comes out of the lobby with a pale orange silk parasol like a floating moon.*]

OLYMPE. Oh, there you are, I've looked for you high and low!—mostly low . . .

[*They float vaguely out into the dazzling plaza as though a capricious wind took them, finally drifting through the Moorish arch downstage right.*]

[*The song dies out.*]

GUTMAN [*lighting a thin cigar*]. Block Two on the Camino Real.

Block two

After GUTMAN'S *announcement, a hoarse cry is heard.
A figure in rags, skin blackened by the sun, tumbles
crazily down the steep alley to the plaza. He turns
about blindly, murmuring: "A donde la fuente?" He
stumbles against the hideous old prostitute* ROSITA *who
grins horribly and whispers something to him, hitching
up her ragged, filthy skirt. Then she gives him a jocu-
lar push toward the fountain. He falls upon his belly
and thrusts his hands into the dried-up basin. Then he
staggers to his feet with a despairing cry.*

SURVIVOR. La fuente está seca!

[ROSITA *laughs madly but the other* STREET PEOPLE
moan. A dry gourd rattles.]

ROSITA. The fountain is dry, but there's plenty to drink
in the Siete Mares!

[*She shoves him toward the hotel. The proprietor,* GUT-
MAN, *steps out, smoking a thin cigar, fanning himself with a palm leaf. As the* SURVIVOR *advances,* GUT-
MAN *whistles. A man in military dress comes out
upon the low terrace.*]

OFFICER. Go back!

[*The* SURVIVOR *stumbles forward. The* OFFICER *fires at
him. He lowers his hands to his stomach, turns
slowly about with a lost expression, looking up at
the sky, and stumbles toward the fountain. During
the scene that follows, until the entrance of* LA
MADRECITA *and* HER SON, *the* SURVIVOR *drags himself
slowly about the concrete rim of the fountain, almost entirely ignored, as a dying pariah dog in a
starving country.* JACQUES CASANOVA *comes out upon
the terrace of the Siete Mares. Now he passes the
hotel proprietor's impassive figure, descending a*

*step beneath and a little in advance of him, and
without looking at him.*]

JACQUES [*with infinite weariness and disgust*]. What
has happened?

GUTMAN [*serenely*]. We have entered the second in a
progress of sixteen blocks on the Camino Real. It's
five o'clock. That angry old lion, the Sun, looked
back once and growled and then went switching his
tail toward the cool shade of the Sierras. Our guests
have taken their afternoon siestas ...

[*The* SURVIVOR *has come out upon the forestage, now,
not like a dying man but like a shy speaker who has
forgotten the opening line of his speech. He is only
a little crouched over with a hand obscuring the red
stain over his belly. Two or three* STREET PEOPLE
*wander about calling their wares: "Tacos, tacos,
fritos . . ."—"Loteria, loteria"—*ROSITA *shuffles
around, calling "Love? Love?"—pulling down the
filthy décolletage of her blouse to show more of her
sagging bosom. The* SURVIVOR *arrives at the top of
the stairs descending into the orchestra of the theatre, and hangs onto it, looking out reflectively as a
man over the rail of a boat coming into a somewhat
disturbingly strange harbor.*]

GUTMAN [*continuing*]. —They suffer from extreme fatigue, our guests at the Siete Mares, all of them
have a degree or two of fever. Questions are passed
amongst them like something illicit and shameful,
like counterfeit money or drugs or indecent post-
cards— [*He leans forward and whispers.*] —"What is
this place? Where are we? What is the meaning of—
Shhhh!"—Ha ha ...

SURVIVOR [*very softly to the audience*]. I once had a
pony named Peeto. He caught in his nostrils the
scent of thunderstorms coming even before the
clouds had crossed the Sierra ...

VENDOR. Tacos, tacos, fritos ...

ROSITA. Love? Love?

LADY MULLIGAN [*to waiter on terrace*]. Are you sure no one called me? I was expecting a call . . .

GUTMAN [*smiling*]. My guests are confused and exhausted but at this hour they pull themselves together, and drift downstairs on the wings of gin and the lift, they drift into the public rooms and exchange notes again on fashionable couturiers and custom tailors, restaurants, vintages of wine, hairdressers, plastic surgeons, girls and young men susceptible to offers . . . [*There is a hum of light conversation and laughter within.*] —Hear them? They're exchanging notes . . .

JACQUES [*striking the terrace with his cane*]. I asked you what has happened in the plaza!

GUTMAN. Oh, in the plaza, ha ha!— Happenings in the plaza don't concern us . . .

JACQUES. I heard shots fired.

GUTMAN. Shots were fired to remind you of your good fortune in staying here. The public fountains have gone dry, you know, but the Siete Mares was erected over the only perpetual never-dried-up spring in Tierra Caliente, and of course that advantage has to be—protected—sometimes by—martial law . . .

[*The guitar resumes.*]

SURVIVOR. When Peeto, my pony, was born—he stood on his four legs at once, and accepted the world!— He was wiser than I . . .

VENDOR. Fritos, fritos, tacos!

ROSITA. Love!

SURVIVOR. —When Peeto was one year old he was wiser than God! [*A wind sings across the plaza; a dry gourd rattles.*] "Peeto, Peeto!" the Indian boys call after him, trying to stop him—trying to stop the wind!

[*The* SURVIVOR's *head sags forward. He sits down as slowly as an old man on a park bench.* JACQUES *strikes the terrace again with his cane and starts toward the* SURVIVOR. *The* GUARD *seizes his elbow.*]

JACQUES. Don't put your hand on *me!*

GUARD. *Stay here.*

GUTMAN. Remain on the terrace, please, Signor Casanova.

JACQUES [*fiercely*]. —*Cognac!*

[*The* WAITER *whispers to* GUTMAN. GUTMAN *chuckles.*]

GUTMAN. The Maître 'D' tells me that your credit has been discontinued in the restaurant and bar, he says that he has enough of your tabs to pave the terrace with!

JACQUES. What a piece of impertinence! I told the man that the letter that I'm expecting has been delayed in the mail. The postal service in this country is fantastically disorganized, and you know it! You also know that Mlle. Gautier will guarantee my tabs!

GUTMAN. Then let her pick them up at dinner tonight if you're hungry!

JACQUES. I'm not accustomed to this kind of treatment on the Camino Real!

GUTMAN. Oh, you'll be, you'll be, after a single night at the "Ritz Men Only." That's where you'll have to transfer your patronage if the letter containing the remittance check doesn't arrive tonight.

JACQUES. I assure you that I shall do nothing of the sort!— Tonight or ever!

GUTMAN. Watch out, old hawk, the wind is ruffling your feathers! [JACQUES *sinks trembling into a chair.*] —Give him a thimble of brandy before he collapses . . . Fury is a luxury of the young, their veins are resilient, but his are brittle . . .

JACQUES. Here I sit, submitting to insult for a thimble of brandy—while directly in front of me— [*The singer,* LA MADRECITA, *enters the plaza. She is a blind woman led by a ragged* YOUNG MAN. *The* WAITER *brings* JACQUES *a brandy.*] —a man in the plaza dies like a pariah dog!— I take the brandy! I sip it!— My heart is too tired to break, my heart is too tired to— break . . .

[LA MADRECITA *chants softly. She slowly raises her arm to point at the* SURVIVOR *crouched on the steps from the plaza.*]

GUTMAN [*suddenly*]. Give me the phone! Connect me with the Palace. Get me the Generalissimo, quick, quick, quick! [*The* SURVIVOR *rises feebly and shuffles very slowly toward the extended arms of "The Little Blind One."*] Generalissimo? Gutman speaking! Hello, sweetheart. There has been a little incident in the plaza. You know that party of young explorers that attempted to cross the desert on foot? Well, one of them's come back. He was very thirsty. He found the fountain dry. He started toward the hotel. He was politely advised to advance no further. But he disregarded this advice. Action had to be taken. And now, and now—that old blind woman they call "La Madrecita"?— She's come into the plaza with the man called "The Dreamer" . . .

SURVIVOR. Donde?

THE DREAMER. Aquí!

GUTMAN [*continuing*]. You remember those two! I once mentioned them to you. You said "They're harmless dreamers and they're loved by the people."— "What," I asked you, "is harmless about a dreamer, and what," I asked you, "is harmless about the love of the people?— Revolution only needs good dreamers who remember their dreams, and the love of the people belongs safely only to you—their Generalissimo!"— Yes, now the blind woman has recovered her sight and is extending her arms to the wounded Survivor, and the man with the guitar is leading him to her . . . [*The described action is being enacted.*] *Wait one moment!* There's a possibility that the forbidden word may be spoken! Yes! The forbidden word is about to be spoken!

[*The* DREAMER *places an arm about the blinded* SURVIVOR, *and cries out:*]

THE DREAMER. *Hermano!*

[*The cry is repeated like springing fire and a loud murmur sweeps the crowd. They push forward with cupped hands extended and the gasping cries of starving people at the sight of bread. Two* MILITARY GUARDS *herd them back under the colonnades with clubs and drawn revolvers.* LA MADRECITA *chants softly with her blind eyes lifted. A* GUARD *starts toward her. The* PEOPLE *shout "NO!"*]

LA MADRECITA [*chanting*]. "Rojo está el sol! Rojo está el sol de sangre! Blanca está la luna! Blanca está la luna de miedo!"

[*The crowd makes a turning motion.*]

GUTMAN [*to the* WAITER]. *Put up the ropes!* [*Velvet ropes are strung very quickly about the terrace of the Siete Mares. They are like the ropes on decks of steamers in rough waters.* GUTMAN *shouts into the phone again.*] The word was spoken. The crowd is agitated. Hang on! [*He lays down instrument.*]

JACQUES [*hoarsely, shaken*]. He said "Hermano." That's the word for brother.

GUTMAN [*calmly*]. Yes, the most dangerous word in any human tongue is the word for brother. It's inflammatory.— I don't suppose it can be struck out of the language altogether but it must be reserved for strictly private usage in back of soundproof walls. Otherwise it disturbs the population . . .

JACQUES. The people need the word. They're thirsty for it!

GUTMAN. What are these creatures? Mendicants. Prostitutes. Thieves and petty vendors in a bazaar where the human heart is a part of the bargain.

JACQUES. Because they need the word and the word is forbidden!

GUTMAN. The word is said in pulpits and at tables of council where its volatile essence can be contained. But on the lips of these creatures, what is it? A wanton incitement to riot, without understanding. For what is a brother to them but someone to get ahead of, to·cheat, to lie to, to undersell in the market. Brother, you say to a man whose wife you sleep with!— But now, you see, the word has disturbed the people and made it necessary to invoke martial law!

[*Meanwhile the* DREAMER *has brought the* SURVIVOR *to* LA MADRECITA, *who is seated on the cement rim of the fountain. She has cradled the dying man in her arms in the attitude of a* Pietà. *The* DREAMER *is crouched beside them, softly playing a guitar. Now he springs up with a harsh cry.*]

THE DREAMER. *Muerto!*

[*The* STREETCLEANERS' *piping commences at a distance.* GUTMAN *seizes the phone again.*]

GUTMAN [*into phone*]. Generalissimo, the Survivor is no longer surviving. I think we'd better have some public diversion right away. Put the Gypsy on! Have her announce the Fiesta!

LOUDSPEAKER [*responding instantly*]. Damas y Caballeros! The next voice you hear will be the voice of— the Gypsy!

GYPSY [*over loudspeaker*]. Hoy! Noche de Fiesta! Tonight the moon will restore the virginity of my daughter!

GUTMAN. Bring on the Gypsy's daughter, Esmeralda. Show the virgin-to-be!

[ESMERALDA *is led from* THE GYPSY'S *stall by a severe duenna,* "NURSIE," *out upon the forestage. She is manacled by the wrist to the duenna. Her costume is vaguely Levantine.*]

[GUARDS *are herding the crowd back again.*]

GUTMAN. Ha ha! Ho ho ho! Music! [*There is gay music.* ROSITA *dances.*] Abdullah! You're on!

[ABDULLAH *skips into the plaza, shouting histrionically.*]

ABDULLAH. Tonight the moon will restore the virginity of my sister, Esmeralda!

GUTMAN. *Dance, boy!*

[ESMERALDA *is led back into the stall. Throwing off his burnoose,* ABDULLAH *dances with* ROSITA. *Behind their dance, armed* GUARDS *force* LA MADRECITA *and the* DREAMER *to retreat from the fountain, leaving the lifeless body of the* SURVIVOR. *All at once there is a discordant blast of brass instruments.*]

[KILROY *comes into the plaza. He is a young American vagrant, about twenty-seven. He wears dungarees and a skivvy shirt, the pants faded nearly white from long wear and much washing, fitting him as closely as the clothes of sculpture. He has a pair of golden boxing gloves slung about his neck and he carries a small duffle bag. His belt is ruby-and-emerald-studded with the word CHAMP in bold letters. He stops before a chalked inscription on a wall downstage which says: "Kilroy Is Coming!" He scratches out "Coming" and over it prints "Here!"*]

GUTMAN. Ho ho!—a clown! The Eternal Punchinella! That's exactly what's needed in a time of crisis! Block Three on the Camino Real. [[

Block three

KILROY [*genially, to all present*]. Ha ha! [*Then he walks up to the* OFFICER *by the terrace of the Siete Mares.*] Buenas dias, señor. [*He gets no response—barely even a glance.*] Habla Inglesia? Usted?

OFFICER. What is it you want?

KILROY. Where is Western Union or Wells-Fargo? I got to send a wire to some friends in the States.

OFFICER. No hay Western Union, no hay Wells-Fargo.

KILROY. That is very peculiar. I never struck a town yet that didn't have one or the other. I just got off a boat. Lousiest frigging tub I ever shipped on, one continual hell it was, all the way up from Rio. And

me sick, too. I picked up one of those tropical fevers.
No sick-bay on that tub, no doctor, no medicine or
nothing, not even one quinine pill, and I was burning up with Christ knows how much fever. I couldn't
make them understand I was sick. I got a bad heart,
too. I had to retire from the prize ring because of
my heart. I was the light heavyweight champion of
the West Coast, won these gloves!—before my ticker
went bad.— Feel my chest! Go on, feel it! Feel it.
I've got a heart in my chest as big as the head of a
baby. Ha ha! They stood me in front of a screen that
makes you transparent and that's what they seen inside me, a heart in my chest as big as the head of a
baby! With something like that you don't need the
Gypsy to tell you, "Time is short, Baby—get ready
to hitch on wings!" The medics wouldn't okay me
for no more fights. They said to give up liquor and
smoking and sex!— To give up sex!— I used to believe a man couldn't live without sex—but he can—if
he wants to! My real true woman, my wife, she
would of stuck with me, but it was all spoiled with
her being scared and me, too, that a real hard kiss
would kill me!— So one night while she was sleeping
I wrote her good-bye . . . [*He notices a lack of attention in the* OFFICER: *he grins.*] No comprendo the
lingo?

OFFICER. What is it you want?

KILROY. Excuse my ignorance, but what place is this?
What is this country and what is the name of this
town? I know it seems funny of me to ask such a
question. Loco! But I was so glad to get off that rotten tub that I didn't ask nothing of no one except
my pay—and I got short-changed on that. I have
trouble counting these pesos or Whatzit-you-call-'em.
[*He jerks out his wallet.*] All-a-this-here. In the States
that pile of lettuce would make you a plutocrat!—
But I bet you this stuff don't add up to fifty dollars
American coin. Ha ha!

OFFICER. Ha ha.

KILROY. Ha ha!

OFFICER [*making it sound like a death-rattle*]. Ha-ha-ha-ha-ha. [*He turns and starts into the cantina.* KIL-ROY *grabs his arm.*]

KILROY. Hey!

OFFICER. What is it you want?

KILROY. What is the name of this country and this town? [*The* OFFICER *thrusts his elbow in* KILROY'S *stomach and twists his arm loose with a Spanish curse. He kicks the swinging doors open and enters the cantina.*] Brass hats are the same everywhere.

[*As soon as the* OFFICER *goes, the* STREET PEOPLE *come forward and crowd about* KILROY *with their wheedling cries.*]

STREET PEOPLE. Dulces, dulces! Lotería! Lotería! Pasteles, café con leche!

KILROY. No caree, no caree!

[*The* PROSTITUTE *creeps up to him and grins.*]

ROSITA. Love? Love?

KILROY. What did you say?

ROSITA. *Love?*

KILROY. Sorry—I don't feature that. [*To audience.*] I have ideals.

[*The* GYPSY *appears on the roof of her establishment with* ESMERALDA *whom she secures by handcuffs to the iron railing.*]

GYPSY. Stay there while I give the pitch! [*She then advances with a portable microphone.*] Testing! One, two, three, four!

NURSIE [*from offstage*]. You're on the air!

GYPSY'S LOUDSPEAKER. Are you perplexed by something? Are you tired out and confused? Do you have a fever? [KILROY *looks around for the source of the voice.*] Do you feel yourself to be spiritually unprepared for the age of exploding atoms? Do you distrust the newspapers? Are you suspicious of governments? Have you arrived at a point on the Camino

Real where the walls converge not in the distance but right in front of your nose? Does further progress appear impossible to you? Are you afraid of anything at all? Afraid of your heartbeat? Or the eyes of strangers! Afraid of breathing? Afraid of not breathing? Do you wish that things could be straight and simple again as they were in your childhood? Would you like to go back to Kindy Garten?

[ROSITA *has crept up to* KILROY *while he listens. She reaches out to him. At the same time a* PICKPOCKET *lifts his wallet.*]

KILROY [*catching the whore's wrist*]. Keep y'r hands off me, y' dirty ole bag! No caree putas! No loteria, no dulces, nada—so get away! Vamoose! All of you! Quit picking at me! [*He reaches in his pocket and jerks out a handful of small copper and silver coins which he flings disgustedly down the street. The grotesque people scramble after it with their inhuman cries.* KILROY *goes on a few steps—then stops short—feeling the back pocket of his dungarees. Then he lets out a startled cry.*] Robbed! My God, I've been robbed! [*The* STREET PEOPLE *scatter to the walls.*] Which of you got my wallet? *Which* of you dirty—? Shh— Uh! [*They mumble with gestures of incomprehension. He marches back to the entrance to the hotel.*] Hey! Officer! Official!— General! [*The* OFFICER *finally lounges out of the hotel entrance and glances at* KILROY.] Tiende? One of them's got my wallet! Picked it out of my pocket while that old whore there was groping me! Don't you comprendo?

OFFICER. Nobody rob you. You don't have no pesos.

KILROY. Huh?

OFFICER. You just dreaming that you have money. You don't ever have money. Nunca! Nada! [*He spits between his teeth.*] Loco . . .

[*The* OFFICER *crosses to the fountain.* KILROY *stares at him, then bawls out:*]

KILROY [*to the* STREET PEOPLE]. We'll see what the

American Embassy has to say about this! I'll go to the American Consul. Whichever of you rotten spivs lifted my wallet is going to jail—calaboose! I hope I have made myself plain. If not, I will make myself plainer! [*There are scattered laughs among the crowd. He crosses to the fountain. He notices the body of the no longer* SURVIVOR, *kneels beside it, shakes it, turns it over, springs up and shouts.*] Hey! This guy is dead! [*There is the sound of the* STREET-CLEANERS' *piping. They trundle their white barrel into the plaza from one of the downstage arches. The appearance of these men undergoes a progressive alteration through the play. When they first appear they are almost like any such public servants in a tropical country; their white jackets are dirtier than the musicians' and some of the stains are red. They have on white caps with black visors. They are continually exchanging sly jokes and giggling unpleasantly together.* LORD MULLIGAN *has come out upon the terrace and as they pass him, they pause for a moment, point at him, snicker. He is extremely discomfited by this impertinence, touches his chest as if he felt a palpitation and turns back inside.* KILROY *yells to the advancing* STREETCLEANERS.] There's a dead man layin' here! [*They giggle again. Briskly they lift the body and stuff it into the barrel; then trundle it off, looking back at* KILROY, *giggling, whispering. They return under the downstage arch through which they entered.* KILROY, *in a low, shocked voice.*] What *is* this place? What kind of a hassle have I got myself into?

LOUDSPEAKER. If anyone on the Camino is bewildered, come to the Gypsy. A poco dinero will tickle the Gypsy's palm and give her visions!

ABDULLAH [*giving* KILROY *a card*]. If you got a question, ask my mama, the Gypsy!

KILROY. Man, whenever you see those three brass balls on a street, you don't have to look a long ways for a

Gypsy. Now le' me think. I am faced with three problems. One: I'm hungry. Two: I'm lonely. Three: I'm in a place where I don't know what it is or how I got there! First action that's indicated is to —cash in on something— Well . . . let's see . . .

[*Honky-tonk music fades in at this point and the Skid Row façade begins to light up for the evening. There is the* GYPSY's *stall with its cabalistic devices, its sectional cranium and palm, three luminous brass balls overhanging the entrance to the* LOAN SHARK *and his window filled with a vast assortment of hocked articles for sale: trumpets, banjos, fur coats, tuxedos, a gown of scarlet sequins, loops of pearls and rhinestones. Dimly behind this display is a neon sign in three pastel colors, pink, green, and blue. It fades softly in and out and it says: "Magic Tricks Jokes." There is also the advertisement of a flea-bag hotel or flophouse called "Ritz Men Only." This sign is also pale neon or luminous paint, and only the entrance is on the street floor, the rooms are above the* LOAN SHARK *and* GYPSY's *stall. One of the windows of this upper story is practical. Figures appear in it sometimes, leaning out as if suffocating or to hawk and spit into the street below. This side of the street should have all the color and animation that are permitted by the resources of the production. There may be moments of dancelike action (a fight, a seduction, sale of narcotics, arrest, etc.).*]

KILROY [*to the audience from the apron*]. What've I got to cash in on? My golden gloves? Never! I'll say that once more, never! The silver-framed photo of my One True Woman? Never! Repeat that! Never! What else have I got of a detachable and a negotiable nature? Oh! My ruby-and-emerald-studded belt with the word CHAMP on it. [*He whips it off his pants.*] This is not necessary to hold on my pants, but this is a precious reminder of the sweet used-to-be. Oh, well. Sometimes a man has got to hock his sweet used-to-be in order to finance his present situation . . .

[*He enters the* LOAN SHARK'S. *A* DRUNKEN BUM *leans out the practical window of the "Ritz Men Only" and shouts.*]

BUM. O Jack o' Diamonds, you robbed my pockets, you robbed my pockets of silver and gold! [*He jerks the window shade down.*]

GUTMAN [*on the terrace*]. Block Four on the Camino Real!

Block four

There is a phrase of light music as the BARON DE CHARLUS, *an elderly foppish sybarite in a light silk suit, a carnation in his lapel, crosses from the Siete Mares to the honky-tonk side of the street. On his trail is a wild-looking young man of startling beauty called* LOBO. CHARLUS *is aware of the follower and, during his conversation with* A. RATT, *he takes out a pocket mirror to inspect him while pretending to comb his hair and point his moustache. As* CHARLUS *approaches, the* MANAGER *of the flea-bag puts up a vacancy sign and calls out:*

A. RATT. Vacancy here! A bed at the "Ritz Men Only"! A little white ship to sail the dangerous night in . . .

THE BARON. Ah, bon soir, Mr. Ratt.

A. RATT. Cruising?

THE BARON. No, just—walking!

A. RATT. That's all you need to do.

THE BARON. I sometimes find it suffices. You have a vacancy, do you?

A. RATT. For you?

THE BARON. And a possible guest. You know the requirements. An iron bed with no mattress and a considerable length of stout knotted rope. No! Chains this evening, metal chains. I've been very bad, I have a lot to atone for . . .

A. RATT. Why don't you take these joy-rides at the Siete Mares?

THE BARON [*with the mirror focused on* LOBO]. They don't have Ingreso Libero at the Siete Mares. Oh, I don't like places in the haute saison, the alta staggione, and yet if you go between the fashionable seasons, it's too hot or too damp or appallingly overrun by all the wrong sort of people who rap on the wall if canaries sing in your bed-springs after midnight. I don't know why such people don't stay at home. Surely a Kodak, a Brownie, or even a Leica works just as well in Milwaukee or Sioux City as it does in these places they do on their whirlwind summer tours, and don't look now, but I think I am being followed!

A. RATT. Yep, you've made a pickup!

THE BARON. Attractive?

A. RATT. That depends on who's driving the bicycle, Dad.

THE BARON. Ciao, Caro! Expect me at ten. [*He crosses elegantly to the fountain.*]

A. RATT. Vacancy here! A little white ship to sail the dangerous night in!

[*The music changes.* KILROY *backs out of the* LOAN SHARK'S, *belt unsold, engaged in a violent dispute. The* LOAN SHARK *is haggling for his golden gloves.* CHARLUS *lingers, intrigued by the scene.*]

LOAN SHARK. I don't want no belt! I want the gloves! Eight-fifty!

KILROY. No dice.

LOAN SHARK. Nine, nine-fifty!

KILROY. Nah, nah, nah!

LOAN SHARK. Yah, yah, yah.

KILROY. I say nah.

LOAN SHARK. I say yah.

KILROY. The nahs have it.

LOAN SHARK. Don't be a fool. What can you do with a pair of golden gloves?

KILROY. I can remember the battles I fought to win them! I can remember that I used to be—CHAMP!

[*Fade in Band Music: "March of the Gladiators"— ghostly cheers, etc.*]

LOAN SHARK. You can remember that you *used to be*— Champ?

KILROY. Yes! I used to be—CHAMP!

THE BARON. Used to be is the past tense, meaning useless.

KILROY. Not to me, Mister. These are my gloves, these gloves are gold, and I fought a lot of hard fights to win 'em! I broke clean from the clinches. I never hit a low blow, the referee never told me to mix it up! And the fixers never got to me!

LOAN SHARK. In other words, a sucker!

KILROY. Yep, I'm a sucker that won the golden gloves!

LOAN SHARK. Congratulations. My final offer is a piece of green paper with Alexander Hamilton's picture on it. Take it or leave it.

KILROY. I leave it for you to *stuff* it! I'd hustle my heart on this street, I'd peddle my heart's true blood before I'd leave my golden gloves hung up in a loan shark's window between a rusted trombone and some poor lush's long ago mildewed tuxedo!

LOAN SHARK. So you say but I will see you later.

THE BARON. The name of the Camino is not unreal!

[*The* BUM *sticks his head out of the window and shouts.*]

BUM. Pa dam, Pa dam, Pa dam!

THE BARON [*continuing the* BUM'S *song*]. Echoes the beat of my heart!
Pa dam, Pa dam—hello! [*He has crossed to* KILROY *as he sings and extends his hand to him.*]

KILROY [*uncertainly*]. Hey, mate. It's wonderful to see you.

THE BARON. Thanks, but why?

KILROY. A normal American. In a clean white suit.

THE BARON. My suit is pale yellow. My nationality is French, and my normality has been often subject to question.

KILROY. I still say your suit is clean.

THE BARON. Thanks. That's more than I can say for your apparel.

KILROY. Don't judge a book by the covers. I'd take a shower if I could locate the "Y."

THE BARON. What's the "Y"?

KILROY. Sort of a Protestant church with a swimmin' pool in it. Sometimes it also has an employment bureau. It does good in the community.

THE BARON. Nothing in this community does much good.

KILROY. I'm getting the same impression. This place is confusing to me. I think it must be the aftereffects of fever. Nothing seems real. Could you give me the scoop?

THE BARON. Serious questions are referred to the Gypsy. Once upon a time. Oh, once upon a time. I used to wonder. Now I simply wander. I stroll about the fountain and hope to be followed. Some people call it corruption. I call it—simplification ...

BUM [*very softly at the window*]. I wonder what's become of Sally, that old gal of mine? [*He lowers the blind.*]

KILROY. Well, anyhow ...

THE BARON. Well, anyhow?

KILROY. How about the hot-spots in this town?

THE BARON. Oh, the hot-spots, ho ho! There's the Pink Flamingo, the Yellow Pelican, the Blue Heron, and the Prothonotary Warbler! They call it the Bird Circuit. But I don't care for such places. They stand three-deep at the bar and look at themselves in the mirror and what they see is depressing. One sailor comes in—they faint! My own choice of resorts is the Bucket of Blood downstairs from the "Ritz Men Only."— How about a match?

KILROY. Where's your cigarette?

THE BARON [*gently and sweetly*]. Oh, I don't smoke. I just wanted to see your eyes more clearly ...

KILROY. Why?

THE BARON. The eyes are the windows of the soul, and yours are too gentle for someone who has as much as I have to atone for. [*He starts off.*] Au revoir ...

KILROY. —A very unusual type character ... [CASANOVA *is on the steps leading to the arch, looking out at the desert beyond. Now he turns and descends a few steps, laughing with a note of tired incredulity.* KILROY *crosses to him.*] Gee, it's wonderful to see you, a normal American in a— [*There is a strangulated outcry from the arch under which the* BARON *has disappeared.*] Excuse me a minute! [*He rushes toward the source of the outcry.* JACQUES *crosses to the bench before the fountain. Rhubarb is heard through the arch.* JACQUES *shrugs wearily as if it were just a noisy radio.* KILROY *comes plummeting out backwards, all the way to* JACQUES.] I tried to interfere, but what's th' use?!

JACQUES. No use at all!

[*The* STREETCLEANERS *come through the arch with the* BARON *doubled up in their barrel. They pause and exchange sibilant whispers, pointing and snickering at* KILROY.]

KILROY. Who are they pointing at? At me, Kilroy? [*The* BUM *laughs from the window.* A. RATT *laughs from his shadowy doorway. The* LOAN SHARK *laughs from his.*] Kilroy is here and he's not about to be there!— If he can help it ... [*He snatches up a rock and throws it at the* STREETCLEANERS. *Everybody laughs louder and the laughter seems to reverberate from the mountains. The light changes, dims a little in*

the plaza.] Sons a whatever you're sons of! Don't
look at me, I'm not about to take no ride in the
barrel!

[*The* BARON, *his elegant white shoes protruding from
the barrel, is wheeled up the Alleyway Out. Figures
in the square resume their dazed attitudes and one
or two* GUESTS *return to the terrace of the Siete Mares
as—*]

GUTMAN. Block Five on the Camino Real! [*He strolls
off.*]

Block five

KILROY [*to* JACQUES]. Gee, the blocks go fast on this
street!

JACQUES. Yes. The blocks go fast.

KILROY. My name's Kilroy. I'm here.

JACQUES. Mine is Casanova. I'm here, too.

KILROY. But you been here longer than me and
maybe could brief me on it. For instance, what do
they do with a stiff picked up in this town? [*The*
GUARD *stares at them suspiciously from the terrace.*
JACQUES *whistles "La Golondrina" and crosses downstage.* KILROY *follows.*] Did I say something untact-
ful?

JACQUES [*smiling into a sunset glow*]. The exchange of
serious questions and ideas, especially between persons from opposite sides of the plaza, is regarded
unfavorably here. You'll notice I'm talking as if I
had acute laryngitis. I'm gazing into the sunset. If
I should start to whistle "La Golondrina" it means
we're being overheard by the Guards on the terrace.
Now you want to know what is done to a body from
which the soul has departed on the Camino Real!—
Its disposition depends on what the Streetcleaners

happen to find in its pockets. If its pockets are empty as the unfortunate Baron's turned out to be, and as mine are at this moment—the "stiff" is wheeled straight off to the Laboratory. And there the individual becomes an undistinguished member of a collectivist state. His chemical components are separated and poured into vats containing the corresponding elements of countless others. If any of his vital organs or parts are at all unique in size or structure, they're placed on exhibition in bottles containing a very foul-smelling solution called formaldehyde. There is a charge of admission to this museum. The proceeds go to the maintenance of the military police. [*He whistles "La Golondrina" till the* GUARD *turns his back again. He moves toward the front of the stage.*]

KILROY [*following*]. —I guess that's—sensible . . .

JACQUES. Yes, but not romantic. And romance is important. Don't you think?

KILROY. Nobody thinks romance is more important than me!

JACQUES. Except possibly me!

KILROY. Maybe that's why fate has brung us together! We're buddies under the skin!

JACQUES. Travelers born?

KILROY. Always looking for something!

JACQUES. Satisfied by nothing!

KILROY. Hopeful?

JACQUES. Always!

OFFICER. Keep moving!

[*They move apart till the* OFFICER *exits.*]

KILROY. And when a joker on the Camino gets fed up with one continual hassle—how does he get *off* it?

JACQUES. You see the narrow and very steep stairway that passes under what is described in the travel brochures as a "Magnificent Arch of Triumph"?— Well, that's the Way Out!

KILROY. That's the way out? [KILROY *without hesitation*

*plunges right up to almost the top step; then pauses
with a sound of squealing brakes. There is a sudden
loud wind.*]

JACQUES [*shouting with hand cupped to mouth*]. Well,
how does the prospect please you, Traveler born?

KILROY [*shouting back in a tone of awe*]. It's too unknown for my blood. Man, I seen nothing like it except through a telescope once on the pier on Coney
Island. "Ten cents to see the craters and plains of
the moon!"— And here's the same view in three di-
mensions for nothing!

[*The desert wind sings loudly:* KILROY *mocks it.*]

JACQUES. Are you—ready to cross it?

KILROY. Maybe sometime with someone but not right
now and alone! How about you?

JACQUES. I'm not alone.

KILROY. You're with a party?

JACQUES. No, but I'm sweetly encumbered with a—
lady . . .

KILROY. It wouldn't do with a lady. I don't see nothing
but nothing—and then more nothing. And then I
see some mountains. But the mountains are covered
with snow.

JACQUES. Snowshoes would be useful!

[*He observes* GUTMAN *approaching through the passage
at upper left. He whistles "La Golondrina" for* KIL-
ROY's *attention and points with his cane as he exits.*]

KILROY [*descending steps disconsolately*]. Mush, mush.

[*The* BUM *comes to his window.* A. RATT *enters his
doorway.* GUTMAN *enters below* KILROY.]

BUM. It's sleepy time down South!

GUTMAN [*warningly as* KILROY *passes him*]. Block Six
in a progress of sixteen blocks on the Camino Real.

Block six

KILROY [*from the stairs*]. Man, I could use a bed now.—
I'd like to make me a cool pad on this camino now
and lie down and sleep and dream of being with
someone—friendly . . . [*He crosses to the "Ritz Men
Only."*]

A. RATT [*softly and sleepily*]. Vacancy here! I got a
single bed at the "Ritz Men Only," a little white
ship to sail the dangerous night in.

[KILROY *crosses down to his doorway.*]

KILROY. —You got a vacancy here?

A. RATT. I got a vacancy here if you got the one-fifty
there.

KILROY. Ha ha! I been in countries where money was
not legal tender. I mean it was legal but it wasn't
tender. [*There is a loud groan from offstage above.*]
—Somebody dying on you or just drunk?

A. RATT. Who knows or cares in this pad, Dad?

KILROY. I heard once that a man can't die while he's
drunk. Is that a fact or a fiction?

A. RATT. Strictly a fiction.

VOICE ABOVE. *Stiff in number seven! Call the Streetcleaners!*

A. RATT [*with absolutely no change in face or voice*].
Number seven is vacant.

[STREETCLEANERS' *piping is heard.*]

[*The* BUM *leaves the window.*]

KILROY. Thanks, but tonight I'm going to sleep under
the stars.

[A. RATT *gestures "Have it your way" and exits.*]

[KILROY, *left alone, starts downstage. He notices that*
LA MADRECITA *is crouched near the fountain, holding something up, inconspicuously, in her hand.*

Coming to her he sees that it's a piece of food. He takes it, puts it in his mouth, tries to thank her but her head is down, muffled in her rebozo and there is no way for him to acknowledge the gift. He starts to cross. STREET PEOPLE *raise up their heads in their Pit and motion him invitingly to come in with them. They call softly, "Sleep, sleep . . ."*]

GUTMAN [*from his chair on the terrace*]. Hey, Joe.

[*The* STREET PEOPLE *duck immediately.*]

KILROY. Who? Me?

GUTMAN. Yes, you, Candy Man. Are you disocupado?

KILROY. —That means—unemployed, don't it? [*He sees* OFFICERS *converging from right.*]

GUTMAN. Jobless. On the bum. Carrying the banner!

KILROY. —Aw, no, aw, no, don't try to hang no vagrancy rap on me! I was robbed on this square and I got plenty of witnesses to prove it.

GUTMAN [*with ironic courtesy*]. Oh? [*He makes a gesture asking "Where?"*]

KILROY [*coming down to apron left and crossing to the right*]. Witnesses! Witness! Witnesses! [*He comes to* LA MADRECITA.] You were a witness! [*A gesture indicates that he realizes her blindness. Opposite the* GYPSY's *balcony he pauses for a second.*] Hey, Gypsy's daughter! [*The balcony is dark. He continues up to the Pit. The* STREET PEOPLE *duck as he calls down.*] You were witnesses!

[*An* OFFICER *enters with a Patsy outfit. He hands it to* GUTMAN.]

GUTMAN. Here, Boy! Take these. [GUTMAN *displays and then tosses on the ground at* KILROY's *feet the Patsy outfit—the red fright wig, the big crimson nose that lights up and has horn rimmed glasses attached, a pair of clown pants that have a huge footprint on the seat.*]

KILROY. What is this outfit?

GUTMAN. The uniform of a Patsy.

KILROY. I know what a Patsy is—he's a clown in the circus who takes prat-falls but *I'm no Patsy!*

GUTMAN. Pick it up.

KILROY. Don't give me orders. Kilroy is a free agent—

GUTMAN [*smoothly*]. But a Patsy isn't. Pick it up and put it on, Candy Man. You are now the Patsy.

KILROY. So you say but you are completely mistaken. [*Four* OFFICERS *press in on him.*] And don't crowd me with your torpedoes! I'm a stranger here but I got a clean record in all the places I been, I'm not in the books for nothin' but vagrancy and once when I was hungry I walked by a truck-load of pineapples without picking one, because I was brought up good— [*Then, with a pathetic attempt at making friends with the* OFFICER *to his right.*] and there was a cop on the corner!

OFFICER. Ponga selo!

KILROY. What'd you say? [*Desperately to audience he asks.*] What did he say?

OFFICER. Ponga selo!

KILROY. What'd you say? [*The* OFFICER *shoves him down roughly to the Patsy outfit.* KILROY *picks up the pants, shakes them out carefully as if about to step into them and says very politely:*] Why, surely. I'd be delighted. My fondest dreams have come true. [*Suddenly he tosses the Patsy dress into* GUTMAN'S *face and leaps into the aisle of the theatre.*]

GUTMAN. Stop him! Arrest that vagrant! Don't let him get away!

LOUDSPEAKER. Be on the lookout for a fugitive Patsy. The Patsy has escaped. Stop him, stop that Patsy!

[*A wild chase commences. The two* GUARDS *rush madly down either side to intercept him at the back of the house.* KILROY *wheels about at the top of the center aisle, and runs back down it, panting, gasping out questions and entreaties to various persons occupying aisle seats, such as:*]

KILROY. How do I git out? Which way do I go, which way do I get out? Where's the Greyhound depot? Hey, do you know where the Greyhound bus depot is? What's the best way out, if there is any way out? I got to find one. I had enough of this place. I had too much of this place. I'm free. I'm a free man with equal rights in this world! You better believe it because that's news for you and you had better believe it! Kilroy's a free man with equal rights in this world! All right, now, help me, somebody, help me find a way out, I got to find one, I don't like this place! It's not for me and I am not buying any! Oh! Over there! I see a sign that says EXIT. That's a sweet word to me, man, that's a lovely word, EXIT! That's the entrance to paradise for Kilroy! Exit, I'm coming, Exit, I'm coming!

[*The* STREET PEOPLE *have gathered along the forestage to watch the chase.* ESMERALDA, *barefooted, wearing only a slip, bursts out of the* GYPSY's *establishment like an animal broken out of a cage, darts among the* STREET PEOPLE *to the front of the* CROWD *which is shouting like the spectators at the climax of a corrida. Behind her,* NURSIE *appears, a male actor, wigged and dressed austerely as a duenna, crying out in both languages.*]

NURSIE. Esmeralda! Esmeralda!

GYPSY. Police!

NURSIE. Come back here, Esmeralda!

GYPSY. Catch her, idiot!

NURSIE. Where is my lady bird, where is my precious treasure?

GYPSY. Idiot! I told you to keep her door locked!

NURSIE. She jimmied the lock, Esmeralda!

[*These shouts are mostly lost in the general rhubarb of the chase and the shouting* STREET PEOPLE. ESMERALDA *crouches on the forestage, screaming encouragement in Spanish to the fugitive.* ABDULLAH *catches sight of her, seizes her wrist, shouting:*]

ABDULLAH. Here she is! I got her!

[ESMERALDA *fights savagely. She nearly breaks loose, but* NURSIE *and the* GYPSY *close upon her, too, and she is overwhelmed and dragged back, fighting all the way, toward the door from which she escaped.*]

[*Meanwhile—timed with the above action—shots are fired in the air by* KILROY'S PURSUERS. *He dashes, panting, into the boxes of the theatre, darting from one box to another, shouting incoherently, now, sobbing for breath, crying out.*]

KILROY. Mary, help a Christian! Help a Christian, Mary!

ESMERALDA. *Yankee! Yankee, jump!* [*The* OFFICERS *close upon him in the box nearest the stage. A dazzling spot of light is thrown on him. He lifts a little gilded chair to defend himself. The chair is torn from his grasp. He leaps upon the ledge of the box.*] Jump! Jump, Yankee!

[*The* GYPSY *is dragging the girl back by her hair.*]

KILROY. *Watch out down there! Geronimo!*

[*He leaps onto the stage and crumples up with a twisted ankle.* ESMERALDA *screams demoniacally, breaks from her mother's grasp and rushes to him, fighting off his pursuers who have leapt after him from the box.* ABDULLAH, NURSIE *and the* GYPSY *seize her again, just as* KILROY *is seized by his pursuers. The* OFFICERS *beat him to his knees. Each time he is struck,* ESMERALDA *screams as if she received the blow herself. As his cries subside into sobbing, so do hers, and at the end, when he is quite helpless, she is also overcome by her captors and as they drag her back to the* GYPSY'S *she cries to him:*]

ESMERALDA. *They've got you! They've got me!* [*Her mother slaps her fiercely.*] Caught! Caught! We're caught!

[*She is dragged inside. The door is slammed shut on her continuing outcries. For a moment nothing is heard but* KILROY'S *hoarse panting and sobbing.*

GUTMAN *takes command of the situation, thrusting his way through the crowd to face* KILROY *who is pinioned by two* GUARDS.]

GUTMAN [*smiling serenely*]. Well, well, how do you do! I understand that you're seeking employment here. We need a Patsy and the job is yours for the asking!

KILROY. I don't. Accept. This job. I been. Shanghaied!
[KILROY *dons Patsy outfit.*]

GUTMAN. Hush! The Patsy doesn't talk. He lights his nose, that's all!

GUARD. Press the little button at the end of the cord.

GUTMAN. That's right. Just press the little button at the end of the cord!

[KILROY *lights his nose. Everybody laughs.*]

GUTMAN. Again, ha ha! Again, ha ha! Again!

[*The nose goes off and on like a firefly as the stage dims out.*]

[*The curtain falls. There is a short intermission.*]

Block seven

The DREAMER *is singing with mandolin,* "*Noche de Ronde.*" *The* GUESTS *murmur,* "*cool—cool . . .*" GUTMAN *stands on the podiumlike elevation downstage right, smoking a long thin cigar, signing an occasional tab from the bar or café. He is standing in an amber spot. The rest of the stage is filled with blue dusk. At the signal the song fades to a whisper and* GUTMAN *speaks.*

GUTMAN. Block Seven on the Camino Real—
I like this hour. [*He gives the audience a tender gold-toothed smile.*] The fire's gone out of the day but the light of it lingers . . . In Rome the continual fountains are bathing stone heroes with silver, in

Copenhagen the Tivoli gardens are lighted, they're selling the lottery on San Juan de Latrene . . .

[*The* DREAMER *advances a little, playing the mandolin softly.*]

LA MADRECITA [*holding up glass beads and shell necklaces*]. Recuerdos, recuerdos?

GUTMAN. And these are the moments when we look into ourselves and ask with a wonder which never is lost altogether: "Can this be all? Is there nothing more? Is this what the glittering wheels of the heavens turn for?" [*He leans forward as if conveying a secret.*] —Ask the Gypsy! Un poco dinero will tickle the Gypsy's palm and give her visions!

[ABDULLAH *emerges with a silver tray, calling:*]

ABDULLAH. Letter for Signor Casanova, letter for Signor Casanova!

[JACQUES *springs up but stands rigid.*]

GUTMAN. Casanova, you have received a letter. Perhaps it's the letter with the remittance check in it!

JACQUES [*in a hoarse, exalted voice*]. Yes! It is! The letter! With the remittance check in it!

GUTMAN. Then why don't you take it so you can maintain your residence at the Siete Mares and so avoid the more somber attractions of the "Ritz Men Only"?

JACQUES. My hand is—

GUTMAN. Your hand is paralyzed? . . . By what? *Anxiety? Apprehension?* . . . Put the letter in Signor Casanova's pocket so he can open it when he recovers the use of his digital extremities. Then give him a shot of brandy on the house before he falls on his face!

[JACQUES *has stepped down into the plaza. He looks down at* KILROY *crouched to the right of him and wildly blinking his nose.*]

JACQUES. Yes. I know the Morse code. [KILROY'S *nose again blinks on and off.*] Thank you, brother. [*This*

is said as if acknowledging a message.] I knew without asking the Gypsy that something of this sort
would happen to you. You have a spark of anarchy
in your spirit and that's not to be tolerated. Nothing
wild or honest is tolerated here! It has to be extin-
guished or used only to light up your nose for Mr.
Gutman's amusement . . . [JACQUES *saunters around*
KILROY *whistling "La Golondrina." Then satisfied
that no one is suspicious of this encounter . . .*] Before the final block we'll find some way out of here!
Meanwhile, patience and courage, little brother!
[JACQUES, *feeling he's been there too long, starts
away giving* KILROY *a reassuring pat on the shoulder
and saying:*] Patience! . . . Courage!

LADY MULLIGAN [*from the* MULLIGANS' *table*]. Mr. Gutman!

GUTMAN. Lady Mulligan! And how are you this evening, Lord Mulligan?

LADY MULLIGAN [*interrupting* LORD MULLIGAN'S *rum-
blings*]. He's not at all well. This . . . climate is so
enervating!

LORD MULLIGAN. I was so weak this morning . . . I
couldn't screw the lid on my tooth paste!

LADY MULLIGAN. Raymond, tell Mr. Gutman about
those two impertinent workmen in the square! . . .
These two idiots pushing a white barrel! Pop up
every time we step outside the hotel!

LORD MULLIGAN. —point and giggle at me!

LADY MULLIGAN. Can't they be discharged?

GUTMAN. They can't be discharged, disciplined nor
bribed! All you can do is pretend to ignore them.

LADY MULLIGAN. I can't eat! . . . Raymond, stop stuff-
ing!

LORD MULLIGAN. *Shut up!*

GUTMAN [*to the audience*]. When the big wheels crack
on this street it's like the fall of a capital city,
the destruction of Carthage, the sack of Rome by
the white-eyed giants from the North! I've seen them

fall! I've seen the destruction of them! Adventurers suddenly frightened of a dark room! Gamblers unable to choose between odd and even! Con men and pitchmen and plume-hatted cavaliers turned babysoft at one note of the Streetcleaners' pipes! When I observe this change, I say to myself: "Could it happen to ME?"— The answer is "YES!" And that's what curdles my blood like milk on the doorstep of someone gone for the summer!

[*A* HUNCHBACK MUMMER *somersaults through his hoop of silver bells, springs up and shakes it excitedly toward a downstage arch which begins to flicker with a diamond-blue radiance; this marks the advent of each legendary character in the play. The music follows: a waltz from the time of Camille in Paris.*]

GUTMAN [*downstage to the audience*]. Ah, there's the music of another legend, one that everyone knows, the legend of the sentimental whore, the courtesan who made the mistake of love. But now you see her coming into this plaza not as she was when she burned with a fever that cast a thin light over Paris, but changed, yes, faded as lanterns and legends fade when they burn into day! [*He turns and shouts.*] Rosita, sell her a flower!

[MARGUERITE *has entered the plaza. A beautiful woman of indefinite age. The* STREET PEOPLE *cluster about her with wheedling cries, holding up glass beads, shell necklaces and so forth. She seems confused, lost, half-awake.* JACQUES *has sprung up at her entrance but has difficulty making his way through the cluster of vendors.* ROSITA *has snatched up a tray of flowers and cries out:*]

ROSITA. Camellias, camellias! Pink or white, whichever a lady finds suitable to the moon!

GUTMAN. That's the ticket!

MARGUERITE. Yes, I would like a camellia.

ROSITA [*in a bad French accent*]. Rouge ou blanc ce soir?

MARGUERITE. It's always a white one, now . . . but there used to be five evenings out of the month when a pink camellia, instead of the usual white one, let my admirers know that the moon those nights was unfavorable to pleasure, and so they called me—Camille . . .

JACQUES. Mia cara! [*Imperiously, very proud to be with her, he pushes the* STREET PEOPLE *aside with his cane.*] Out of the way, make way, let us through, please!

MARGUERITE. Don't push them with your cane.

JACQUES. If they get close enough they'll snatch your purse. [MARGUERITE *utters a low, shocked cry.*] What is it?

MARGUERITE. *My purse is gone! It's lost! My papers were in it!*

JACQUES. Your passport was in it?

MARGUERITE. My passport and my permiso de residencia! [*She leans faint against the arch during the following scene.*]

[ABDULLAH *turns to run.* JACQUES *catches him.*]

JACQUES [*seizing* ABDULLAH'S *wrist*]. Where did you take her?

ABDULLAH. Oww!— P'tit Zoco.

JACQUES. The Souks?

ABDULLAH. The Souks!

JACQUES. Which cafés did she go to?

ABDULLAH. Ahmed's, she went to—

JACQUES. Did she smoke at Ahmed's?

ABDULLAH. Two kif pipes!

JACQUES. Who was it took her purse? Was it *you?* We'll see!

[*He strips off the boy's burnoose. He crouches whimpering, shivering in a ragged slip.*]

MARGUERITE. Jacques, let the boy go, he didn't take it!

JACQUES. He doesn't have it on him but knows who does!

ABDULLAH. No, no, I don't know!

JACQUES. You little son of a Gypsy! Senta! . . . You know who I am? I am Jacques Casanova! I belong to the Secret Order of the Rose-colored Cross! . . . Run back to Ahmed's. Contact the spiv that took the lady's purse. Tell him to keep it but give her back her papers! There'll be a large reward.

[*He thumps his cane on the ground to release* ABDULLAH *from the spell. The boy dashes off.* JACQUES *laughs and turns triumphantly to* MARGUERITE.]

LADY MULLIGAN. Waiter! That adventurer and his mistress must not be seated next to Lord Mulligan's table!

JACQUES [*loudly enough for* LADY MULLIGAN *to hear*]. This hotel has become a mecca for black marketeers and their expensively kept women!

LADY MULLIGAN. Mr. Gutman!

MARGUERITE. Let's have dinner upstairs!

WAITER [*directing them to terrace table*]. *This* way, M'sieur.

JACQUES. We'll take our usual table. [*He indicates one.*]

MARGUERITE. Please!

WAITER [*overlapping* MARGUERITE'S *"please!"*]. This table is reserved for Lord Byron!

JACQUES [*masterfully*]. This table is always our table.

MARGUERITE. I'm not hungry.

JACQUES. Hold out the lady's chair, cretino!

GUTMAN [*darting over to* MARGUERITE'S *chair*]. Permit me!

[JACQUES *bows with mock gallantry to* LADY MULLIGAN *as he turns to his chair during seating of* MARGUERITE.]

LADY MULLIGAN. We'll move to *that* table!

JACQUES. —You must learn how to carry the banner of Bohemia into the enemy camp.

[*A screen is put up around them.*]

MARGUERITE. Bohemia has no banner. It survives by discretion.

JACQUES. I'm glad that you value discretion. *Wine list!*

Was it discretion that led you through the bazaars this afternoon wearing your cabochon sapphire and diamond ear-drops? You were fortunate that you lost only your purse and papers!

MARGUERITE. Take the wine list.

JACQUES. Still or sparkling?

MARGUERITE. Sparkling.

GUTMAN. May I make a suggestion, Signor Casanova?

JACQUES. Please do.

GUTMAN. It's a very cold and dry wine from only ten metres below the snowline in the mountains. The name of the wine is Quando!—meaning when! Such as "When are remittances going to be received?" "When are accounts to be settled?" Ha ha ha! Bring Signor Casanova a bottle of Quando with the compliments of the house!

JACQUES. I'm sorry this had to happen in—your presence . . .

MARGUERITE. That doesn't matter, my dear. But why don't you *tell* me when you are short of money?

JACQUES. I thought the fact was apparent. It is to everyone else.

MARGUERITE. The letter you were expecting, it still hasn't come?

JACQUES [*removing it from his pocket*]. It came this afternoon— Here it is!

MARGUERITE. You haven't opened the letter!

JACQUES. I haven't had the nerve to! I've had so many unpleasant surprises that I've lost my faith in my luck.

MARGUERITE. Give the letter to me. Let me open it for you.

JACQUES. Later, a little bit later, after the—wine . . .

MARGUERITE. Old hawk, anxious old hawk! [*She clasps his hand on the table: he leans toward her: she kisses her fingertips and places them on his lips.*]

JACQUES. Do you call that a kiss?

MARGUERITE. I call it the ghost of a kiss. It will have to do for now. [*She leans back, her blue-tinted eyelids closed.*]

JACQUES. Are you tired? Are you tired, Marguerite? You know you should have rested this afternoon.

MARGUERITE. I looked at silver and rested.

JACQUES. You looked at silver at Ahmed's?

MARGUERITE. No, I rested at Ahmed's, and had mint-tea.

[*The* DREAMER *accompanies their speech with his guitar. The duologue should have the style of an antiphonal poem, the cues picked up so that there is scarcely a separation between the speeches, and the tempo quick and the voices edged.*]

JACQUES. You had mint-tea downstairs?

MARGUERITE. No, upstairs.

JACQUES. Upstairs where they burn the poppy?

MARGUERITE. Upstairs where it's cool and there's music and the haggling of the bazaar is soft as the murmur of pigeons.

JACQUES. That sounds restful. Reclining among silk pillows on a divan, in a curtained and perfumed alcove above the bazaar?

MARGUERITE. Forgetting for a while where I am, or that I don't know where I am . . .

JACQUES. Forgetting alone or forgetting with some young companion who plays the lute or the flute or who had silver to show you? Yes. That sounds very restful. And yet you do seem tired.

MARGUERITE. If I seem tired, it's your insulting solicitude that I'm tired of!

JACQUES. Is it insulting to feel concern for your safety in this place?

MARGUERITE. Yes, it is. The implication is.

JACQUES. What is the implication?

MARGUERITE. You know what it is: that I am one of those *aging—voluptuaries—*who used to be paid for pleasure but now have to pay!— Jacques, I won't be followed, I've gone too far to be followed!— *What is it?*

[*The* WAITER *has presented an envelope on a salver.*]

WAITER. A letter for the lady.

MARGUERITE. How strange to receive a letter in a place where nobody knows I'm staying! Will you open it for me?

[*The* WAITER *withdraws.* JACQUES *takes the letter and opens it.*]

Well! What is it?

JACQUES. Nothing important. An illustrated brochure from some resort in the mountains.

MARGUERITE. What is it called?

JACQUES. Bide-a-While.

[*A chafing dish bursts into startling blue flame at the* MULLIGANS' *table.* LADY MULLIGAN *clasps her hands and exclaims with affected delight, the* WAITER *and* MR. GUTMAN *laugh agreeably.* MARGUERITE *springs up and moves out upon the forestage.* JACQUES *goes to her.*]

Do you know this resort in the mountains?

MARGUERITE. Yes. I stayed there once. It's one of those places with open sleeping verandahs, surrounded by snowy pine woods. It has rows and rows of narrow white iron beds as regular as tombstones. The invalids smile at each other when axes flash across valleys, ring, flash, ring again! Young voices shout across valleys Hola! And mail is delivered. The friend that used to write you ten-page letters contents himself now with a postcard bluebird that tells you to "Get well Quick!" [JACQUES *throws the brochure away.*] —And when the last bleeding comes, not much later nor earlier than expected, you're wheeled discreetly into a little tent of white gauze, and the last thing you know of this world, of which you've known so little and yet so much, is the smell of an empty ice box.

[*The blue flame expires in the chafing dish.* GUTMAN *picks up the brochure and hands it to the* WAITER, *whispering something.*]

JACQUES. You won't go back to that place.

[*The* WAITER *places the brochure on the salver again and approaches behind them.*]

MARGUERITE. I wasn't released. I left without permission. They sent me this to remind me.

WAITER [*presenting the salver*]. You dropped this.

JACQUES. We threw it away!

WAITER. Excuse me.

JACQUES. Now, from now on, Marguerite, you must take better care of yourself. Do you hear me?

MARGUERITE. I hear you. No more distractions for me? No more entertainers in curtained and perfumed alcoves above the bazaar, no more young men that a pinch of white powder or a puff of gray smoke can almost turn to someone devoutly remembered?

JACQUES. No, from now on—

MARGUERITE. What "from now on," old hawk?

JACQUES. Rest. Peace.

MARGUERITE. Rest in peace is that final bit of advice they carve on gravestones, and I'm not ready for it! Are you? Are *you* ready for it? [*She returns to the table. He follows her.*]
Oh, Jacques, when are we going to leave here, how are we going to leave here, you've got to tell me!

JACQUES. I've told you all I know.

MARGUERITE. Nothing, you've given up hope!

JACQUES. I haven't, that's not true.

[GUTMAN *has brought out the white cockatoo which he shows to* LADY MULLIGAN *at her table.*]

GUTMAN [*his voice rising above the murmurs*]. Her name is Aurora.

LADY MULLIGAN. Why do you call her Aurora?

GUTMAN. She cries at daybreak.

LADY MULLIGAN. Only at daybreak?

GUTMAN. Yes, at daybreak only.

[*Their voices and laughter fade under.*]

MARGUERITE. How long is it since you've been to the travel agencies?

JACQUES. This morning I made the usual round of Cook's, American Express, Wagon-lits Universal, and it was the same story. There are no flights out of here till further orders from someone higher up.

MARGUERITE. Nothing, nothing at all?

JACQUES. Oh, there's a rumor of something called the Fugitivo, but—

MARGUERITE. The What!!! ?

JACQUES. The Fugitivo. It's one of those non-scheduled things that—

MARGUERITE. When, when, when?

JACQUES. I told you it was non-scheduled. Non-scheduled means it comes and goes at no predictable—

MARGUERITE. Don't give me the dictionary! I want to know how does one get on it? Did you bribe them? Did you offer them money? No. Of course you didn't! And I know why! You really don't want to leave here. You *think* you don't want to go because you're brave as an old hawk. But the truth of the matter—the real not the royal truth—is that you're terrified of the Terra Incognita outside that wall.

JACQUES. You've hit upon the truth. I'm terrified of the unknown country inside or outside this wall or any place on earth without you with me! The only country, known or unknown that I can breathe in, or care to, is the country in which we breathe together, as we are now at this table. And later, a little while later, even closer than this, the sole inhabitants of a tiny world whose limits are those of the light from a rose-colored lamp—beside the sweetly, completely known country of your cool bed!

MARGUERITE. The little comfort of love?

JACQUES. Is that comfort so little?

MARGUERITE. Caged birds accept each other but flight is what they long for.

JACQUES. I want to stay here with you and love you and guard you until the time or way comes that we both can leave with honor.

MARGUERITE. "Leave with honor"? Your vocabulary is almost as out-of-date as your cape and your cane. How could anyone quit this field with honor, this place where there's nothing but the gradual wasting away of everything decent in us . . . the sort of desperation that comes after even desperation has been worn out through long wear! . . . Why have they put these screens around the table? [*She springs up and knocks one of them over.*]

LADY MULLIGAN. There! You see? I don't understand why you let such people stay here.

GUTMAN. They pay the price of admission the same as you.

LADY MULLIGAN. What price is that?

GUTMAN. Desperation!— With cash here! [*He indicates the Siete Mares.*] Without cash there! [*He indicates Skid Row.*] Block Eight on the Camino Real!

Block eight

There is the sound of loud desert wind and a flamenco cry followed by a dramatic phrase of music.

A flickering diamond blue radiance floods the hotel entrance. The crouching, grimacing HUNCHBACK *shakes his hoop of bells which is the convention for the appearance of each legendary figure.*

LORD BYRON *appears in the doorway readied for departure.* GUTMAN *raises his hand for silence.*

GUTMAN. You're leaving us, Lord Byron?

BYRON. Yes, I'm leaving you, Mr. Gutman.

GUTMAN. What a pity! But this is a port of entry and

departure. There are no permanent guests. Possibly you are getting a little restless?

BYRON. The luxuries of this place have made me soft. The metal point's gone from my pen, there's nothing left but the feather.

GUTMAN. That may be true. But what can you do about it?

BYRON. Make a departure!

GUTMAN. From yourself?

BYRON. From my present self to myself as I used to be!

GUTMAN. *That's* the *furthest* departure a man could make! I guess you're sailing to Athens? There's another war there and like all wars since the beginning of time it can be interpreted as a—struggle for *what?*

BYRON. —For *freedom!* You may laugh at it, but it still means something to *me!*

GUTMAN. Of course it does! I'm not laughing a bit, I'm beaming with admiration.

BYRON. I've allowed myself many distractions.

GUTMAN. Yes, indeed!

BYRON. But I've never altogether forgotten my old devotion to the—

GUTMAN. —To the *what,* Lord Byron? [BYRON *passes nervous fingers through his hair.*] You can't remember the object of your one-time devotion?

[*There is a pause.* BYRON *limps away from the terrace and goes toward the fountain.*]

BYRON. When Shelley's corpse was recovered from the sea . . . [GUTMAN *beckons the* DREAMER *who approaches and accompanies* BYRON'S *speech.*] —It was burned on the beach at Viareggio.— I watched the spectacle from my carriage because the stench was revolting . . . Then it—fascinated me! I got out of my carriage. Went nearer, holding a handkerchief to my nostrils!— I saw that the front of the skull had broken away in the flames, and there— [*He advances out upon the stage apron, followed by* ABDULLAH *with the pine torch or lantern.*] And there was the brain of Shelley, indistinguishable from a cooking stew!—*boiling, bubbling, hissing!*—in the *blackening* —*cracked*—*pot*—of his skull! [MARGUERITE *rises abruptly.* JACQUES *supports her.*] —Trelawney, his friend, Trelawney, threw salt and oil and frankincense in the flames and finally the almost intolerable stench— [ABDULLAH *giggles.* GUTMAN *slaps him.*] —was *gone* and the burning was *pure!*—as a man's burning should be ...

A man's burning *ought* to be pure!—*not* like mine— (a crepe suzette—burned in brandy ...)

Shelley's burning was finally very *pure!*

But the body, the corpse, split open like a grilled pig! [ABDULLAH *giggles irrepressibly again.* GUTMAN *grips the back of his neck and he stands up stiff and assumes an expression of exaggerated solemnity.*] —And then Trelawney—as the ribs of the corpse unlocked—reached into them as a baker reaches quickly into an oven! [ABDULLAH *almost goes into another convulsion.*] —And snatched out —as a baker would a biscuit!—the *heart* of Shelley! Snatched the heart of Shelley out of the blistering corpse!— Out of the purifying—blue-flame . . . [MARGUERITE *resumes her seat;* JACQUES *his.*] —And it was *over!*— I thought— [*He turns slightly from the audience and crosses upstage from the apron. He faces* JACQUES *and* MARGUERITE.] —I thought it was a disgusting thing to do, to snatch a man's heart from his body! What can one man do with another man's heart? [JACQUES *rises and strikes the stage with his cane.*]

JACQUES [*passionately*]. He can do this with it! [*He seizes a loaf of bread on his table, and descends from the terrace.*] He can twist it like this! [*He twists the loaf.*] He can tear it like this! [*He tears the loaf in two.*] He can crush it under his foot! [*He drops the bread and stamps on it.*] —And kick it away—like this! [*He kicks the bread off the terrace.* LORD BYRON *turns away from him and limps again out upon the stage apron and speaks to the audience.*]

BYRON. That's very true, Señor. But a poet's vocation, which used to be my vocation, is to influence the heart in a gentler fashion than you have made your mark on that loaf of bread. He ought to purify it and lift it above its ordinary level. For what is the heart but a sort of— [*He makes a high, groping gesture in the air.*] —A sort of—*instrument!*—that translates *noise* into *music,* chaos into—*order* . . . [ABDULLAH *ducks almost to the earth in an effort to stifle his mirth.* GUTMAN *coughs to cover his own amusement.*] —*a mysterious order!* [*He raises his voice till it fills the plaza.*] —That was my vocation once upon a time, before it was obscured by vulgar plaudits!— Little by little it was lost among gondolas and palazzos!—masked balls, glittering salons, huge shadowy courts and torch-lit entrances!— Baroque façades, canopies and carpets, candelabra and gold plate among snowy damask, ladies with throats as slender as flower-stems, bending and breathing toward me their fragrant breath—

—Exposing their breasts to me!

Whispering, half-smiling!— And everywhere marble, the visible grandeur of marble, pink and gray marble, veined and tinted as flayed corrupting flesh,—all these provided agreeable distractions from the rather frightening solitude of a poet. Oh, I wrote many cantos in Venice and Constantinople and in Ravenna and Rome, on all of those Latin and Levantine excursions that my twisted foot led me into—but I wonder about them a little. They seem to improve as the wine in the bottle—dwindles . . . *There is a passion for declivity in this world!*

And lately I've found myself listening to hired musicians behind a row of artificial palm trees—instead of the single—pure-stringed instrument of my heart . . .

Well, then, it's time to leave here! [*He turns back to
the stage.*] —There is a time for departure even when
there's no certain place to go!

I'm going to look for one, now. I'm sailing to
Athens. At least I can look up at the Acropolis, I
can stand at the foot of it and look up at broken
columns on the crest of a hill—if not purity, at least
its recollection . . .

I can sit quietly looking for a long, long time in ab-
solute silence, and possibly, yes, *still* possibly—

The old pure music will come to me again. Of course
on the other hand I may hear only the little noise of
insects in the grass . . .

But I am sailing to Athens! *Make voyages!— Attempt them!*—there's nothing else . . .

MARGUERITE [*excitedly*]. *Watch where he goes!* [LORD
BYRON *limps across the plaza with his head bowed,
making slight, apologetic gestures to the wheedling
BEGGARS who shuffle about him. There is music. He
crosses toward the steep Alleyway Out. The following is played with a quiet intensity so it will be in a
lower key than the later Fugitivo Scene.*] Watch him,
watch him, see which way he goes. Maybe he knows
of a way that we haven't found out.

JACQUES. Yes, I'm watching him, Cara.

[LORD *and* LADY MULLIGAN *half rise, staring anxiously
through monocle and lorgnon.*]

MARGUERITE. Oh, my God, I believe he's going up that
alley.

JACQUES. Yes, he is. He has.

LORD and LADY MULLIGAN. Oh, the fool, the idiot, he's
going under the arch!

MARGUERITE. Jacques, run after him, warn him, tell
him about the desert he has to cross.

JACQUES. I think he knows what he's doing.

MARGUERITE. I can't look!

[*She turns to the audience, throwing back her head*

and closing her eyes. The desert wind sings loudly as
BYRON *climbs to the top of the steps.*]

BYRON [*to several porters carrying luggage—which is
mainly caged birds*]. THIS WAY! [*He exits.*]

[KILROY *starts to follow. He stops at the steps, cring-
ing and looking at* GUTMAN. GUTMAN *motions him to
go ahead.* KILROY *rushes up the stairs. He looks out,
loses his nerve and sits—blinking his nose.* GUTMAN
laughs as he announces—]

GUTMAN. Block Nine on the Camino Real! [*He goes
into the hotel.*]

Block nine

ABDULLAH *runs back to the hotel with the billowing
flambeau. A faint and far away humming sound becomes audible . . .* MARGUERITE *opens her eyes with a
startled look. She searches the sky for something. A
very low percussion begins with the humming sound,
as if excited hearts were beating.*

MARGUERITE. Jacques! I hear something in the sky!

JACQUES. I think what you hear is—

MARGUERITE [*with rising excitement*]. —No, it's a plane,
a great one, I see the lights of it, now!

JACQUES. Some kind of fireworks, Cara.

MARGUERITE. Hush! LISTEN! [*She blows out the candle to see better above it. She rises, peering into the
sky.*] I see it! I see it! There! It's circling over us!

LADY MULLIGAN. Raymond, Raymond, sit down, your
face is flushed!

HOTEL GUESTS [*overlapping*].

—What is it?

—The FUGITIVO!

—THE FUGITIVO! THE FUGITIVO!

—Quick, get my jewelry from the hotel safe!

—Cash a check!

—Throw some things in a bag! I'll wait here!

—Never mind luggage, we have our money and papers!

—Where is it now?

—There, there!

—It's turning to land!

—To go like this?

—Yes, go anyhow, just go anyhow, just go!

—Raymond! Please!

—Oh, it's rising again!

—Oh, it's—*SHH! MR. GUTMAN!*

[GUTMAN *appears in the doorway. He raises a hand in a commanding gesture.*]

GUTMAN. Signs in the sky should not be mistaken for wonders! [*The Voices modulate quickly.*] Ladies, gentlemen, please resume your seats! [*Places are resumed at tables, and silver is shakily lifted. Glasses are raised to lips, but the noise of concerted panting of excitement fills the stage and a low percussion echoes frantic heart beats.* GUTMAN *descends to the plaza, shouting furiously to the* OFFICER.] Why wasn't I told the Fugitivo was coming?

[*Everyone, almost as a man, rushes into the hotel and reappears almost at once with hastily collected possessions.* MARGUERITE *rises but appears stunned.*]

[*There is a great whistling and screeching sound as the aerial transport halts somewhere close by, accompanied by rainbow splashes of light and cries like children's on a roller-coaster. Some incoming* PASSENGERS *approach the stage down an aisle of the theatre, preceded by* REDCAPS *with luggage.*]

PASSENGERS.

—What a heavenly trip!

—The scenery was thrilling!

—It's so quick!

—The only way to travel! Etc., etc.

[*A uniformed man, the* PILOT, *enters the plaza with a megaphone.*]

PILOT [*through megaphone*]. Fugitivo now loading for departure! Fugitivo loading immediately for departure! Northwest corner of the plaza!

MARGUERITE. Jacques, it's the Fugitivo, it's the non-scheduled thing you heard of this afternoon!

PILOT. All out-going passengers on the Fugitivo are requested to present their tickets and papers immediately at this station.

MARGUERITE. He said "out-going passengers"!

PILOT. Out-going passengers on the Fugitivo report immediately at this station for customs inspection.

MARGUERITE [*with a forced smile*]. Why are you just standing there?

JACQUES [*with an Italian gesture*]. Che cosa possa fare!

MARGUERITE. Move, move, do something!

JACQUES. *What!*

MARGUERITE. Go to them, ask, find out!

JACQUES. I have no idea what the damned thing is!

MARGUERITE. I do, I'll tell you! It's a way to escape from this abominable place!

JACQUES. Forse, forse, non so!

MARGUERITE. It's a way *out* and *I'm* not going to miss it!

PILOT. Ici la Douane! Customs inspection here!

MARGUERITE. Customs. That means luggage. Run to my room! Here! Key! Throw a few things in a bag, my jewels, my furs, but hurry! Vite, vite, vite! I don't believe there's much time! No, everybody is— [*Out-going* PASSENGERS *storm the desk and table.*] —Clamoring for tickets! There must be limited space! Why don't you do what I tell you? [*She rushes to a man with a rubber stamp and a roll of tickets.*] Monsieur! Señor! Pardonnez-moi! I'm going, I'm going out! I want my ticket!

PILOT [*coldly*]. Name, please.

MARGUERITE. Mademoiselle—Gautier—but I—

PILOT. Gautier? Gautier? We have no Gautier listed.

MARGUERITE. I'm—*not* listed! I mean I'm—traveling under another name.

TRAVEL AGENT. What name are you traveling under?

[PRUDENCE *and* OLYMPE *rush out of the hotel half dressed, dragging their furs. Meanwhile* KILROY *is trying to make a fast buck or two as a Redcap. The scene gathers wild momentum, is punctuated by crashes of percussion. Grotesque mummers act as demon custom inspectors and immigration authorities, etc. Baggage is tossed about, ripped open, smuggled goods seized, arrests made, all amid the wildest importunities, protests, threats, bribes, entreaties; it is a scene for improvisation.*]

PRUDENCE. Thank God I woke up!

OLYMPE. Thank God I wasn't asleep!

PRUDENCE. I knew it was non-scheduled but I *did* think they'd give you time to get in your girdle.

OLYMPE. Look, who's trying to crash it! I know damned well *she* don't have a reservation!

PILOT [*to* MARGUERITE]. What name did you say, Mademoiselle? Please! People—are waiting, you're holding up the line!

MARGUERITE. I'm so confused! Jacques! What name did you make my reservation under?

OLYMPE. She has no reservation!

PRUDENCE. *I have, I got mine!*

OLYMPE. *I got mine!*

PRUDENCE. *I'm* next!

OLYMPE. Don't push *me,* you old bag!

MARGUERITE. I was here first! I was here before anybody! Jacques, quick! Get my money from the hotel safe!

[JACQUES *exits.*]

AGENT. *Stay in line!*

[*There is a loud warning whistle.*]

PILOT. Five minutes. The Fugitivo leaves in five minutes. Five, five minutes only!

[*At this announcement the scene becomes riotous.*]

TRAVEL AGENT. *Four minutes! The Fugitivo leaves in four minutes!* [PRUDENCE *and* OLYMPE *are shrieking at him in French. The warning whistle blasts again.*] *Three minutes, the Fugitivo leaves in three minutes!*

MARGUERITE [*topping the turmoil*]. Monsieur! Please! I was here first, I was here before anybody! Look! [JACQUES *returns with her money.*] I have thousands in francs! Take whatever you want! Take all of it, it's yours!

PILOT. Payment is only accepted in pounds sterling or dollars. Next, please.

MARGUERITE. You don't accept francs? They do at the hotel! They accept my francs at the Siete Mares!

PILOT. Lady, don't argue with me, I don't make the rules!

MARGUERITE [*beating her forehead with her fist*]. Oh, God, Jacques! Take these back to the cashier! [*She thrusts the bills at him.*] Get them changed to dollars or— Hurry! Tout de suite! I'm—going to faint . . .

JACQUES. But Marguerite—

MARGUERITE. *Go! Go! Please!*

PILOT. Closing, we're closing now! The Fugitivo leaves in two minutes!

[LORD *and* LADY MULLIGAN *rush forward.*]

LADY MULLIGAN. Let Lord Mulligan through.

PILOT [*to* MARGUERITE]. You're standing in the way.

[OLYMPE *screams as the* CUSTOMS INSPECTOR *dumps her jewels on the ground. She and* PRUDENCE *butt heads as they dive for the gems: the fight is renewed.*]

MARGUERITE [*detaining the* PILOT]. Oh, look, Monsieur! Regardez ça! My diamond, a solitaire—two carats! Take that as security!

PILOT. Let me go. The Loan Shark's across the plaza!

[*There is another warning blast.* PRUDENCE *and* OLYMPE *seize hat boxes and rush toward the whistle.*]

MARGUERITE [*clinging desperately to the* PILOT]. You don't understand! Señor Casanova has gone to change money! He'll be here in a second. And I'll pay five, ten, twenty times the price of—*JACQUES! JACQUES! WHERE ARE YOU?*

VOICE [*back of auditorium*]. We're closing the gate!

MARGUERITE. You can't close the gate!

PILOT. Move, Madame!

MARGUERITE. I won't move!

LADY MULLIGAN. I tell you, Lord Mulligan is the Iron & Steel man from Cobh! Raymond! They're closing the gate!

LORD MULLIGAN. I can't seem to get through!

GUTMAN. Hold the gate for Lord Mulligan!

PILOT [*to* MARGUERITE]. Madame, stand back or I will have to use force!

MARGUERITE. Jacques! Jacques!

LADY MULLIGAN. Let us through! We're clear!

PILOT. Madame! Stand back and let these passengers through!

MARGUERITE. No, No! I'm first! I'm next!

LORD MULLIGAN. Get her out of our way! That woman's a whore!

LADY MULLIGAN. How dare you stand in our way?

PILOT. Officer, take this woman!

LADY MULLIGAN. Come on, Raymond!

MARGUERITE [*as the* OFFICER *pulls her away*]. Jacques! Jacques! Jacques! [JACQUES *returns with changed money.*] Here! Here is the money!

PILOT. All right, give me your papers.

MARGUERITE. —My papers? Did you say my papers?

PILOT. Hurry, hurry, your passport!

MARGUERITE. —Jacques! He wants my papers! Give him my papers, Jacques!

JACQUES. —The lady's papers are lost!

MARGUERITE [*wildly*]. No, no, no, THAT IS NOT

TRUE! HE WANTS TO KEEP ME HERE! HE'S
LYING ABOUT IT!

JACQUES. Have you forgotten that your papers were
stolen?

MARGUERITE. I gave you my papers, I gave you my papers to keep, you've got my papers.

[*Screaming,* LADY MULLIGAN *breaks past her and descends the stairs.*]

LADY MULLIGAN. Raymond! Hurry!

LORD MULLIGAN [*staggering on the top step*]. I'm sick!
I'm sick!

[*The* STREETCLEANERS *disguised as expensive morti-
cians in swallowtail coats come rapidly up the aisle
of the theatre and wait at the foot of the stairway
for the tottering tycoon.*]

LADY MULLIGAN. You cannot be sick till we get on the
Fugitivo!

LORD MULLIGAN. Forward all cables to Guaranty Trust
in Paris.

LADY MULLIGAN. Place de la Concorde.

LORD MULLIGAN. Thank you! All purchases C.O.D. to
Mulligan Iron & Steel Works in Cobh— Thank you!

LADY MULLIGAN. Raymond! Raymond! Who are these
men?

LORD MULLIGAN. I know these men! I recognize their
faces!

LADY MULLIGAN. Raymond! They're the Streetcleaners!
[*She screams and runs up the aisle screaming re-
peatedly, stopping half-way to look back. The* TWO
STREETCLEANERS *seize* LORD MULLIGAN *by either arm
as he crumples.*] Pack Lord Mulligan's body in dry
ice! Ship Air Express to Cobh care of Mulligan Iron
& Steel Works, in Cobh! [*She runs sobbing out of the
back of the auditorium as the whistle blows repeat-
edly and a Voice shouts.*] I'm coming! I'm coming!

MARGUERITE. Jacques! Jacques! Oh, God!

PILOT. The Fugitivo is leaving, all aboard! [*He starts*

toward the steps. MARGUERITE *clutches his arm.*] Let go of me!

MARGUERITE. You can't go without me!

PILOT. Officer, hold this woman!

JACQUES. Marguerite, let him go!

[*She releases the* PILOT'S *arm and turns savagely on* JACQUES. *She tears his coat open, seizes a large envelope of papers and rushes after the* PILOT *who has started down the steps over the orchestra pit and into a center aisle of the house. Timpani build up as she starts down the steps, screaming—*]

MARGUERITE. Here! I have them here! Wait! I have my papers now, I have my papers!

[*The* PILOT *runs cursing up the center aisle as the* FUGITIVO *whistle gives repeated short, shrill blasts; timpani and dissonant brass are heard.*]

[*Outgoing* PASSENGERS *burst into hysterical song, laughter, shouts of farewell. These can come over a loudspeaker at the back of the house.*]

VOICE IN DISTANCE. Going! Going! Going!

MARGUERITE [*attempting as if half-paralyzed to descend the steps*]. NOT WITHOUT ME, NO, NO, NOT WITHOUT ME!

[*Her figure is caught in the dazzling glacial light of the follow-spot. It blinds her. She makes violent, crazed gestures, clinging to the railing of the steps; her breath is loud and hoarse as a dying person's, she holds a blood-stained handkerchief to her lips.*]

[*There is a prolonged, gradually fading, rocketlike roar as the* FUGITIVO *takes off. Shrill cries of joy from departing passengers; something radiant passes above the stage and streams of confetti and tinsel fall into the plaza. Then there is a great calm, the ship's receding roar diminished to the hum of an insect.*]

GUTMAN [*somewhat compassionately*]. Block Ten on the Camino Real.

Block ten

There is something about the desolation of the plaza that suggests a city devastated by bombardment. Reddish lights flicker here and there as if ruins were smoldering and wisps of smoke rise from them.

LA MADRECITA [*almost inaudibly*]. Donde?
THE DREAMER. Aquí. Aquí, Madrecita.
MARGUERITE. Lost! Lost! Lost! Lost!
[*She is still clinging brokenly to the railing of the steps. JACQUES descends to her and helps her back up the steps.*]
JACQUES. Lean against me, Cara. Breathe quietly, now.
MARGUERITE. Lost!
JACQUES. Breathe quietly, quietly, and look up at the sky.
MARGUERITE. Lost ...
JACQUES. These tropical nights are so clear. There's the Southern Cross. Do you see the Southern Cross, Marguerite? [*He points through the proscenium. They are now on the bench before the fountain; she is resting in his arms.*] And there, over there, is Orion, like a fat, golden fish swimming North in the deep clear water, and we are together, breathing quietly together, leaning together, quietly, quietly together, completely, sweetly together, not frightened, now, not alone, but completely quietly together ... [LA MADRECITA, *led into the center of the plaza by her* SON, *has begun to sing very softly; the reddish flares dim out and the smoke disappears.*] All of us have a desperate bird in our hearts, a memory of—some distant mother with—wings ...
MARGUERITE. I would have—left—without you ...

JACQUES. I know, I know!

MARGUERITE. Then how can you—still—?

JACQUES. Hold you? [MARGUERITE *nods slightly*.] Because you've taught me that part of love which is tender. I never knew it before. Oh, I had—mistresses that circled me like moons! I scrambled from one bed-chamber to another bed-chamber with shirttails always aflame, from girl to girl, like buckets of coal-oil poured on a conflagration! But never loved until now with the part of love that's tender . . .

MARGUERITE. —We're used to each other. That's what you think is love . . . You'd better leave me now, you'd better go and let me go because there's a cold wind blowing out of the mountains and over the desert and into my heart, and if you stay with me now, I'll say cruel things, I'll wound your vanity, I'll taunt you with the decline of your male vigor!

JACQUES. Why does disappointment make people unkind to each other?

MARGUERITE. Each of us is very much alone.

JACQUES. Only if we distrust each other.

MARGUERITE. We have to distrust each other. It is our only defense against betrayal.

JACQUES. I think our defense is love.

MARGUERITE. Oh, Jacques, we're used to each other, we're a pair of captive hawks caught in the same cage, and so we've grown used to each other. That's what passes for love at this dim, shadowy end of the Camino Real . . .

What are we sure of? Not even of our existence, dear comforting friend! And whom can we ask the questions that torment us? "What is this place?" "Where are we?"—a fat old man who gives sly hints that only bewilder us more, a fake of a Gypsy squinting at cards and tea-leaves. What else are we offered? The never-broken procession of little events that assure us that we and strangers about us are still going on! Where? Why? and the perch that we hold is unstable! We're threatened with eviction, for this is a port of entry and departure, there are no permanent guests! And where else have we to go when we leave here? Bide-a-While? "Ritz Men Only"? Or under that ominous arch into Terra Incognita? We're lonely. We're frightened. We hear the Street-cleaners' piping not far away. So now and then, although we've wounded each other time and again—we stretch out hands to each other in the dark that we can't escape from—we huddle together for some dim-communal comfort—and that's what passes for love on this terminal stretch of the road that used to be royal. What is it, this feeling between us? When you feel my exhausted weight against your shoulder—when I clasp your anxious old hawk's head to my breast, what is it we feel in whatever is left of our hearts? Something, yes, something—delicate, unreal, bloodless! The sort of violets that could grow on the moon, or in the crevices of those far away mountains, fertilized by the droppings of carrion birds. Those birds are familiar to us. Their shadows inhabit the plaza. I've heard them flapping their wings like old charwomen beating worn-out carpets with gray brooms . . .

But tenderness, the violets in the mountains—can't break the rocks!

JACQUES. The violets in the mountains can break the rocks if you believe in them and allow them to grow!

[*The plaza has resumed its usual aspect.* ABDULLAH *enters through one of the downstage arches.*]

ABDULLAH. Get your carnival hats and noisemakers here! Tonight the moon will restore the virginity of my sister!

MARGUERITE [*almost tenderly touching his face*]. Don't you know that tonight I am going to betray you?

JACQUES. —Why would you do that?

MARGUERITE. Because I've out-lived the tenderness of

my heart. Abdullah, come here! I have an errand
for you! Go to Ahmed's and deliver a message!

ABDULLAH. I'm working for Mama, making the Yankee
dollar! Get your carnival hats and—

MARGUERITE. *Here, boy!* [*She snatches a ring off her
finger and offers it to him.*]

JACQUES. —Your cabochon sapphire?

MARGUERITE. Yes, my cabochon sapphire!

JACQUES. Are you mad?

MARGUERITE. Yes, I'm mad, or nearly! The specter of
lunacy's at my heels tonight! [JACQUES *drives* ABDUL-
LAH *back with his cane.*] Catch, boy! The other side
of the fountain! Quick! [*The guitar is heard molto
vivace. She tosses the ring across the fountain.*
JACQUES *attempts to hold the boy back with his cane.*
ABDULLAH *dodges in and out like a little terrier,
laughing.* MARGUERITE *shouts encouragement in
French. When the boy is driven back from the ring,
she snatches it up and tosses it to him again, shouting.*] Catch, boy! Run to Ahmed's! Tell the charming young man that the French lady's bored with
her company tonight! Say that the French lady
missed the Fugitivo and wants to forget she missed
it! Oh, and reserve a room with a balcony so I can
watch your sister appear on the roof when the moonrise makes her a virgin! [ABDULLAH *skips shouting
out of the plaza.* JACQUES *strikes the stage with his
cane. She says, without looking at him:*] Time be-
trays us and we betray each other.

JACQUES. Wait, Marguerite.

MARGUERITE. No! I can't! The wind from the desert is
sweeping me away!

[*A loud singing wind sweeps her toward the terrace,
away from him. She looks back once or twice as if
for some gesture of leave-taking but he only stares at
her fiercely, striking the stage at intervals with his
cane, like a death-march.* GUTMAN *watches, smiling,*

from the terrace, bows to MARGUERITE *as she passes into the hotel. The drum of* JACQUES' *cane is taken up by other percussive instruments, and almost unnoticeably at first, weird-looking celebrants or carnival mummers creep into the plaza, silently as spiders descending a wall.*]

[*A sheet of scarlet and yellow rice paper bearing some cryptic device is lowered from the center of the plaza. The percussive effects become gradually louder.* JACQUES *is oblivious to the scene behind him, standing in front of the plaza, his eyes closed.*]

GUTMAN. Block Eleven on the Camino Real.

Block eleven

GUTMAN. The Fiesta has started. The first event is the coronation of the King of Cuckolds.

[*Blinding shafts of light are suddenly cast upon* CASANOVA *on the forestage. He shields his face, startled, as the crowd closes about him. The blinding shafts of light seem to strike him like savage blows and he falls to his knees as—*]

[*The* HUNCHBACK *scuttles out of the* GYPSY'S *stall with a crown of gilded antlers on a velvet pillow. He places it on* JACQUES' *head. The celebrants form a circle about him chanting.*]

JACQUES. What is this?—a crown—

GUTMAN. A crown of horns!

CROWD. Cornudo! Cornudo! Cornudo! Cornudo! Cornudo!

GUTMAN. Hail, all hail, the King of Cuckolds on the Camino Real!

[JACQUES *springs up, first striking out at them with his cane. Then all at once he abandons self-defense, throws off his cape, casts away his cane, and fills the plaza with a roar of defiance and self-derision.*]

JACQUES. Si, si, sono cornudo! Cornudo! Cornudo! Casanova is the King of Cuckolds on the Camino Real! Show me crowned to the world! Announce the honor! Tell the world of the honor bestowed on Casanova, Chevalier de Seingalt! Knight of the Golden Spur by the Grace of His Holiness the Pope . . . Famous adventurer! Con man Extraordinary! Gambler! Pitch-man par excellence! Shill! Pimp! Spiv! *And—great—lover* . . . [*The* CROWD *howls with applause and laughter but his voice rises above them with sobbing intensity.*] Yes, I said GREAT LOVER! The greatest lover wears the longest horns on the Camino! GREAT! LOVER!

GUTMAN. Attention! Silence! The moon is rising! The restoration is about to occur!

[*A white radiance is appearing over the ancient wall of the town. The mountains become luminous. There is music. Everyone, with breathless attention, faces the light.*]

[KILROY *crosses to* JACQUES *and beckons him out behind the crowd. There he snatches off the antlers and returns him his fedora.* JACQUES *reciprocates by removing* KILROY's *fright wig and electric nose. They embrace as brothers. In a Chaplinesque dumb-play,* KILROY *points to the wildly flickering three brass balls of the* LOAN SHARK *and to his golden gloves: then with a terrible grimace he removes the gloves from about his neck, smiles at* JACQUES *and indicates that the two of them together will take flight over the wall.* JACQUES *shakes his head sadly, pointing to his heart and then to the Siete Mares.* KILROY *nods with regretful understanding of a human and manly folly. A* GUARD *has been silently approaching them in a soft shoe dance.* JACQUES *whistles "La Golondrina."* KILROY *assumes a very nonchalant pose. The* GUARD *picks up curiously the discarded fright wig and electric nose. Then glancing suspiciously at the pair, he advances.* KILROY *makes a run for it. He does a baseball slide into the* LOAN SHARK'S *welcoming doorway. The door slams. The* COP *is about to crash it when a gong sounds and* GUTMAN *shouts:*]

GUTMAN. SILENCE! ATTENTION! THE GYPSY!

GYPSY [*appearing on the roof with a gong*]. The moon has restored the virginity of my daughter Esmeralda!

[*The gong sounds.*]

STREET PEOPLE. Ahh!

GYPSY. The moon in its plenitude has made her a virgin!

[*The gong sounds.*]

STREET PEOPLE. Ahh!

GYPSY. Praise her, celebrate her, give her suitable homage!

[*The gong sounds.*]

STREET PEOPLE. Ahh!

GYPSY. Summon her to the roof! [*She shouts.*] ESMERALDA! [DANCERS *shout the name in rhythm.*] RISE WITH THE MOON, MY DAUGHTER! CHOOSE THE HERO!

[ESMERALDA *appears on the roof in dazzling light. She seems to be dressed in jewels. She raises her jeweled arms with a harsh flamenco cry.*]

ESMERALDA. OLE!

DANCERS. OLE!

[*The details of the Carnival are a problem for director and choreographer but it has already been indicated in the script that the Fiesta is a sort of serio-comic, grotesque-lyric "Rites of Fertility" with roots in various pagan cultures.*]

[*It should not be over-elaborated or allowed to occupy much time. It should not be more than three minutes from the appearance of* ESMERALDA *on the* GYPSY'S *roof till the return of* KILROY *from the* LOAN SHARK'S.]

[KILROY *emerges from the Pawn Shop in grotesque disguise, a turban, dark glasses, a burnoose and an umbrella or sunshade.*]

KILROY [*to* JACQUES]. So long, pal, I wish you could come with me.

[JACQUES *clasps his cross in* KILROY'S *hands.*]

ESMERALDA. Yankee!

KILROY [*to the audience*]. So long, everybody. Good luck to you all on the Camino! I hocked my golden gloves to finance this expedition. I'm going. Hasta luega. I'm going. I'm gone!

ESMERALDA. Yankee!

[*He has no sooner entered the plaza than the riotous women strip off everything but the dungarees and skivvy which he first appeared in.*]

KILROY [*to the women*]. Let me go. Let go of me! Watch out for my equipment!

ESMERALDA. Yankee! Yankee!

[*He breaks away from them and plunges up the stairs of the ancient wall. He is half-way up them when* GUTMAN *shouts out:*]

GUTMAN. Follow-spot on that gringo, light the stairs!

[*The light catches* KILROY. *At the same instant* ESMERALDA *cries out to him.*]

ESMERALDA. *Yankee! Yankee!*

GYPSY. What's goin' on down there? [*She rushes into the plaza.*]

KILROY. Oh, no, I'm on my way out!

ESMERALDA. Espere un momento!

[*The* GYPSY *calls the police, but is ignored in the crowd.*]

KILROY. Don't tempt me, baby! I hocked my golden gloves to finance this expedition!

ESMERALDA. Querido!

KILROY. Querido means sweetheart, a word which is hard to resist but I must resist it.

ESMERALDA. Champ!

KILROY. I used to be Champ but why remind me of it?

ESMERALDA. Be champ again! Contend in the contest! Compete in the competition!

GYPSY [*shouting*]. *Naw, naw, not eligible!*

ESMERALDA. *Pl-eeeeeeze!*

GYPSY. Slap her, Nursie, she's flippin'.

[ESMERALDA *slaps* NURSIE *instead.*]

ESMERALDA. Hero! Champ!

KILROY. I'm not in condition!

ESMERALDA. You're still the Champ, the undefeated Champ of the golden gloves!

KILROY. Nobody's called me that in a long, long time!

ESMERALDA. Champ!

KILROY. My resistance is crumbling!

ESMERALDA. Champ!

KILROY. It's crumbled!

ESMERALDA. Hero!

KILROY. GERONIMO! [*He takes a flying leap from the stairs into the center of the plaza. He turns toward* ESMERALDA *and cries:*] DOLL!! [KILROY *surrounded by cheering* STREET PEOPLE *goes into a triumphant eccentric dance which reviews his history as fighter, traveler and lover.*]

[*At finish of the dance, the music is cut off, as* KILROY *lunges, arm uplifted toward* ESMERALDA, *and cries:*]

KILROY. *Kilroy the Champ!*

ESMERALDA. *KILROY the Champ!* [*She snatches a bunch of red roses from the stunned* NURSIE *and tosses them to* KILROY.]

CROWD [*sharply*]. OLE!

[*The* GYPSY, *at the same instant, hurls her gong down, creating a resounding noise.*]

[KILROY *turns and comes down toward the audience, saying to them:*]

KILROY. *Y'see?*

[*Cheering* STREET PEOPLE *surge toward him and lift him in the air. The lights fade as the curtain descends.*]

CROWD [*in a sustained yell*]. *OLE!*
[*The curtain falls. There is a short intermission.*]

Block twelve

The stage is in darkness except for a spot light which picks out ESMERALDA *on the* GYPSY'S *roof.*

ESMERALDA. Mama, what happened? —Mama, the lights went out!— Mama, where are you? It's so dark I'm scared!— MAMA!
[*The lights are turned on displaying a deserted plaza. The* GYPSY *is seated at a small table before her stall.*]

GYPSY. Come on downstairs, Doll. The mischief is done. You've chosen your hero!

GUTMAN [*from the balcony of the Siete Mares*]. Block Twelve on the Camino Real.

NURSIE [*at the fountain*]. Gypsy, the fountain is still dry!

GYPSY. What d'yuh expect? There's nobody left to up-hold the old traditions! You raise a girl. She watches television. Plays be-bop. Reads *Screen Secrets*. Comes the Big Fiesta. The moonrise makes her a virgin—which is the neatest trick of the week! And what does she do? Chooses a Fugitive Patsy for the Chosen Hero! Well, show him in! Admit the joker and get the virgin ready!

NURSIE. You're going through with it?

GYPSY. Look, Nursie! I'm operating a legitimate joint! This joker'll get the same treatment he'd get if he breezed down the Camino Real in a blizzard of G-notes! Trot, girl! Lubricate your means of loco-motion!

[NURSIE *goes into the* GYPSY's *stall. The* GYPSY *rubs her hands together and blows on the crystal ball, spits on it and gives it the old one-two with a "shammy" rag . . . She mutters "Crystal ball, tell me all . . . crystal ball tell me all" . . . as:*]

[KILROY *bounds into the plaza from her stall . . . a rose between his teeth.*]

GYPSY. Siente se, por favor.

KILROY. No comprendo the lingo.

GYPSY. Put it down!

NURSIE [*offstage*]. Hey, Gypsy!

GYPSY. Address me as Madam!

NURSIE [*entering*]. *Madam!* Winchell has scooped you!

GYPSY. In a pig's eye!

NURSIE. The Fugitivo has "*fftt . . .*"!

GYPSY. In Elizabeth, New Jersey . . . ten fifty seven p.m. . . . Eastern Standard Time—while you were putting them kiss-me-quicks in your hair-do! Furthermore, my second exclusive is that the solar system is drifting toward the constellation of Hercules: *Skiddoo!* [NURSIE *exits. Stamping is heard offstage.*] *Quiet, back there! God damn it!*

NURSIE [*offstage*]. She's out of control!

GYPSY. Give her a double-bromide! [*To* KILROY:] Well, how does it feel to be the Chosen Hero?

KILROY. I better explain something to you.

GYPSY. Save your breath. You'll need it.

KILROY. I want to level with you. Can I level with you?

GYPSY [*rapidly stamping some papers*]. How could you help but level with the Gypsy?

KILROY. I don't know what the hero is chosen for.

[ESMERALDA *and* NURSIE *shriek offstage.*]

GYPSY. Time will brief you . . . Aw, I hate paper work! . . . NURSEHH! [NURSIE *comes out and stands by the table.*] This filing system is screwed up six ways from Next Sunday . . . File this crap under crap!—

[*To* KILROY:] The smoking lamp is lit. Have a stick on me! [*She offers him a cigarette.*]

KILROY. No thanks.

GYPSY. Come on, indulge yourself. You got nothing to lose that won't be lost.

KILROY. If that's a professional opinion, I don't respect it.

GYPSY. Resume your seat and give me your full name.

KILROY. Kilroy.

GYPSY [*writing all this down*]. Date of birth and place of that disaster?

KILROY. Both unknown.

GYPSY. Address?

KILROY. Traveler.

GYPSY. Parents?

KILROY. Anonymous.

GYPSY. Who brought you up?

KILROY. I was brought up and down by an eccentric old aunt in Dallas.

GYPSY. Raise both hands simultaneously and swear that you have not come here for the purpose of committing an immoral act.

ESMERALDA [*from offstage*]. Hey, Chico!

GYPSY. *QUIET!* Childhood diseases?

KILROY. Whooping cough, measles and mumps.

GYPSY. Likes and dislikes?

KILROY. I like situations I can get out of. I don't like cops and—

GYPSY. Immaterial! Here! Signature on this! [*She hands him a blank.*]

KILROY. What is it?

GYPSY. You always sign something, don't you?

KILROY. Not till I know what it is.

GYPSY. It's just a little formality to give tone to the establishment and make an impression on our out-of-town trade. Roll up your sleeve.

KILROY. What for?

GYPSY. A shot of some kind.

KILROY. What kind?

GYPSY. Any kind. Don't they always give you some kind of a shot?

KILROY. "They"?

GYPSY. Brass-hats, Americanos! [*She injects a hypo.*]

KILROY. I am no guinea pig!

GYPSY. Don't kid yourself. We're all of us guinea pigs in the laboratory of God. Humanity is just a work in progress.

KILROY. I don't make it out.

GYPSY. Who does? The Camino Real is a funny paper read backwards! [*There is weird piping outside.* KILROY *shifts on his seat. The* GYPSY *grins.*] Tired? The altitude makes you sleepy?

KILROY. It makes me nervous.

GYPSY. I'll show you how to take a slug of tequila! It dilates the capillaries. First you sprinkle salt on the back of your hand. Then lick it off with your tongue. Now then you toss the shot down! [*She demonstrates.*] —And then you bite into the lemon. That way it goes down easy, but what a bang! —You're next.

KILROY. No, thanks, I'm on the wagon.

GYPSY. There's an old Chinese proverb that says, "When your goose is cooked you might as well have it cooked with plenty of gravy." [*She laughs.*] Get up, baby. Let's have a look at yuh!— You're not a bad-looking boy. Sometimes working for the Yankee dollar isn't a painful profession. Have you ever been attracted by older women?

KILROY. Frankly, no, ma'am.

GYPSY. Well, there's a first time for everything.

KILROY. That is a subject I cannot agree with you on.

GYPSY. You think I'm an old bag? [KILROY *laughs awkwardly. The* GYPSY *slaps his face.*] Will you take the cards or the crystal?

KILROY. It's immaterial.

GYPSY. All right, we'll begin with the cards. [*She shuffles and deals.*] Ask me a question.

KILROY. Has my luck run out?

GYPSY. Baby, your luck ran out the day you were born.
Another question.

KILROY. Ought I to leave this town?

GYPSY. It don't look to me like you've got much choice
in the matter . . . Take a card.

[KILROY *takes one.*]

GYPSY. Ace?

KILROY. Yes, ma'am.

GYPSY. What color?

KILROY. Black.

GYPSY. Oh, oh— That does it. How big is your heart?

KILROY. As big as the head of a baby.

GYPSY. It's going to break.

KILROY. That's what I was afraid of.

GYPSY. The Streetcleaners are waiting for you outside
the door.

KILROY. Which door, the front one? I'll slip out the
back!

GYPSY. Leave us face it frankly, your number is up!
You must've known a long time that the name of
Kilroy was on the Streetcleaners' list.

KILROY. Sure. But not on top of it!

GYPSY. It's always a bit of a shock. Wait a minute!
Here's good news. The Queen of Hearts has turned
up in proper position.

KILROY. What's that mean?

GYPSY. Love, Baby!

KILROY. Love?

GYPSY. The Booby Prize!—Esmeralda!

[*She rises and hits a gong. A divan is carried out. The
GYPSY'S DAUGHTER is seated in a reclining position,
like an odalisque, on this low divan. A spangled veil
covers her face. From this veil to the girdle below
her navel, that supports her diaphanous bifurcated
skirt, she is nude except for a pair of glittering em-*

erald snakes coiled over her breasts. KILROY'S *head moves in a dizzy circle and a canary warbles inside it.*]

KILROY. WHAT'S—WHAT'S *HER* SPECIALTY?— Tea-leaves?

[*The* GYPSY *wags a finger.*]

GYPSY. You know what curiosity did to the tom cat!— Nursie, give me my glamour wig and my forty-five. I'm hitting the street! I gotta go down to Walgreen's for change.

KILROY. What change?

GYPSY. The change from that ten-spot you're about to give me.

NURSIE. Don't argue with her. She has a will of iron.

KILROY. I'm not arguing! [*He reluctantly produces the money.*] But let's be *fair* about this! I hocked my golden gloves for this saw-buck!

NURSIE. All of them Yankee bastids want something for nothing!

KILROY. I want a receipt for this bill.

NURSIE. No one is gypped at the Gypsy's!

KILROY. That's wonderful! How do I know it?

GYPSY. It's in the cards, it's in the crystal ball, it's in the tea-leaves! Absolutely no one is gypped at the Gypsy's! [*She snatches the bill. The wind howls.*] Such changeable weather! I'll slip on my summer furs! Nursie, break out my summer furs!

NURSIE [*leering grotesquely*]. Mink or sable?

GYPSY. *Ha ha, that's a doll!* Here! Clock him! [NURSIE *tosses her a greasy blanket, and the* GYPSY *tosses* NURSIE *an alarm clock. The* GYPSY *rushes through the beaded string curtains.*] *Adios!* Ha ha!

[*She is hardly offstage when two shots ring out.* KILROY *starts.*]

ESMERALDA [*plaintively*]. Mother has such an awful time on the street.

KILROY. You mean that she is insulted on the street?

ESMERALDA. By strangers.

KILROY [*to the audience*]. I shouldn't think acquaintances would do it. [*She curls up on the low divan.* KILROY *licks his lips.*] —You seem very different from —this afternoon . . .

ESMERALDA. This afternoon?

KILROY. Yes, in the plaza when I was being roughed up by them gorillas and you was being dragged in the house by your Mama! [ESMERALDA *stares at him blankly.*] You don't remember?

ESMERALDA. I never remember what happened before the moonrise makes me a virgin.

KILROY. —That—comes as a shock to you, huh?

ESMERALDA. Yes. It comes as a shock.

KILROY [*smiling*]. You have a little temporary amnesia they call it!

ESMERALDA. Yankee . . .

KILROY. Huh?

ESMERALDA. I'm glad I chose you. I'm glad that you were chosen. [*Her voice trails off.*] I'm glad. I'm very glad . . .

NURSIE. Doll!

ESMERALDA. —What is it, Nursie?

NURSIE. How are things progressing?

ESMERALDA. Slowly, Nursie—

[NURSIE *comes lumbering in.*]

NURSIE. I want some light reading matter.

ESMERALDA. He's sitting on *Screen Secrets.*

KILROY [*jumping up*]. Aw. Here. [*He hands her the fan magazine. She lumbers back out, coyly.*] —I—I feel— —self-conscious . . . [*He suddenly jerks out a silver-framed photo.*] —D'you—like pictures?

ESMERALDA. Moving pictures?

KILROY. No, a—motionless—snapshot!

ESMERALDA. Of you?

KILROY. Of my—real—true woman . . . She was a platinum blonde the same as Jean Harlow. Do you remember Jean Harlow? No, you wouldn't remember Jean Harlow. It shows you are getting old when you remember Jean Harlow. [*He puts the snapshot away*.] . . . They say that Jean Harlow's ashes are kept in a little private cathedral in Forest Lawn . . . Wouldn't it be wonderful if you could sprinkle them ashes over the ground like seeds, and out of each one would spring another Jean Harlow? And when spring comes you could just walk out and pick them off the bush! . . . You don't talk much.

ESMERALDA. You want me to *talk?*

KILROY. Well, that's the way we do things in the States. A little vino, some records on the victrola, some quiet conversation—and then if both parties are in a mood for romance . . . Romance—

ESMERALDA. Music! [*She rises and pours some wine from a slender crystal decanter as music is heard.*] They say that the monetary system has got to be stabilized all over the world.

KILROY [*taking the glass*]. Repeat that, please. My radar was not wide open.

ESMERALDA. I said that *they* said that—uh, skip it! But we couldn't care less as long as we keep on getting the Yankee dollar . . . plus federal tax!

KILROY. That's for surely!

ESMERALDA. How do you feel about the class struggle? Do you take sides in that?

KILROY. Not that I—

ESMERALDA. Neither do we. because of the dialectics.

KILROY. Who! Which?

ESMERALDA. Languages with accents, I suppose. But Mama don't care as long as they don't bring the Pope over here and put him in the White House.

KILROY. Who would do that?

ESMERALDA. Oh, the Bolsheviskies, those nasty old things with whiskers! *Whiskers scratch!* But little moustaches tickle . . . [*She giggles.*]

KILROY. I always get a smooth shave . . .

ESMERALDA. And how do you feel about the Mumbo Jumbo? Do you think they've got the Old Man in the bag yet?

KILROY. The Old Man?

ESMERALDA. God. We don't think so. We think there has been so much of the Mumbo Jumbo it's put Him to sleep!

[KILROY *jumps up impatiently.*]

KILROY. This is not what I mean by a quiet conversation. I mean this is no where! *No where!*

ESMERALDA. What sort of talk do you want?

KILROY. Something more—intimate sort of! You know, like—

ESMERALDA. —Where did you get those eyes?

KILROY. *PERSONAL!* Yeah . . .

ESMERALDA. Well,—where did you get those eyes?

KILROY. Out of a dead cod-fish!

NURSIE [*shouting offstage*]. DOLL!

[KILROY *springs up, pounding his left palm with his right fist.*]

ESMERALDA. What?

NURSIE. Fifteen minutes!

KILROY. I'm no hot-rod mechanic. [*To the audience.*] I bet she's out there holding a stop watch to see that I don't over-stay my time in this place!

ESMERALDA [*calling through the string curtains*]. *Nursie, go to bed, Nursie!*

KILROY [*in a fierce whisper*]. That's right, go to bed, Nursie!!

[*There is a loud crash offstage.*]

ESMERALDA. —Nursie has gone to bed . . . [*She drops the string curtains and returns to the alcove.*]

KILROY [*with vast relief*]. —Ahhhhhhhhhh . . .

ESMERALDA. What've you got your eyes on?

KILROY. Those green snakes on you—what do you wear them for?

ESMERALDA. Supposedly for protection, but really for fun. [*He crosses to the divan.*] What are you going to do?

KILROY. I'm about to establish a beach-head on that sofa. [*He sits down.*] How about—lifting your veil?

ESMERALDA. I can't lift it.

KILROY. Why not?

ESMERALDA. I promised Mother I wouldn't.

KILROY. I thought your mother was the broadminded type.

ESMERALDA. Oh, she is, but you know how mothers are. You can lift it for me, if you say pretty please.

KILROY. Aww—

ESMERALDA. Go on, say it! Say pretty please!

KILROY. No!!

ESMERALDA. Why not?

KILROY. It's silly.

ESMERALDA. Then you can't lift my veil!

KILROY. Oh, all right. Pretty please.

ESMERALDA. Say it again!

KILROY. Pretty please.

ESMERALDA. Now say it once more like you meant it. [*He jumps up. She grabs his hand.*] Don't go away.

KILROY. You're making a fool out of me.

ESMERALDA. I was just teasing a little. Because you're so cute. Sit down again, please—*pretty* please!

[*He falls on the couch.*]

KILROY. What is that wonderful perfume you've got on?

ESMERALDA. Guess!

KILROY. Chanel Number Five?

ESMERALDA. No.

KILROY. Tabu?

ESMERALDA. No.

KILROY. I give up.

ESMERALDA. It's *Noche en Acapulco!* I'm just dying to go to Acapulco. I wish that you would take me to Acapulco. [*He sits up.*] What's the matter?

KILROY. You gypsies' daughters are invariably re-
minded of something without which you cannot do
—just when it looks like everything has been fixed.

ESMERALDA. That isn't nice at all. I'm not the gold-
digger type. Some girls see themselves in silver foxes.
I only see myself in Acapulco!

KILROY. At Todd's Place?

ESMERALDA. Oh, no, at the Mirador! Watching those
pretty boys dive off the Quebrada!

KILROY. Look again, Baby. Maybe you'll see yourself
in Paramount Pictures or having a Singapore Sling
at a Statler bar!

ESMERALDA. You're being sarcastic?

KILROY. Nope. Just realistic. All of you gypsies' daughters have hearts of stone, and I'm not whistling
"Dixie"! But just the same, the night before a man
dies, he says, "Pretty please—will you let me lift your
veil?"—while the Streetcleaners wait for him right
outside the door!— Because to be warm for a little
longer is life. And love?—that's a four-letter word
which is sometimes no better than one you see
printed on fences by kids playing hooky from
school!— Oh, well—what's the use of complaining?
You gypsies' daughters have ears that only catch
sounds like the snap of a gold cigarette case! Or,
pretty please, Baby,—we're going to Acapulco!

ESMERALDA. *Are* we?

KILROY. See what I mean? [*To the audience.*] Didn't I
tell you?! [*To* ESMERALDA.] Yes! In the morning!

ESMERALDA. Ohhhh! I'm dizzy with joy! My little heart
is going pitty-pat!

KILROY. My big heart is going boom-boom! Can I lift
your veil now?

ESMERALDA. If you will be gentle.

KILROY. I would not hurt a fly unless it had on leather
mittens. [*He touches a corner of her spangled veil.*]

ESMERALDA. Ohhh . . .

KILROY. What?

ESMERALDA. Ohhhhhh!!

KILROY. Why! What's the matter?

ESMERALDA. You are not being gentle!

KILROY. I *am* being gentle.

ESMERALDA. You are *not* being gentle.

KILROY. What was I being, then?

ESMERALDA. Rough!

KILROY. I am *not* being rough.

ESMERALDA. Yes, you *are* being rough. You have to be gentle with me because you're the first.

KILROY. Are you kidding?

ESMERALDA. No.

KILROY. How about all of those other fiestas you've been to?

ESMERALDA. Each one's the first one. That is the wonderful thing about gypsies' daughters!

KILROY. You can say that again!

ESMERALDA. I don't like you when you're like that.

KILROY. Like what?

ESMERALDA. Cynical and sarcastic.

KILROY. I am sincere.

ESMERALDA. Lots of boys aren't sincere.

KILROY. Maybe they aren't but I am.

ESMERALDA. Everyone says he's sincere, but everyone isn't sincere. If everyone was sincere who says he's sincere there wouldn't be half so many insincere ones in the world and there would be lots, lots, lots more really sincere ones!

KILROY. I think you have got something there. But how about gypsies' daughters?

ESMERALDA. Huh?

KILROY. Are they one hundred percent in the really sincere category?

ESMERALDA. Well, yes, and no, mostly no! But some of them are for a while if their sweethearts are gentle.

KILROY. Would you believe I am sincere and gentle?

ESMERALDA. I would believe that you believe that you are . . . For a while . . .

KILROY. Everything's for a while. For a while is the stuff that dreams are made of, Baby! Now?— Now?

ESMERALDA. Yes, now, but be gentle!—*gentle* . . .

[*He delicately lifts a corner of her veil. She utters a soft cry. He lifts it further. She cries out again. A bit further . . . He turns the spangled veil all the way up from her face.*]

KILROY. I am sincere.

ESMERALDA. I am sincere.

KILROY. I am sincere.

ESMERALDA. I am sincere.

KILROY. I am sincere.

ESMERALDA. I am sincere.

KILROY. I am sincere.

ESMERALDA. I am sincere. [KILROY *leans back, removing his hand from her veil. She opens her eyes.*] Is that all?

KILROY. I am tired.

ESMERALDA. —Already?

[*He rises and goes down the steps from the alcove.*]

KILROY. I am tired, and full of regret . . .

ESMERALDA. Oh!

KILROY. It wasn't much to give my golden gloves for.

ESMERALDA. You pity yourself?

KILROY. That's right, I pity myself and everybody that goes to the Gypsy's daughter. I pity the world and I pity the God who made it. [*He sits down.*]

ESMERALDA. It's always like that as soon as the veil is lifted. They're all so ashamed of having degraded themselves, and their hearts have more regret than a heart can hold!

KILROY. Even a heart that's as big as the head of a baby!

ESMERALDA. You don't even notice how pretty my face is, do you?

KILROY. You look like all gypsies' daughters, no better, no worse. But as long as you get to Acapulco, your cup runneth over with ordinary contentment.

ESMERALDA. —I've never been so insulted in all my life!

KILROY. Oh, yes, you have, Baby. And you'll be insulted worse if you stay in this racket. You'll be
insulted so much that it will get to be like water off
a duck's back!

[*The door slams. Curtains are drawn apart on the*
GYPSY. ESMERALDA *lowers her veil hastily.* KILROY *pre-
tends not to notice the* GYPSY'S *entrance. She picks
up a little bell and rings it over his head.*]

Okay, Mamacita! I am aware of your presence!

GYPSY. Ha-ha! I was followed three blocks by some awful man!

KILROY. Then you caught him.

GYPSY. Naw, he ducked into a subway! I waited fifteen
minutes outside the men's room and he never came
out!

KILROY. Then you went in?

GYPSY. No! I got myself a sailor!— The streets are brilliant! . . . Have you all been good children? [ESMER-
ALDA *makes a whimpering sound.*] The pussy will
play while the old mother cat is away?

KILROY. Your sense of humor is wonderful, but how
about my change, Mamacita?

GYPSY. What change are you talking about?

KILROY. Are you boxed out of your mind? The change
from that ten-spot you trotted over to Walgreen's?

GYPSY. Ohhhhh—

KILROY. *Oh, what?*

GYPSY [*counting on her fingers*]. Five for the works, one
dollar luxury tax, two for the house percentage and
two more pour la service!—makes ten! Didn't I tell
you?

KILROY. —What kind of a deal is this?

GYPSY [*whipping out a revolver*]. A rugged one, Baby!

ESMERALDA. Mama, don't be unkind!

GYPSY. Honey, the gentleman's friends are waiting outside the door and it wouldn't be nice to detain him!
Come on— Get going— Vamoose!

KILROY. Okay, Mamacita! Me voy! [*He crosses to the beaded string curtains: turns to look back at the* GYPSY *and her daughter. The piping of the* STREET-CLEANERS *is heard outside.*] Sincere?— Sure! That's the wonderful thing about gypsies' daughters!

[*He goes out.* ESMERALDA *raises a wondering fingertip to one eye. Then she cries out.*]

ESMERALDA. Look, Mama! Look, Mama! A tear!

GYPSY. You have been watching television too much . . . [*She gathers the cards and turns off the crystal ball as—*]

[*Light fades out on the phony paradise of the* GYPSY'*s.*]

GUTMAN. Block Thirteen on the Camino Real. [*He exits.*]

Block thirteen

In the blackout the STREETCLEANERS *place a barrel in the center and then hide in the Pit.*

KILROY, *who enters from the right, is followed by a spot light. He sees the barrel and the menacing* STREET-CLEANERS *and then runs to the closed door of the Siete Mares and rings the bell. No one answers. He backs up so he can see the balcony and calls:*

KILROY. Mr. Gutman! Just gimme a cot in the lobby. I'll do odd jobs in the morning. I'll be the Patsy again. I'll light my nose sixty times a minute. I'll take prat-falls and assume the position for anybody that drops a dime on the street . . . Have a heart! Have just a LITTLE heart. Please!

[*There is no response from* GUTMAN'*s balcony.* JACQUES *enters. He pounds his cane once on the pavement.*]

JACQUES. Gutman! Open the door!—*GUTMAN! GUTMAN!*

[EVA, *a beautiful woman, apparently nude, appears on the balcony.*]

GUTMAN [*from inside*]. Eva darling, you're exposing yourself! [*He appears on the balcony with a portmanteau.*]

JACQUES. What are you doing with my portmanteau?

GUTMAN. Haven't you come for your luggage?

JACQUES. Certainly not! I haven't checked out of here!

GUTMAN. Very few do . . . but residences are frequently terminated.

JACQUES. Open the door!

GUTMAN. Open the letter with the remittance check in it!

JACQUES. In the morning!

GUTMAN. Tonight!

JACQUES. Upstairs in my room!

GUTMAN. Downstairs at the entrance!

JACQUES. I won't be intimidated!

GUTMAN [*raising the portmanteau over his head*]. What?!

JACQUES. Wait!— [*He takes the letter out of his pocket.*] Give me some light. [KILROY *strikes a match and holds it over* JACQUES' *shoulder.*] Thank you. What does it say?

GUTMAN. —Remittances?

KILROY [*reading the letter over* JACQUES' *shoulder*]. —discontinued . . .

[GUTMAN *raises the portmanteau again.*]

JACQUES. Careful, I have— [*The portmanteau lands with a crash. The* BUM *comes to the window at the crash.* A. RATT *comes out to his doorway at the same time.*] —fragile—mementoes . . . [*He crosses slowly down to the portmanteau and kneels as* GUTMAN *laughs and slams the balcony door.* JACQUES *turns to* KILROY. *He smiles at the young adventurer.*] —"And so at last it has come, the distinguished thing!"

[A. RATT *speaks as* JACQUES *touches the portmanteau.*]

A. RATT. Hey, Dad— Vacancy here! A bed at the "Ritz Men Only." A little white ship to sail the dangerous night in.

JACQUES. Single or double?

A. RATT. There's only singles in this pad.

JACQUES [*to* KILROY]. Match you for it.

KILROY. What the hell, we're buddies, we can sleep spoons! If we can't sleep, we'll push the wash stand against the door and sing old popular songs till the crack of dawn! . . . "Heart of my heart, I love that melody!" . . . You bet your life I do.

[JACQUES *takes out a pocket handkerchief and starts to grasp the portmanteau handle.*]

—It looks to me like you could use a Redcap and my rates are non-union!

[*He picks up the portmanteau and starts to cross toward the "Ritz Men Only." He stops at right center.*]

Sorry, buddy. Can't make it! The altitude on this block has affected my ticker! And in the distance which is nearer than further, I hear—the Street-cleaners'—piping!

[*Piping is heard.*]

JACQUES. COME ALONG! [*He lifts the portmanteau and starts on.*]

KILROY. NO. Tonight! I prefer! To sleep! Out! Under! The stars!

JACQUES [*gently*]. I understand, Brother!

KILROY [*to* JACQUES *as he continues toward the "Ritz Men Only"*]. Bon Voyage! I hope that you sail the dangerous night to the sweet golden port of morning!

JACQUES [*exiting*]. Thanks, Brother!

KILROY. Excuse the *corn!* I'm sincere!

BUM. Show me the way to go home! . . .

GUTMAN [*appearing on the balcony with white parakeet*]. Block Fourteen on the Camino Real.

Block fourteen

At opening, the BUM *is still at the window.*

The STREETCLEANERS' *piping continues a little louder.* KILROY *climbs, breathing heavily, to the top of the stairs and stands looking out at Terra Incognita as . . .*

MARGUERITE *enters the plaza through alleyway at right. She is accompanied by a silent* YOUNG MAN *who wears a domino.*

MARGUERITE. Don't come any further with me. I'll have to wake the night porter. Thank you for giving me safe conduct through the Medina. [*She has offered her hand. He grips it with a tightness that makes her wince.*] Ohhhh . . . I'm not sure which is more provocative in you, your ominous silence or your glittering smile or— [*He's looking at her purse.*] What do you want? . . . Oh! [*She starts to open the purse. He snatches it. She gasps as he suddenly strips her cloak off her. Then he snatches off her pearl necklace. With each successive despoilment, she gasps and retreats but makes no resistance. Her eyes are closed. He continues to smile. Finally, he rips her dress and runs his hands over her body as if to see if she had anything else of value concealed on her.*] —What else do I have that you want?
THE YOUNG MAN [*contemptuously*]. Nothing.
[*The* YOUNG MAN *exits through the cantina, examining his loot. The* BUM *leans out his window, draws a deep breath and says:*]
BUM. Lonely.
MARGUERITE [*to herself*]. Lonely . . .
KILROY [*on the steps*]. Lonely . . .

[*The* STREETCLEANERS' *piping is heard.*]

[MARGUERITE *runs to the Siete Mares and rings the bell. Nobody answers. She crosses to the terrace.* KILROY, *meanwhile, has descended the stairs.*]

MARGUERITE. Jacques!

[*Piping is heard.*]

KILROY. Lady?

MARGUERITE. What?

KILROY. —I'm—safe . . .

MARGUERITE. I wasn't expecting that music tonight, were you?

[*Piping.*]

KILROY. It's them Streetcleaners.

MARGUERITE. I know.

[*Piping.*]

KILROY. You better go on in, lady.

MARGUERITE. No.

KILROY. GO ON IN!

MARGUERITE. NO! I want to stay out here and I do what I want to do! [KILROY *looks at her for the first time.*] Sit down with me please.

KILROY. They're coming for me. The Gypsy told me I'm on top of their list. Thanks for. Taking my. Hand.

[*Piping is heard.*]

MARGUERITE. Thanks for taking mine.

[*Piping.*]

KILROY. Do me one more favor. Take out of my pocket a picture. My fingers are. Stiff.

MARGUERITE. This one?

KILROY. My one. True. Woman.

MARGUERITE. A silver-framed photo! Was she really so fair?

KILROY. She was so fair and much fairer than they could tint that picture!

MARGUERITE. Then you have been on the street when the street was royal.

KILROY. Yeah . . . when the street was royal!

[*Piping is heard.* KILROY *rises.*]

MARGUERITE. Don't get up, don't leave me!

KILROY. I want to be on my feet when the Street-cleaners come for me!

MARGUERITE. Sit back down again and tell me about your girl.

[*He sits.*]

KILROY. Y'know what it is you miss most? When you're separated. From someone. You lived. With. And loved? It's waking up in the night! With that—warmness beside you!

MARGUERITE. Yes, that *warmness* beside you!

KILROY. Once you get used to that. *Warmness!* It's a hell of a lonely feeling to wake up without it! Specially in some dollar-a-night hotel room on Skid! A hot-water bottle won't do. And a stranger. Won't do. It has to be some one you're used to. And that you. *KNOW LOVES* you! [*Piping is heard.*] Can you see them?

MARGUERITE. I see no one but you.

KILROY. I looked at my wife one night when she was sleeping and that was the night that the medics wouldn't okay me for no more fights . . . Well . . . My wife was sleeping with a smile like a child's. I kissed her. She didn't wake up. I took a pencil and paper. I wrote her. Good-bye!

MARGUERITE. That was the night she would have loved you the most!

KILROY. Yeah, *that* night, but what about *after* that night? Oh, Lady . . . Why should a beautiful girl tie up with a broken-down champ?— The earth still turning and her obliged to turn with it, not out—of dark into light but out of light into dark? Naw, naw, naw, naw!— Washed up!— Finished! [*Piping.*] . . . that ain't a word that a man can't look at . . . There ain't no words in the language a man can't look at . . . and know just what they mean. And be. And act. And *go!* [*He turns to the waiting* STREET-

CLEANERS.] Come on! . . . Come on! . . . COME ON, YOU SONS OF BITCHES! KILROY IS HERE! HE'S READY!

[*A gong sounds.*]

[KILROY *swings at the* STREETCLEANERS. *They circle about him out of reach, turning him by each of their movements. The swings grow wilder like a boxer. He falls to his knees still swinging and finally collapses flat on his face.*]

[*The* STREETCLEANERS *pounce but* LA MADRECITA *throws herself protectingly over the body and covers it with her shawl.*]

[*Blackout.*]

MARGUERITE. Jacques!

GUTMAN [*on balcony*]. Block Fifteen on the Camino Real.

Block fifteen

LA MADRECITA *is seated: across her knees is the body of* KILROY. *Up center, a low table on wheels bears a sheeted figure. Beside the table stands a* MEDICAL IN-STRUCTOR *addressing* STUDENTS *and* NURSES, *all in white surgical outfits.*

INSTRUCTOR. This is the body of an unidentified va-grant.

LA MADRECITA. This was thy son, America—and now mine.

INSTRUCTOR. He was found in an alley along the Ca-mino Real.

LA MADRECITA. Think of him, now, as he was before his luck failed him. Remember his time of greatness, when he was not faded, not frightened.

INSTRUCTOR. More light, please!

LA MADRECITA. More light!

INSTRUCTOR. Can everyone see clearly!

LA MADRECITA. Everyone must see clearly!

INSTRUCTOR. There is no external evidence of disease.

LA MADRECITA. He had clear eyes and the body of a champion boxer.

INSTRUCTOR. There are no marks of violence on the body.

LA MADRECITA. He had the soft voice of the South and a pair of golden gloves.

INSTRUCTOR. His death was apparently due to natural causes.

[*The* STUDENTS *make notes. There are keening voices.*]

LA MADRECITA. Yes, blow wind where night thins! He had many admirers!

INSTRUCTOR. There are no legal claimants.

LA MADRECITA. He stood as a planet among the moons of their longing, haughty with youth, a champion of the prize-ring!

INSTRUCTOR. No friends or relatives having identified him—

LA MADRECITA. You should have seen the lovely monogrammed robe in which he strode the aisles of the Colosseums!

INSTRUCTOR. After the elapse of a certain number of days, his body becomes the property of the State—

LA MADRECITA. Yes, blow wind where night thins—for laurel is not everlasting . . .

INSTRUCTOR. And now is transferred to our hands for the nominal sum of five dollars.

LA MADRECITA. This was thy son,—and now mine . . .

INSTRUCTOR. We will now proceed with the dissection. Knife, please!

LA MADRECITA. Blow wind! [*Keening is heard offstage.*] Yes, blow wind where night thins! You are his passing bell and his lamentation. [*More keening is heard.*] Keen for him, all maimed creatures, deformed and mutilated—his homeless ghost is your own!

INSTRUCTOR. First we will open up the chest cavity and examine the heart for evidence of coronary occlusion.

LA MADRECITA. His heart was pure gold and as big as the head of a baby.

INSTRUCTOR. We will make an incision along the vertical line.

LA MADRECITA. Rise, ghost! Go! Go bird! "Humankind cannot bear very much reality."

[*At the touch of her flowers,* KILROY *stirs and pushes himself up slowly from her lap. On his feet again, he rubs his eyes and looks around him.*]

VOICES [*crying offstage*]. Olé! Olé! Olé!

KILROY. Hey! Hey, somebody! Where am I? [*He notices the dissection room and approaches.*]

INSTRUCTOR [*removing a glittering sphere from a dummy corpse*]. Look at this heart. It's as big as the head of a baby.

KILROY. My heart!

INSTRUCTOR. Wash it off so we can look for the pathological lesions.

KILROY. Yes, siree, that's my heart!

GUTMAN. Block Sixteen!

[KILROY *pauses just outside the dissection area as a* STUDENT *takes the heart and dips it into a basin on the stand beside the table. The* STUDENT *suddenly cries out and holds aloft a glittering gold sphere.*]

INSTRUCTOR. Look! This heart's solid gold!

Block sixteen

KILROY [*rushing forward*]. That's mine, you bastards! [*He snatches the golden sphere from the* MEDICAL IN-

STRUCTOR. *The autopsy proceeds as if nothing had happened as the spot of light on the table fades out, but for* KILROY *a ghostly chase commences, a dream-like re-enactment of the chase that occurred at the end of Block Six.* GUTMAN *shouts from his balcony:*]

GUTMAN. Stop, thief, stop, corpse! That gold heart is the property of the State! Catch him, catch the golden-heart robber!

[KILROY *dashes offstage into an aisle of the theatre. There is the wail of a siren: the air is filled with calls and whistles, roar of motors, screeching brakes, pistol-shots, thundering footsteps. The dimness of the auditorium is transected by searching rays of light—but there are no visible pursuers.*]

KILROY [*as he runs panting up the aisle*]. This is my heart! It don't belong to no State, not even the U.S.A. Which way is out? Where's the Greyhound depot? Nobody's going to put my heart in a bottle in a museum and charge admission to support the rotten police! Where are they? Which way are they going? Or coming? Hey, somebody, help me get out of here! Which way do I—which way—which way do I—*go! go! go! go! go!* [*He has now arrived in the balcony.*] Gee, I'm lost! I don't know where I am! I'm all turned around, I'm *confused,* I don't understand—what's—happened, it's like a—*dream,* it's—just like a—dream . . . Mary! Oh, Mary! Mary! [*He has entered the box from which he leapt in Act One. A clear shaft of light falls on him. He looks up into it, crying:*] Mary, help a Christian!! Help a Christian, Mary!— It's like a dream . . .

[ESMERALDA *appears in a childish nightgown beside her gauze-tented bed on the* GYPSY's *roof. Her* MOTHER *appears with a cup of some sedative drink, cooing . . .*]

GYPSY. Beddy-bye, beddy-bye, darling. It's sleepy-time down South and up North, too, and also East and West!

KILROY [*softly*]. Yes, it's—like a—*dream* . . . [*He leans panting over the ledge of the box, holding his heart like a football, watching* ESMERALDA.]

GYPSY. Drink your Ovaltine, Ducks, and the sandman will come on tip-toe with a bag full of dreams . . .

ESMERALDA. I want to dream of the Chosen Hero, Mummy.

GYPSY. Which one, the one that's coming or the one that is gone?

ESMERALDA. The *only* one, *Kilroy! He* was *sincere!*

KILROY. That's *right! I was,* for a while!

GYPSY. How do you know that Kilroy was sincere?

ESMERALDA. He said so.

KILROY. That's the truth, I *was!*

GYPSY. When did he say that?

ESMERALDA. When he lifted my veil.

GYPSY. Baby, they're always sincere when they lift your veil; it's one of those natural reflexes that don't mean a thing.

KILROY [*aside*]. What a cynical old bitch that Gypsy mama is!

GYPSY. And there's going to be lots of other fiestas for you, baby doll, and lots of other chosen heroes to lift your little veil when Mamacita and Nursie are out of the room.

ESMERALDA. No, Mummy, never, I mean it!

KILROY. I *believe* she means it!

GYPSY. Finish your Ovaltine and say your Now-I-Lay-Me.

[ESMERALDA *sips the drink and hands her the cup.*]

KILROY [*with a catch in his voice*]. I had one true woman, which I can't go back to, but now I've found another. [*He leaps onto the stage from the box.*]

ESMERALDA [*dropping to her knees*]. Now I lay me down to sleep, I pray the Lord my soul to keep. If I should die before I wake, I pray the Lord my soul to take.

GYPSY. God bless Mummy!

ESMERALDA. And the crystal ball and the tea-leaves.

KILROY. *Pssst!*

ESMERALDA. What's that?

GYPSY. A tom-cat in the plaza.

ESMERALDA. God bless all cats without pads in the plaza tonight.

KILROY. Amen! [*He falls to his knees in the empty plaza.*]

ESMERALDA. God bless all con men and hustlers and pitch-men who hawk their hearts on the street, all two-time losers who're likely to lose once more, the courtesan who made the mistake of love, the greatest of lovers crowned with the longest horns, the poet who wandered far from his heart's green country and possibly will and possibly won't be able to find his way back, look down with a smile tonight on the last cavaliers, the ones with the rusty armor and soiled white plumes, and visit with understanding and something that's almost tender those fading legends that come and go in this plaza like songs not clearly remembered, oh, sometime and somewhere, let there be something to mean the word *honor* again!

QUIXOTE [*hoarsely and loudly, stirring slightly among his verminous rags*]. Amen!

KILROY. Amen . . .

GYPSY [*disturbed*]. —That will do, now.

ESMERALDA. *And, oh, God, let me dream tonight of the Chosen Hero!*

GYPSY. Now, sleep. Fly away on the magic carpet of dreams!

[ESMERALDA *crawls into the gauze-tented cot. The* GYPSY *descends from the roof.*]

KILROY. *Esmeralda! My little Gypsy sweetheart!*

ESMERALDA [*sleepily*]. Go away, cat.

[*The light behind the gauze is gradually dimming.*]

KILROY. This is no cat. This is the chosen hero of the big fiesta, Kilroy, the champion of the golden gloves with his gold heart cut from his chest and in his hands to give you!

ESMERALDA. Go away. Let me dream of the Chosen Hero.

KILROY. What a hassle! Mistook for a cat! What can I do to convince this doll I'm real? [*Three brass balls wink brilliantly.*] —Another transaction seems to be indicated! [*He rushes to the* LOAN SHARK'S. *The entrance immediately lights up.*] My heart is gold! What will you give me for it? [*Jewels, furs, sequined gowns, etc., are tossed to his feet. He throws his heart like a basketball to the* LOAN SHARK, *snatches up the loot and rushes back to the* GYPSY'S.] *Doll! Behold this loot! I gave my golden heart for it!*

ESMERALDA. Go away, cat . . .

[*She falls asleep.* KILROY *bangs his forehead with his fist, then rushes to the* GYPSY'S *door, pounds it with both fists. The door is thrown open and the sordid contents of a large jar are thrown at him. He falls back gasping, spluttering, retching. He retreats and finally assumes an exaggerated attitude of despair.*]

KILROY. Had for a button! Stewed, screwed and tattooed on the Camino Real! Baptized, finally, with the contents of a slop-jar!— Did anybody say the deal was rugged?!

[QUIXOTE *stirs against the wall of Skid Row. He hawks and spits and staggers to his feet.*]

GUTMAN. Why, the old knight's awake, his dream is over!

QUIXOTE [*to* KILROY]. Hello! Is that a fountain?

KILROY. —Yeah, but—

QUIXOTE. I've got a mouthful of old chicken feathers . . .

[*He approaches the fountain. It begins to flow.* KILROY *falls back in amazement as the* OLD KNIGHT *rinses his mouth and drinks and removes his jacket to bathe, handing the tattered garment to* KILROY.]

QUIXOTE [*as he bathes*]. Qué pasa, mi amigo?

KILROY. The deal is rugged. D'you know what I mean?

QUIXOTE. Who knows better than I what a rugged deal is! [*He produces a tooth brush and brushes his teeth.*] —Will you take some advice?

KILROY. Brother, at this point on the Camino I will take anything which is offered!

QUIXOTE. *Don't! Pity! Your! Self!* [*He takes out a pocket mirror and grooms his beard and moustache.*] The wounds of the vanity, the many offenses our egos have to endure, being housed in bodies that age and hearts that grow tired, are better accepted with a tolerant smile—like *this!*— You *see?* [*He cracks his face in two with an enormous grin.*]

GUTMAN. Follow-spot on the face of the ancient knight!

QUIXOTE. Otherwise what you become is a bag full of curdled cream—*leche mala,* we call it!—attractive to nobody, least of all to yourself! [*He passes the comb and pocket mirror to* KILROY.] Have you got any plans?

KILROY [*a bit uncertainly, wistfully*]. Well, I was thinking of—going *on* from—*here!*

QUIXOTE. Good! Come with me.

KILROY [*to the audience*]. Crazy old bastard. [*Then to the* KNIGHT:] Donde?

QUIXOTE [*starting for the stairs*]. Quien sabe!

[*The fountain is now flowing loudly and sweetly. The* STREET PEOPLE *are moving toward it with murmurs of wonder.* MARGUERITE *comes out upon the terrace.*]

KILROY. Hey, there's—!

QUIXOTE. Shhh! Listen!

[*They pause on the stairs.*]

MARGUERITE. Abdullah!

[GUTMAN *has descended to the terrace.*]

GUTMAN. Mademoiselle, allow me to deliver the message for you. It would be in bad form if I didn't take some final part in the pageant. [*He crosses the plaza to the opposite façade and shouts "Casanova!" under the window of the "Ritz Men Only." Meanwhile*

KILROY *scratches out the verb "is" and prints the correction "was" in the inscription on the ancient wall.*]

Casanova! Great lover and King of Cuckolds on the Camino Real! The last of your ladies has guaranteed your tabs and is expecting you for breakfast on the terrace!

[CASANOVA *looks first out of the practical window of the flophouse, then emerges from its scabrous doorway, haggard, unshaven, crumpled in dress but bearing himself as erectly as ever. He blinks and glares fiercely into the brilliant morning light.*]

[MARGUERITE *cannot return his look, she averts her face with a look for which anguish would not be too strong a term, but at the same time she extends a pleading hand toward him. After some hesitation, he begins to move toward her, striking the pavement in measured cadence with his cane, glancing once, as he crosses, out at the audience with a wry smile that makes admissions that would be embarrassing to a vainer man than* CASANOVA *now is. When he reaches* MARGUERITE *she gropes for his hand, seizes it with a low cry and presses it spasmodically to her lips while he draws her into his arms and looks above her sobbing, dyed-golden head with the serene, clouded gaze of someone mortally ill as the mercy of a narcotic laps over his pain.*]

[QUIXOTE *raises his lance in a formal gesture and cries out hoarsely, powerfully from the stairs:*]

QUIXOTE. *The violets in the mountains have broken the rocks!*

[QUIXOTE *goes through the arch with* KILROY.]

GUTMAN [*to the audience*]. The Curtain Line has been spoken! [*To the wings:*] Bring it down! [*He bows with a fat man's grace as—*]

[*The curtain falls.*]

TEA AND SYMPATHY

by Robert Anderson

*This is for Phyllis
whose spirit is everywhere
in this play and in my life.*

Copyrighted as an unpublished work, 1953,
By Robert Woodruff Anderson
Copyright, 1953, by Robert Anderson
Reprinted by permission of Random House, Inc.
All rights reserved under International and Pan-American
Copyright Conventions.

CAUTION: *Professionals and amateurs are hereby warned that*
TEA AND SYMPATHY, *being fully protected under the copy-
rights laws of the United States, the British Empire including the Dominion of Canada, and all other countries of the
Copyright Union, is subject to royalty. All rights including
professional, amateur, motion picture, recitation, lecturing,
public reading, radio and television broadcasting, and the
rights of translation into foreign languages, are strictly reserved. Particular emphasis is laid on the question of readings, permission for which must be obtained in writing from
the Author's representative. All inquiries should be addressed to the Author's representative, Liebling-Wood, 551
Fifth Avenue, New York 17.*

First production, September 30, 1953,
at the Ethel Barrymore Theatre, New York,
with the following cast:

LAURA REYNOLDS, *Deborah Kerr*
LILLY SEARS, *Florida Friebus*
TOM LEE, *John Kerr*
DAVID HARRIS, *Richard Midgley*
RALPH, *Alan Sues*
AL, *Dick York*
STEVE, *Arthur Steuer*
BILL REYNOLDS, *Leif Erickson*
PHIL, *Richard Franchot*
HERBERT LEE, *John McGovern*
PAUL, *Yale Wexler*

SCENES

ACT ONE / *A dormitory in a boys' school in New England.*
Late afternoon of a day early in June.

ACT TWO / SCENE I. *Two days later.*
          SCENE II. *Eight-thirty Saturday night.*

ACT THREE / *The next afternoon.*

Act one

The scene is a small old Colonial house which is now being used as a dormitory in a boys' school in New England.

On the ground floor at stage right we see the house-master's study. To stage left is a hall and stairway which leads up to the boys' rooms. At a half-level on stage left is one of the boys' rooms.

The housemaster's study is a warm and friendly room, rather on the dark side, but when the lamps are lighted, there are cheerful pools of light. There is a fireplace in the back wall, bookcases, and upstage right double doors leading to another part of the house. Since there is no common room for the eight boys in this house, there is considerable leniency in letting the boys use the study whenever the door is left ajar.

The boy's bedroom is small, containing a bed, a chair and a bureau. It was meant to be Spartan, but the present occupant has given it a few touches to make it a little more homelike: an Indian print on the bed, India print curtains for the dormer window. There is a phonograph on the ledge of the window. The door to the room is presumed to lead to the sitting room which the roommates share. There is a door from the sitting room which leads to the stair landing. Thus, to get to the bedroom from the stairs, a person must go through the sitting room.

As the curtain rises, it is late afternoon of a day early in June. No lamps have been lighted yet so the study is in a sort of twilight.

Upstairs in his room, TOM LEE *is sitting on his bed playing the guitar and singing softly and casually, the plaintive song, "The Joys of Love"* . . . TOM *is going on eighteen.*

He is young and a little gangling, but intense. He is wearing faded khaki trousers, a white shirt open at the neck and white tennis sneakers.

Seated in the study listening to the singing are LAURA REYNOLDS *and* LILLY SEARS. LAURA *is a lovely, sensitive woman in her mid to late twenties. Her essence is gentleness. She is compassionate and tender. She is wearing a cashmere sweater and a wool skirt. As she listens to* TOM'S *singing, she is sewing on what is obviously a period costume.*

LILLY *is in her late thirties, and in contrast to the simple effectiveness of* LAURA'S *clothes, she is dressed a little too flashily for her surroundings. . . . It would be in good taste on East 57th Street, but not in a small New England town. . . . A smart suit and hat and a fur piece. As she listens to* TOM *singing, she plays with the martini glass in her hand.*

TOM [*singing*].
> The joys of love
> Are but a moment long . . .
> The pains of love
> Endure forever . . .

[*When he has finished, he strums on over the same melody very casually, and hums to it intermittently.*]

LILLY [*while* TOM *is singing*]. Tom Lee?

LAURA. Yes.

LILLY. Doesn't he have an afternoon class?

LAURA. No. He's the only one in the house that doesn't.

LILLY [*when* TOM *has finished the song*]. Do you know what he's thinking of?

LAURA [*bites off a thread and looks up*]. What do you mean?

LILLY. What all the boys in this school are thinking

about. Not only now in the spring, but all the time
. . . Sex! [*She wags her head a little wisely, and
smiles.*]

LAURA. Lilly, you just like to shock people.

LILLY. Four hundred boys from the ages of thirteen to
nineteen. That's the age, Laura. [*Restless, getting
up.*] Doesn't it give you the willies sometimes, having all these boys around?

LAURA. Of course not. I never think of it that way.

LILLY. Harry tells me they put saltpeter in their food
to quiet them down. But the way they look at you, I
can't believe it.

LAURA. At me?

LILLY. At any woman worth looking at. When I first
came here ten years ago, I didn't think I could
stand it. Now I love it. I love watching them look
and suffer.

LAURA. Lilly.

LILLY. This is your first spring here, Laura. You wait.

LAURA. They're just boys.

LILLY. The authorities say the ages from thirteen to
nineteen . . .

LAURA. Lilly, honestly!

LILLY. You sound as though you were in the grave.
How old are you?

LAURA [*smiling*]. Over twenty-one.

LILLY. They come here ignorant as all get out about
women, and then spend the next four years exchanging misinformation. They're so cute, and so damned
intense. [*She shudders again.*]

LAURA. Most of them seem very casual to me.

LILLY. That's just an air they put on. This is the age
Romeo should be played. You'd believe him! So intense! These kids would die for love, or almost anything else. Harry says all their themes end in death.

LAURA. That's boys.

LILLY. Failure; death! Dishonor; death! Lose their
girls; death! It's gruesome.

LAURA. But rather touching too, don't you think?

LILLY. You won't tell your husband the way I was talking?

LAURA. Of course not.

LILLY. Though I don't know why I should care. All the boys talk about me. They have me in and out of bed with every single master in the school—and some married ones, too.

LAURA [*kidding her*]. Maybe I'd better listen to them.

LILLY. Oh, never with your husband, of course.

LAURA. Thanks.

LILLY. Even before he met you, Bill never gave me a second glance. He was all the time organizing teams, planning Mountain Club outings.

LAURA. Bill's good at that sort of thing; he likes it.

LILLY. And you? [LAURA *looks up at* LILLY *and smiles.*] Not a very co-operative witness, are you? I know, mind my own business. But watch out he doesn't drag his usual quota of boys to the lodge in Maine this summer.

LAURA. I've got my own plans for him. [*She picks up some vacation folders.*]

LILLY. Oh really? What?

LAURA. "Come to Canada" . . . I want to get him off on a trip alone.

LILLY. I don't blame you.

LAURA [*reflecting*]. Of course I'd really like to go back to Italy. We had a good time there last summer. It was wonderful then. You should have seen Bill.

LILLY. Look, honey, you married Bill last year on his sabbatical leave, and abroad to boot. Teachers on sabbatical leave abroad are like men in uniform during the war. They never look so good again.

LAURA. Bill looks all right to me.

LILLY. Did Bill ever tell you about the party we gave him before his sabbatical?

LAURA. Yes. I have a souvenir from it. [*She is wearing a rather large Woolworth's diamond ring on a gold chain around her neck . . . She now pulls it out from her sweater.*]

LILLY. I never thought he'd use that Five-and-Dime engagement ring we gave him that night. Even though we gave him an awful ribbing, we all expected him to come back a bachelor.

LAURA. You make it sound as though you kidded him into marrying.

LILLY. Oh, no, honey, it wasn't that.

LAURA [*with meaning*]. No, it wasn't. [LAURA *laughs at* LILLY.]

LILLY. Well, I've got to go. You know, Bill could have married any number of the right kind of girls around here. But I knew it would take more than the right kind of girl to get Bill to marry. It would take something special. And you're something special.

LAURA. How should I take that?

LILLY. As a compliment. Thanks for the drink. Don't tell Harry I had one when you see him at dinner.

LAURA. We won't be over to the hall. I've laid in a sort of feast for tonight.

LILLY. Celebrating something?

LAURA. No, just an impulse.

LILLY. Well, don't tell Harry anyway.

LAURA. You'd better stop talking the way you've been talking, or I won't have to tell him.

LILLY. Now, look, honey, don't you start going puritan on me. You're the only one in this school I can shoot my mouth off to, so don't change, baby. Don't change.

LAURA. I won't.

LILLY. Some day I'm going to wheedle out of you all the juicy stories you must have from when you were in the theater.

LAURA. Lilly, you would make the most hardened chorus girl blush.

LILLY [*pleased*]. Really?

LAURA. Really.

LILLY. That's the sweetest thing you've said to me in days. Good-bye. [*She goes out the door, and a moment later we hear the outside door close.*]

LAURA [*sits for a moment, listening to* TOM'S *rather plaintive whistling. She rises and looks at the Canada vacation literature on the desk, and then, looking at her watch, goes to the door, opens it, and calls up the stairway*]. Tom . . . Oh, Tom.

[*The moment* TOM *hears his name, he jumps from the bed, and goes through the sitting room, and appears on the stairs.*]

TOM. Yes?

LAURA [*she is very friendly with him, comradely*]. If it won't spoil your supper, come on down for a cup of tea.

[TOM *goes back into his room and brushes his hair, then he comes on down the stairs, and enters the study. He enters this room as though it were something rare and special. This is where* LAURA *lives.*]

LAURA [*has gone out to the other part of the house. Comes to doorway for a moment pouring cream from bottle to pitcher*]. I've just about finished your costume for the play, and we can have a fitting.

TOM. Sure. That'd be great. Do you want the door open or shut?

LAURA [*goes off again*]. It doesn't make any difference. [TOM *shuts the door. He is deeply in love with this woman, though he knows nothing can come of it. It is a sort of delayed puppy love. It is very touching and very intense. They are easy with each other, casual, though he is always trying in thinly veiled ways to tell her he loves her.* LAURA *enters with tea tray and sees him closing the door. She puts tray on table.*] Perhaps you'd better leave it ajar, so that if some of the other boys get out of class early, they can come in too.

TOM [*is disappointed*]. Oh, sure.

LAURA [*goes off for the plate of cookies, but pauses long enough to watch* TOM *open the door the merest crack. She is amused. In a moment, she re-enters with a plate of cookies*]. Help yourself.

TOM. Thanks. [*He takes a cookie, and then sits on the floor, near her chair.*]

LAURA. Are the boys warm enough in the rooms? They shut down the heat so early this spring, I guess they didn't expect this little chill.

TOM. We're fine. But this is nice. [*He indicates low fire in fireplace.*]

LAURA [*goes back to her sewing*]. I heard you singing.

TOM. I'm sorry if it bothered you.

LAURA. It was very nice.

TOM. If it ever bothers you, just bang on the radiator.

LAURA. What was the name of the song? It's lovely.

TOM. It's an old French song . . . "The Joys of Love" . . . [*He speaks the lyric.*]

> The joys of love
> Are but a moment long,
> The pain of love
> Endures forever.

LAURA. And is that true? [TOM *shrugs his shoulders.*] You sang as though you knew all about the pains of love.

TOM. And you don't think I do?

LAURA. Well . . .

TOM. You're right.

LAURA. Only the joys.

TOM. Neither, really.

[*Teapot whistles off stage.*]

LAURA. Then you're a fake. Listening to you, one would think you knew everything there was to know. [*Rises and goes to next room for tea.*] Anyway, I don't believe it. A boy like you.

TOM. It's true.

LAURA [*off stage*]. Aren't you bringing someone to the dance after the play Saturday?

TOM. Yes.

LAURA. Well, there.

TOM. You.

LAURA [*reappears in doorway with teapot*]. Me?

TOM. Yes, you're going to be a hostess, aren't you?

LAURA. Yes, of course, but . . .

TOM. As a member of the committee, I'm taking you. All the committee drew lots . . .

LAURA. And you lost.

TOM. I won.

LAURA [*a little embarrassed by this*]. Oh. My husband could have taken me. [*She sits down again in her chair.*]

TOM. He's not going to be in town. Don't you remember, Mountain Climbing Club has its final outing this week-end.

LAURA. Oh, yes, of course. I'd forgotten.

TOM. He's out a lot on that kind of thing, isn't he? [LAURA *ignores his probing.*] I hope you're not sorry that I'm to be your escort.

LAURA. Why, I'll be honored.

TOM. I'm supposed to find out tactfully and without your knowing it what color dress you'll be wearing.

LAURA. Why?

TOM. The committee will send you a corsage.

LAURA. Oh, how nice. Well, I don't have much to choose from, I guess my yellow.

TOM. The boy who's in charge of getting the flowers thinks a corsage should be something like a funeral decoration. So I'm taking personal charge of getting yours.

LAURA. Thank you.

TOM. You must have gotten lots of flowers when you were acting in the theater.

LAURA. Oh, now and then. Nothing spectacular.

TOM. I can't understand how a person would give up the theater to come and live in a school . . . I'm sorry. I mean, I'm glad you did, but, well . . .

LAURA. If you knew the statistics on unemployed actors, you might understand. Anyway, I was never any great shakes at it.

TOM. I can't believe that.

LAURA. Then take my word for it.

TOM [*after a moment, looking into the fire, pretending to be casual, but actually touching on his love for* LAURA]. Did you ever do any of Shaw's plays?

LAURA. Yes.

TOM. We got an assignment to read any Shaw play we wanted. I picked *Candida*.

LAURA. Because it was the shortest?

TOM [*laughs*]. No . . . because it sounded like the one I'd like the best, one I could understand. Did you ever play Candida?

LAURA. In stock—a very small stock company, way up in Northern Vermont.

TOM. Do you think she did right to send Marchbanks away?

LAURA. Well, Shaw made it seem right. Don't you think?

TOM [*really talking about himself*]. That Marchbanks sure sounded off a lot. I could never sound off like that, even if I loved a woman the way he did. She could have made him seem awfully small if she'd wanted to.

LAURA. Well, I guess she wasn't that kind of woman. Now stand up. Let's see if this fits. [*She rises with dress in her hands.*]

TOM [*gets up*]. My Dad's going to hit the roof when he hears I'm playing another girl.

LAURA. I think you're a good sport not to mind. Besides, it's a good part. Lady Teazle in *The School for Scandal*.

TOM [*puts on top of dress*]. It all started when I did Lady Macbeth last year. You weren't here yet for that. Lucky you.

LAURA. I hear it was very good.

TOM. You should have read a letter I got from my father. They printed a picture of me in the *Alumni Bulletin,* in costume. He was plenty peeved about it.

LAURA. He shouldn't have been.

TOM. He wrote me saying he might be up here today on Alumni Fund business. If he comes over here, and you see him, don't tell him about this.

LAURA. I won't . . . What about your mother? Did she come up for the play? [*She helps him button the dress.*]

TOM. I don't see my mother. Didn't you know? [*He starts to roll up pants legs.*]

LAURA. Why no. I didn't.

TOM. She and my father are divorced.

LAURA. I'm sorry.

TOM. You needn't be. They aren't. I was supposed to hold them together. That was how I happened to come into the world. I didn't work. That's a terrible thing, you know, to make a flop of the first job you've got in life.

LAURA. Don't you ever see her?

TOM. Not since I was five. I was with her till five, and then my father took me away. All I remember about my mother is that she was always telling me to go outside and bounce a ball.

LAURA [*handing him skirt of the dress*]. You must have done something before Lady Macbeth. When did you play that character named Grace?

TOM [*stiffens*]. I never played anyone called Grace.

LAURA. But I hear the boys sometimes calling you Grace. I thought . . . [*She notices that he's uncomfortable.*] I'm sorry. Have I said something terrible?

TOM. No.

LAURA. But I have. I'm sorry.

TOM. It's all right. But it's a long story. Last year over at the movies, they did a revival of Grace Moore in *One Night of Love.* I'd seen the revival before the picture came. And I guess I oversold it, or something. But she was wonderful! ... Anyway, some of the guys started calling me Grace. It was my own fault, I guess.

LAURA. Nicknames can be terrible. I remember at one time I was called "Beany." I can't remember why, now, but I remember it made me mad. [*She adjusts the dress a little.*] Hold still a moment. We'll have to let this out around here. [*She indicates the bosom.*] What size do you want to be?

TOM [*he is embarrassed, but rather nicely, not obviously and farcically. In his embarrassment he looks at* LAURA'S *bosom, then quickly away*]. I don't know. Whatever you think.

LAURA [*she indicates he is to stand on a small wooden footstool*]. I should think you would have invited some girl up to see you act, and then take her to the dance.

TOM [*gets on stool*]. There's nobody I could ask.

LAURA [*working on hem of dress*]. What do you mean?

TOM. I don't know any girls, really.

LAURA. Oh, certainly back home ...

TOM. Last ten years I haven't been home, I mean really home. Summers my father packs me off to camps, and the rest of the time I've been at boarding schools.

LAURA. What about Christmas vacation, and Easter?

TOM. My father gets a raft of tickets to plays and concerts, and sends me and my aunt.

LAURA. I see.

TOM. So I mean it when I say I don't know any girls.

LAURA. Your roommate, Al, knows a lot of girls. Why not ask him to fix you up with a blind date?

TOM. I don't know ... I can't even dance. I'm telling you this so you won't expect anything of me Saturday night.

LAURA. We'll sit out and talk.

TOM. Okay.

LAURA. Or I could teach you how to dance. It's quite simple.

TOM [*flustered*]. You?

LAURA. Why not?

TOM. I mean, isn't a person supposed to go to some sort of dancing class or something? [*He gets down from footstool.*]

LAURA. Not necessarily. Look, I'll show you how simple it is. [*She assumes the dancing position.*] Hold your left hand out this way, and put your right hand around my— [*She stops, as she sees him looking at her.*] Oh, now you're kidding me. A boy your age and you don't know how to dance.

TOM. I'm not kidding you.

LAURA. Well, then, come on. I had to teach my husband. Put your arm around me. [*She raises her arms.*]

TOM [*looks at her a moment, afraid to touch this woman he loves. Then to pass it off*]. We better put it off. We'd look kind of silly, both of us in skirts.

LAURA. All right. Take it off, then. No, wait a minute. Just let me stand off and take a look ... [*She walks around him.*] You're going to make a very lovely girl.

TOM. Thank you, ma'am ... [*He kids a curtsy, like a girl, and starts out of his costume.* MR. HARRIS, *a good-looking young master, comes in the hallway and starts up to* TOM'S *room. On the landing, he knocks on* TOM'S *door.*]

LAURA. I wonder who that is?

TOM. All the other fellows have late afternoon classes.

LAURA [*opens the door wider, and looks up the stairs*]. Yes? Oh, David.

HARRIS [*turns and looks down the stairs*]. Oh, hello, Laura.

LAURA. I just was wondering who was coming in. [*TOM proceeds to get out of the costume.*]

HARRIS. I want to see Tom Lee.

LAURA. He's down here. I'm making his costume for the play.

HARRIS. I wonder if I could see him for a moment?

LAURA. Why yes, of course. Tom, Mr. Harris would like to see you. Do you want to use our study, David? I can go into the living room.

HARRIS. No, thanks. I'll wait for him in his room. Will you ask him to come up? [*He opens the door and goes in.*]

LAURA [*is puzzled at his intensity, the urgency in his voice. Comes back in the study*]. Tom, Mr. Harris would like to see you in your room. He's gone along.

TOM. That's funny.

LAURA. Wait a minute . . . take this up with you, try it on in front of your mirror . . . see if you can move in it . . . [*She hands him skirt of costume.*] When Mr. Harris is through, bring the costume back.

TOM [*anxious over what* HARRIS *wants to see him about*]. Yeah, sure. [*He starts out, then stops and picks up a cookie. He looks at her lovingly.*] Thanks for tea.

LAURA. You're welcome.

[TOM *goes to the door as* LAURA *turns to the desk. He stands in the door a moment and looks at her back, then he turns and shuts the door and heads upstairs.* HARRIS *has come into* TOM'S *bedroom, and is standing there nervously clenching and unclenching his hands.*]

TOM [*off stage, presumably in the study he shares with his roommate*]. Mr. Harris?

[LAURA *wanders off into the other part of the house after looking for a moment at the Canada vacation material on the desk.*]

HARRIS. I'm in here.

TOM [*comes in a little hesitantly*]. Oh. Hello, sir.

[HARRIS *closes the door to the bedroom.* TOM *regards this action with some nervousness.*]

HARRIS. Well?

TOM [*has dumped some clothes from a chair to his bed. Offers chair to* HARRIS]. Sir?

HARRIS. What did you tell the Dean?

TOM. What do you mean, Mr. Harris?

HARRIS. What did you tell the Dean?

TOM. When? What are you talking about, sir?

HARRIS. Didn't the Dean call you in?

TOM. No. Why should he?

HARRIS. He didn't call you in and ask you about last Saturday afternoon?

TOM. Why should he? I didn't do anything wrong.

HARRIS. About being with me?

TOM. I'm allowed to leave town for the day in the company of a master.

HARRIS. I don't believe you. You must have said something.

TOM. About what?

HARRIS. About you and me going down to the dunes and swimming.

TOM. Why should I tell him about that?

HARRIS [*threatening*]. Why didn't you keep your mouth shut?

TOM. About what? What, for God's sake?

HARRIS. I never touched you, did I?

TOM. What do you mean, touch me?

HARRIS. Did you say to the Dean I touched you?

TOM [*turning away from* HARRIS]. I don't know what you're talking about.

HARRIS. Here's what I'm talking about. The Dean's had me on the carpet all afternoon. I probably won't be reappointed next year . . . and all because I took you swimming down off the dunes on Saturday.

TOM. Why should he have you on the carpet for that?

HARRIS. You can't imagine, I suppose.

TOM. What did you do wrong?

HARRIS. Nothing! Nothing, unless you made it seem like something wrong. Did you?

TOM. I told you I didn't see the Dean.

HARRIS. You will. He'll call for you. Bunch of gossiping old busybodies! Well . . . [*He starts for the door, stops, turns around and softens. He comes back to the puzzled* TOM.] I'm sorry . . . It probably wasn't your fault. It was my fault. I should have been more . . . discreet . . . Good-bye. Good luck with your music.

[TOM *hasn't understood. He doesn't know what to say. He makes a helpless gesture with his hands.* HARRIS *goes into the other room on his way out. Three boys, about seventeen, come in from the downstairs hall door and start up the stairs. They're carrying books. All are wearing sports jackets, khaki or flannel trousers, white or saddle rubber-soled shoes.*]

AL. I don't believe a word of it.

RALPH [*he is large and a loud-mouthed bully*]. I'm telling you the guys saw them down at the dunes.

AL [*he is* TOM'S *roommate, an athlete*]. So what?

RALPH. They were bare-assed.

AL. Shut up, will you? You want Mrs. Reynolds to hear you?

RALPH. Okay. You watch and see. Harris'll get bounced, and I'm gonna lock my room at night as long as Tom is living in this house.

AL. Oh, dry up!

RALPH. Jeeze, you're his roommate and you're not worried.

HARRIS [*comes out the door and starts down the stairs*]. Hello. [*He goes down stairs and out.*]

AL. Sir.

RALPH. Do you believe me now? You aren't safe. Believe me.

STEVE [*he is small,* RALPH'S *appreciative audience. He comes in the front door.*] Hey, Al, can I come in watch Mrs. Morrison nurse her kid?

RALPH. You're the loudest-mouthed bastard I ever heard. You want to give it away.

STEVE. It's time. How about it, Al?

AL [*grudgingly*]. Come on.

[TOM *hears them coming, and moves to bolt his door, but* STEVE *and* RALPH *break in before he gets to the door. He watches them from the doorway.* STEVE *rushes to the bed and throws himself across it, looking out the window next to the bed.* RALPH *settles down next to him.*]

AL [*to* TOM *as he comes in*]. Hi. These horny bastards.

STEVE. Al, bring the glasses. [AL *goes into sitting room.*]

RALPH. Some day she's going to wean that little bastard and spoil all our fun.

STEVE. Imagine sitting in a window . . .

TOM [*has been watching this with growing annoyance*]. Will you guys get out of here?

RALPH [*notices* TOM *for the first time*]. What's the matter with you, Grace?

TOM. This is my damned room.

RALPH. Gracie's getting private all of a sudden.

TOM. I don't want a lot of Peeping Toms lying on my bed watching a . . . a . . .

STEVE. You want it all for yourself, don't you?

RALPH. Or aren't you interested in women?

AL [*comes back in with field glasses*]. Shut up! [*Looks out window, then realizes* TOM *is watching him. Embarrassed.*] These horny bastards.

STEVE [*looking*]. Geeze!

RALPH [*a bully, riding down on* TOM]. I thought you were going to play ball with us Saturday.

TOM. I didn't feel like it.

RALPH. What *did* you feel like doing, huh?

AL. Will you shut up?

STEVE. Hey, lookit. [*Grabs glasses from* AL. AL *leaves room.*]

TOM [*climbing over* STEVE *and* RALPH *and trying to pull*

the shade]. I told you to get out. I told you last time . . .

RALPH [*grabbing hold of* TOM, *and holding him down*]. Be still, boy, or she'll see, and you'll spoil everything.

TOM. Horny bastard. Get out of here.

RALPH. Who are you calling a horny bastard? [*He grabs hold of* TOM *more forcefully, and slaps him a couple of times across the face, not trying to hurt him, but just to humiliate him.* STEVE *gets in a few pokes and in a moment, it's not in fun, but verging on the serious.*] You don't mean that now, boy, do you . . . Do you, Grace? [*He slaps him again.*]

AL [*hearing the scuffle, comes in and hauls* RALPH *and* STEVE *off* TOM]. Come on, come on, break it up. Clear out. [*He has them both standing up now,* TOM *still on the bed.*]

RALPH. I just don't like that son of a bitch calling me a horny bastard. Maybe if it was Dr. Morrison instead of Mrs. Morrison, he'd be more interested. Hey, wouldn't you, Grace? [*He tries to stick his face in front of* TOM, *but* AL *holds him back.*]

AL. Come on, lay off the guy, will you? Go on. Get ready for supper.

[*He herds them out during this. When they have left the room,* TOM *gets up and goes to bureau and gets a handkerchief. He has a bloody nose. He lies down on the bed, his head tilted back to stop the blood.*]

AL [*in doorway*]. You all right?

TOM. Yeah.

[RALPH *and* STEVE *go up the stairway singing in raucous voices, "One Night of Love." The downstairs outside door opens, and* BILL REYNOLDS *enters the hall with a student,* PHIL. BILL *is* LAURA'S *husband. He is large and strong with a tendency to be gruff. He's wearing gray flannel trousers, a tweed jacket, a blue button-down shirt. He is around forty.*]

BILL. Okay, boy, we'll look forward to— [*He notices* RALPH *still singing. He goes to the bend in the stairs and calls.*] Hey, Ralph. . . . Ralph!

RALPH [*stops singing up out of sight*]. You calling me, Mr. Reynolds, sir?

BILL. Yeah. Keep it down to a shout, will you?

RALPH. Oh, *yes, sir.* Sorry, I didn't know I was disturbing you, Mr. Reynolds.

BILL [*comes back and talks with* PHIL *at the bend in the stairway*]. Phil, you come on up to the lodge around . . . Let's see . . . We'll open the lodge around July first, so you plan to come up say, July third, and stay for two weeks. Okay?

PHIL. That'll be swell, sir.

BILL. Frank Hocktor's coming then. You get along with Frank, don't you? He's a regular guy.

PHIL. Oh, sure.

BILL. The float's all gone to pieces. We can make that your project to fix it up. Okay?

PHIL. Thanks a lot, Mr. Reynolds. [*He goes on up the stairs.*]

BILL. See you. [*He comes in and crosses to phone and starts to call.*]

LAURA [*off stage*]. Tom?

[BILL *looks around in the direction of the voice, but says nothing.*]

LAURA [*comes on*]. Oh, Bill. Tom was down trying on his costume. I thought . . . You're early.

BILL. Yes. I want to catch the Dean before he leaves his office. [LAURA *goes up to him to be kissed, but he's too intent on the phone, and she compromises by kissing his cheek.*] Hello, this is Mr. Reynolds. Is the Dean still in his office?

LAURA. What's the matter, Bill?

BILL. Nothing very pretty. Oh? How long ago? All right. Thanks. I'll give him a couple of minutes, then I'll call him home. [*Hangs up.*] Well, they finally caught up with Harris. [*He goes into the next room to take off his jacket.*]

LAURA. What do you mean, "caught up" with him?

BILL [*off stage*]. You're going to hear it anyhow . . . so . . . last Saturday they caught him down in the dunes, naked.

LAURA [*crosses to close door to hall*]. What's wrong with that?

BILL [*enters and crosses to fireplace and starts to go through letters propped there. He has taken off his jacket*]. He wasn't alone.

LAURA. Oh.

BILL. He was lying there naked in the dunes, and one of the students was lying there naked too. Just to talk about it is disgusting.

LAURA. I see.

BILL. I guess you'll admit that's something.

LAURA. I can't see that it's necessarily conclusive.

BILL. With a man like Harris, it's conclusive enough. [*Then casually:*] The student with him was—

LAURA [*interrupting*]. I'm not sure I care to know.

BILL. I'm afraid you're going to have to know sooner or later, Laura. It was Tom Lee.

[TOM *rises from bed, grabs a towel and goes out up the stairs.* LAURA *just looks at* BILL *and frowns.*]

BILL. Some of the boys down on the Varsity Club outing came on them . . . or at least saw them . . . And Fin Hadley saw them too, and he apparently used his brains for once and spoke to the Dean.

LAURA. And?

BILL. He's had Harris on the carpet this afternoon. I guess he'll be fired. I certainly hope so. Maybe Tom too, I don't know.

LAURA. They put two and two together?

BILL. Yes, Laura.

LAURA. I suppose this is all over school by now.

BILL. I'm afraid so.

LAURA. And most of the boys know.

BILL. Yes.

LAURA. So what's going to happen to Tom?

BILL [*takes pipe from mantelpiece and cleans it*]. I know you won't like this, Laura, but I think he should be kicked out. I think you've got to let people know the school doesn't stand for even a hint of this sort of thing. He should be booted.

LAURA. For what?

BILL. Look, a boy's caught coming out of Ellie Martin's rooms across the river. That's enough evidence. Nobody asks particulars. They don't go to Ellie's rooms to play Canasta. It's the same here.

LAURA [*hardly daring to suggest it*]. But, Bill . . . you don't think Tom is . . . [*She stops.* BILL *looks at her a moment, his answer is in his silence.*] Oh, Bill!

BILL. And I'm ashamed and sorry as hell for his father. Herb Lee was always damned good to me . . . came down from college when I was playing football here . . . helped me get into college . . . looked after me when I was in college and he was in law school . . . And I know he put the boy in my house hoping I could do something with him. [*He dials number.*]

LAURA. And you feel you've failed.

BILL. Yes. [*He pauses.*] With your help, I might say. [*Busy signal. He hangs up.*]

LAURA. How?

BILL. Because, Laura, the boy would rather sit around here and talk with you and listen to music and strum his guitar.

LAURA. Bill, I'm not to blame for everything. Everything's not my fault.

BILL [*disregarding this*]. What a lousy thing for Herb. [*He looks at a small picture of a team on his desk.*] That's Herb. He was Graduate Manager of the team when I was a sophomore in college. He was always the manager of the teams, and he really wanted his son to be there in the center of the picture.

LAURA. Why are you calling the Dean?

BILL. I'm going to find out what's being done.

LAURA. I've never seen you like this before.

BILL. This is something that touches me very closely. The name of the school, its reputation, the reputation of all of us here. I went here and my father before me, and one day I hope our children will come here, when we have them. And, of course, one day I hope to be headmaster.

LAURA. Let's assume that you're right about Harris. It's a terrible thing to say on the evidence you've got, but let's assume you're right. Does it necessarily follow that Tom—

BILL. Tom was his friend. Everyone knew that.

LAURA. Harris encouraged him in his music.

BILL. Come on, Laura.

LAURA. What if Tom's roommate, Al, or some other great big athlete had been out with Harris?

BILL. He wouldn't have been.

LAURA. I'm saying what if he had been? Would you have jumped to the same conclusion?

BILL. It would have been different. Tom's always been an off-horse. And now it's quite obvious why. If he's kicked out, maybe it'll bring him to his senses. But he won't change if nothing's done about it. [LAURA *turns away.* BILL *starts to look over his mail again.*] Anyway, why are you so concerned over what happens to Tom Lee?

LAURA. I've come to know him. You even imply that I am somewhat responsible for his present reputation.

BILL. All right. I shouldn't have said that. But you watch, now that it's out in the open. Look at the way he walks, the way he sometimes stands.

LAURA. Oh, Bill!

BILL. All right, so a woman doesn't notice these things. But a man knows a queer when he sees one. [*He has opened a letter. Reads.*] The bookstore now has the

book you wanted . . . *The Rose and The Thorn.*
What's that?

LAURA. A book of poems. Do you know, Bill, I'll bet
he doesn't even know the meaning of the word . . .
queer.

BILL. What do you think he is?

LAURA. I think he's a nice sensitive kid who doesn't
know the meaning of the word.

BILL. He's eighteen, or almost. I don't know.

LAURA. How much did you know at eighteen?

BILL. A lot. [*At the desk he now notices the Canada literature.*] What are these?

LAURA. What?

BILL. These.

LAURA. Oh, nothing.

BILL [*he throws them in wastebasket, then notices her
look*]. Well, they're obviously something. [*He takes
them out of wastebasket.*]

LAURA [*the joy of it gone for her*]. I was thinking we
might take a motor trip up there this summer.

BILL [*dialing phone again*]. I wish you'd said something about it earlier. I've already invited some of
the scholarship boys up to the lodge. I can't disap-
point them.

LAURA. Of course not.

BILL. If you'd said something earlier.

LAURA. It's my fault.

BILL. It's nobody's fault, it's just— Hello, Fitz, Bill
Reynolds— I was wondering if you're going to be in
tonight after supper . . . Oh . . . oh, I see . . . Supper?
Well, sure I could talk about it at supper. . . . Well,
no, I think I'd better drop over alone. . . . All right.
I'll see you at the house then . . . Good-bye.

[LAURA *looks at him, trying to understand him.* BILL
*comes to her to speak softly to her. Seeing him come,
she holds out her arms to be embraced, but he just
takes her chin in his hand.*]

BILL. Look, Laura, when I brought you here a year

ago, I told you it was a tough place for a woman with a heart like yours. I told you you'd run across boys, big and little boys, full of problems, problems which for the moment seem gigantic and heartbreaking. And you promised me then you wouldn't get all taken up with them. Remember?

LAURA. Yes.

BILL. When I was a kid in school here, I had my problems too. There's a place up by the golf course where I used to go off alone Sunday afternoons and cry my eyes out. I used to lie on my bed just the way Tom does, listening to phonograph records hour after hour. [LAURA, *touched by this, kneels at his side.*] But I got over it, Laura. I learned how to take it. [LAURA *looks at him. This touches her.*] When the headmaster's wife gave you this teapot, she told you what she tells all the new masters' wives. You have to be an interested bystander.

LAURA. I know.

BILL. Just as she said, all you're supposed to do is every once in a while give the boys a little tea and sympathy. Do you remember?

LAURA. Yes, I remember. It's just that . . .

BILL. What?

LAURA. This age—seventeen, eighteen—it's so . . .

BILL. I know.

LAURA. John was this age when I married him.

BILL. Look, Laura . . .

LAURA. I know. You don't like me to talk about John, but . . .

BILL. It's not that. It's . . .

LAURA. He was just this age, eighteen or so, when I married him. We both were. And I know now how this age can suffer. It's a heartbreaking time . . . no longer a boy . . . not yet a man . . . Bill? Bill?

BILL [*looks at her awkwardly a moment, then starts to move off*]. I'd better clean up if I'm going to get to the Dean's for supper. You don't mind, do you?

LAURA [*very quietly*]. I got things in for dinner here. But they'll keep.

BILL [*awkwardly*]. I'm sorry, Laura. But you understand, don't you? About this business? [LAURA *shakes her head, "No." * BILL *stands over her, a little put out that she has not understood his reasoning. He starts to say something several times, then stops. Finally he notices the Five-and-Dime engagement ring around her neck. He touches it.*] You're not going to wear this thing to the dining hall, are you?

LAURA. Why not?

BILL. It was just a gag. It means something to you, but to them . . .

LAURA [*bearing in, but gently*]. Does it mean anything to you, Bill?

BILL. Well, it did, but . . . [*He stops with a gesture, unwilling to go into it all.*]

LAURA. I think you're ashamed of the night you gave it to me. That you ever let me see you needed help. That night in Italy, in some vague way you cried out . . .

BILL. What is the matter with you today? *Me* crying out for help. [*He heads for the other room. A knock on study door is heard.*]

BILL. It's probably Tom.

[LAURA *goes to door.*]

HERB [*this is* HERBERT LEE, TOM'S *father. He is a middle-sized man, fancying himself a man of the world and an extrovert. He is dressed as a conservative Boston businessman, but with still a touch of the collegiate in his attire—button-down shirt, etc.*]. Mrs. Reynolds?

LAURA. Yes?

BILL [*stopped by the voice, turns*]. Herb! Come in.

HERB [*coming in*]. Hiya, Bill. How are you, fella?

BILL [*taking his hand*]. I'm fine, Herb.

HERB [*poking his finger into* BILL'S *chest*]. Great to see you. [*Looks around to* LAURA.] Oh, uh . . .

BILL. I don't think you've met Laura, Herb. This is
Laura. Laura, this is Herb Lee, Tom's father.

HERB [*hearty and friendly, meant to put people at
their ease*]. Hello, Laura.

LAURA. I've heard so much about you.

HERB [*after looking at her for a moment*]. I like her,
Bill. I like her very much. [LAURA *blushes, and is a
little taken aback by this. To* LAURA.] What I'd like
to know is how did you manage to do it? [*Cuffing*
BILL.] I'll bet you make her life miserable . . . You
look good, Bill.

BILL. You don't look so bad yourself. [*He takes in a
notch in his belt.*]

HERB. No, *you're* in shape. I never had anything to
keep in shape, but you . . . You should have seen
this boy, Laura.

LAURA. I've seen pictures.

HERB. Only exercise I get these days is bending the
elbow.

LAURA. May I get you something? A drink?

HERB. No, thanks. I haven't got much time.

BILL. You drive out from Boston, Herb?

HERB. No, train. You know, Bill, I think that's the
same old train you and I used to ride in when we
came here.

BILL. Probably is.

HERB. If I don't catch the six-fifty-four, I'll have to stay
all night, and I'd rather not.

BILL. We'll be glad to put you up.

HERB. No. You're putting me up in a couple of weeks
at the reunion. That's imposing enough. [*There is
an awkward pause. Both men sit down.*] I . . . uh . . .
was over at the Dean's this afternoon.

BILL. Oh, he called you?

HERB. Why, no. I was up discussing Alumni Fund matters with him . . . and . . . Do you know about it?

BILL. You mean about Tom?

HERB. Yes. [*Looks at* LAURA.]

BILL. Laura knows too. [*He reaches for her to come to him, and he puts his arm around her waist.*]

HERB. Well, after we discussed the Fund, he told me about that. Thought I ought to hear about it from him. Pretty casual about it, I thought.

BILL. Well, that's Fitz.

HERB. What I want to know is, what was a guy like Harris doing at the school?

BILL. I tried to tell them.

HERB. Was there anyone around like that in our day, Bill?

BILL. No. You're right.

HERB. I tried to find the guy. I wanted to punch his face for him. But he's cleared out. Is Tom around?

LAURA. He's in his room.

HERB. How'd he get mixed up with a guy like that?

BILL. I don't know, Herb . . .

HERB. I know. I shouldn't ask you. I know. Of course I don't believe Tom was really involved with this fellow. If I believed that, I'd . . . well, I don't know what I'd do. You don't believe it, do you, Bill?

BILL. Why . . . [*Looks at* LAURA.]

HERB [*cutting in*]. Of course you don't. But what's the matter? What's happened, Bill? Why isn't my boy a regular fellow? He's had every chance to be since he was knee-high to a grasshopper—boys' camps every summer, boarding schools. What do you think, Laura?

LAURA. I'm afraid I'm not the one to ask, Mr. Lee. [*She breaks away from* BILL.]

HERB. He's always been with men and boys. Why doesn't some of it rub off?

LAURA. You see, I feel he's a "regular fellow" . . . whatever that is.

HERB. You do?

LAURA. If it's sports that matter, he's an excellent tennis player.

HERB. But Laura, he doesn't even play tennis like a regular fellow. No hard drives and cannon-ball serves. He's a cut artist. He can put more damn twists on that ball.

LAURA. He wins. He's the school champion. And isn't he the champion of your club back home?

[TOM *comes down the stairs and enters his bedroom with the costume skirt and towel.*]

HERB. I'm glad you mentioned that . . . because that's just what I mean. Do you know, Laura, his winning that championship brought me one of my greatest humiliations? I hadn't been able to watch the match. I was supposed to be in from a round of golf in time, but we got held up on every hole . . . And when I got back to the locker room, I heard a couple of men talking about Tom's match in the next locker section. And what they said, cut me to the quick, Laura. One of them said, "It's a damn shame Tom Lee won the match. He's a good player, all right, but John Batty is such a regular guy." John Batty was his opponent. Now what pleasure was there for me in that?

BILL. I know what you mean.

HERB. I *want* to be proud of him. My God, that's why I had him in the first place. That's why I took him from his mother when we split up, but . . . Look, this is a terrible thing to say, but you know the scholarships the University Club sponsors for needy kids . . .

BILL. Sure.

HERB. Well, I contribute pretty heavily to it, and I happened to latch on to one of the kids we help—an orphan. I sort of talk to him like a father, go up to see him at his school once in a while, and that kid listens to me . . . and you know what, he's shaping up better than my own son.

[*There is an awkward pause. Upstairs* TOM *has put a record on the phonograph. It starts playing now.*]

BILL. You saw the Dean, Herb?

HERB. Yes.

BILL. And?

HERB. He told me the circumstances. Told me he was confident that Tom was innocently involved. He actually apologized for the whole thing. He did say that some of the faculty had suggested—though he didn't go along with this—that Tom would be more comfortable if I took him out of school. But I'm not going to. He's had nothing but comfort all his life, and look what's happened. My associates ask me what he wants to be, and I tell them he hasn't made up his mind. Because I'll be damned if I'll tell them he wants to be a singer of folk songs.

[TOM *lies on the bed listening to the music.*]

BILL. So you're going to leave him in?

HERB. Of course. Let him stick it out. It'll be a good lesson.

LAURA. Mightn't it be more than just a lesson, Mr. Lee?

HERB. Oh, he'll take some kidding. He'll have to work extra hard to prove to them he's . . . well, manly. It may be the thing that brings him to his senses.

LAURA. Mr. Lee, Tom's a very sensitive boy. He's a very lonely boy.

HERB. Why should he be lonely? I've always seen to it that he's been with people . . . at camps, at boarding schools.

BILL. He's certainly an off-horse, Herb.

HERB. That's a good way of putting it, Bill. An off-horse. Well, he's going to have to learn to run with the other horses. Well, I'd better be going up.

LAURA. Mr. Lee, this may sound terribly naïve of me, and perhaps a trifle indelicate, but I don't believe your son knows what this is all about. Why Mr. Harris was fired, why the boys will kid him.

HERB. You mean . . . [*Stops.*]

LAURA. I'm only guessing. But I think when it comes

to these boys, we often take too much knowledge for granted. And I think it's going to come as a terrible shock when he finds out what they're talking about. Not just a lesson, a shock.

HERB. I don't believe he's as naïve as all that. I just don't. Well . . . [*He starts for the door.*]

BILL [*takes* HERB's *arm and they go into the hall*]. I'm going over to the Dean's for supper, Herb. If you're through with Tom come by here and I'll walk you part way to the station.

HERB. All right. [*Stops on the stairs.*] How do you talk to the boys, Bill?

BILL. I don't know. I just talk to them.

HERB. They're not your sons. I only talked with Tom, I mean, really talked with him, once before. It was after a Sunday dinner and I made up my mind it was time we sat in a room together and talked about important things. He got sick to his stomach. That's a terrible effect to have on your boy . . . Well, I'll drop down. [*He takes a roll of money from his pocket and looks at it, then starts up the stairs.*]

BILL [*coming into his study*]. Laura, you shouldn't try to tell him about his own son. After all, if he doesn't know the boy, who does?

LAURA. I'm sorry.

[BILL *exits into the other part of the house, pulling off his tie.* HERB *has gone up the stairs. Knocks on the study door.* LAURA *settles down in her chair and eventually goes on with her sewing.*]

AL [*inside, calls*]. Come in.

[HERB *goes in and shuts the door.*]

HERB [*opens* TOM's *bedroom door and sticks his head in*]. Hello, there.

TOM [*looks up from the bed, surprised*]. Oh . . . Hi . . .

HERB. I got held up at the Dean's.

TOM. *Oh.* [*He has risen, and attempts to kiss his father on the cheek. But his father holds him off with a firm handshake.*]

HERB. How's everything? You look bushed.

TOM. I'm okay.

HERB [*looking at him closely*]. You sure?

TOM. Sure.

HERB [*looking around room*]. This room looks smaller than I remember. [*He throws on light switch.*] I used to have the bed over here. Used to rain in some nights. [*Comes across phonograph.*] This the one I gave you for Christmas?

TOM. Yeah. It works fine.

HERB [*turns phonograph off*]. You're neater than I was. My vest was always behind the radiator, or somewhere. [*Sees part of dress costume.*] What's this?

TOM [*hesitates for a moment. Then*]. A costume Mrs. Reynolds made for me. I'm in the play.

HERB. You didn't write about it.

TOM. I know.

HERB. What are you playing? [*Looks at dress.*]

TOM. You know *The School for Scandal*. I'm playing Lady Teazle.

HERB. Tom, I want to talk to you. Last time we tried to talk, it didn't work out so well.

TOM. What's up?

HERB. Tom, I'd like to be your friend. I guess there's something between fathers and sons that keeps them from being friends, but I'd like to try.

TOM [*embarrassed*]. Sure, Dad. [*He sits on the bed.*]

HERB. Now when you came here, I told you to make friends slowly. I told you to make sure they were the right kind of friends. You're known by the company you keep. Remember I said that?

TOM. Yes.

HERB. And I told you if you didn't want to go out for sports like football, hockey . . . that was all right with me. But you'd get in with the right kind of fellow if you managed these teams. They're usually pretty good guys. You remember.

TOM. Yes.

HERB. Didn't you believe me?

TOM. Yes, I believed you.

HERB. Okay, then let's say you believed me, but you decided to go your own way. That's all right too, only you see what it's led to.

TOM. What?

HERB. You made friends with people like this Harris guy who got himself fired.

TOM. Why is he getting fired?

HERB. He's being fired because he was seen in the dunes with you.

TOM. Look, I don't—

HERB. Naked.

TOM. You too?

HERB. So you know what I'm talking about?

TOM. No, I don't.

HERB. You do too know. I heard my sister tell you once. She warned you about a janitor in the building down the street.

TOM [*incredulous*]. Mr. Harris . . . ?

HERB. Yes. He's being fired because he's been doing a lot of suspicious things around apparently, and this finished it. All right, I'll say it plain, Tom. He's a fairy. A homosexual.

TOM. Who says so?

HERB. Now, Tom—

TOM. And seeing us on the beach . . .

HERB. Yes.

TOM. And what does that make me?

HERB. Listen, I know you're all right.

TOM. Thanks.

HERB. Now wait a minute.

TOM. Look, we were just swimming.

HERB. All right, all right. So perhaps you didn't know.

TOM. What do you mean perhaps?

HERB. It's the school's fault for having a guy like that around. But it's your fault for being a damned fool in picking your friends.

TOM. So that's what the guys meant.

HERB. You're going to get a ribbing for a while, but you're going to be a man about it and you're going to take it and you're going to come through much more careful how you make your friends.

TOM. He's kicked out because he was seen with me on the beach, and I'm telling you that nothing, absolutely nothing . . . Look, I'm going to the Dean and tell him that Harris did nothing, that—

HERB [*stopping him*]. Look, don't be a fool. It's going to be hard enough for you without sticking your neck out, asking for it.

TOM. But, Dad!

HERB. He's not going to be reappointed next year. Nothing you can say is going to change anyone's mind. You got to think about yourself. Now, first of all, get your hair cut. [TOM *looks at father, disgusted.*] Look, this isn't easy for me. Stop thinking about yourself, and give me a break. [TOM *looks up at this appeal.*] I suppose you think it's going to be fun for *me* to have to live this down back home. It'll get around, and it'll affect me, too. So we've got to see this thing through together. You've got to do your part. Get your hair cut. And then . . . No, the first thing I want you to do is call whoever is putting on this play, and tell them you're not playing this lady whatever her name is.

TOM. Why shouldn't I play it? It's the best part in the play, and I was chosen to play it.

HERB. I should think you'd have the sense to see why you shouldn't.

TOM. Wait a minute. You mean . . . do you mean, you think I'm . . . whatever you call it? Do you, Dad?

HERB. I told you "no."

TOM. But the fellows are going to think that I'm . . . and Mrs. Reynolds?

HERB. Yes. You're going to have to fight their thinking

it. Yes. [TOM *sits on the bed, the full realization of it dawning.*]

RALPH [*sticks his head around the stairs from upstairs, and yells*]. Hey, Grace, who's taking you to the dance Saturday night? Hey, Grace! [*He disappears again up the stairs.*]

HERB. What's that all about?

TOM. I don't know.

[LAURA, *as the noise comes in, rises and goes to door to stop it, but* AL *comes into the hall and goes upstairs yelling at the boys and* LAURA *goes back to her chair.*]

HERB [*looks at his watch*]. Now . . . Do you want me to stay over? If I'm not going to stay over tonight, I've got to catch the six-fifty-four.

TOM. Stay over?

HERB. Yes, I didn't bring a change of clothes along, but if you want me to stay over . . .

TOM. Why should you stay over?

HERB [*stung a little by this*]. All right. Now come on down to Bill's room and telephone this drama fellow. So I'll know you're making a start of it. And bring the dress.

TOM. I'll do it tomorrow.

HERB. I'd feel better if you did it tonight. Come on. I'm walking out with Bill. And incidentally, the Dean said if the ribbing goes beyond bounds . . . you know . . . you're to come to him and he'll take some steps. He's not going to do anything now, because these things take care of themselves. They're better ignored . . .

[*They have both started out of the bedroom, but during the above* HERB *goes back for the dress.* TOM *continues out and stands on the stairs looking at the telephone in the hall.*]

HERB [*comes out of the study. Calls back*]. See you Al. Take good care of my boy here. [*Starts down stairs. Stops.*] You need any money?

TOM. No.

HERB. I'm lining you up with a counselor's job at camp this year. If this thing doesn't spoil it. [*Stops.*] You sure you've got enough money to come home?

TOM. Yes, sure. Look Dad, let me call about the play from here. [*He takes receiver off hook.*]

HERB. Why not use Bill's phone? He won't mind. Come on. [TOM *reluctantly puts phone back on hook.*] Look, if you've got any problems, talk them over with Bill—Mr. Reynolds. He's an old friend, and I think he'd tell you about what I'd tell you in a spot. [*Goes into master's study.*] Is Bill ready?

LAURA. He'll be right down. How does the costume work?

TOM. I guess it's all right, only . . .

HERB. I'd like Tom to use your phone if he may—to call whoever's putting on the play. He's giving up the part.

LAURA. Giving up the part?

HERB. Yes. I've . . . I want him to. He's doing it for me.

LAURA. Mr. Lee, it was a great honor for him to be chosen to play the part.

HERB. Bill will understand. Bill! [*He thrusts costume into* LAURA'S *hand and goes off through alcove.*] Bill, what's the number of the man putting on the play? Tom wants to call him.

[LAURA *looks at* TOM *who keeps his eyes from her. She makes a move toward him, but he takes a step away.*]

BILL [*off stage*]. Fred Mayberry . . . Three-two-six . . . You ready, Herb?

HERB [*off stage*]. Yes. You don't mind if Tom uses your phone, do you?

BILL. Of course not.

HERB [*comes in*]. When do you go on your mountain-climbing week-end, Bill?

BILL [*comes in*]. This week-end's the outing.

HERB. Maybe Tom could go with you.

BILL. He's on the dance committee, I think. Of course he's welcome if he wants to. Always has been.

HERB [*holds out phone to* TOM]. Tom. [TOM *hesitates to cross to phone. As* LAURA *watches him with concern, he makes a move to escape out the door.*] Three-two-six.

[TOM *slowly and painfully crosses the stage, takes the phone and sits.*]

BILL. Will you walk along with us as far as the dining hall, Laura?

LAURA. I don't think I feel like supper, thanks.

BILL [*looks from her to* TOM]. What?

HERB. I've got to get along if I want to catch my train. [TOM *dials phone.*]

BILL. Laura?

[LAURA *shakes her head, tight-lipped.*]

HERB. Well, then, good-bye, Laura . . . I still like you.

LAURA. Still going to the Dean's, Bill?

BILL. Yes. I'll be right back after supper. Sure you don't want to walk along with us to the dining hall?

[LAURA *shakes her head.*]

TOM. Busy.

HERB [*pats his son's arm*]. Keep trying him. We're in this together. Anything you want? [TOM *shakes his head "no."*] Just remember, anything you want, let me know. [*To* LAURA.] See you at reunion time . . . This'll all be blown over by then. [*He goes.*]

BILL. Laura, I wish you'd . . . Laura! [*He is disturbed by her mood. He sees it's hopeless, and goes after* HERB, *leaving door open.*]

TOM [*at phone*]. Hello, Mr. Mayberry . . . This is Tom Lee . . . Yes, I know it's time to go to supper, Mr. Mayberry . . . [*Looks around at open door.* LAURA *shuts it.*] but I wanted you to know . . . [*This comes hard.*] I wanted you to know I'm not going to be able to play in the play . . . No . . . I . . . well, I just can't. [*He is about to break. He doesn't trust himself to speak.*]

LAURA [*quickly crosses and takes phone from* TOM].
Give it to me. Hello, Fred . . . Laura. Yes, Tom's
father, well, he wants Tom—he thinks Tom is tired,
needs to concentrate on his final exams. You had
someone covering the part, didn't you? . . . Yes, of
course it's a terrible disappointment to Tom. I'll see
you tomorrow.

[*She hangs up.* TOM *is ashamed and humiliated. Here
is the woman he loves, hearing all about him . . .
perhaps believing the things . . .* LAURA *stands above
him for a moment, looking at the back of his head
with pity. Then he rises and starts for the door without looking at her.* RALPH *and* STEVE *come stamped-
ing down the stairway.*]

RALPH [*as he goes*]. Okay, you can sit next to him if you
want. Not me.

STEVE. Well, if you won't . . . why should I?

RALPH. Two bits nobody will.

[*They slam out the front door.* TOM *has shut the door
quickly again when he has heard* RALPH *and* STEVE
start down. Now stands against the door listening.]

AL [*comes out from his door, pulling on his jacket.
Calls*]. Tom . . . Tom ! [*Getting no answer, he goes
down the stairs and out.*]

LAURA. Tom . . .

TOM [*opens the study door*]. I'll bet my father thinks
I'm . . . [*Stops.*]

LAURA. Now, Tom! I thought I'd call Joan Harrison
and ask her to come over for tea tomorrow. I want
you to come too. I want you to ask her to go to the
dance with you.

TOM [*turns in anguish and looks at her for several moments. Then*]. You were to go with me.

LAURA. I know, but . . .

TOM. Do you think so too, like the others? Like my
father?

LAURA. Tom!

TOM. Is that why you're shoving me off on Joan?

LAURA [*moving toward him*]. Tom, I asked her over so that we could lick this thing.

TOM [*turns on her*]. What thing? What thing?

[*He looks at her a moment, filled with indignation, then he bolts up the stairs. But on the way up,* PHIL *is coming down.* TOM *feels like a trapped rat. He starts to turn down the stairs again, but he doesn't want to face* LAURA, *as he is about to break. He tries to hide his face and cowers along one side going up.*]

PHIL. What's the matter with you?

[TOM *doesn't answer. Goes on up and into the study door.* PHIL *shrugs his shoulders and goes on down the stairs and out.* TOM *comes into his own bedroom and shuts the door and leans against the doorjamb.* LAURA *goes to the partly opened door. Her impulse is to go up to* TOM *to comfort him, but she checks herself, and turns in the doorway and closes the door, then walks back to her chair and sits down and reaches out and touches the teapot, as though she were half-unconsciously rubbing out a spot. She is puzzled and worried. Upstairs we hear the first few sobs from* TOM *as the lights dim out, and*

THE CURTAIN FALLS

Act two

SCENE I

The scene is the same.
The time is two days later.
As the curtain rises, AL *is standing at the public telephone fastened to the wall on the first landing. He seems to be doing more listening than talking.*

AL. Yeah . . . [*He patiently waits through a long tirade.*] Yeah, Dad. I know, Dad . . . No, I haven't done anything about it, yet . . . Yes, Mr. Hudson says he has a room in his house for me next year . . . But I haven't done anything about it here yet . . . Yeah, okay, Dad . . . I know what you mean . . . [*Gets angry.*] I swear to God I don't . . . I lived with him a year, and I don't . . . All right, okay, Dad . . . No, don't *you* call. I'll do it. Right now. [*He hangs up. He stands and puts his hands in his pockets and tries to think this out. It's something he doesn't like.*]

RALPH [*comes in the house door and starts up the steps*]. Hey, Al?

AL. Yeah?

RALPH. The guys over at the Beta house want to know has it happened yet?

AL. Has what happened?

RALPH. Has Tom made a pass at you yet?

AL [*reaches out to swat* RALPH]. For crying out loud!

RALPH. Okay, okay! You can borrow my chastity belt if you need it.

AL. That's not funny.

RALPH [*shifting his meaning to hurt* AL]. No, I know it's not. The guys on the ball team don't think it's funny at all.

AL. What do you mean?

RALPH. The guy they're supposed to elect captain rooming with a queer.

AL [*looks at him for a moment, then rejects the idea*]. Aw . . . knock it off, huh!

RALPH. So you don't believe me . . . Wait and see. [*Putting on a dirty grin.*] Anyway, my mother said I should save myself for the girl I marry. Hell, how would you like to have to tell your wife, "Honey, I've been saving myself for you, except for one night when a guy—" [AL *roughs* RALPH *up with no intention of hurting him.*] Okay, okay. So you don't want to be captain of the baseball team. So who the hell cares. I don't, I'm sure.

AL. Look. Why don't you mind your own business?

RALPH. What the hell fun would there be in that?

AL. Ralph, Tom's a nice kid.

RALPH. Yeah. That's why all the guys leave the shower room at the gym when he walks in.

AL. When?

RALPH. Yesterday . . . Today. You didn't hear about it?

AL. No. What are they trying to do?

RALPH. Hell, they don't want some queer looking at them and—

AL. Oh, can it! Go on up and bury your horny nose in your *Art Models* magazine.

RALPH. At least I'm normal. I like to look at pictures of naked girls, not men, the way Tom does.

AL. Jeeze, I'm gonna push your face in in a—

RALPH. Didn't you notice all those strong man poses he's got in his bottom drawer?

AL. Yes, I've noticed them. His old man wants him to be a muscle man, and he wrote away for this course in muscle building and they send those pictures. Any objections?

RALPH. Go on, stick up for him. Stick your neck out. You'll get it chopped off with a baseball bat, you crazy bastard.

[*Exits upstairs.* AL *looks at the phone, then up the way* RALPH *went. He is upset. He throws himself into a few push-ups, using the bannisters. Then still not happy with what he's doing, he walks down the stairs and knocks on the study door.*]

LAURA [*comes from inside the house and opens the door*]. Oh, hello, Al.

AL. Is Mr. Reynolds in?

LAURA. Why, no, he isn't. Can I do something?

AL. I guess I better drop down when he's in.

LAURA. All right. I don't really expect him home till after supper tonight.

AL [*thinks for a moment*]. Well . . . well, you might tell him just so's he'll know and can make other plans . . . I won't be rooming in this house next year. This is the last day for changing, and I want him to know that.

LAURA [*moves into the room to get a cigarette*]. I see. Well, I know he'll be sorry to hear that, Al.

AL. I'm going across the street to Harmon House.

LAURA. Both you and Tom going over?

AL. No.

LAURA. Oh.

AL. Just me.

LAURA. I see. Does Tom know this?

AL. No. I haven't told him.

LAURA. You'll have to tell him, won't you, so he'll be able to make other plans.

AL. Yes, I suppose so.

LAURA. Al, won't you sit down for a moment, please? [AL *hesitates, but comes in and sits down. Offers* AL *a cigarette.*] Cigarette?

AL [*reaches for one automatically, then stops*]. No, thanks. I'm in training. [*He slips a pack of cigarettes from his shirt pocket to his trousers pocket.*]

LAURA. That's right. I'm going to watch you play Saturday afternoon. [AL *smiles at her.*] You're not looking forward to telling Tom, are you, Al? [AL *shakes his head, "No."*] I suppose I can guess why you're not rooming with him next year. [AL *shrugs his shoulders.*] I wonder if you know how much it has meant for him to room with you this year. It's done a lot for him too. It's given him a confidence to know he was rooming with one of the big men of the school.

AL [*embarrassed*]. Oh . . .

LAURA. You wouldn't understand what it means to be befriended. You're one of the strong people. I'm surprised, Al.

AL [*blurting it out*]. My father's called me three times. How he ever found out about Harris and Tom, I don't know. But he did. And some guy called him and asked him, "Isn't that the boy your son is rooming with?" . . . and he wants me to change for next year.

LAURA. What did you tell your father?

AL. I told him Tom wasn't so bad, and . . . I'd better wait and see Mr. Reynolds.

LAURA. Al, you've lived with Tom. You know him better than anyone else knows him. If you do this, it's as good as finishing him so far as this school is concerned, and maybe farther.

AL [*almost whispering it*]. Well, he *does* act sort of queer, Mrs. Reynolds. He . . .

LAURA. You never said this before. You never paid any attention before. What do you mean, "queer?"

AL. Well, like the fellows say, he sort of walks lightly, if you know what I mean. Sometimes the way he moves . . . the things he talks about . . . long hair music all the time.

LAURA. All right. He wants to be a singer. So he talks about it.

AL. He's never had a girl up for any of the dances.

LAURA. Al, there are good explanations for all these things you're saying. They're silly . . . and prejudiced . . . and arguments all dug up to suit a point of view. They're all after the fact.

AL. I'd better speak to Mr. Reynolds. [*He starts for the door.*]

LAURA. Al, look at me. [*She holds his eyes for a long time, wondering whether to say what she wants to say.*]

AL. Yes?

LAURA [*she decides to do it*]. Al, what if I were to start the rumor tomorrow that you were . . . well, queer, as you put it.

AL. No one would believe it.

LAURA. Why not?

AL. Well, because . . .

LAURA. Because you're big and brawny and an athlete. What they call a top guy and a hard hitter?

AL. Well, yes.

LAURA. You've got some things to learn, Al. I've been around a little, and I've met men, just like you—same setup—who weren't men, some of them married and with children.

AL. Mrs. Reynolds, you wouldn't do a thing like that.

LAURA. No, Al, I probably wouldn't. But I could, and I almost would to show you how easy it is to smear a person, and once I got them believing it, you'd be surprised how quickly your . . . manly virtues would be changed into suspicious characteristics.

AL [*has been standing with his hands on his hips.* LAURA *looks pointedly at this stance.* AL *thrusts his hands down to his side, and then behind his back*]. Mrs. Reynolds, I got a chance to be captain of the baseball team next year.

LAURA. I know. And I have no right to ask you to give up that chance. But I wish somehow or other you could figure out a way . . . so it wouldn't hurt Tom.

[TOM *comes in the hall and goes up the stairs. He's pretty broken up, and mad. After a few moments he appears in his room, shuts the door, and sits on the bed, trying to figure something out.*]

AL [*as* TOM *enters house*]. Well . . .

LAURA. That's Tom now. [AL *looks at her, wondering how she knows.*] I know all your footsteps. He's coming in for tea. [AL *starts to move to door.*] Well, Al? [AL *makes a helpless motion.*] You still want me to tell Mr. Reynolds about your moving next year?

AL [*after a moment*]. No.

LAURA. Good.

AL. I mean, I'll tell him when I see him.

LAURA. Oh.

AL [*turns on her*]. What can I do?

LAURA. I don't know.

AL. Excuse me for saying so, but it's easy for you to talk

the way you have. You're not involved. You're just
a bystander. You're not going to be hurt. Nothing's
going to happen to you one way or the other. I'm
sorry.

LAURA. That's a fair criticism, Al. I'm sorry I asked
you ... As you say, I'm not involved.

AL. I'm sorry. I think you're swell, Mrs. Reynolds.
You're the nicest housemaster's wife I've ever ran
into ... I mean ... Well, you know what I mean.
It's only that ... [*He is flustered. He opens the
door.*] I'm sorry.

LAURA. I'm sorry, too, Al.

[*She smiles at him.* AL *stands in the doorway for a moment, not knowing whether to go out the hall door
or go upstairs. Finally, he goes upstairs, and into the
study door.* LAURA *stands thinking over what* AL *has
said, even repeating to herself, "I'm not involved."
She then goes into the alcove and off.*]

AL [*outside* TOM'S *bedroom door*]. Tom? [TOM *moves
quietly away from the door.*] Tom? [*He opens the
door.*] Hey.

TOM. I was sleeping.

AL. Standing up, huh? [TOM *turns away.*] You want to
be alone?

TOM. No. You want to look. Go ahead. [*He indicates
the window.*]

AL. No, I don't want to look, I ... [*He looks at* TOM,
not knowing how to begin ... He stalls ... smiling.]
Nice tie you got there.

TOM [*starts to undo tie*]. Yeah, it's yours. You want it?

AL. No. Why? I can only wear one tie at a time. [TOM
*leaves it hanging around his neck. After an awkward
pause.*] I ... uh ...

TOM. I guess I don't need to ask you what's the matter?

AL. It's been rough today, huh?

TOM. Yeah. [*He turns away, very upset. He's been holding it in ... but here's his closest friend asking him
to open up.*] Jesus Christ! [AL *doesn't know what to*

say. He goes to TOM's *bureau and picks up his hair-brush, gives his hair a few brushes.*] Anybody talk to you?

AL. Sure. You know they would.

TOM. What do they say?

AL [*yanks his tie off*]. Hell, I don't know.

TOM. I went to a meeting of the dance committee. I'm no longer on the dance committee. Said that since I'd backed out of playing the part in the play, I didn't show the proper spirit. That's what they *said* was the reason.

AL [*loud*]. Why the hell don't you do something about it?

TOM [*yelling back*]. About what?

AL. About what they're saying.

TOM. What the hell can I do?

AL. Geez, you could . . . [*He suddenly wonders what* TOM *could do.*] I don't know.

TOM. I tried to pass it off. Christ, you can't pass it off. You know, when I went into the showers today after my tennis match, everyone who was in there, grabbed a towel and . . . and . . . walked out.

AL. They're stupid. Just a bunch of stupid bastards. [*He leaves the room.*]

TOM [*following him into sitting room*]. Goddamn it, the awful thing I found myself . . . Jesus, I don't know . . . I found myself self-conscious about things I've been doing for years. Dressing, undressing . . . I keep my eyes on the floor . . . [*Re-enters his own room.*] Geez, if I even look at a guy that doesn't have any clothes on, I'm afraid someone's gonna say something, or . . . Jesus, I don't know.

AL [*during this,* AL *has come back into the room, un-buttoning his shirt, taking it off. Suddenly he stops*]. What the hell am I doing? I've had a shower today. [*He tries to laugh.*]

TOM [*looks at him a moment*]. Undress in your own

room, will ya? You don't want them talking about you too, do you?

AL. No I don't. [*He has said this very definitely and with meaning.*]

TOM [*looks up at his tone of voice*]. Of course you don't. [*He looks at* AL *a long time. He hardly dares say this.*] You ... uh ... you moving out?

AL [*doesn't want to answer*]. Look, Tom, do you mind if I try to help you?

TOM. Hell, no. How?

AL. I know this is gonna burn your tail, and I know it sounds stupid as hell. But it isn't stupid. It's the way people look at things. You could do a lot for yourself, just the way you talk and look.

TOM. You mean get my hair cut?

AL. For one thing.

TOM. Why the hell should a man with a crew cut look more manly than a guy who—

AL. Look, I don't know the reasons for these things. It's just the way they are.

TOM [*looking at himself in bureau mirror*]. I tried a crew cut a coupla times. I haven't got that kind of hair, or that kind of head. [*After a moment.*] Sorry, I didn't mean to yell at you. Thanks for trying to help.

AL [*finds a baseball on the radiator and throws it at* TOM. TOM *smiles, and throws it back*]. Look, Tom, the way you walk ...

TOM. Oh, Jesus.

AL [*flaring*]. Look, I'm trying to help you.

TOM. No one gave a goddamn about how I walked till last Saturday!

AL [*starts to go*]. Okay, okay. Forget it. [*He goes out.*]

TOM [*stands there a few moments, then slams the baseball into the bed and walks out after* AL *into sitting room*]. Al?

AL [*off*]. Yeah?

TOM. Tell me about how I walk.

AL [*in the sitting room*]. Go ahead, walk!

TOM [*walks back into the bedroom.* AL *follows him, wiping his face on a towel and watching* TOM *walk. After he has walked a bit*]. Now I'm not going to be able to walk any more. Everything I been doing all my life makes me look like a fairy.

AL. Go on.

TOM. All right, now I'm walking. Tell me.

AL. Tom, I don't know. You walk sort of light.

TOM. Light? [*He looks at himself take a step.*]

AL. Yeah.

TOM. Show me.

AL. No, I can't do it.

TOM. Okay. You walk. Let me watch you. I never noticed how you walked. [AL *stands there for a moment, never having realized before how difficult it could be to walk if you think about it. Finally he walks.*] Do it again.

AL. If you go telling any of the guys about this ...

TOM. Do you think I would? ... [AL *walks again.*] That's a good walk. I'll try to copy it. [*He tries to copy the walk, but never succeeds in taking even a step.*] Do you really think that'll make any difference?

AL. I dunno.

TOM. Not now it won't. Thanks anyway.

AL [*comes and sits on bed beside* TOM. *Puts his arm around* TOM's *shoulder and thinks this thing out*]. Look, Tom ... You've been in on a lot of bull sessions. You heard the guys talking about stopping over in Boston on the way home ... getting girls ... you know.

TOM. Sure. What about it?

AL. You're not going to the dance Saturday night?

TOM. No. Not now.

AL. You know Ellie Martin. The gal who waits on table down at the soda joint?

TOM. Yeah. What about her?

AL. You've heard the guys talking about her.

TOM. Come on, come on.

AL. Why don't you drop in on Ellie Saturday night?

TOM. What do you mean?

AL. Hell, do you want me to draw a picture?

TOM [*with disgust*]. Ellie Martin?

AL. Okay. I know she's a dog, but . . .

TOM. So what good's that going to do? I get caught there, I get thrown out of school.

AL. No one ever gets caught. Sunday morning people'd hear about it . . . not the Dean . . . I mean the fellows. Hell, Ellie tells and tells and tells . . . Boy, you'd be made!

TOM. Are you kidding?

AL. No.

TOM [*with disgust*]. Ellie Martin!

AL [*after a long pause*]. Look, I've said so much already, I might as well be a complete bastard . . . You ever been with a woman?

TOM. What do you think?

AL. I don't think you have.

TOM. So?

AL. You want to know something?

TOM. What?

AL. Neither have I. But if you tell the guys, I'll murder you.

TOM. All those stories you told . . .

AL. Okay, I'll be sorry I told you.

TOM. Then why don't you go see Ellie Martin Saturday night?

AL. Why the hell should I?

TOM. You mean you don't have to prove anything?

AL. Aw, forget it. It's probably a lousy idea anyway. [*He starts out.*]

TOM. Yeah.

AL [*stops*]. Look, about next— [*Stops.*]

TOM. Next year? Yes?

AL. Hap Hudson's asked me to come to his house. He's got a single there. A lot of the fellows from the team are over there, and . . . well . . . [*He doesn't look at* TOM.]

TOM. Sure, sure . . . I understand.

AL. Sorry I didn't tell you till now, after we'd made our plans. But I didn't know. I mean, I just found out about the . . . the opening.

TOM. I understand!

AL [*looks up at last. He hates himself but he's done it, and it's a load off his chest*]. See ya. [*He starts to go.*]

TOM [*as* AL *gets to door*]. Al . . . [AL *stops and looks back. Taking tie from around his neck.*] Here.

AL [*looks at tie, embarrassed*]. I said wear it. Keep it.

TOM. It's yours.

AL [*looks at the tie for a long time, then without taking it, goes through the door*]. See ya.

[TOM *folds the tie neatly, dazed, then seeing what he's doing, he throws it viciously in the direction of the bureau, and turns and stares out the window. He puts a record on the phonograph.*]

BILL [*comes in to the study from the hall, carrying a pair of shoes and a slim book. As he opens his study door, he hears the music upstairs. He stands in the door and listens, remembering his miserable boyhood. Then he comes in and closes the door*]. Laura. [*Throws shoes on floor near footstool.*]

LAURA [*off stage, calling*]. Bill?

BILL. Yes.

LAURA [*coming in with tea things*]. I didn't think you'd be back before your class. Have some tea.

BILL. I beat young Harvey at handball.

LAURA. Good.

BILL. At last. It took some doing, though. He was after my scalp because of that D minus I gave him in his last exam. [*Gives her book.*] You wanted this . . . book of poems.

LAURA [*looks at book. Her eyes shift quickly to the*

same book in the chair]. Why yes. How did you know?

BILL [*trying to be very offhand about it*]. The notice from the bookstore.

LAURA. That's very nice of you. [*She moves toward him to kiss him, but at this moment, in picking some wrapping paper from the armchair, he notices the duplicate copy.*]

BILL [*a little angry*]. You've already got it.

LAURA. Why, yes . . . I . . . well, I . . . [BILL *picking it up . . . opens it.*] That is, someone gave it to me. [BILL *reads the inscription.*] Tom knew I wanted it, and . . .

BILL [*looks at her, a terrible look coming into his face. Then he slowly rips the book in two and hurls it into the fireplace*]. Damn!

LAURA. Bill! [BILL *goes to footstool and sits down and begins to change his shoes.*] Bill, what difference does it make that he gave me the book? He knew I wanted it too.

BILL. I don't know. It's just that every time I try to do something . . .

LAURA. Bill, how can you say that? It isn't so.

BILL. It is.

LAURA. Bill, this thing of the book is funny.

BILL. I don't think it's very funny.

LAURA [*going behind him, and kneeling by his side*]. Bill, I'm very touched that you should have remembered. Thank you. [*He turns away from her and goes on with his shoes.*] Bill, don't turn away. I want to thank you. [*As she gets no response from him, she rises.*] Is it such a chore to let yourself be thanked? [*She puts her hands on his shoulders, trying to embrace him.*] Oh, Bill, we so rarely touch any more. I keep feeling I'm losing contact with you. Don't you feel that?

BILL [*looking at his watch*]. Laura, I . . .

LAURA [*she backs away from him*]. I know, you've got

to go. But it's just that, I don't know, we don't touch any more. It's a silly way of putting it, but you seem to hold yourself aloof from me. A tension seems to grow between us . . . and then when we do . . . touch . . . it's a violent thing . . . almost a compulsive thing. [BILL *is uncomfortable at this accurate description of their relationship. He sits troubled. She puts her arms around his neck and embraces him, bending over him.*] You don't feel it? You don't feel yourself holding away from me until it becomes overpowering? There's no growing together any more . . . no quiet times, just holding hands, the feeling of closeness, like it was in Italy. Now it's long separations and then this almost brutal coming together, and . . . Oh, Bill, you do see, you do see. [BILL *suddenly straightens up, toughens, and looks at her.* LAURA *repulsed, slowly draws her arms from around his shoulders.*]

BILL. For God's sake, Laura, what are you talking about? [*He rises and goes to his desk.*] It can't always be a honeymoon.

[*Upstairs in his room,* TOM *turns off the phonograph, and leaves the room, going out into the hall and up the stairs.*]

LAURA. Do you think that's what I'm talking about?

BILL. I don't know why you chose a time like this to talk about things like . . .

LAURA. . . . I don't know why, either. I just wanted to thank you for the book . . . [*Moves away and looks in book.*] What did you write in it?

BILL [*starts to mark exam papers*]. Nothing. Why? Should I write in it? I just thought you wanted the book.

LAURA. Of course . . . Are you sure you won't have some tea? [*She bends over the tea things.*]

BILL. Yes.

LAURA [*straightening up, trying another tack of return-*

ing to normality]. Little Joan Harrison is coming over for tea.

BILL. No, she isn't. [LAURA *looks inquiringly.*] I just saw her father at the gym. I don't think that was a very smart thing for you to do, Laura.

LAURA. I thought Tom might take her to the dance Saturday. He's on the committee, and he has no girl to take.

BILL. I understand he's no longer on the committee. You're a hostess, aren't you?

LAURA. Yes.

BILL. I've got the mountain-climbing business this week-end. Weather man predicts rain.

LAURA [*almost breaks. Hides her face in her hands. Then recovers*]. That's too bad. [*After a moment.*] Bill?

BILL. Yes?

LAURA. I think someone should go to the Dean about Tom and the hazing he's getting.

BILL. What could the Dean do? Announce from chapel, "You've got to stop riding Tom. You've got to stop calling him Grace?" Is that what you'd like him to do?

LAURA. No. I suppose not.

BILL. You know we're losing Al next year because of Tom.

LAURA. Oh, you've heard?

BILL. Yes, Hudson tells me he's moving over to his house. He'll probably be captain of the baseball team. Last time we had a major sport captain was eight years ago.

LAURA. Yes, I'm sorry.

BILL. However, we'll also be losing Tom.

LAURA. Oh?

BILL [*noting her increased interest*]. Yes. We have no singles in this house, and he'll be rooming alone.

LAURA. I'm sorry to hear that.

BILL [*he turns to look at her*]. I knew you would be.

LAURA. Why should my interest in this boy make you angry?

BILL. I'm not angry.

LAURA. You're not only angry. It's almost as though you were, well, jealous.

BILL. Oh, come on now.

LAURA. Well, how else can you explain your . . . your vindictive attitude toward him?

BILL. Why go into it again? Jealous! [*He has his books together now. Goes to the door.*] I'll go directly from class to the dining hall. All right?

LAURA. Yes, of course.

BILL. And please, please, Laura . . . [*He stops.*]

LAURA. I'll try.

BILL. I know you like to be different, just for the sake of being different . . . and I like you for that . . . But this time, lay off. Show your fine free spirit on something else.

LAURA. On something that can't hurt us?

BILL. All right. Sure. I don't mind putting it that way. And Laura?

LAURA. Yes?

BILL. Seeing Tom so much . . . having him down for tea alone all the time . . .

LAURA. Yes?

BILL. I think you should have him down only when you have the other boys . . . for his own good. I mean that. Well, I'll see you in the dining hall. Try to be on time. [*He goes out.* LAURA *brings her hands to her face, and cries, leaning against the back of the chair.* AL *has come tumbling out of the door to his room with books in hand, and is coming down the stairs. Going down the hall.*] You going to class, Al?

AL. Hello, Mr. Reynolds. Yes I am.

BILL [*as they go*]. Let's walk along together. I'm sorry to hear that you're moving across the street next year. [*And they are gone out the door.*]

TOM [*has come down the stairs, and now stands looking at the hall telephone. He is carrying his coat. After a long moment's deliberation, he puts in a coin and dials*]. Hello, I'd like to speak to Ellie Martin, please. [LAURA *has moved to pick up the torn book which her husband has thrown in the fireplace. She is smoothing it out, as she suddenly hears* TOM'S *voice in the hall. She can't help but hear what he is saying. She stands stock still and listens, her alarm and concern showing on her face.*] Hello, Ellie? This is Tom Lee ... Tom Lee. I'm down at the soda fountain all the time with my roommate, Al Thompson ... Yeah, the guys do sometimes call me that ... Well, I'll tell you what I wanted. I wondered if ... you see, I'm not going to the dance Saturday night, and I wondered if you're doing anything? Yeah, I guess that is a hell of a way to ask for a date ... but I just wondered if I could maybe drop by and pick you up after work on Saturday ... I don't know what's *in* it for you, Ellie ... but something I guess. I just thought I'd like to see you ... What time do you get through work? ... Okay, nine o'clock. [LAURA *having heard this, goes out through the alcove. About to hang up.*] Oh, thanks. [*He stands for a moment, contemplating what he's done, then he slips on his jacket, and goes to the study door and knocks. After a moment, he opens the door and enters.*]

LAURA [*coming from the other room with a plate of cookies*]. Oh, there you are. I've got your favorites today.

TOM. Mrs. Reynolds, do you mind if I don't come to tea this afternoon?

LAURA. Why ... if you don't want to ... How are you? [*She really means this question.*]

TOM. I'm okay.

LAURA. Good.

TOM. I just don't feel like tea.

LAURA. Perhaps, it's just as well . . . Joan can't make it today, either.

TOM. I didn't expect she would. She's nothing special; just a kid.

LAURA. Something about a dentist appointment or something.

TOM. It wouldn't have done any good anyway. I'm not going to the dance.

LAURA. Oh?

TOM. Another member of the committee will stop around for you.

LAURA. What will you be doing?

TOM. I don't know. I can take care of myself.

LAURA. If you're not going, that gives me an easy out. I won't have to go.

TOM. Just because I'm not going?

LAURA [*in an effort to keep him from going to* ELLIE]. Look, Tom . . . now that neither of us is going, why don't you drop down here after supper, Saturday night. We could listen to some records, or play gin, or we can just talk.

TOM. I . . . I don't think you'd better count on me.

LAURA. I'd like to.

TOM. No, really. I don't want to sound rude . . . but I . . . I may have another engagement.

LAURA. Oh?

TOM. I'd like to come. Please understand that. It's what I'd like to do . . . but . . .

LAURA. Well, I'll be here just in case, just in case you decide to come in. [LAURA *extends her hand.*] I hope you'll be feeling better.

TOM [*hesitates, then takes her hand*]. Thanks.

LAURA. Maybe your plans will change.

[TOM *looks at her, wishing they would; knowing they won't. He runs out and down the hall as the lights fade out on* LAURA *standing at the door.*]

CURTAIN

SCENE II

The time is eight-forty-five on Saturday night.

In the study a low fire is burning. As the curtain rises, the town clock is striking the three quarter hour. LAURA *is sitting in her chair sipping a cup of coffee. The door to the study is open slightly. She is waiting for* TOM. *She is wearing a lovely but informal dress, and a single flower. In his room,* TOM *listens to the clock strike. He has just been shaving. He is putting shaving lotion on his face. His face is tense and nervous. There is no joy in the preparations. In a moment, he turns and leaves the room, taking off his belt as he goes.*

After a moment, LILLY *comes to the study door, knocks and comes in.*

LILLY. Laura?

LAURA. Oh, Lilly.

LILLY [*standing in the doorway, a raincoat held over her head. She is dressed in a low-cut evening gown, which she wears very well*]. You're not dressed yet. Why aren't you dressed for the dance?

LAURA [*still in her chair*]. I'm not going. I thought I told you.

LILLY [*deposits raincoat and goes immediately to look at herself in mirror next to the door*]. Oh, for Heaven's sake, why not? Just because Bill's away with his loathsome little mountain climbers?

LAURA. Well . . .

LILLY. Come along with us. It's raining on and off, so Harry's going to drive us in the car.

LAURA. No, thanks.

LILLY. If you come, Harry will dance with you all evening. You won't be lonely, I promise you. [LAURA *shakes her head, "no."*] You're the only one who can dance those funny steps with him.

LAURA. It's very sweet of you, but no.

LILLY [*at the mirror*]. Do you think this neck is too low?

LAURA. I think you look lovely.

LILLY. Harry says this neck will drive all the little boys crazy.

LAURA. I don't think so.

LILLY. Well, that's not very flattering.

LAURA. I mean, I think they'll appreciate it, but as for driving them crazy . . .

LILLY. After all I want to give them some reward for dancing their duty dances with me.

LAURA. I'm sure when they dance with you, it's no duty, Lilly. I've seen you at these dances.

LILLY. It's not this . . . [*Indicating her bosom.*] it's my line of chatter. I'm oh so interested in what courses they're taking, where they come from and where they learned to dance so divinely.

LAURA [*laughing*]. Lilly, you're lost in a boys' school. You were meant to shine some place much more glamorous.

LILLY. I wouldn't trade it for the world. Where else could a girl indulge in three hundred innocent flirtations a year?

LAURA. Lilly, I've often wondered what you'd do if one of the three hundred attempted to go, well, a little further than innocent flirtation.

LILLY. I'd slap him down . . . the little beast. [*She laughs and admires herself in mirror.*] Harry says if I'm not careful I'll get to looking like Ellie Martin. You've seen Ellie.

LAURA. I saw her this afternoon for the first time.

LILLY. Really? The first time?

LAURA. Yes. I went into the place where she works . . . the soda shop . . .

LILLY. You!

LAURA. Yes . . . uh . . . for a package of cigarettes. [*After a moment she says with some sadness.*] She's not even pretty, is she?

LILLY [*turns from admiring herself at the tone in* LAURA'S *voice*]. Well, honey, don't sound so sad. What difference should it make to you if she's pretty or not?

LAURA. I don't know. It just seems so . . . they're so young.

LILLY. If they're stupid enough to go to Ellie Martin, they deserve whatever happens to them. Anyway, Laura, the boys *talk* more about Ellie than anything else. So don't fret about it.

LAURA [*arranges chair for* TOM *facing fireplace. Notices* LILLY *primping*]. You look lovely, Lilly.

LILLY. Maybe I'd better wear that corsage the dance committee sent, after all . . . right here. [*She indicates low point in dress.*] I was going to carry it—or rather Harry was going to help me carry it. You know, it's like one of those things people put on Civil War monuments on Decoration Day.

LAURA. Yes, I've seen them.

LILLY [*indicating the flower* LAURA *is wearing*]. Now that's tasteful. Where'd you get that?

LAURA. Uh . . . I bought it for myself.

LILLY. Oh, now.

LAURA. It's always been a favorite of mine and I saw it in the florist's window.

LILLY. Well, Harry will be waiting for me to tie his bow tie. [*Starts toward door.*] Will you be up when we get back?

LAURA [*giving* LILLY *her raincoat*]. Probably not.

LILLY. If there's a light on, I'll drop in and tell you how many I had to slap down . . . Night-night.

[*She leaves.* LAURA *stands at the closed door until she hears the outside door close. Then she opens her door a bit. She takes her cup of coffee and stands in front of the fireplace and listens.*]

TOM [*as* LILLY *goes, he returns to his room, dressed in a blue suit. He stands there deliberating a moment, then reaches under his pillow and brings out a pint bottle of whisky. He takes a short swig. It gags him. He corks it and puts it back under the pillow*]. Christ, I'll never make it. [*He reaches in his closet and pulls out a raincoat, then turns and snaps out the room light, and goes out. A moment later, he appears on the stairs. He sees* LAURA's *door partly open, and while he is putting on his raincoat, he walks warily past it.*]

LAURA [*when she hears* TOM's *door close, she stands still and listens more intently. She hears him pass her door and go to the front door. She puts down the cup of coffee, and goes to the study door. She calls*]. Tom? [*After some moments,* TOM *appears in the door, and she opens it wide.*] I've been expecting you.

TOM. I . . . I . . .

LAURA [*opening the door wide*]. Are you going to the dance, after all?

TOM [*comes in the door*]. No . . . You can report me if you want. Out after hours. Or . . . [*He looks up at her finally.*] Or you can give me permission. Can I have permission to go out?

LAURA [*moving into the room, says pleasantly*]. I think I'd better get you some coffee.

TOM [*at her back, truculent*]. You can tell them that, too . . . that I've been drinking. There'll be lots to tell before— [*He stops.*] I didn't drink much. But I didn't eat much either.

LAURA. Let me get you something to eat.

TOM [*as though convincing himself*]. No. I can't stay!

LAURA. All right. But I'm glad you dropped in. I was counting on it.

TOM [*chip on shoulder*]. I said I might not. When you invited me.

LAURA. I know. [*She looks at him a moment. He is to her a heartbreaking sight . . . all dressed up as though he were going to a prom, but instead he's going to* ELLIE *. . . the innocence and the desperation touch her deeply . . . and this shows in her face as she circles behind him to the door.*] It's a nasty night out, isn't it?

TOM. Yes.

LAURA. I'm just as glad I'm not going to the dance. [*She shuts the door gently.* TOM, *at the sound of the door, turns and sees what she has done.*] It'll be nice just to stay here by the fire.

TOM. I wasn't planning to come in.

LAURA. Then why the flower . . . and the card? "For a pleasant evening?"

TOM. It was for the dance. I forgot to cancel it.

LAURA. I'm glad you didn't.

TOM. Why? [*He stops studying the curtains and looks at her.*]

LAURA [*moving into the room again*]. Well, for one thing I like to get flowers. For another thing . . . [TOM *shakes his head a little to clear it.*] Let me make you some coffee.

TOM. No. I'm just about right.

LAURA. Or you can drink this . . . I just had a sip. [*She holds up the cup.* TOM *looks at the proffered coffee.*] You can drink from this side. [*She indicates the other side of the cup.*]

TOM [*takes the cup, and looks at the side where her lips have touched and then slowly turns it around to the other and takes a sip*]. And for another thing?

LAURA. What do you mean?

TOM. For one thing you like to get flowers . . .

LAURA. For another it's nice to have flowers on my anniversary.

TOM. Anniversary?

LAURA. Yes.

TOM [*waving the cup and saucer around*]. And Mr. Reynolds on a mountain top with twenty stalwart youths, soaking wet . . . Didn't he remember?

LAURA [*rescues the cup and saucer*]. It's not that anniversary. [TOM *looks at her wondering. Seeing that she has interested him, she moves toward him.*] Let me take your coat.

TOM [*definitely*]. I can't—

LAURA. I know. You can't stay. But . . . [*She comes up behind him and puts her hand on his shoulders to take off his coat. He can hardly stand her touch. She gently peels his coat from him and stands back to look at him.*] How nice you look!

TOM [*disarranging his hair or tie*]. Put me in a blue suit and I look like a kid.

LAURA. How did you know I liked this flower?

TOM. You mentioned it.

LAURA. You're very quick to notice these things. So was he.

TOM [*after a moment, his curiosity aroused*]. Who?

LAURA. My first husband. That's the anniversary.

TOM. I didn't know.

LAURA [*sits in her chair*]. Mr. Reynolds doesn't like me to talk about my first husband. He was, I'd say, about your age. How old are you, Tom?

TOM. Eighteen . . . tomorrow.

LAURA. Tomorrow . . . We must celebrate.

TOM. You'd better not make any plans.

LAURA. He was *just* your age then. [*She looks at him again with slight wonder.*] It doesn't seem possible now, looking at you . . .

TOM. Why, do I look like such a child?

LAURA. Why no.

TOM. Men are married at my age.

LAURA. Of course, they are. *He* was. Maybe a few months older. Such a lonely boy, away from home for the first time . . . and . . . and going off to war. [TOM *looks up inquiringly.*] Yes, he was killed.

TOM. I'm sorry ... but I'm glad to hear about him.

LAURA. Glad?

TOM. Yes. I don't know ... He sounds like someone you *should* have been married to, not ... [*Stops.*] I'm sorry if I ... [*Stops.*]

LAURA [*after a moment*]. He was killed being conspicuously brave. He had to be conspicuously brave, you see, because something had happened in training camp ... I don't know what ... and he was afraid the others thought him a coward ... He showed them he wasn't.

TOM. He had that satisfaction.

LAURA. What was it worth if it killed him?

TOM. I don't know. But I can understand.

LAURA. Of course you can. You're very like him.

TOM. Me?

LAURA [*holding out the coffee cup*]. Before I finish it all? [TOM *comes over and takes a sip from his side of the cup.*] He was kind and gentle, and lonely. [TOM *turns away in embarrassment at hearing himself so described.*] We knew it wouldn't last ... We sensed it ... But he always said, "Why must the test of everything be its durability?"

TOM. I'm sorry he was killed.

LAURA. Yes, so am I. I'm sorry he was killed the way he was killed ... trying to prove how brave he was. In trying to prove he was a man, he died a boy.

TOM. Still he must have died happy.

LAURA. Because he proved his courage?

TOM. That ... and because he was married to you. [*Embarrassed, he walks to his coat which she has been holding in her lap.*] I've got to go.

LAURA. Tom, please.

TOM. I've got to.

LAURA. It must be a very important engagement.

TOM. It is.

LAURA. If you go now, I'll think I bored you, talking all about myself.

TOM. You haven't.

LAURA. I probably shouldn't have gone on like that. It's just that I felt like it . . . a rainy spring night . . . a fire. I guess I'm in a reminiscent mood. Do you ever get in reminiscing moods on nights like this?

TOM. About what?

LAURA. Oh, come now . . . there must be something pleasant to remember, or someone. [TOM *stands by the door beginning to think back, his raincoat in his hand, but still dragging on the floor.*] Isn't there? . . . Of course there is. Who was it, or don't you want to tell?

TOM [*after a long silence*]. May I have a cigarette?

LAURA [*relieved that she has won another moment's delay*]. Yes. Of course. [*Hands him a box, then lights his cigarette.*]

TOM. My seventh-grade teacher.

LAURA. What?

TOM. That's who I remember.

LAURA. Oh.

TOM. Miss Middleton . . .

LAURA. How sweet.

TOM [*drops the raincoat again, and moves into the room*]. It wasn't sweet. It was terrible.

LAURA. At that time, of course . . . Tell me about her.

TOM. She was just out of college . . . tall, blonde, honey-colored hair . . . and she wore a polo coat, and drove a convertible.

LAURA. Sounds very fetching.

TOM. Ever since then I've been a sucker for girls in polo coats.

LAURA [*smiling*]. I have one somewhere.

TOM. Yes, I know. [*He looks at her.*]

LAURA. What happened?

TOM. What could happen? As usual I made a fool of myself. I guess everyone knew I was in love with her. People I like, I can't help showing it.

LAURA. That's a good trait.

TOM. When she used to go on errands and she needed one of the boys to go along and help carry something, there I was.

LAURA. She liked you too, then.

TOM. This is a stupid thing to talk about.

LAURA. I can see why she liked you.

TOM. I thought she . . . I thought she loved me. I was twelve years old.

LAURA. Maybe she did.

TOM. Anyway, when I was in eighth grade, she got married. And you know what they made me do? They gave a luncheon at school in her honor, and I had to be the toastmaster and wish her happiness and everything . . . I had to write a poem . . . [*He quotes.*]

"Now that you are going to be married,
And away from us be carried,
Before you promise to love, honor and obey,
There are a few things I want to say."

[*He shakes his head as they both laugh.*] From there on it turned out to be more of a love poem than anything else.

LAURA [*as she stops laughing*]. Puppy love can be heartbreaking.

TOM [*the smile dying quickly as he looks at her. Then after what seems like forever*]. I'm always falling in love with the wrong people.

LAURA. Who isn't?

TOM. You too?

LAURA. It wouldn't be any fun if we didn't. Of course, nothing ever comes of it, but there are bittersweet memories, and they can be pleasant. [*Kidding him as friend to friend, trying to get him to smile again.*] Who else have you been desperately in love with?

TOM [*he doesn't answer. Then he looks at his watch*]. It's almost nine . . . I'm late. [*Starts to go.*]

LAURA [*rising*]. I can't persuade you to stay? [TOM *shakes his head, "no."*] We were getting on so well.

TOM. Thanks.

LAURA. In another moment I would have told you all the deep, dark secrets of my life.

TOM. I'm sorry. [*He picks up his coat from the floor.*]

LAURA [*desperately trying to think of something to keep him from going*]. Won't you stay even for a dance?

TOM. I don't dance.

LAURA. I was going to teach you. [*She goes over to the phonograph and snaps on the button.*]

TOM [*opens the door*]. Some other time . . .

LAURA. Please, for me. [*She comes back.*]

TOM [*after a moment he closes the door*]. Tell me something.

LAURA. Yes?

[*The record starts to play, something soft and melodic. It plays through to the end of the act.*]

TOM. Why are you so nice to me?

LAURA. Why . . . I . . .

TOM. You're not this way to the rest of the fellows.

LAURA. No, I know I'm not. Do you mind my being nice to you?

TOM [*shakes his head, "no"*]. I just wondered why.

LAURA [*in a perfectly open way*]. I guess, Tom . . . I guess it's because I like you.

TOM. No one else seems to. Why do you?

LAURA. I don't know . . . I . . .

TOM. Is it *because* no one else likes me? Is it just pity?

LAURA. No, Tom, no, of course not . . . It's, well . . . it's because you've been very nice to me . . . very considerate. It wasn't easy for me, you know, coming into a school, my first year. You seemed to sense that. I don't know, we just seem to have hit it off. [*She smiles at him.*]

TOM. Mr. Reynolds knows you like me.

LAURA. I suppose so. I haven't kept it a secret.

TOM. Is that why he hates me so?

LAURA. I don't think he hates you.

TOM. Yes, he hates me. Why lie? I think everyone here hates me but you. But they won't.

LAURA. Of course they won't.

TOM. He hates me because he made a flop with me. I know all about it. My father put me in this house when I first came here, and when he left he said to your husband, "Make a man out of him." He's failed, and he's mad, and then you came along, and were nice to me . . . out of pity.

LAURA. No, Tom, not pity. I'm too selfish a woman to like you just out of pity.

TOM [*he has worked himself up into a state of confusion, and anger, and desperation*]. There's so much I . . . there's so much I don't understand.

LAURA [*reaches out and touches his arm*]. Tom, don't go out tonight.

TOM. I've got to. That's one thing that's clear. I've got to!

LAURA [*holds up her arms for dancing*]. Won't you let me teach you how to dance?

TOM [*suddenly and impulsively he throws his arms around her, and kisses her passionately, awkwardly, and then in embarrassment he buries his head in her shoulder*]. Oh, God . . . God.

LAURA. Tom . . . Tom . . . [TOM *raises his face and looks at her, and would kiss her again.*] No, Tom . . . No, I . . . [*At the first "No,"* TOM *breaks from her and runs out the door halfway up the stairs. Calling.*] Tom! . . . Tom! [TOM *stops at the sound of her voice and turns around and looks down the stairs.* LAURA *moves to the open door.*] Tom, I . . .

[*The front door opens and two of the mountain-climbing boys,* PHIL *and* PAUL *come in, with their packs.*]

PHIL [*seeing* TOM *poised on the stairs*]. What the hell are you doing? [TOM *just looks at him.*] What's the matter with you? [*He goes on and up the stairs.*]

TOM. What are you doing back?

PAUL. The whole bunch is back. Who wants to go mountain climbing in the rain?

BILL [*outside his study door*]. Say, any of you fellows who want to go across the street for something to eat when you get changed, go ahead. [PHIL *and* PAUL *go up the stairs past* TOM. BILL *goes into his own room, leaving door open.*] Hi. [*He takes off his equipment and puts it on the floor.*]

LAURA [*has been standing motionless where* TOM *has left her*]. Hello.

BILL [*comes to her and kisses her on the cheek*]. One lousy week-end a year we get to go climbing and it rains. [*Throws the rest of his stuff down.*] The fellows are damned disappointed.

LAURA [*hardly paying any attention to him*]. That's too bad.

BILL [*going up to alcove*]. I think they wanted me to invite them down for a feed. But I didn't want to. I thought we'd be alone. Okay? [*He looks across at her.*]

LAURA [*she is listening for footsteps outside*]. Sure. [BILL *goes out through alcove.* LAURA *stoops and picks up the raincoat which* TOM *has dropped and hides it in the cabinet by the fireplace.*]

BILL [*appears in door momentarily wiping his hands with towel*]. Boy it really rained. [*He disappears again.* LAURA *sadly goes to the door and slowly and gently closes it. When she is finished, she leans against the door, listening, hoping against hope that* TOM *will go upstairs. When* TOM *sees the door close, he stands there for a moment, then turns his coat collar up and goes down the hall and out. Off stage as* TOM *starts to go down the hall.*] We never made it to the timberline. The rain started to come down. Another hour or so and we would have got to the hut and spent the night, but the fellows wouldn't hear of it . . . [*The door slams.* LAURA *turns away from the study door in despair. Still off stage.*] What was that?

LAURA. Nothing ... Nothing at all.

BILL [*enters and gets pipe from mantelpiece*]. Good to get out, though. Makes you feel alive. Think I'll go out again next Saturday, alone. Won't be bothered by the fellows wanting to turn back.

[*He has settled down in the chair intended for* TOM. *The school bells start to ring nine.* BILL *reaches out his hand for* LAURA. *Standing by the door, she looks at his outstretched hand, as the lights fade, and*

THE CURTAIN FALLS

Act three

The time is late the next afternoon.

As the curtain rises, TOM *is in his room. His door is shut and bolted. He is lying on his back on the bed, staring up at the ceiling.*

RALPH [*he is at the phone*]. Hello, Mary ... Ralph ... Yeah, I just wanted you to know I'd be a little delayed picking you up ... Yeah ... everyone was taking a shower over here, and there's only one shower for eight guys ... No it's not the same place as last night ... The tea dance is at the Inn ... [*He suddenly looks very uncomfortable.*] Look, I'll tell you when I see you ... Okay ... [*Almost whispers it.*] I love you ... [STEVE, RALPH's *sidekick, comes running in from the outside. He's all dressed up and he's got something to tell.*] Yeah, Mary. Well, I can't say it over again ... Didn't you hear me the first time? [*Loud so she'll hear it.*] Hi, Steve.

STEVE. Come on, get off. I got something to tell you.

RALPH. Mary—Mary, I'll get there faster if I stop talking now. Okay? Okay. See you a little after four. [*He hangs up.*] What the hell's the matter with you?

STEVE. Have you seen Tom?

RALPH. No.

STEVE. You know what the hell he did last night?

RALPH. What?

STEVE. He went and saw Ellie.

RALPH. Who are you bulling?

STEVE. No, honest. Ellie told Jackson over at the kitchen. Everybody knows now.

RALPH. What did he want to go and do a thing like that for?

STEVE. But wait a minute. You haven't heard the half of it.

RALPH. Listen, I gotta get dressed. [*Starts upstairs.*]

STEVE [*on their way up the stairs*]. The way Ellie tells it, he went there, all the hell dressed up like he was going to the dance, and . . .

[*They disappear up the stairs.* BILL *after a moment, comes in the hall, and goes quickly up the stairs. He goes right into* AL *and* TOM'S *main room without knocking. We then hear him try the handle of* TOM'S *bedroom door.* TOM *looks at the door defiantly and sullenly.*]

BILL [*knocks sharply*]. Tom! [*Rattles door some more.*] Tom, this is Mr. Reynolds. Let me in.

TOM. I don't want to see anyone.

BILL. You've got to see me. Come on. Open up! I've got to talk to the Dean at four, and I want to speak to you first.

TOM. There's nothing to say.

BILL. I can break the door down. Then your father would have to pay for a new door. Do you want that? Are you afraid to see me? [TOM *after a moment, goes to the door and pulls back the bolt.* BILL *comes in quickly.*] Well. [TOM *goes back and sits on the bed. Doesn't look at* BILL.] Now I've got to have the full story. All the details so that when I see the Dean ...

TOM. You've got the full story. What the hell do you want?

BILL. We don't seem to have the full story.

TOM. When the school cops brought me in last night they told you I was with Ellie Martin.

BILL. That's just it. It seems you weren't *with* her.

TOM [*after a moment*]. What do you mean?

BILL. You weren't *with* her. You couldn't be *with* her. Do you understand what I mean?

TOM [*trying to brave it out*]. Who says so?

BILL. She says so. And she ought to know. [TOM *turns away.*] She says that you couldn't ... and that you jumped up and grabbed a knife in her kitchen and tried to kill yourself ... and she had to fight with you and that's what attracted the school cops.

TOM. What difference does it make?

BILL. I just wanted the record to be straight. You'll undoubtedly be expelled, no matter what ... but I wanted the record straight.

TOM [*turning on him*]. You couldn't have stood it, could you, if I'd proved you wrong?

BILL. Where do you get off talking like that to a master?

TOM. You'd made up your mind long ago, and it would have killed you if I'd proved you wrong.

BILL. Talking like that isn't going to help you any.

TOM. Nothing's going to help. I'm gonna be kicked out, and then you're gonna be happy.

BILL. I'm not going to be happy. I'm going to be very sorry ... sorry for your father.

TOM. All right, now you know. Go on, spread the news. How can you wait?

BILL. I won't tell anyone ... but the Dean, of course.

TOM. And my father ...

BILL. Perhaps ...

TOM [*after a long pause*]. And Mrs. Reynolds.

BILL [*looks at* TOM]. Yes. I think she ought to know. [*He turns and leaves the room. Goes through the sitting room and up the stairs, calling "Ralph."* TOM *closes the door and locks it, goes and sits down in the chair.*]

LAURA [*as* BILL *goes upstairs to* RALPH, *she comes into the master's study. She is wearing a wool suit. She goes to the cupboard and brings out* TOM'S *raincoat. She moves with it to the door. There is a knock. She opens the door*]. Oh, hello, Mr. Lee.

HERB [*coming in, he seems for some reason rather pleased*]. Hello, Laura.

LAURA. Bill isn't in just now, though I'm expecting him any moment.

HERB. My train was twenty minutes late. I was afraid I'd missed him. We have an appointment with the Dean in a few minutes . . .

LAURA [*is coolly polite*]. Oh, I see.

HERB. Have I done something to displease you, Laura? You seem a little . . . [HERB *shrugs and makes a gesture with his hands meaning cool.*]

LAURA. I'm sorry. Forgive me. Won't you sit down?

HERB. I remember that you were displeased at my leaving Tom in school a week ago. Well, you see I was right in a sense. Though, perhaps being a lady you wouldn't understand.

LAURA. I'm not sure that I do.

HERB. Well, now, look here. If I had taken Tom out of school after that scandal with Mr. . . . uh . . . what was his name?

LAURA. Mr. Harris.

HERB. Yes. If I'd taken Tom out then, he would have been marked for the rest of his life.

LAURA. You know that Tom will be expelled, of course.

HERB. Yes, but the circumstances are so much more normal.

LAURA [*after looking at him a moment*]. I think, Mr.

Lee, I'm not quite sure, but I think, in a sense, you're proud of Tom.

HERB. Well.

LAURA. Probably for the first time you're proud of him because the school police found him out of bounds with a . . .

HERB. I shouldn't have expected you to understand. Bill will see what I mean.

[BILL *starts down the stairs.*]

LAURA. Yes. He probably will.

[BILL *comes in the room.*]

HERB. Bill.

BILL. Hello, Herb.

[HERB *looks from* LAURA *to* BILL. *Notices the coldness between them.*]

BILL. I was just up seeing Tom.

HERB. Yes. I intend to go up after we've seen the Dean. How is he?

BILL. All right.

HERB [*expansive*]. Sitting around telling the boys all about it.

BILL. No, he's in his room alone. The others are going to the tea dance at the Inn. Laura . . . [*Sees* LAURA *is leaving the room.*] Oh, Laura, I wish you'd stay.

[LAURA *takes one step back into the room.*]

HERB. I was telling your wife here, trying to make her understand the male point of view on this matter. I mean, how being kicked out for a thing like this, while not exactly desirable, is still not so serious. It's sort of one of the calculated risks of being a man. [*He smiles at his way of putting it.*]

BILL [*preparing to tell* HERB]. Herb?

HERB. Yes, Bill. I mean, you agree with me on that, don't you?

BILL. Yes, Herb, only the situation is not exactly as it was reported to you over the phone. It's true that Tom went to this girl Ellie's place, and it's true that he went for the usual purpose. However . . . however, it didn't work out that way.

HERB. What do you mean?

BILL. Nothing happened.

HERB. You mean she . . . she wouldn't have him?

BILL. I mean, Tom . . . I don't know . . . he didn't go through with it. He couldn't. [*He looks at* LAURA.] It's true. The girl says so. And when it didn't work, he tried to kill himself with a knife in the kitchen, and she struggled with him, and that brought the school cops, and that's that. [LAURA *turns away, shocked and moved.* MR. LEE *sits down in a chair bewildered.*] I'm sorry, Herb. Of course the fact that he was with Ellie at her place is enough to get him expelled.

HERB. Does everyone know this?

BILL. Well, Ellie talks. She's got no shame . . . and this is apparently something to talk about.

LAURA [*to* MR. LEE]. Do you still think it will make a good smoking-car story?

BILL. What do you mean?

HERB. Why did he do it? Before, maybe he could talk it down, but to go do a thing like this and leave no doubts.

LAURA. In whose mind?

BILL. Laura, please.

LAURA [*angry*]. You asked me to stay.

BILL [*flaring back at her*]. Well, now you've heard. We won't keep you.

LAURA [*knowing, without asking*]. Why did you want me to hear?

BILL [*going to her*]. I wanted you to know the facts. That's all. The whole story.

[LAURA *stands in the alcove.*]

HERB. Bill, Bill! Maybe there's some way of getting to this girl so she wouldn't spread the story.

BILL. I'm afraid it's too late for that.

HERB. I don't know. Some things don't make any sense. What am I going to do now?

LAURA [*re-entering*]. Mr. Lee, please don't go on drawing the wrong conclusions!

HERB. I'm drawing no conclusions. This sort of thing can happen to a normal boy. But it's what the others will think . . . Added to the Harris business. And that's all that's important. What they'll think.

LAURA. Isn't it important what Tom thinks?

BILL. Herb, we'd better be getting on over to the Dean's . . .

HERB [*indicating upstairs*]. Is he in his room?

BILL. Yes.

HERB. Packing?

BILL. No.

HERB. I told him to come to you to talk things over. Did he?

BILL. No.

HERB. What am I going to say to him now?

BILL. We're expected at four.

HERB. I know. But I've got to go up . . . Maybe I should have left him with his mother. She might have known what to do, what to say . . . [*He starts out.*] You want to come along with me?

BILL [*moving to hall*]. All right.

LAURA [*serious*]. Bill, I'd like to talk with you.

BILL. I'll be back. [*Goes with* HERB *to the landing.* LAURA *exits, taking off her jacket.*]

HERB. Maybe I ought to do this alone.

BILL. He's probably locked in his bedroom.

[HERB *goes up the stairs and inside the study.* BILL *stays in the hall.* TOM, *as he hears his father knocking on the bedroom door, stiffens.* HERB *tries the door handle.*]

HERB [*off, in the study*]. Tom . . . Tom . . . it's Dad. [TOM *gets up, but just stands there.*] Tom, are you asleep? [*After a few moments, he reappears on the landing. He is deeply hurt that his son wouldn't speak to him.*] I think he's asleep.

BILL [*making a move to go in and get* TOM]. He can't be . . .

HERB [*stops*]. Yes, I think he is. He was always a sound sleeper. We used to have to drag him out of bed when he was a kid.

BILL. But he should see you.

HERB. It'll be better later, anyhow. [*He starts down the stairs, troubled, puzzled.*]

BILL. I'll go right with you, Herb.

[*They re-enter the study, and* BILL *goes out through the alcove.* HERB *stays in the master's study.*]

TOM [*when his father is downstairs, he opens his bedroom door and faintly calls*]. Dad?

[HERB *looks up, thinking he's heard something but then figures it must have been something else.* RALPH, STEVE *and* PHIL *come crashing down the stairs, dressed for the tea dance, ad libbing comments about the girls at the dance.* TOM *closes his door. When they have gone, he opens it again and calls "Dad" faintly. When there is no response, he closes the door, and goes and lies on the bed.*]

BILL [*re-entering*]. Laura, I'm going to the Dean's now with Herb. I'm playing squash with the headmaster at five. So I'll see you at the dining room at six-thirty.

LAURA [*entering after him*]. I wish you'd come back here after.

BILL. Laura, I can't.

LAURA. Bill, I wish you would.

BILL [*sees that there is some strange determination in* LAURA'S *face*]. Herb, I'll be with you in a minute. Why don't you walk along?

HERB. All right . . . Good-bye, Laura. See you again.

BILL. You'll see her in a couple of days at the reunion.

HERB. I may not be coming up for it now . . . Maybe I will. I don't know. I'll be walking along. Good-bye,

Laura. Tell Tom I tried to see him. [*He goes out.*]

BILL. Now, Laura, what's the matter? I've got to get to the Dean's rooms to discuss this matter.

LAURA. Yes, of course. But first I'd like to discuss the boys who made him do this . . . the men and boys who made him do this.

BILL. No one made him do anything.

LAURA. Is there to be no blame, no punishment for the boys and men who taunted him into doing this? What if he had succeeded in killing himself? What then?

BILL. You're being entirely too emotional about this.

LAURA. If he had succeeded in killing himself in Ellie's rooms, wouldn't you have felt some guilt?

BILL. I?

LAURA. Yes, you.

BILL. I wish you'd look at the facts and not be so emotional about this.

LAURA. The facts! What facts! An innocent boy goes swimming with an instructor . . . an instructor whom he likes because this instructor is one of the few who encourage him, who don't ride him . . . And because he's an off-horse, you and the rest of them are only too glad to put two and two together and get a false answer . . . anything which will let you go on and persecute a boy whom you basically don't like. If it had happened with Al or anybody else, you would have done nothing.

BILL. It would have been an entirely different matter. You can't escape from what you are . . . your character. Why do they spend so much time in the law courts on character witnesses? To prove this was the kind of man who could or couldn't commit such and such a crime.

LAURA. I resent this judgment by prejudice. He's not like me, therefore, he is capable of all possible crimes. He's not one of us . . . a member of the tribe!

BILL. Now look, Laura, I know this is a shock to you, because you were fond of this boy. But you did all you could for him, more than anyone would expect. After all, your responsibility doesn't go beyond—

LAURA. I know. Doesn't go beyond giving him tea and sympathy on Sunday afternoons. Well, I want to tell you something. It's going to shock you . . . but I'm going to tell you.

BILL. Laura, it's late.

LAURA. Last night I knew what Tom had in mind to do.

BILL. How did you know?

LAURA. I heard him making the date with Ellie on the phone.

BILL. And you didn't stop him? Then you're the one responsible.

LAURA. Yes, I am responsible, but not as you think. I did try to stop him, but not by locking him in his room, or calling the school police. I tried to stop him by being nice to him, by being affectionate. By showing him that he was liked . . . yes, even loved. I knew what he was going to do . . . and why he was going to do it. He had to prove to you bullies that he was a man, and he was going to prove it with Ellie Martin. Well . . . last night . . . last night, I wished he had proved it with me.

BILL. What in Christ's name are you saying?

LAURA. Yes, I shock you. I shock myself. But you are right. I am responsible here. I know what I should have done. I knew it then. My heart cried out for this boy in his misery . . . a misery imposed by my husband. And I wanted to help him as one human being to another . . . and I failed. At the last moment, I sent him away . . . sent him to . . .

BILL. You mean you managed to overcome your exaggerated sense of pity.

LAURA. No, it was not just pity. My heart in its own loneliness . . . Yes, I've been lonely here, miserably lonely . . . and my heart in its loneliness cried out for this boy . . . cried out for the comfort he could give me too.

BILL. You don't know what you're saying.

LAURA. But I was a good woman. Good in what sense of the word? Good to whom . . . and for whom?

BILL. Laura, we'll discuss this, if we must, later on . . .

LAURA. Bill! There'll be no later on. I'm leaving you.

BILL. Over this thing?

LAURA [*after a moment*]. Yes, this *thing*, and all the other *things* in our marriage.

BILL. For God's sake, Laura, what are you talking about?

LAURA. I'm talking about love and honor and manliness, and tenderness, and persecution. I'm talking about a lot. You haven't understood any of it.

BILL. Laura, you can't leave over a thing like this. You know what it means.

LAURA. I wouldn't worry too much about it. When I'm gone, it will probably be agreed by all that I was an off-horse too, and didn't really belong to the clan, and it's good riddance.

BILL. And you're doing this . . . all because of this . . . this fairy?

LAURA [*after a moment*]. This boy, Bill . . . this boy is more of a man than you are.

BILL. Sure. Ask Ellie.

LAURA. Because it was distasteful for him. Because for him there has to be love. He's more of a man than you are.

BILL. Yes, sure.

LAURA. Manliness is not all swagger and swearing and mountain climbing. Manliness is also tenderness, gentleness, consideration. You men think you can decide on who is a man, when only a woman can really know.

BILL. Ellie's a woman. Ask Ellie.

LAURA. I don't need to ask anyone.

BILL. What do you know about a man? Married first to that boy . . . again, a poor pitiable boy . . . You want to mother a boy, not love a man. That's why you never really loved me. Because I was not a boy you could mother.

LAURA. You're quite wrong about my not loving you. I did love you. But not just for your outward show of manliness, but because you needed me . . . For one unguarded moment you let me know you needed me, and I have tried to find that moment again the year we've been married . . . Why did you marry me, Bill? In God's name, why?

BILL. Because I loved you. Why else?

LAURA. You've resented me . . . almost from the day you married me, you've resented me. You never wanted to marry really . . . Did they kid you into it? Does a would-be headmaster have to be married? Or what was it, Bill? You would have been far happier going off on your jaunts with the boys, having them to your rooms for feeds and bull sessions . . .

BILL. That's part of being a master.

LAURA. Other masters and their wives do not take two boys always with them whenever they go away on vacations or weekends.

BILL. They are boys without privileges.

LAURA. And I became a wife without privileges.

BILL. You became a wife . . . [*He stops.*]

LAURA. Yes?

BILL. You did *not* become a wife.

LAURA. I know. I know I failed you. In some terrible way I've failed you.

BILL. You were more interested in mothering that fairy up there than in being my wife.

LAURA. But you wouldn't let me, Bill. You wouldn't let me.

BILL [*grabbing her by the shoulders*]. What do you mean I wouldn't let you?

LAURA [*quietly, almost afraid to say it*]. Did it ever

occur to you that you persecute in Tom, that boy up there, you persecute in him the thing you fear in yourself? [BILL *looks at her for a long moment of hatred. She has hit close to the truth he has never let himself be conscious of. There is a moment when he might hurt her, but then he draws away, still staring at her. He backs away, slowly, and then turns to the door.*] Bill!

BILL [*not looking at her*]. I hope you will be gone when I come back from dinner.

LAURA [*quietly*]. I will be . . . [*Going toward him.*] Oh, Bill, I'm sorry. I shouldn't have said that . . . it was cruel. [*She reaches for him as he goes out the door.*] This was the weakness you cried out for me to save you from, wasn't it . . . And I have tried. [*He is gone.*] I have tried. [*Slowly she turns back into the room and looks at it.*] I did try. [*For a few minutes she stands stunned and tired from her outburst. Then she moves slowly to* TOM'S *raincoat, picks it up and turns and goes out of the room and to the stair-landing. She goes to the boy's study door and knocks.*] Tom. [*She opens it and goes in out of sight. At* TOM'S *door, she calls again.*] Tom. [TOM *turns his head slightly and listens.* LAURA *opens* TOM'S *door and comes in.*] Oh, I'm sorry. May I come in? [*She sees she's not going to get an answer from him, so she goes in.*] I brought back your raincoat. You left it last night. [*She puts it on chair. She looks at him.*] This is a nice room . . . I've never seen it before . . . As a matter of fact I've never been up here in this part of the house. [*Still getting no response, she goes on.* TOM *slowly turns and looks at her back, while she is examining something on the walls. She turns, speaking.*] It's very cozy. It's really quite . . . [*She stops when she sees he has turned around looking at her.*] Hello.

TOM [*barely audible*]. Hello.

LAURA. Do you mind my being here?

TOM. You're not supposed to be.

LAURA. I know. But everyone's out, and will be for some time . . . I wanted to return your raincoat.

TOM. Thank you. [*After a pause he sits up on the bed, his back to her.*] I didn't think you'd ever want to see me again.

LAURA. Why not?

TOM. After last night. I'm sorry about what happened downstairs.

LAURA [*she looks at him a while, then*]. I'm not.

TOM [*looks at her. Can't quite make it out*]. You've heard everything, I suppose.

LAURA. Yes.

TOM. Everything?

LAURA. Everything.

TOM. I knew your husband would be anxious to give you the details.

LAURA. He did. [*She stands there quietly looking down at the boy.*]

TOM. So now you know too.

LAURA. What?

TOM. That everything they said about me is true.

LAURA. Tom!

TOM. Well, it is, isn't it?

LAURA. Tom?

TOM. I'm no man. Ellie knows it. Everybody knows it. It seems everybody knew it, except me. And now I know it.

LAURA [*moves toward him*]. Tom . . . Tom . . . dear. [TOM *turns away from her.*] You don't think that just because . . .

TOM. What else am I to think?

LAURA [*very gently*]. Tom, that didn't work because you didn't believe in it . . . in such a test.

TOM [*with the greatest difficulty*]. I touched her, and there was nothing.

LAURA. You aren't in love with Ellie.

TOM. That's not supposed to matter.

LAURA. But it does.

TOM. I wish they'd let me kill myself.

LAURA. Tom, look at me. [TOM *shakes his head.*] Tom, last night you kissed me.

TOM. Jesus!

LAURA. Why did you kiss me?

TOM [*turns suddenly*]. And it made you sick, didn't it? Didn't it? [*Turns away from her again.*]

LAURA. How can you think such a thing?

TOM. You sent me away . . . you . . . Anyway, when you heard this morning it must have made you sick.

LAURA [*sits on edge of bed*]. Tom, I'm going to tell you something. [TOM *won't turn.*] Tom? [*He still won't turn.*] It was the nicest kiss I've ever had . . . from anybody. [TOM *slowly turns and looks at her.*] Tom, I came up to say good-bye. [TOM *shakes his head, looking at her.*] I'm going away . . . I'll probably never see you again. I'm leaving Bill. [TOM *knits his brows questioning.*] For a lot of reasons. . . one of them, what he's done to you. But before I left, I wanted you to know, for your own comfort, you're more of a man now than he ever was or will be. And one day you'll meet a girl, and it will be right. [TOM *turns away in disbelief.*] Tom, believe me.

TOM. I wish I could. But a person knows . . . knows inside. Jesus, do you think after last night I'd ever . . . [*He stops. After a moment, he smiles at her.*] But thanks . . . thanks a lot.

[*He closes his eyes.* LAURA *looks at him a long time. Her face shows the great compassion and tenderness she feels for this miserable boy. After some time, she gets up and goes out the door. A moment later she appears in the hall door. She pauses for a moment, then reaches out and closes it, and stays inside.*

TOM, *when he hears the door close, his eyes open. He sees she has left his bedroom. Then in complete misery, he lies down on the bed, like a wounded animal, his head at the foot of the bed.*

LAURA *in a few moments appears in the bedroom door-*

way. She stands there, and comes in, always looking at the slender figure of the boy on the bed. She closes the bedroom door.

TOM *hears the sound and looks around. When he sees she has come back, he turns around slowly, wonderingly, and lies on his back, watching her.*

LAURA *seeing a bolt on the door, slides it to. Then she stands looking at* TOM, *her hand at her neck. With a slight and delicate movement, she unbuttons the top button of her blouse, and moves toward* TOM. *When she gets alongside the bed, she reaches out her hand, still keeping one hand at her blouse.* TOM *makes no move. Just watches her.*

LAURA *makes a little move with the outstretched hand, asking for his hand.* TOM *slowly moves his hand to hers.*]

LAURA [*stands there holding his hand and smiling gently at him. Then she sits and looks down at the boy, and after a moment, barely audible*]. And now . . . nothing?

[TOM'S *other hand comes up and with both his hands he brings her hand to his lips.*]

LAURA [*smiles tenderly at this gesture, and after a moment*]. Years from now . . . when you talk about this . . . and you will . . . be kind. [*Gently she brings the boy's hands toward her opened blouse, as the lights slowly dim out . . . and . . .*]

THE CURTAIN FALLS

A HATFUL OF RAIN

by Michael Vincente Gazzo

to my fathers, Michael and David

Copyright, as an unpublished work, 1954,
by Michael V. Gazzo
© Copyright, 1956, by Michael V. Gazzo
Reprinted by permission of Random House, Inc.
All rights including the right of reproduction in whole or in part,
in any form, are reserved under International and Pan-American
Copyright Conventions.

CAUTION: *Professionals and amateurs are hereby warned that*
A HATFUL OF RAIN *being fully protected under the Copy-*
right Laws of the United States of America, the British
Empire, including the Dominion of Canada, and all other
countries of the Copyright Union, is subject to royalty. All
rights, including professional, amateur, motion picture, reci-
tation, lecturing, public reading, radio and television
broadcasting, and the rights of translation into foreign
languages are strictly reserved. Particular emphasis is laid
on the question of readings, permission for which must be
secured from the author's agent in writing. All inquiries
should be addressed to the author's agent, Audrey Wood,
M.C.A. Artists Ltd., 598 Madison Avenue, New York, N.Y.

First production, November 9, 1955,
at the Lyceum Theatre, New York,
with the following cast:

JOHN POPE, SR., *Frank Silvera*
JOHNNY POPE, *Ben Gazzara*
CELIA POPE, *Shelley Winters*
MOTHER, *Henry Silva*
APPLES, *Paul Richards*
CHUCH, *Harry Guardino*
POLO POPE, *Anthony Franciosa*
MAN, *Steve Gravers*
PUTSKI, *Christine White*

SCENES

The action takes place in a remodeled apartment
on New York's Lower East Side.
ACT ONE / SCENE I: *Early evening.*
      SCENE II: *Very late that night.*

ACT TWO / SCENE I: *Early the next morning.*
      SCENE II: *A few hours later.*
      SCENE III: *Early the same evening.*

ACT THREE / *Several hours later.*

Act one

A tenement apartment on New York's Lower East Side. To our left we see a small kitchen, and to our right a combination living room-bedroom. There are two doors in the kitchen—one leading to the hallway, left, and the other, in the rear wall, leading to a bedroom. Looking through the living-room windows, we see the worn brick of the building next door and—beyond the fire-escape railing, which is just outside—distant window lights that outline a suspension bridge, marred only by the occasional suggestion of rooftops with jutting black chimneys.

It is only because of what is seen from these windows that we can place the apartment in the Lower East Side. Within the apartment itself there is everywhere the suggestion of a ceaseless effort to transform bedraggled rooms into rooms of comfort and taste. All the woodwork—formerly coated with twenty coats of paint—has been scraped, cleaned, stained and varnished. The windows have been refurbished; cases have been built beneath them, and they are spotlessly clean, as are the shades and draw curtains. Though the sink-and-tub combination is outdated in design, plywood has been used to cover up the intricacies of old-fashioned piping. Between the kitchen and bedroom, a partition of shelving has been built, and on each shelf are flowerpots, some of glass, others of copper, containing green plants. There is a sense of life.

In the kitchen, we see a cupboard, its paint removed, a table and four chairs. The chairs are old—picked up from one of the antique shops along Third Avenue. The table is solid and of heavy wood, something that might have been picked up from a farmer along a Jersey road.

In the living room, we see an armchair in a corner and a bed against the side wall. There is an unusual and startling use of color in the room; the bedspread is particularly lively, and all the objects in the room are colorful. Homemade bookcases made of wood planks and bricks line another wall.

The hallway, off the kitchen, is clearly in contrast to the apartment. Its walls are a drab brown and, off it, we see a suggestion of a stairway, leading to the roof, the railing of painted iron. Overhead there is a dim light, covered with a dusty and cracked skylight.

When the curtain rises, we hear the sound of rain. In the kitchen area, at the table, are JOHNNY *and his* FATHER. *The meal is almost at an end.*

FATHER [*moves away from the table, toward an umbrella which he picks up and works with difficulty, opening it and closing it*]. I almost missed the plane up because of this umbrella . . . it's made of Japanese silk, the handle is ivory . . . and it was designed in Germany . . . and they make the damn things in Peru. This guy down in Palm Beach who sold me the thing . . . Anyway, I kept looking at my watch. He wouldn't tell me how much it was . . . I thought he was crazy until he told me the price. Twenty-seven dollars for an umbrella . . . Seven minutes from plane time he tells me the price . . .

JOHNNY [*calls off to* CELIA, *who is in* POLO'S *room*]. Honey! What's the trouble in there?

CELIA [*stands in the doorway*]. I can't get Polo's windows closed. . . .

FATHER. Polo? That's Polo's room?

CELIA. Johnny . . . ? I can't close his windows and his bed is going to float out here any minute. The dampness has them jammed. . . .

FATHER. I thought you and Johnny slept in there—and Polo slept out here.

CELIA. That room isn't big enough for two people. Johnny and I tried to sleep in there but—

FATHER. What are you going to call him?

CELIA. Her. Not him. Her.

FATHER. I was counting on a grandson.

CELIA. Well, you'll have to settle for a granddaughter.

FATHER. Wow! Whew . . . That's strong coffee. Turkish?

CELIA. No, it's not Turkish. It's just plain ordinary everyday coffee.

JOHNNY. What did you put in that pot?

CELIA. I don't understand it. Last night I put nine tablespoons of coffee in the pot and it came out like weak tea.

JOHNNY. Which pot? You know you got four pots and they're all different sizes . . .

CELIA. Well, I didn't ask for all those pots.

JOHNNY. If you'd just put three of those pots away—

CELIA. It's a curse, that's all. For as long as I could remember I could never make coffee . . .

JOHNNY. They gave her four pots . . . one of those showers when we got married.

CELIA. And you went out and bought one too—so never mind.

JOHNNY. How did I know that all your girl friends were coffee-pot happy? There were only six girls at the shower, and four of them show up with a coffee pot.

CELIA. This morning I had a headache—and I wanted to have my coffee, and I dropped an Alka Seltzer in my coffee. I thought for a minute the house was going to blow up . . .

FATHER. Sorry, honey, I didn't mean to knock your coffee.

CELIA. It's not you, Pop. I was late for work this morning . . . I had to go to the doctor's on my lunch hour—and I took a bus on the way back . . . and the bus had to wait ten minutes at an intersection while a parade passed by . . .

JOHNNY. Honey, you're behaving like a woman.

CELIA. Darling, if you'll just take a good look at me, you'll confirm the fact that I am a woman.

FATHER. What's this your wife writes me, you're not going to school any more . . .

JOHNNY. I'm going to start again soon, Pop. Working days and school nights, I—

FATHER. I don't want you to think that I'm pushing you, but I was down there feeling good about the fact that you got the government picking up the bill with that G.I. Rights thing . . . How long will it take you to finish, I mean if you started soon again . . . ?

CELIA. Another two years and he'll have his degree . . . Excuse me, Pop, I've got some ironing to do for work.

FATHER. Working in a machine shop, being a toolmaker, that must help you with engineering studies, huh?

JOHNNY. I'm a machinist, Pop. I'm not a toolmaker . . .

FATHER. You lost two years in the Army, another damn year laying in a hospital bed, now that's a big chunk of time—so look to the clock, Johnny.

JOHNNY. I was going to write and tell you myself about my not going to school any more, but I didn't want to worry you—

FATHER. You don't have any pains, I mean, you're all cured.

JOHNNY. Yeh, I'm all cured . . .

FATHER. Sometimes things like that act up . . . you

know, guys with rheumatism, their teeth start to hurt when it rains. I'm just asking you . . .

JOHNNY. I'm all right, Pop.

FATHER. I was proud of you, Johnny. I told everybody down the Club . . . how you laid in a cave for thirteen days. I showed them that picture you took at the hospital . . . I told them all—how you went down to ninety pounds. How you kept your mouth shut, no matter what they did to you.

JOHNNY. Aw, come on now, Pop—there's nothing to be proud of.

CELIA. You'd think it was something to be ashamed of.

JOHNNY. Can we just forget about it . . . ?

FATHER. Well, I couldn't have held out—and I don't think there are many men who could. And I'm proud of you, kid!

JOHNNY. All right, Pop, you're proud of me.

CELIA. He tore up all the newspaper clippings. . . .

JOHNNY. Honey, will you please forget it?

FATHER. It's really coming down . . . every time I think of having to get on that plane tomorrow my stomach starts doing flip flops. . . . We got a glass wall they just put in, the sun comes in and from behind the bar you can see the water. Exclusive, private, only for the big wheels. Corporation lawyers, senators, department-store heads and a few judges thrown in. It was a good job. Well, maybe I can get it back.

JOHNNY. You mean you quit your job?

FATHER. What do you think I was shouting about before. Your brother wrote me a hundred times. Pop, I've got twenty-five hundred stashed away. Any time you want it, it's yours. I put money down on the option, and I started the renovations. The carpenters have been working there for a week, and I got the plumbers fixing the pipes. . . .

CELIA. Can you get your job back?

FATHER. I wish you could see this new place. It's all

good hard wood, the dining room's got heavy beams two feet thick, and there's a long oak bar.

CELIA. You could have wired Polo and confirmed the loan before you put any money down . . . certainly before you got men in to go to work.

FATHER. It's not the first time his brother's disappointed me, and look what he's doing now. A bouncer. He calls that place a cocktail lounge? That's no cocktail lounge. I've been in chippie joints in my time, it's more like a cat house. Excuse me, honey, I mean whore house.

JOHNNY. You could have made a two-dollar phone call.

FATHER. For what? Seven months ago when I thought I was going to buy that bar on the Bay, he sent me a check for twenty-five hundred bucks. The deal fell through, and I sent the money back to him. . . . That was seven lousy months ago! The bank never promised me a loan! My son promised me. Now he tells me the money is gone! Gone where? Where did it go?

JOHNNY. Now look, Pop, I know Polo as well as I know myself. If he had the money he'd give it to you.

FATHER. I don't want to be here when he gets back.

JOHNNY. You're not going to hold a grudge against him.

CELIA. I'm going to talk to Polo when he comes home.

JOHNNY. Pop, how about some wine?

FATHER. O.K., let's have some wine. Hey, that looks like homemade red.

CELIA. Yes, I buy it from a grocer in the neighborhood.

JOHNNY. He makes it in the cellar. The grocery store is just a front.

FATHER. Hey Johnny, remember the farm we used to have. Remember how we used to hitch those big bay horses to the trees and tear them up by the roots so's we could plant. Look at my hands . . . mixing pink ladies and daiquiris. It's embarrassing.

JOHNNY. What's embarrassing?

FATHER. I have to get a manicure twice a week.

CELIA. I can't imagine Johnny on a farm. He's got a face like the city.

FATHER. Yeh, well, he'd pick tomatoes until he'd fall on his face—walk right under the horse's belly, right, Johnny?

JOHNNY. Right, Pop.

FATHER. I was thinking about getting a farm while you were in the Army, Johnny. Every once in a while now, I feel a funny thing in the air. People look lost to me. All I see is movement. Trains, boats, planes. Look at an oak tree, it doesn't move so that you can notice it. I was thinking about a farm again. I just had the feeling that the time had come to stop . . . and really add up what counts. Maybe look back and see if we didn't pass something by.

CELIA. That's a lovely thought . . .

FATHER. Ah . . . It's all talk. When you come right down to it. Nothing is right. Nothing is wrong. Nobody's for, and nobody's against. Something happened somewhere along the line!

JOHNNY. Happened to who, Pop? I don't follow you . . .

FATHER. Happened to us, the people.

CELIA. Well, what happened to us?

FATHER. This is the age of the vacuum. The people—they don't believe any more.

CELIA. You know there's a joke now about *"they."* It's said that when you find out who *they* are, you don't need a psychiatrist any more.

FATHER. Now look, young lady—before psychiatrists struck oil, the bartenders did their job. There's no better place to feel the pulse of the nation.

CELIA. I hope the Senate and the rest of the legislators aren't making a survey of the bars.

JOHNNY. Honey, you're getting red in the face.

CELIA. I've heard this before—the age of the vacuum, everybody's waiting—and no one believes. It's been said enough in the last few years. What's the sense of having a child? Another war may come. Look out for the white light when you hear the siren . . . every time I hear this kind of talk my blood boils. . . .

FATHER. You have to be young to get excited. There's an old Italian saying—

CELIA. I'm not interested in old Italian sayings. Just what do you believe in?

FATHER. What do you suggest I believe in? I'm sorry, I'm trying to take you seriously—

CELIA. You have two sons! You have a grandchild coming—some day Polo will have a wife and there'll be more children.

FATHER. Oh Hell, there will always be children.

CELIA. No, there will not! Because people don't believe in staying married any more. If you can't be happy together, why stay together? Johnny has been back two years, and there hasn't been a married couple in this house for over two years. They're all divorced or separated, and they've excused themselves, and granted one another pardons. No, there will not always be children. Not if people go around talking about the age of the vacuum as if it were an indestructible fact.

JOHNNY. Honey! Calm down, you're going to get the neighbors in here.

CELIA. The neighbors should know that too . . . And I don't want to apologize for anything I've said.

[*The hall lights brighten slightly. A figure scurries down the fire escape. Two men appear in the hallway.*]

FATHER. She's all woman, Johnny—all woman. You know, you look just like Johnny's mother did. That light hair, and—

CELIA. I thought she had dark hair, in the pictures Johnny showed me, she—

FATHER. Sure, she had dark hair, but you look just like her.

[*Another figure has scurried down the fire escape. The three men whisper in the hallway; then the figure scurries up the fire escape again. The tall silhouetted man,* MOTHER, *raps him playfully with the umbrella as he goes up. The smaller figure,* APPLES, *knocks gently at the door.*]

JOHNNY [*opens the door*]. Hi!

CELIA. Well, tell them to come in, Johnny. Don't have them standing out in the hall.

JOHNNY. Come on in . . .

[MOTHER *and* APPLES *appear and take a few steps into the doorway.* MOTHER *is tall, sleekly dressed and wears a pair of dark glasses.* APPLES, *at his side, has on a dirty raincoat. Both are wet.*]

MOTHER [*looking at shoes*]. Our feet are wet, Johnny. We just want to see you for a minute.

JOHNNY. This is my wife—and this is my father.

FATHER. How do you do?

CELIA. I'm sorry I didn't get your names?

FATHER. Take off your glasses and stay a while.

APPLES. I got your floor all dirty. Maybe I'd better wait out in the hall.

MOTHER. Yeh, wait out in the hall. Could you step out for a few minutes, Johnny. Nice meeting you—

[*They both go out and stand out in the hallway, closing the door after them.* JOHNNY *walks to closet, gets out jacket.*]

CELIA. Who are they?

JOHNNY [*smiling*]. They're a couple of guys I play poker with. They probably want to borrow a few bucks. . . .

CELIA. I don't care about the floor, tell them to come in.

JOHNNY. Why don't you get the album out and show the old man the pictures you were talking about? I'll be right back. . . .

CELIA. Put your coat on. It's damp.

[JOHNNY *goes out. Lights dim in apartment area and come up in the hallway.*]

JOHNNY. Look, Mother, everything went wrong. I called the clubhouse, I called Ginnino's, I've been trying to get you all day long.

APPLES. Every junkey in the city has been trying to call us. Right, Mother?

MOTHER. That's right. They picked up Alby this afternoon.

APPLES. We been walking in the shadows all day long. We can't stay in one place more than ten minutes.

MOTHER. The lid is all over the city.

APPLES. This is no three-day affair. They're hitting this city like a hurricane. In a week the city's going to be dry.

JOHNNY. I'm thin, Mother.

MOTHER. I'm no doctor, I'm a businessman.

APPLES. You got it for free in the hospital, Johnny, but Mother's no charity ward.

MOTHER. You got it?

JOHNNY. No.

MOTHER. You ain't even got a hunk of it?

JOHNNY. Where can I get it? All of a sudden you start to close in on me. That kind of money isn't easy to get.

[*The third figure,* CHUCH, *comes slowly down the ladder and hangs over* JOHNNY's *head; in the darkness he could pass for an ape.*]

MOTHER. What have you been trying to get us for then?

JOHNNY. My old man came in tonight. He's going to be here for a few days. I wanted you to give me enough to hold me over, until he gets on his plane. As soon as he goes, I'll try to get the money I owe you.

APPLES. How you going to pay? Two dollars a week for the next five years?

MOTHER. You'll get it by tomorrow morning! Every penny of it ...

JOHNNY. Oh, Mother, you must be crazy. Where am I going to get seven hundred dollars by tomorrow morning?

APPLES. Your wife must have something for a rainy day.... Huh?

JOHNNY. What do you expect me to do! Go to my wife and say—

MOTHER. Chuchie! [*Instantly* CHUCH'S *arm comes down and wraps itself around* JOHNNY, *holding him pressed against the fire-escape ladder.*] Now you listen to me, you junkey bastard! I don't care how many jokes you told me, or how long I know you. I'd never press you, if they didn't press me. Your eyes can rattle out of your head. Just good faith . . . five hundred, and I'll carry you for the rest. Let him go, Chuchie. . . .

[CHUCH *lets his arm loose.*]

JOHNNY. What am I going to do for the next few days . . . ?

MOTHER. Riddle arm, that's your problem. [MOTHER *takes a small packet out of his pocket. He holds it up.*] Here. Feel it? Give me the weight minus the paper. And what do you have? Not even an ounce . . . one lousy spoon of morphine, and I put my life on the block every time I put it in my pocket. How many times did I bring it to you? They'll give me ten years for carrying that.

JOHNNY. Thanks, Mother. I'll pay you tomorrow.

MOTHER. Look! You need forty dollars a day now. You can't make it working. I don't care how you make it—push the stuff, steal . . .

APPLES [*handing* JOHNNY *a gun*]. Here.

JOHNNY. You guys must be crazy. I don't want that.

APPLES. Keep it. It's not loaded.

JOHNNY. No!

MOTHER. Leave it on the floor, Apples. Gimme back that packet, Johnny!

JOHNNY. Look, I walked around all day long trying to—

[*Suddenly* MOTHER *kicks* JOHNNY *in the groin.*]
Sshhhh . . . for. Quiet. My old man's here. . . .

CHUCH. His old man's here, Mother . . . his old man's here. Give him a break, willya. Can't you see he's going to curdle?

MOTHER [*taking packet*]. His old man's here, and mine's dead. You go over the roof—and we'll meet you by Ginnino's.

CHUCH. Okay.

MOTHER. Five hundred . . . tomorrow morning, Johnny. [MOTHER *and* APPLES *walk out.*]

CHUCH. Johnny, you all right? Look, Johnny, he's not kidding. It's a shame what they did to Willy De-Carlo this afternoon. He didn't even owe as much as you do. He's no good: Mother . . . he'll do everything but kill you. Be a good guy, pick it up— It's not even loaded.

JOHNNY. Chuchie . . . You got anything at all?

CHUCH. No.

JOHNNY. Even half . . .

CHUCH. I ain't got enough for myself.

JOHNNY. When you tried to kick it, and you couldn't stand it—you called me, and I gave you my last drop.

CHUCH. All right. You come by my house later. And, Johnny, don't say nothing about my dog. I mean if the ole lady says anything, just change the subject. My dog fell out the window last night . . .

JOHNNY. All right, Chuch.

CHUCH. He died, Johnny. Right in my arms.

[CHUCH *scurries up the ladder.* JOHNNY *bends down, picks up the gun and puts it in his jacket pocket. The lights dim in the hallway and come up in the apartment area.*]

FATHER. It wasn't a big farm but you could eat and live off it. A cosmetic factory squeezed me on the mortgage. I built that barn and I was the last one to go. Johnny's mother died a short time after and the kid went to live with his Aunt Grace— No, Polo went to live with his Aunt Grace; Johnny went to live with his Uncle Louis. [JOHNNY *has entered.*] What did those characters want?

CELIA. I don't like those men . . .

JOHNNY. They're only a couple of guys I play poker with.

FATHER. Who ever heard of seeing people out in the hall? There's a room right here . . .

JOHNNY. Now, what in the world's the trouble— You've never seen them before.

CELIA. I've seen them with that Willy DeCarlo standing on a corner. And I never liked him coming up here either . . . and you never know where he's looking. He just stares in space.

JOHNNY. You don't see him coming around here any more.

CELIA. How much money did you lose?

JOHNNY. Couple of bucks.

CELIA. Should I try to make some more coffee . . . ?

FATHER. No, not for me, thanks. I'd better get back to the hotel. Oh— I brought a package in. What happened to it?

CELIA. I think I put it with your coat.

FATHER. When your brother comes in, don't say anything to him, Johnny. It's all water under the bridge. I bought a half a dozen Oxford shirts down there . . . they're all brand-new . . . I figured you and your brother could wear them. Put four of them in your drawer and give him two.

JOHNNY. Here, honey, put three in Polo's drawer . . .

FATHER. Keep four of them for yourself.

CELIA. You come early for dinner tomorrow night . . . and you come over for breakfast too. . . .

FATHER. I'll get a couple of box seats for the ball game, Johnny.

JOHNNY. He's got a back like a gorilla . . . he dumped Benny Leonard once . . . Isn't that right, Pop?

FATHER. Yeh, and I swam the English Channel both ways.

CELIA. Watch your step, Pop. [*Goes out and starts down the stairs with* FATHER.]

FATHER. See you in the morning, kid.

JOHNNY. Good night, Pop.

FATHER. Heh, Johnny . . . and if I drop my hat crossing the street . . .

JOHNNY. Oh . . . don't bend down to pick it up.

FATHER [*like an old vaudevillian*]. Why not?

JOHNNY. You'll get an assful of taxicab bumpers . . . [*The* FATHER *goes.*]

FATHER [*off*]. That's an old standing gag we used to have.

[*We hear their voices trail off.* JOHNNY *moves to his jacket, takes out the gun, looks about the room and goes to a drawer to hide the gun. He walks to the kitchen, starts to roll up his sleeves without thinking—catches himself and rolls them down. As he begins to remove objects from the table, he notices the shirts his* FATHER *left and throws them into* POLO's *room. For a split second, he stops moving; he throws his head back, blinks his eyes and shakes his head as if to ward off sleep. He goes to the sink and throws water on his face; then he again begins to clear the table, as* CELIA *enters.*]

CELIA. There's no hot water, is there? Aren't we speaking to one another? The clock has stopped again? I guess we're not speaking to one another. Thanks for clearing the table. The cream belongs in the icebox.

JOHNNY. The refrigerator . . .

CELIA. Johnny, I'm sorry about this morning. It's silly, I don't even know what it was that I said now.

JOHNNY. You said I was useless . . . Something like that.

CELIA. Why should you be afraid to tell me that you lost a job? I felt like a fool when I called . . . your boss must have thought I was a fool, too . . . out of

work three days and I have to find out by acci-
dent...

JOHNNY. I ruined a day's work. A whole day's work
just botched ... I don't know how I did it.

CELIA. Ruining a day's work—losing a job is no reason
to go into hiding!

JOHNNY. Honey, I didn't lose that job—I was thrown
out. I put fifteen shafts into the lathe that day and I
undercut every one by twenty lousy thousandths of
an inch. It's the fourth job I've lost in six months.

CELIA. All right—but this isn't 1929—so you lost four
jobs.

JOHNNY. Where do these go?

CELIA. The top shelf.

JOHNNY. Don't start shouting now...

CELIA. I haven't even raised my voice...

JOHNNY. I know when you're shouting even when you
don't raise your voice.

CELIA. Well, they go on the top shelf. The dishes go
on the top shelf. The cream belongs in the ice—refrigerator. Your shoes are to be found in the closet
... your shirts and shorts are in the bottom drawer.
And we live at 967 Rivington Street! Let's not do
the dishes. Can't we sit down in the front room.
Let's just for once, sit down and talk. Come on, put
that down.

JOHNNY. All right. Where do you want to sit? Where
do I sit?

CELIA. Can we try to talk...

JOHNNY. I thought everything was decided. Do you
leave, or do I leave?

CELIA. I thought we had more to talk about than that.

JOHNNY. Well, go ahead, I'm listening.

CELIA. You'll have to do more than listen.

JOHNNY. I can't talk. I just can't seem to talk to people
any more.

CELIA. I'm not people. I'm your wife. I married you to

live with you. I married you to have your child in me.

JOHNNY. Look, do we have to sit down like we're holding a class. Well—?

CELIA. Well, what about her? Is she rich? Is she pretty?

JOHNNY. I've told you I haven't even shaken hands with another woman since we've been married. And that's four years.

CELIA. One year, Johnny—that's all the marriage we ever had. The first year. I never said this before, I think I'm ashamed of it . . . but there were many times while you were gone, that I just wanted to be near a man. Sometimes I thought I'd go crazy. I just wanted to go out and watch people dance, I never went anywhere, I waited for you . . .

JOHNNY. I didn't go anywhere either. They told me where to go.

CELIA. I can understand how you might . . . Maybe I haven't given you what you want . . . or need. All right—who is she? Why do you have to lie to me?

JOHNNY. I'm not lying.

CELIA. You must think I've been stupid all these months . . . I thought that if I let you go and not say anything . . . I kept saying to myself, you love me and only me . . .

JOHNNY. I love you, and only you.

CELIA. God, I would like to know where you are! I waited for you and you never came home . . . I was here when you left, while you were gone, and I'm here now. Johnny, I spend more time with your brother than I do with you. Polo and I are together every night of the week. He never mentions you and neither do I. We just pretend that you don't exist . . . being lonely at night is nothing new, but last night I was lonely in a different way. I almost threw myself in Polo's arms.

JOHNNY. What are you talking about?

CELIA. We can't go on living like this any more. Not the three of us in one house. . . . Johnny, we used to talk all night long and wake up bleary-eyed. But it didn't matter because we were together. Don't you remember?

JOHNNY. All week-end long too . . . that week-end we spent at the Point. We didn't sleep from Friday to Sunday. . . .

CELIA. And that poor house detective—he thought we weren't married.

JOHNNY. I told you to get out of the sun and you got sunburned.

CELIA. And I told you we shouldn't go out on the rocks . . . You hobbled around for a week with a stubbed toe.

JOHNNY. And you walked around for a week with that white stuff on your nose—you looked like a clown.

CELIA. The old man who climbed out to where we were, and caught us kissing.

JOHNNY. Caught us kissing . . . ? He must have been watching us for five minutes.

CELIA. Well, that's all we were doing.

JOHNNY. You're not remembering that day . . .

CELIA. I remember that day most of all. . . . It was your week-end, before you went away. All I wanted to do was hold you and never let you go.

JOHNNY. You cried at the train station.

CELIA. I know. But I didn't know where you were going and how long you'd be gone. You cried too. . . .

JOHNNY. No, I didn't.

CELIA. I saw you through the window of the train, just as it was pulling out. You were smiling, but you were crying.

JOHNNY. Well—for crissake—you looked like a kid who lost her rag doll . . .

CELIA. And—we weren't just kissing. The old man saw us—

JOHNNY. Playing. The old man saw us playing.

CELIA. Playing . . . well, that's a new word for—Johnny, please love me.

JOHNNY. Love you? I love you more than I can say. Sometimes at night, when you sleep I walk the streets like I'm looking for something, and yet I know all the while what I want is sleeping. It's like I walk the streets looking for you . . . and you're right here.

CELIA. What's the matter?

JOHNNY. Nothing . . .

CELIA. I didn't mean to offend you by touching you . . .

JOHNNY. I'm sorry . . .

CELIA. Were you with her today . . . ?

JOHNNY. Never mind where I was today.

CELIA. Oh, yes, I'm going to mind . . . You walk the streets at night, you go out any time you want and come home any time you want. A day isn't just a day. It's no longer your day or my day—a day belongs to us both. All right, you didn't work today, you'll get another job, but what was today? What was your day? Did you take her to a movie or—

JOHNNY. This morning you said that the marriage was a bust, that we were on the rocks . . . After you left . . . Did you ever feel like you were going crazy? Ever since I knew the old man was coming up . . . I just can't stop remembering things . . . like all night long I've been hearing that whistle . . . The old man used to whistle like that when he used to call us . . . I was supposed to come right home from school, but I played marbles. Maybe every half-hour he'd whistle . . . I'd be on my knees in the schoolyard, with my immie glove on—you take a woman's glove and you cut off the fingers . . . so your fingers are free and your knuckles don't bleed in the wintertime . . . and I just kept on playing and the whistle got madder and madder. It starts to get dark and I'd get worried but I wouldn't go home until I won all the marbles . . . and he'd be up on that porch whistling away. I'd cross myself at the door . . . and there was a grandmother I had who taught me to cross myself to protect myself from lightning . . . I'd open the door and go in . . . hold up the chamois bag of marbles and I'd say, hey, Pop, I won! Wham! Pow! . . . I'd wind up in the corner saying, Pop, I didn't hear you. I didn't hear you . . .

CELIA. What did you do today? You didn't play marbles today, did you? You weren't home all day because I called here five times if I called once . . .

JOHNNY. I'm trying to tell you what I did today . . .

CELIA. You're trying to avoid telling me what you did today.

JOHNNY. I took a train see . . . then I took a bus . . . I went to look at the house I was born in. It's only an hour away . . . but in fifteen years, I've never gone anywhere near that house . . . or that town! I had to go back . . . I can't explain the feeling, but I was ten years old when I left there . . . The way I looked around, they must have thought I was crazy . . . because I kept staring at the old house—I was going to knock at the door and ask the people if I could just look around . . . and then I went to that Saybrook school where I used to hear the old man whistle . . . and those orange fire escapes . . . and ivy still climbing up the walls. Then I took the bus and the train, and I went to meet the old man's plane . . . and we came here.

CELIA. You came here. Not home . . . but here.

JOHNNY. I mean home.

CELIA. You said here . . .

JOHNNY. All right, here, not home. You know, I've lived in a lot of places since I left that town. There was always a table, some cups and some windows . . . and somebody was the boss, somebody to tell you what to do and what not to do, always somebody to slap you down, pep you up, or tell you to use will power ... there was always a bed. What do I know about a home?

CELIA. Johnny? Johnny! Do you want to run away from here ... ?

JOHNNY. I want to live here.

CELIA. With me ...

JOHNNY. Honey, there is no other woman. Look, baby —you don't know how much I need you, how much I love you, sometimes I want to bury myself in you ...

CELIA. Well, do. ...

JOHNNY. Honey—Honey, I've got to go out tonight ... but, I'm ... I love you ...

CELIA. The rain's stopped. I think I'd better open the windows ... everything's so damp in here.

[*We hear rollicking, happy laughter in the hallway, and* POLO's *voice.*]

POLO [*off*]. Hey, boy, hey, Johnny, the walls are crooked.

JOHNNY. Hold on to those walls.

CELIA. Help him before he falls down the stairs.

[JOHNNY *goes out.* POLO *appears, hanging on* JOHNNY's *arm and shoulder. He is quite drunk.*]

POLO. Hey, come on ... we're all going dancing. Hey, Celia, come on, we're all going dancing. The floors are crooked, Johnny.

CELIA. You ought to be ashamed of yourself.

POLO. I'm so drunk I couldn't walk a chalk line.

JOHNNY. Hold on. Let's see if we can get over to that chair.

POLO. I don't know what that would prove ... if I could walk a chalk line. Leave me alone, Johnny, I'm all right. Come on, lemme alone ...

JOHNNY. Come on, let's get those clothes off.

POLO. Hey, Johnny, who are you going to vote for Miss Rheingold of 1955?

JOHNNY. I haven't made my mind up yet.

POLO. I voted twenty-three times for Miss Woods . . . You think she cares, Johnny? She doesn't care.

CELIA. Here . . . drink this.

POLO. Oh, no, honey—I don't want any of that coffee. I'm not *that* drunk. Hey, hey . . . handle those shoes with care. They're Florsheim shoes . . . Hey, hey . . . le's get some good music on . . . hey, Johnny . . . take it easy with that shirt. That's an Arrow shirt. Hey, Celia, le's get some good music on.

CELIA. You get your clothes off and get to bed.

POLO. Aw come on, don't be a party pooper! Hey, Celia, you know there's a lady lives up there by the second-floor fire escape. . . . Every day, she hangs out her clothes—right, Popo . . . Dopo, Mopo. She dreamt she washed her windows in her Maidenform bra. . . . [*Growl.*] Rub-a-dub, dub, three men in her tub . . . blow you March sonofabitchin winds blow. . . .

CELIA. I think we should undress you and put you to bed.

POLO. Oh, no, no . . . You're not undressing me. I'm ashamed. I got a big appendix scar. We all got scars. Johnny's got scars all the way down his back, huh? Johnny was fourteen days in a cave . . . all the way down his back. Celia, meet my brother . . . my guests are his guests . . . but his guests aren't my guests. Celia, Johnny's got a heart like a snake.

JOHNNY. All right, you said enough.

POLO. If I ever catch those sonsabitches around here again, Johnny, I'll tear their heads off.

JOHNNY. Shut up. Why don't you shut up?

POLO. I shut up. I'm shut up. I'm like you, Johnny . . . all you ever gave was your rank, your name and your serial number . . . I don't tell the old man.

JOHNNY. Let's forget the old man and get to bed.

POLO. That's right, Johnny. Let's forget the old man . . . let's forget everybody. We don't need anybody. I got . . . Florsheim shoes . . . Paris belt . . . hey, where's my Paris belt . . . ? Thanks, Celia . . . You're an angel in disguise.

CELIA. Good night, Polo.

POLO. Don't worry about me. I got everything I need . . . except a Bond suit. I dreamt I fell asleep in my Bond suit.

[JOHNNY *leads him off; then comes back.*]

JOHNNY. Just a little high, that's all—like Christmas, once a year.

CELIA. I'd better put this on him. He'll freeze to death. [*The moment she goes into the room,* JOHNNY *goes to the drawer, takes out the gun and puts it in his pocket.* CELIA *stops in the doorway.*] Where are you going?

JOHNNY. Out, I'm going out, I'll take a walk for myself. Oh, no, leave your coat where it is. I don't want you coming with me . . .

CELIA. Why not . . . ?

JOHNNY. 'Cause, I just want to think . . .

CELIA. I won't even talk, I'll just hold on to your arm.

JOHNNY. You *can't* come with me . . . I'll be back.

CELIA. *When?* Tell me when so I can wait. Tonight, and—tomorrow, at dawn . . . Noon . . . When?

JOHNNY. Don't be mad, willya?

CELIA. Oh, no, no, no. I won't be mad. Do you know that I fell so in love with you all over again tonight? I wanted you. Do you understand what it means to want someone!

JOHNNY. Look, all the things you said tonight about trying—

CELIA. Trying? I've tried . . . if they gave out medals for trying I'd sink right through this floor. And every week, every day you keep slipping away— Why don't you look around you? You worked on the woodwork like a beaver, you built everything . . . but—nothing here belongs to you. This is yours . . . I'm yours . . . Go on tell her she's welcome to you . . .

JOHNNY. It's not another woman. Will you get that out of your mind . . . get it out, I love you . . . and believe me it's not another woman!

CELIA. Then what is it . . . ? This is the last time you'll ever do this to me.

JOHNNY. I'm sorry.

CELIA. Don't stand with one hand on the doorknob like that. You look like Mickey Rooney leaving Boy's Town forever . . .

[JOHNNY *goes out, closing the door sharply behind him. He walks down the hall; at the end of it he stops.* CELIA *has walked away from the door. For a moment, they start to walk toward the door and each other—but they both stop.* JOHNNY *goes down the stairs.*]

THE LIGHTS DIM OUT

SCENE II

It is about two o'clock in the morning. The lights are dim. In the darkness we see the city beyond—glowing. There is the sound of a dog barking in the distance. The door to POLO'S *room opens, and, in the lighted doorway, we see* POLO *standing in shorts. He moves to the sink shakily and begins throwing water down his throat. . . . The lights are flicked on.*

CELIA. Don't do that, Polo! You'll give yourself a stomach cramp.

POLO. I got no choice . . . stomach cramp or I'll die of thirst . . . Where's my pants . . . who robbed my pants? Hey Johnny, where did you put my pants?

CELIA. Johnny went out.

POLO. You're mad at me too, huh?

CELIA. You ought to be ashamed of yourself. Your father was hurt . . . you almost took the door off the hinges slamming it.

POLO. He was hurt, huh? His boy Johnny was here so he shouldn't feel so bad. Nobody said I was a bum, huh? All right, I never graduated high school . . . What's that make me, a bum?

CELIA. You're jealous . . .

POLO. Why should I be jealous? It's always been the same. It's not only him . . . it's all my damn relatives. As long as I can remember, always laughing at me . . .

CELIA. You don't like your father very much, do you? Why didn't you lend your father the money? He said you promised . . . he said that—

POLO. I know what he said—what I said . . . The money's gone. It flew south with the birds. I bet it on one of Ali Khan's horses—gone is gone, any kid knows that. Gone doesn't come back.

CELIA. I only asked a simple question, Polo.

POLO. I'm glad you didn't ask a difficult one. I don't like my father, huh? He comes over to that nightly circus I work in, he tells me it's a joint. People don't come in there to drink, that's what he says— that's bright on his part. There's thirteen whores leaning on the bar and he tells me people don't come in there to drink.

CELIA. What's the matter with you, Polo? I've never seen you like this before.

POLO. I'm drunk, that's all.

CELIA. I can see that you're drunk.

POLO. Well, can't a guy drink just because he likes to drink? Do you have to have a reason to drink?

CELIA. You don't like Johnny any more, do you? Why does he have a heart like a snake?

POLO. You're starting to sound like the 47th Precinct. Why? What? Who?

CELIA. Sometimes I get the feeling that you hate your brother ...

POLO. I'll tell you one thing, I used to hate him ... When I was a kid ... Johnny kept getting adopted, nobody ever adopted me. *And I wanted to get adopted.* They'd line us up, and he'd get picked— then he'd run away and come back to the home the old man put us in ... and I used to think to myself ... just let me get adopted once and I'll stay. I used to hate him every time he left—and every time he came back. He'd say the same goddamn thing ... We gotta stick together, Polo ... we're the only family we got.

CELIA. Johnny never told me that ...

POLO. Johnny never told you a lot of things. What I mean is ... it's not a nice thing to say about the old man, is it?

CELIA. Polo, I want you to tell me what the matter is!

POLO. Why don't you ask your husband Johnny what's the matter with him and leave me alone?

CELIA. Everybody wants to be left alone. We're getting to be a house full of Garbos.

POLO. Just leave me alone ...

CELIA. Just like Johnny. If I closed my eyes, I'd think you were Johnny.

POLO. You ask the old man who I am, he'll tell you. I'm Polo, the no-good sonofabitch. He'll never forget anything. I threw a lemon at a passing car once ... and hit the driver in the head. I set fire to a barn once ... and I never graduated high school. No, I'm not Johnny, he's my brother and he's a son-ofabitch. That sonofabitch is going to kill me.

[CELIA *throws a glass of water in* POLO'S *face.*]

CELIA. I'm sorry I did that.

POLO. It's a sign of the times ... a sign of the times. All the king's men, and all the king's horses ... Oh, what's the difference. [*He goes into his room.*]

CELIA. Polo? Polo? Will you come out and talk to me.

POLO. No!

CELIA. Polo, please, I'm lonely.

[POLO *comes out.*]

CELIA. There's some muffins from tonight's supper. Would you like one?

POLO. No.

CELIA. Well, I'm going to have one.

POLO. I'll have one too. How's the job . . . ?

CELIA. Johnny got fired.

POLO. I know Johnny got fired. I was asking about your job.

CELIA. Well, why didn't you come and tell me that, Polo?

POLO. Honey, I'm not a personnel manager, I'm just a boarder.

CELIA. You're a bouncer in a cat house . . .

POLO. Who said that?

CELIA. Your father . . .

POLO. There must have been a full moon last night . . . boy, they showed up last night, mean, ugly and out of their minds . . . That slap-happy bouncer I work with, if he'd just learn to try to talk these bums out of the place—he's always grabbing somebody by the seat of their pants, and we're off. You know that sonofabitchin bouncer is six foot three and, as God is my witness, honey, every time hell breaks loose I'm in there getting the hell kicked out of me and that big bastard is up against the wall cheering me on! Atta boy, Polo! Atta boy! You got him going. Who have I got going? Who? I'll be punchy before Christmas.

CELIA. You're too light to be a bouncer, Polo. Why don't you quit?

POLO. Quit? Where can I make a hundred and twenty-five dollars a week? Where? Well, you can't beat it. You come into the world poor and you go out owing money. . . .

CELIA. You can say that again. . . .

POLO. You come into the world poor, and , . .

CELIA. All right, smarty, forget it. . . . The Union Metal Company of America . . . that's where you should work, Polo. At least there's a little excitement at your job . . . Do you know that when I started working in the carpeted air-conditioned desert I could take dictation at the rate of 120 words a minute? I could type ninety words . . . Today I was sitting at my desk, pretending to be busy. I have papers in all the drawers. I keep shuffling them from drawer to drawer. I break pencils and sharpen them. Mr. Wagner called me in his office today and I bustled in with my steno pad and . . . you know what he called me in for? He wanted to know. Was I happy? Was Union Metals treating me right? I've been there five years come Ash Wednesday . . . and every six months they call you in and ask you the same thing. . . . Are you happy?

POLO. Why don't you quit?

CELIA. Nobody ever quits Union Metals . . . and no one ever gets fired. A bonus on Christmas, a turkey on Thanksgiving, long holiday week-ends. They've insured Johnny and I against sickness, and the plague, everything for the employees . . . boat rides, picnics, sick leave, a triple-savings interest, the vacations keep getting longer, we have a doctor, a nurse, and a cafeteria, four coffee breaks a day, if it gets too hot they send you home, and if it rains it's perfectly all right if you're late . . . and it's the dullest job in the whole world.

POLO. Honey . . . you know what? You've got a real problem there.

CELIA. I don't know whether to laugh or cry. . . .

POLO. Why?

CELIA. I got another raise today. . . .

POLO. Boy, I wish I didn't know right from wrong . . .

CELIA. What?

POLO. Nothing. . . .

CELIA. Polo, I've been wanting to talk to you every night this week.

POLO. We've been here every night this week . . . That's all we've done is talked.

CELIA. You're not listening to me, Polo. I've always liked you and Johnny thinks the world of you, but . . . but . . . I'm afraid you'll have to find a different place to live. . . . Maybe you could take a room somewhere in the neighborhood and still come over to dinner.

POLO. I could, huh? And what about breakfast . . . ?

CELIA. You could come over for breakfast too . . . And I could do your shirts and everything but you'll have to find a different place to live.

POLO. I can do my own shirts . . . Why do I have to move?

CELIA. I know how you feel about me and it's embarrassing.

POLO. Love shouldn't be embarrassing.

CELIA. It's not really embarrassing, but I don't think the three of us can live together any more. I want you out of this house tomorrow. Tomorrow night— after dinner, your father gets his plane. I want you to leave.

POLO. Why?

CELIA. Because I don't want to take any chances.

POLO. What chances?

CELIA. Polo, let's not be children. You do know the difference between right and wrong and so do I. Tomorrow . . . I don't want you to go, but you have to. . . .

POLO. Tomorrow, for crissakes, even Simon Legree gave Little Eva two weeks' notice.

CELIA. I'm going to bed.

POLO. Yeh, go to bed. You're tired. Lay your head down on the pillow and close your eyes. If you want me to go, I'll go, but tonight I'll be in the room next to yours . . . I'll say I love you, but you won't be able to hear me because you'll be asleep. Maybe I'll sing you a lullaby.

CELIA. Polo, why are you doing this? Why now? We've been together so many nights and you've never been like this. . . . Why?

POLO. I'm drunk, that's the prize excuse for anything. I'm drunk and I don't know what I'm saying or doing. I could never say anything if I was sober . . . Celia?

CELIA. What?

POLO. Look, you know how I feel about you. How do you feel about me?

CELIA. I don't know.

POLO. Let's feel and find out.

CELIA. Please . . . don't.

POLO. Why didn't you slap me! I'll bet I could kiss you again and you wouldn't raise your hand.

CELIA. Why don't you? Go ahead, don't stop . . . pick me up in your arms and carry me to your brother's bed; I'm going to have a baby, Polo, so I might be a little heavy.

POLO. I'm sorry, but I love you. I didn't ask to. I didn't want to, but I do.

CELIA. Johnny . . . please go to bed.

POLO. I'm not Johnny, I'm Polo. . . .

CURTAIN

Act two

SCENE I

It is about eight o'clock the following morning. CELIA *is in the kitchen and* POLO *in his bedroom.*

CELIA. Polo, your coffee's poured. Polo? Are you up?

POLO. I'm up.

CELIA. On your feet? I've called you three times.

POLO. All right. [*A moment later* POLO *appears in the doorway. He is wearing pajamas that are three sizes too big for him.*] Good morning.

CELIA. Good morning . . . Those pajamas? They're big enough for two people. [*Rolling up his sleeve.*]

POLO. Christmas present. My relatives.

CELIA. They're absolutely precious. . . . I'm sorry, Polo, but they're hysterical.

POLO. Honey, what do you put in this coffee?

CELIA. Coffee and water and don't kid me about my coffee.

POLO. Well, for crissakes, do you know it has to boil?

CELIA. Give it back. I'll let it boil.

CELIA. See that Johnny gets these things for supper. I think you *should* come to supper and apologize to your father.

POLO. Since when do you have to apologize because you don't have money? If it's all the same to you I'll stop in Nedicks. They're running a special this week, two skinless franks and all the orange juice you can drink.

CELIA. You'll come to supper tonight.

POLO. Who said so?

CELIA. I said so.

POLO. I'll come to supper tonight. Boy, you're really going this morning. Did you have a long talk with God last night? You're like a new washing machine— pa ta-poom, pa ta-poom.

CELIA. You know what? You're blushing. Is your head killing you?

POLO. It isn't bleeding, is it?

CELIA. You're red as a beet.

POLO. I said an awful lot last night. I'm sorry. . . . I'm not sorry, I just think I should say I'm sorry. Just roll the sleeve up. Don't sit in my lap.

CELIA. I wasn't going to sit in your lap, Polo. What's so funny?

POLO. Nothing. I'm just so tired I'm silly. Did you ever get that tired? I'm so tired that nothing matters. I think if you dropped dead right now I'd laugh.

CELIA. That's sweet.

POLO. Where is Johnny?

CELIA. I don't know.

POLO. Well, where is he? Isn't that any of your business? I'll tell you the truth, sometimes . . . you just get me sick. He's your husband, isn't he? He hasn't been home all night . . . that happens two, three times a week. Honest it's been like living in a nut house.

CELIA. Polo! Johnny never asked me whether it would be all right if you came here and lived with us. He said you needed a home and brought you here.

POLO. I'm getting out. When I get good and ready and not before. I paid my rent this week.

CELIA. All right.

POLO. You see, you're like a dishrag. I thought I had to get out tonight—you didn't want to take any chances. Why don't you stand up on your feet!

CELIA. I've been standing on my feet all night long, Polo.

POLO. I must be going out of my mind. I could of sworn that I heard you come to my door . . . like a mirage, you want something and you see it . . . even when it's not there.

CELIA. Would you ask Johnny to take the laundry out when he comes in?

POLO. I'll take it out.

CELIA. Let Johnny do it.

POLO. All right! I'll let Johnny do it!

CELIA. There's no need to shout at me, Polo!

POLO. No, huh . . . You don't think so. For six months I kept my peace . . . You had your life to live and I let you live it, but I'm so in love with you . . . that I don't know what to do. But I'm just so fed up watch-

ing you being thrown away— What'll I do, go to
Alaska—join the Foreign Legion? All right, I love
you and I'll get out of here as soon as I can. Now
leave me alone! And if my sleeves roll down, just
keep your hands off me. . . . I'll roll them up myself.

CELIA. Now you shut up!

POLO. Boy, that's getting to be a habit with you.

CELIA. I don't need you to tell me what I've been
doing or what I haven't been doing.

POLO. Then you tell me. Why don't you ask—where he
is? Where has he been? What has he been doing?
How do you stand it day in and day out? Don't you
want to know where your kid's going to live? You're
going to have a baby, how do you live a life turning
your back on what's been happening? You tell me.

CELIA. Because I don't love Johnny.

POLO. That's not true.

CELIA. It is— I don't love him.

POLO. All right.

CELIA. He hasn't even so much as held my hands in
months. When he comes home at night, when he
comes home, I pretend I'm sleeping . . . you'd think
he'd touch my back, or kiss me good night. He
wouldn't know the difference if he found Santa
Claus in bed. He doesn't talk, he's always going . . .
I'm having a baby, his baby and he never mentions
the child or anything about it. Like anyone else . . .
I need. Love, children . . . a home. He used to be like
you . . . but he's not any more, and it's too late . . .
it's too late.

POLO. We're all nice people. . . . Come on, now, stop
crying.

CELIA. I can't tell him.

POLO. Why not?

CELIA. I don't know. I don't even know who he is. He's
a stranger . . . I never married that person. . . . I
thought he was so full of love. I don't know what it

is . . . but it doesn't matter any more because I don't love him, and I can't tell him that.

POLO. Listen, are you sure? Maybe you're—maybe you just want to get even, show him something.

CELIA. Last night—and it wasn't a mirage, Polo— That was me at your door.

POLO. But you couldn't come in the door—and I couldn't open it.

CELIA. You take the laundry out.

POLO. Do you think I could . . . just put my arms around you? Do you think it would be all right?

CELIA. I think so.

POLO. When will you tell him?

CELIA. Tonight. You'll be here tonight?

POLO. Yes.

CELIA. Have the laundry bleached and dried.

POLO. All right.

CELIA. I don't want to go to work.

POLO. You'd better.

CELIA. I think I'd better. When he comes home, make him take a bath and put on his flannel pajamas.

THE LIGHTS DIM OUT

SCENE II

It is about ten in the morning. As the lights dim up, JOHNNY *is seen coming down the fire escape. Halfway down, he slips; panicked, he grabs the railing and stops his fall. He steadies himself and then climbs down to the hall. He opens the door and enters the kitchen. The door to* POLO's *room is ajar.*

JOHNNY. Polo! Hi!
POLO. Welcome home.

JOHNNY. Celia go to work?

POLO. It's ten o'clock in the morning. She starts at nine . . . she's not here, so figure it out for yourself.

JOHNNY. The old man wanted you to have those shirts. How do they fit?

POLO. I haven't put it on yet.

JOHNNY. I was out all night.

POLO. No kidding. Your wife wants you to get these things for supper.

JOHNNY. Where are you going?

POLO. I'm going to take the laundry out. . . .

JOHNNY. You know what's happening . . .

POLO. I read the papers. Where you been?

JOHNNY. All over.

POLO. Where's all over?

JOHNNY. All over . . . Harlem, Lower East Side . . . everybody's disappeared.

POLO. It'll all blow over in a few weeks. . . .

JOHNNY. No. No . . . they dropped the net, Polo . . . they're starting to tie the knot. Every pusher in the city's vanished. . . . Look, Polo. . . . I was lucky. I met Ginnino. I told him to hold some for me . . . I have to get to him in fifteen minutes.

POLO. Who fixed you last night?

JOHNNY. Chuchie . . . I stopped over his place. He gave me half of his . . . enough to carry me through the night . . . but I'm thin now, Polo.

POLO. I told you yesterday, Johnny, the cupboard's bare. I'm out of the box and that's all there is to it. If I inherited the Chrysler building right now I wouldn't give you another dime. Try to understand that.

JOHNNY. Don't start lecturing me now. All I need is twenty bucks—and he won't do business on credit.

POLO. Take the kitchen set down and sell it to the Salvation Army. This linoleum isn't in bad shape. If you sell it at night in the dark, maybe you can get a few bucks for it. . . .

JOHNNY. Polo, you know I never sold a thing out of this house and I never will.

POLO. Try to listen, Johnny, try to hear me. I felt great refusing the old man that twenty-five hundred because I know the money went to a good cause. . . . It's only something he wanted all his life. You were right in the middle when he shouted, "Where? Where did it go?"

JOHNNY. Yeh, I was right in the middle. And I almost said, "Here!" It went here. [*Thrusting his arm forward.*]

POLO. You went through that twenty-five hundred like grease through a tin horn. . . . I'm afraid to park my car out front . . . you might steal it some night.

JOHNNY. I'm quitting tomorrow. Tomorrow I'm quitting. . . .

POLO. It's been tomorrow for months, Johnny, the calendar never moves.

JOHNNY. Polo! This is the last time I'll ask you . . . I need twenty bucks. . . .

POLO. Twenty bucks, twice a day.

JOHNNY. Where am I gonna get it?

POLO. Get yourself a black felt hat, cut holes in it for eyes, and go down in the men's room of the subway like Apples does and clobber some poor bastard over the head. . . .

JOHNNY. The answer is no?

POLO. You look tired. . . .

JOHNNY. Here. . . . [*Tosses gun on bed.*] I almost used it four times last night . . . I picked dark streets and I waited. Four times . . . and they were set-ups. An old guy . . . must have been eighty years old . . . all alone. A guy and his girl, a young kid coming home from a dance drunk . . . some woman. Four times I left the doorway—I was on top of them . . . They weren't even afraid of me. I asked for a match, which way Fifty-sixth Street was . . . and would you give me a light please. Dust—that's all. Tired feet, tired eyes, and jammed up log tight.

POLO. Where did you get this . . . ?

JOHNNY. The lousy bastards told me it wasn't loaded. I'm into them for seven or eight hundred . . . on top of your twenty-five hundred cash. They want their money today . . . They'll be coming for me.

POLO. What do you mean?

JOHNNY. What do you think I mean?

POLO. It's not going to be Mother and Apples alone . . . they know I'm here, they'll bring company. Put those shoes on and let's get out of here.

JOHNNY. No more running, Polo. I'm through running. I can't run any more. If they don't get me today, they'll get me tomorrow.

POLO. You saw what happened to Willy DeCarlo . . .

JOHNNY. I'm not running away from them . . . and that's that! I'm going to stay right here. . . .

POLO. You're crazy, you're going crazy!

JOHNNY. I'm not moving. . . .

POLO. I haven't got seven or eight hundred dollars, Johnny . . . there's nothing I can do.

JOHNNY. Take the laundry out . . . and go to a movie or something.

POLO. What are you going to do?

JOHNNY. I'm going to wait for them . . .

POLO. You going to fight back . . . ?

JOHNNY. Well, I'm not going to stand still while they beat the hell out of me. . . .

POLO. You can't win . . . they'll kick your ribs in.

[FATHER *knocks and enters.*]

JOHNNY. Hi ya, Pop, you're up early . . .

FATHER. Good morning, Johnny—

POLO. Good morning, Pop. . . . I said good morning, Pop . . .

FATHER. Good morning.

POLO. I'm sorry about last night—

FATHER. How's the boy, Johnny . . . ?

POLO. I'm sorry about not getting to dinner last night . . . Pop, I got looped. Come on, Pop, how about shaking hands and turning over a new leaf . . .

FATHER. I made a long-distance call to Palm Beach this morning trying to get the carpenter . . . and the plumber but I can't. They're putting in eight hours today, maybe copper tubing behind the bar . . .

JOHNNY. Have you had your breakfast—maybe I can whip you up a few scrambled. . . .

FATHER. I'll bet I could throw dollar bills out that window all morning long and there wouldn't be enough on the sidewalk to pay off the money I'm losing today. . . .

JOHNNY. We got an electric orange-juice squeezer—how about if I squeeze up some juice . . .

FATHER. I'm renovating a building I'll never be able to buy . . .

POLO. I'm sorry, Pop. I said I was sorry and I mean it.

FATHER. You said a lot of other things.

POLO. Let's shake hands on it, what do you say?

JOHNNY. The kid's got his hand out waiting for yours. . . .

POLO. I'd like to go to that ball game with you, Pop. Today's my day off . . .

FATHER. You made a jackass out of me! They'll laugh at me down there. I tell all my friends about you kids . . .

JOHNNY. Take the laundry out . . .

POLO. For crissakes, Pop, I haven't got the money. I'm not holding out on you.

JOHNNY. Take the laundry out!

POLO. I don't want to take it out.

JOHNNY. Take it out.

POLO. All right, Johnny. [*He goes out.*]

FATHER. A good rain cleans the streets . . . huh?

JOHNNY. You're up early, Pop.

FATHER. I didn't get much sleep. I was wondering about something, Johnny. Is today your day off? I mean, how can you take in the ball game if you're working?

JOHNNY. I'm not working.

FATHER. You say you and your wife are getting along . . . ?

JOHNNY. Yeh . . .

FATHER. Last night, when I went back to the hotel, I kept thinking about what your wife said, about believing. About what do I believe in. She's right, I got you kids to believe in. Like I come up here—you got a wife, a little home, a kid on the way, you're making a home for your brother. You did a good job of bringing yourself up . . . but what the hell's your brother doing? Holing up in some dame's apartment? Twenty-five hundred is a—

JOHNNY. I don't know. . . .

FATHER. You talk in awful short phrases, Johnny. . . .

JOHNNY. I'm not used to talking to you, Pop.

FATHER. That's right, we don't talk very much, do we?

JOHNNY. No. . . .

FATHER. I like the letters you write me, Johnny . . . Life plays funny tricks on people. Hello and Good-bye . . . and nothing in between, but I like the letters you write me.

JOHNNY. I'm glad you do, Pop.

FATHER. You take this believing thing—after your mother died, I used to read to you and your brother . . . Hi Diddle Diddle, the Cat and the Fiddle, Easter Bunny, Santa Claus and all that crap. You'd believe everything. I'd tell Polo Santa Claus was coming, and he'd look at me like I was out of my mind. You understand what I mean . . . ?

JOHNNY. I'm trying to, Pop. . . .

FATHER. Well, some people can talk, they have all the words. There are some things I feel that I don't have the words for. Maybe you're a little bit like me because you don't seem to be able to talk to me. . . .

JOHNNY. I always wanted to talk to you, Pop, but it's like you never wanted to talk to me, like you were afraid . . .

FATHER. What I want to say is that I care what happens to you. . . .

JOHNNY. Thanks. . . .

FATHER. And I love you—that's the thing, see?

JOHNNY. You what?

FATHER. You heard me the first time. Don't make me say it again.

JOHNNY. I feel the same way, Pop—

FATHER. How's that?

JOHNNY. You know what I mean—Polo, you and me, we're all kinda— Pop, willya do something for me. I never asked you for anything. When the kid comes back, tell him it's all water under the bridge. . . . Oh. . . .

FATHER. What's the matter?

JOHNNY. Headache . . .

FATHER. You wouldn't know anything about what happened to that money. Or would you? He doesn't pay a hundred dollars a week board here, does he?

JOHNNY. I'm asking you for something now. When Polo comes—

FATHER. That's the difference between you and Polo, you never asked me for anything.

JOHNNY. He never asked you for anything either, Pop.

FATHER. Yeh, but the way he looked at me sometimes— Maybe I never gave you much either.

JOHNNY. You gave me a coat once!

FATHER. A coat?

JOHNNY. Yeh, you came to the home, and you took me out to a department store—and you let me pick out a coat. And then you took me to a restaurant and made the guy give me some wine. . . .

FATHER. Your brother doesn't gamble, does he?

JOHNNY. No. . . .

FATHER. I always kinda thought that you and your

brother and I had a special thing. I thought we were just kinda three men . . . Your brother did a lot of shouting last night.

JOHNNY. Pop, you did a little shouting yourself last night.

FATHER. I lived with my father until I was twenty-two years old, and I never raised my voice above a whisper . . .

JOHNNY. He lived with his father for nine years. What did you expect, Little Lord Fauntleroy?

FATHER. I expect the same thing I get from you. You don't go around crying like a kid in a crib. I like the letters you write me—'cause they're a man's letter. Dammit, you had a tough life but you made the best of it. Ever since he left home . . .

JOHNNY. He didn't leave home. He was sent away. Every time he gets a letter from you, he goes into his room and reads it. He's got a box of them in there. . . .

FATHER. Yeh . . . ?

JOHNNY. Yeh.

FATHER. Well, how would I know that!

JOHNNY. He's missed you for a long time, Pop. You shipped him out to uncles and aunts . . .

FATHER. And what was I doing? Gambling, drinking, laying on my can in Bermuda. I don't know anything about him. . . .

JOHNNY. Well, when he comes in, you ask him about that time in the orphan home when he wet the bed, and they made him stand on a staircase all day long with the wet sheet over his head . . .

FATHER. I shipped him— What was I supposed to do, buy a house, work nights, wash clothes during the day? Uncles and aunts, thank God he had them . . .

JOHNNY. All right, Pop . . .

FATHER. A man has only two hands.

JOHNNY. All right, Pop . . .

FATHER. And don't go around all-righting me. When I

came yesterday, I had a funny feeling. Right now I
got it again. You're not glad to see me, are you?

JOHNNY. Pop, I don't want to talk about it.

FATHER. You're not glad to see me, are you?

JOHNNY. Nobody's blaming you for anything. . . .

FATHER. You both always had a roof over your heads.

JOHNNY. Yeh, but when we woke up we didn't know
what roof we were under.

FATHER. Waking up in a hotel room is no fun . . .

JOHNNY. Nobody's blaming you. When you stand in
the snow your feet get cold—if you fall in the water
and you can't swim, you drown. We call you Pop,
and you call us Son, but it never was . . .

FATHER. You're a pretty cold-hearted cookie, Johnny.

JOHNNY. I don't save your letters . . . and I never saved
my money to try to help you out. Don't come around
knocking Polo to me . . . because he's my brother.

FATHER. And I'm not your father?

JOHNNY. Don't put words in my mouth . . .

FATHER. What the hell's the matter with you—all the
things you say? What are you—the lawyer in the
case . . . !

JOHNNY. I know you, Pop—either you clam up, or you
start to push . . .

FATHER. As I listen to you, it sounds like I don't even
know you. . . .

JOHNNY. Don't start to steam!

FATHER. I don't even know you!

JOHNNY. All right, you don't even know me.

FATHER. I don't even know you!

JOHNNY. How the hell could you know me? The last
time I saw you I was in the hospital. You came to see
me for three days. Before that . . . I saw you for two
days, when I graduated school. How the hell could
you know me? When you came to the hospital . . .
you said, Jesus, it must have been rough, kid, but it's
all over . . . that's all you had to say . . . we shook
hands, like two big men.

FATHER. If you felt that was wrong, why didn't you tell me?

JOHNNY. Tell you what? All I remember is laying there and smiling, thinking the old man's come to take me home.

FATHER. I live in a hotel, Johnny!

JOHNNY. Three big days. Six lousy visiting hours, and you run out. I was so glad to see you. . . .

FATHER. Your wife was there to take you home.

JOHNNY. I knew my wife for one year. I've known you for twenty-seven. Twenty-seven years. Your son! My boy Johnny. I didn't even know who she was.

[POLO *enters.*]

FATHER. That's a helluva thing to tell me—you didn't know who your wife was. You're not gonna blame me, are you? What's the matter with your brother?

POLO. Come on, Johnny, sit down. Sit down, will you.

JOHNNY. No, no, come on, let me stand up. I'd like to tell you right now what's standing in front of you . . . and it's not your Johnny boy.

POLO. No, Johnny, don't!

JOHNNY. I told you about the Sergeant, Polo. I told you all about that sonofabitchin Sergeant.

POLO. Come on, Pop, take a walk.

[JOHNNY *is not only disturbed by the pent-up emotion, but the narcotic's absence is beginning to become physically apparent.*]

JOHNNY. Tell him what they give you, Polo, tell him. He walked out, like the Sergeant ran out . . . The nurse came, and the doctor . . . They roll up your sleeve—one—then two—then another. You know what I'm talking about? Your son's trying to tell you something. . . .

FATHER. What have you been doing—hitting cheap gin?

POLO. You'd better go, Pop.

JOHNNY. And you come around here talking about an oak tree.

FATHER. Don't shake your finger in my face . . .

JOHNNY. I'm trying to tell you something, old man. . . .

POLO. Johnny, lay off . . .

FATHER. Are we still going to have supper tonight?

JOHNNY. Sure, we're going to have supper tonight. Why not?

FATHER. Why don't you meet me at the hotel in an hour or so? We'll go up and see the ball game.

POLO. Johnny and I will both be there. . . .

FATHER. You better see that he gets to bed. Make him get some sleep. [*The* FATHER *moves into the hallway.* POLO *follows him.*]

POLO. He's not feeling good, Pop. He doesn't mean—

FATHER. He means it, Polo.

JOHNNY. Okay, Sergeant. It's okay. Every man for himself. It's okay, Sarge. I got your number.

POLO [*off*]. I'll see you in an hour. . . . [*Returning.*] Come, Johnny, on your feet and walk around. Come on, get up. Take your shirt off, you're starting to sweat.

JOHNNY. Close the window, it's cold.

POLO. Johnny, I'm going to turn you in. [*Moves to phone.*] Johnny? Tell me to pick it up. Nobody will hate you, tell me to pick it up, will you?

JOHNNY. Tomorrow. Don't touch that . . . don't touch it, Sarge. Look, we'll get out of here alive.

POLO. Johnny! Johnny. This is Polo.

JOHNNY. The Sergeant—where's the Sergeant?

POLO. He's not here.

JOHNNY. You don't know what it is to need something, Sergeant. All alone in a cave and not a crumb in the whole cave.

POLO. Johnny, get up!

JOHNNY. You're not going to leave me, Sergeant.

POLO. No, Johnny. I'm not going to leave you. Come on get up. Now slow, go slow, Johnny.

JOHNNY. I'm all right, I'm all right. You go to sleep, Sarge. I'll watch for you. . . . Twenty dollars, that's all I need. Twenty dollars and I'll be the night watchman. . . . Twenty dollars, Sarge. I'll go to the desk myself. I'll turn myself in. [POLO *is at the phone.*] What are you doing with that? What are you taking my goddamn shoes for? You leave me something to eat, 'ya hear! [JOHNNY *grabs the phone.*] What are you taking my shoes for?

POLO. Johnny, give me the phone.

JOHNNY. You're not going to leave me, Sergeant, are you? Don't leave me, all I need is twenty lousy bucks.

POLO. Twenty bucks twice a day.

JOHNNY. Leave me something to eat, you hear? Go ahead, run! Run! Run and leave me alone, you son-ofabitch. I can't move but you run, run and leave me here to die by myself, you sonofabitch.

POLO. Johnny!

JOHNNY. Sssssshhhh. Quiet. Be quiet. Here they come, run for it, run for it. Oh God, here they come. Hit it! Hit it! [*He cowers on the bed.*]

POLO. For the love of God, Johnny, it's Polo. . . . It's your brother. It's Polo. . . . Polo!

JOHNNY. Hit me, go ahead. Hit me. I don't have to tell you anything. There was nobody here with me. No-body. Corporal John Pope, 122036617. Name, rank, serial number. I don't know who took my shoes.

[MOTHER *and* APPLES *appear.*]

POLO. Come on, will you snap out of it. Mother, do something for him. I'll make good for it.

MOTHER. I'd like to laugh, but I can't. The pocket's in trouble.

JOHNNY. Go ahead, beat me. I'm bleeding, but beat me. You sonsabitches—go ahead! Watch my back—will you watch my back—beat me, 1220—122036617—John Pope.

POLO. Give him something to quiet him down. I'll make good for it.

APPLES. He must think you're the Chase National Bank, Mother. We don't wake up and find our money in a rain barrel.

POLO. On my word of honor, I'll pay you tomorrow.

MOTHER. All eight hundred. You got enough to cover this trip.

POLO. I swore if it killed me I wasn't going to put another nickel into that arm!

JOHNNY. Don't hit me—will you watch my back. I didn't have a gun. I don't know who took my shoes.

POLO. Take it. You're the Mother of them all. Go ahead, count it.

APPLES. Mother's got a Horn and Hardart mentality. Nickels and dimes, right, Mother. Right?

MOTHER. I'll tell you what I'm going to do. I'll set him straight for twelve bucks. . . . We'll give him back his spine. Then we're going to work him over.

POLO. You'll get yours someday, Mother. I'll see that you get paid in full someday.

JOHNNY. 122036617! That's all I have to tell you. Nobody with me . . . that's all.

MOTHER [*picking up* JOHNNY]. Just take it easy, Corporal—the General's here.

JOHNNY [*as he is carried out by* MOTHER]. Watch my back. . . . Watch my back.

APPLES. Old Mother's got some sense of humor—the General's here. You shouldn't treat Mother like a smell. You know the British Government's been sending tax collectors into the bush for years . . . trying to get them pygmy bastards to pay up their back taxes. That's right. Flies don't have brains . . . and the pygmies don't have money, but they got goats. They got to pay their back taxes with goats . . . you understand. Flies don't have brains, but he's got brains.

[MOTHER *has returned.*]

MOTHER. You don't need a car in the city, no place to park.

APPLES. Allus getting parkin' tickets . . .

MOTHER. You got your keys . . . ?

POLO. Yeh.

MOTHER. You got your pink slip?

POLO. Yeh.

MOTHER. You get to the nearest used-car lot and sell that car! I want eight hundred dollars. We'll be back tonight. We don't get that money—we put your brother in the hospital with Willy DeCarlo. . . . Maybe we send you along too. Let's move it!

[*He and* APPLES *leave.*]

JOHNNY [*comes into the kitchen*]. Where'd they go?

POLO. Are you all right?

JOHNNY. I'm all right. Polo—

POLO. Johnny— The shopping list is on the table, Johnny. I got something to do before I meet the old man. Do you want us to pick you up . . . go to the game with us?

JOHNNY. No, I think I'd better stay here.

POLO. I'll see you at supper.

JOHNNY. Polo . . . I have to tell her, but what can I say? I don't know what the hell's happening to me . . . that's the trouble . . . yesterday, I went all the way over to that Summittown . . . and I stand there like an idiot looking at the house. It's all gone, what the hell am I looking for? I trust you, Polo—how can I tell her?

POLO. Tell her, Johnny, just tell her.

JOHNNY. What'll I say for crissakes?

POLO. Just say . . . uh . . . I'm a junkey. That's what you are, isn't it, Johnny?

THE LIGHTS DIM OUT

SCENE III

It is early the same evening. As the lights fade in, we hear faintly the music of a street carousel and the eager, happy voices of children in the street below. Odd fragments of the phrases, "Ma, Ma, I wanna go again...." JOHNNY, wearing a neatly pressed shirt, is in the kitchen, spreading a tablecloth. He moves to the sink, and, as he turns around, we see that he has a bouquet of flowers; he sets them on the table. As he hears CELIA approach, he moves hurriedly into POLO'S room, leaving the door ajar. CELIA enters.

CELIA. Polo.

JOHNNY [*from within*]. Yeh.

CELIA. Did Johnny go to the game?

JOHNNY [*still inside*]. Yeh.

CELIA. The flowers are beautiful. What smells so good? What are you doing in there? The kids are riding the carousel. The old horse looks like he wants to go home and sleep. [JOHNNY *sneaks up behind her and puts his hands over her eyes.*] What are you doing? A surprise ... what's the surprise?

JOHNNY. Me.

CELIA. I thought you were going to the game with your father.

JOHNNY. Let's go down and ride the carousel.

CELIA. I've got to get things ready. Did Polo go to the game?

JOHNNY. Yeh. Come on, let's go down and take one ride on it.

CELIA. We'd break the horses.

JOHNNY. How was your day?

CELIA. What?

JOHNNY. I said, how was your day?

CELIA. Like any other day. Why?

JOHNNY. Why? I thought you said that a day wasn't just a day.

CELIA. Oh. I'll have to make a salad.

JOHNNY. It's in the icebox.

CELIA. I'll have to make the dressing.

JOHNNY. It's in the blue cup. I've looked for the shoe polish all day and I can't find it. Where do you hide it?

CELIA. The cabinet . . . under the sink. You did the floors.

JOHNNY. I swished a mop around. I took all my clothes to the cleaners, and I fixed that clock.

CELIA. You didn't look for a job today, did you?

JOHNNY. No, I didn't have time.

CELIA. I didn't mean anything. I was just curious . . . that's all.

JOHNNY. Yeh. You want to sit in a tub of hot water . . . I'll rub your back with alcohol.

CELIA. What is this? Flowers, the floors mopped, meat in the oven, shining your shoes—what's the occasion? I mean, what's all this for?

JOHNNY. Don't you like the flowers?

CELIA. Of course, I like the flowers. I didn't expect to find you home, flowers and the floor mopped.

JOHNNY. You just said that.

CELIA. Said what?

JOHNNY. Flowers and the floor mopped, you said that twice.

CELIA. All right, supposing I did say that twice, what difference does it make!

JOHNNY. No difference, I wasn't criticizing you, I was just—

CELIA. Can we forget it, Johnny, please?

JOHNNY. Forget what?

CELIA. That I said something twice!

JOHNNY. What is it? I was out last night again, is that it?

CELIA. No.

JOHNNY. How many more guesses do I get?

CELIA. It's over.

JOHNNY. What's over? What are you talking about?

CELIA. We've tried.

JOHNNY. I'm behind the times. I thought it was just

going to begin. What you said yesterday, that I never came home . . . all the things you said, I've been thinking about them.

CELIA. I'll leave tonight.

JOHNNY. Is it because I lost my job?

CELIA. It's not the job, Johnny.

JOHNNY. What is it?

CELIA. I don't love you.

JOHNNY. And we snap our fingers and that's that?

CELIA. That's the way it is.

JOHNNY. I don't like this talk. Everything's so cold. What is this, a formal dance or something?

CELIA. Johnny, I refuse to get emotional. . . . I just refuse to. My mind is made up. It's not easy, but it's something that has to be done. Now I refuse to get emotional. I'm not going to blame you for anything and I don't want to be blamed for anything. We have to concede that the marriage has failed, not you, not I . . . but we have. I refuse to get emotional. Nothing will be settled by emotion.

JOHNNY. A day isn't just a day, that's what you said. It's not my day or your day. It's not just you and I now.

CELIA. If I understand you correctly, you are talking about the baby?

JOHNNY. Yeh, you understand me correctly.

CELIA. It's amazing, honestly.

JOHNNY. What's amazing? What?

CELIA. For four months I've been waiting for you to say something, one word, one syllable about the baby.

JOHNNY. Today isn't yesterday . . . things can change, you know?

CELIA. Johnny. I don't want to talk any more because I don't want to get emotional.

JOHNNY. I'm home! Do you understand that? I'm home now! I haven't been but I am now. Here! I bought this today. [*Gives package to her.*]

CELIA. What is it?

JOHNNY. You said it was going to be a girl, didn't you? Five dresses, one for every day of the week . . . that's another thing I did today.

CELIA. Where did you get the money?

JOHNNY. We don't need electric orange-juice squeezers. I can squeeze oranges with my hands.

CELIA. Well, thank you, Johnny. Thank you very much.

JOHNNY. Look, it's my turn to cry, to beg . . . you reached out your hand and I turned my back, you've looked at me and I've closed my eyes. You're not listening to me. Please listen to me. . . . Please.

CELIA. I'm listening.

JOHNNY. All right, you don't love me any more. There was something in me worthwhile loving. You must have loved me for some reason! What was the reason? Celia? Celia? I haven't even used your name. I say baby . . . and I say honey . . . but now I'm saying Celia. Celia. I love you.

CELIA. Oh, Johnny, please. Please stop . . . please.

JOHNNY. I know I've been deaf, dumb and blind but please don't do to me what I did to you. Something happened to me. It's something that's hard to understand. Honey, I don't know whether I'm laughing or crying, but, Celia, you don't have to love me . . . not for a long time. You just don't even have to bother . . .

CELIA. Oh . . . oh . . . oh . . . Do you want to feel something? Johnny, give me your hand . . . Lightly, do you feel it . . . [*She has taken* JOHNNY's *hand and put it gently over her stomach.*] You see?

JOHNNY. Oh— Wow! Holy cats . . . I felt it move. I swear I felt it move. Let me feel that again. I don't feel anything. What happened?

CELIA. Nothing happened. It doesn't move all day long. Just every once in a while.

JOHNNY. Well, let me know the next time you think it's going to move.

CELIA. I will.

JOHNNY. That's a real miracle, you know. Heh . . .

CELIA. Hold me, Johnny. Please . . . hold me.

JOHNNY. Oh, you're going to see some changes . . . I've been making plans all day. I've been like a kid waiting for you to come home. I kept looking at the clock.

CELIA. I don't have a handkerchief.

JOHNNY. You're not going to leave me? Are you? Tell me?

CELIA. No, Johnny, I'm gonna get an apron.

[POLO *comes in.*]

POLO. The old man's down in Garrity's. He wants to buy you a drink.

JOHNNY. Is he sore?

POLO. He says he wants bygones to be bygones.

JOHNNY. You got a little windburn. Who won the game?

POLO. Who played?

JOHNNY. What's eating you?

POLO. The old man. He thinks I still have that money . . . on the way home he started talking it up again. Gone where? You didn't buy a new car, what do you pay—five hundred dollars a week board? This time he's using the happy-time-U.S.A. approach.

JOHNNY. I'll go down and talk to him.

CELIA. I want you to forget this morning, Polo.

POLO. All right.

JOHNNY. What are you two talking about?

CELIA. Nothing that concerns you, Johnny.

POLO. It's forgotten. Did you tell her, Johnny? Did you tell her?

CELIA. Now what are you two talking about?

JOHNNY. Nothing that concerns you, honey.

POLO. The old man will wait a minute.

JOHNNY. Not now, Polo. I'll take care of it. I give you my word, but not now.

POLO. Johnny, I'm going away. I don't know where. I'd like to leave tonight . . . but I can't.

JOHNNY. Let the old man get on his plane and go back to Palm Beach. He doesn't have to know anything.

CELIA. Know what?

POLO. I'm not leaving her with you, Johnny.

JOHNNY. Will you leave us alone for a minute.

CELIA. Johnny! What's the matter!

POLO. I'll stay, Johnny. I've been part of it.

JOHNNY. Look, Celia—now it's nothing to get excited about. [*From off, we hear the* FATHER'*s whistle.*] Will you just sit down for a minute. Polo had the money that the old man wanted, but I took it all.

CELIA. What do you mean?

JOHNNY. Look, honey, I'm . . . the thing is, I . . . I'll go down with the old man. He's whistling.

POLO. Tell her, will you please tell her.

CELIA. What is it?

JOHNNY. Get out of my way, Polo . . . you hear me. Get out of my way!

POLO. I'm not in your way. Go ahead, run.

JOHNNY. Honey, my father's whistling. Will you get away from that door. Let me out.

CELIA. Johnny, you can tell me . . . you can tell me anything. What have you done?

FATHER [*off*]. Heh, Johnny . . .

POLO. Nobody's going to hate you, Johnny.

FATHER [*off*]. Heh, Johnny boy . . .

JOHNNY. Honey, I'm hooked . . . I'm a junkey . . . I take dope. I'm hooked.

CELIA. You're what?

JOHNNY. I'm hooked!

CELIA. That's silly.

JOHNNY. No, it's not silly. I need it, two times . . . every day . . . and it costs money.

CELIA. It's all right. Whatever it is, it's all right. It's all right.

JOHNNY. Don't say anything to the old man.

CELIA. We'll call a doctor.

JOHNNY. Not until the old man goes. He doesn't have to know.

CELIA. Johnny, it doesn't matter. There's nothing to be ashamed of, it's all right, everything's going to be all right.

[FATHER *comes in.*]

FATHER. Where the hell were you? I been downstairs whistling my brains out.

JOHNNY. I didn't hear you, Pop.

FATHER. Didn't hear you, Pop . . . do you know these bums of mine . . . these bums . . . ?

CELIA. They're not bums.

FATHER. These bums. I spent more time on the back porch whistling. I'd get all the cats and the dogs in the neighborhood . . . but not Johnny, not Polo . . . isn't that right, Johnny?

POLO. That's right, Pop.

FATHER. Got a towel for me, honey? [*Moving off into the john; out of sight.*] Did Johnny ever tell you about the time he was a kid I came home and found him digging up the backyard? I asked him what the hell are you doing? Workin', daddy . . . me workin' . . . I told him the only way you get money in your pockets is to work. He'd dig a hole, and then look in the pockets, dig another hole and in the pockets, and no money . . . Johnny was convinced . . . Work and you make money. One day I came home and it was raining . . . and there's the little bum there digging away . . . he had his hat laying alongside a big empty hole . . . and finally I convinced him not to believe what I told him in the first place, then . . . he bends down and picks up his hat—and the water goes running all over him . . . he worked and worked and all he got was a hatful of rain.

CELIA. I was on time for work today.

POLO. You were?

CELIA. Yes, I was.

POLO. Good!

FATHER. There's no napkins on the table. [*Coming out of the john.*] What's everybody so quiet about . . . ?

CELIA. Pass me the pepper and salt . . . please, Polo.

FATHER. Let me have that salt after you.

JOHNNY. How about you, Polo, you want some salt too?

POLO. It needs it.

JOHNNY. I thought I put salt in.

CELIA. We're putting it in now. It doesn't matter.

FATHER. The soup's flat as Kelsey's.

CELIA. Johnny cooked that soup.

FATHER. Let's not start the Trojan war over a bowl of soup.

JOHNNY. How'd you like the ball game, Pop?

FATHER. When that Snider steps up to the plate . . . he looks like he owns the ball park. How about you, Johnny—do you get out and see a ball game?

JOHNNY. No, Pop, I don't . . .

FATHER. You ought to—get out in the air. Fresh air—it's good for you. What the . . . ? What is this, the last supper? What did I do now? Well, go ahead, you guys . . . Did I say something wrong?

JOHNNY. No—we're all a little tired, that's all . . .

FATHER. Talking in short phrases again? Johnny? All right, yes, Pop, no, Pop—

POLO. It's your imagination . . .

CELIA. Can we just pretend that we are—

FATHER. Will you let me say what I want to say! Now look—last night you gave me a working over, right, Polo? And today you really laced into me. Did you see me walking around with my tail between my legs? You didn't come through with the money you promised me. We're eating here now—we're all together, now for crissakes let's have a song or something. Let's get a few laughs . . .

JOHNNY. I'm a junkey, Pop . . .

CELIA. Johnny's sick . . .

FATHER. You don't know what you're talking about . . .

POLO. He knows what he's talking about . . .

FATHER. You mean you take . . . dope? That's a junkey, isn't it?

JOHNNY. That's it.

FATHER. You've known about this, Polo?

POLO. All the time . . .

FATHER. Well, where do you get it . . . I mean, how?

POLO. Let's forget it.

FATHER. I'm asking your brother a question. I'm not asking you for orders . . .

[CELIA *moves off into the living room.*]

POLO. I'm giving you one—shut up!

FATHER. Don't say "shut up" to me.

POLO. Keep your hat on.

FATHER. What do you mean, "keep my hat on?"

JOHNNY. Geez, I'm not so hungry. [*Calls to* CELIA.] Honey, why don't you sit down and try to eat . . .

CELIA. I was looking for lipstick on your shirts.

FATHER. All the time you knew it . . . ? How long is all the time?

JOHNNY. I've been hooked . . . this time, seven months . . .

FATHER. This time? There was another time . . . ?

JOHNNY. Yeh . . . for a few months after I came out of the hospital, but I told Polo, and he helped me. I kicked it . . .

FATHER. You kicked it . . .

JOHNNY. Yeh, I kicked it . . . I got off the habit.

CELIA. Johnny, please! Don't start getting touchy!

JOHNNY. Well, go to a public library and read up on it! What do you expect me to do, sit here and—

FATHER. Look, I'm going to find out now whose fault this is and who's to blame. And you knew about it, so you talk.

POLO. I don't know whose fault it is. . . .

CELIA. What difference does it make who's to blame. Maybe it's my fault?

FATHER. You're his wife! What do you know about

this? You been sleeping in the same bed with him and you don't even know you been sleeping with a dope addict!

POLO. Pop, will you shut up.

CELIA. I haven't been sleeping with a dope addict. We've just been sharing the bed for—

FATHER. For crissakes, it's disgusting. You sit down to dinner and your kid turns out to be a—

JOHNNY. Will you lay off.

CELIA. Why don't you tell me?

JOHNNY. I told you.

FATHER. I can't understand how a boy like you—

JOHNNY. Will you be quiet! And don't turn your back on me like I'm dead . . . I know what I am.

FATHER. What are you?

JOHNNY. I'm a *junkey!*

FATHER. I ought to beat the hell out of you!

POLO. Pop, the kid is trying . . .

FATHER. How could you sit at that table . . . ?

POLO [*between* JOHNNY *and the enraged* FATHER]. Lay off him . . . come on now . . .

FATHER. Mind your own business!

CELIA. Please, please . . .

JOHNNY. I'm asking you to be quiet, Pop, I'm not begging . . . Be quiet!

FATHER. Polo, get out of my way . . .

JOHNNY. You raise that hand to me and I'll—

FATHER. Polo, get out of my way—

POLO. He told you, Pop . . .

JOHNNY. I'm trying to tell you something, Pop . . .

POLO. He told you—and telling you hasn't changed anything. He's still a junkey . . . For crissakes he's sick . . . don't you understand that he's sick . . . ?

JOHNNY. I'm not . . . I'm not . . . Oh, what the hell's the use. [*He rushes out.*]

FATHER. Johnny, come back here . . . ! Come back! Come back!

CELIA. Johnny . . . Johnny—oh, Johnny, I'm afraid.

POLO. He'll come back . . .

FATHER. He ran away.

POLO. I'll go out and find him.

CELIA. No, Polo. Don't leave me. Stay right here. Just let me sit for a minute. Something is wrong . . .

POLO. The baby?

CELIA. Polo? I think you'd better call a cab . . . Something is going wrong inside of me. I'm afraid to move. . . .

POLO. Get her coat, Pop. [POLO *runs downstairs.*]

CELIA. He'll come back. He's got to come back . . .

FATHER. Put your arms around me. [*He picks her up.*] Just hold tight . . .

POLO. Taxi! Yo . . . Yo . . . taxi . . . heh, taxi!

[*The* FATHER *moves with* CELIA *toward the door.*]

FATHER. Shhhhh . . . shhhhh. . . .

CURTAIN

Act three

When the curtain rises, there are no lights in the apartment area. We see the glow of the skylight. In the distance we hear MOTHER *and* APPLES *laughing hysterically as they climb up the stairs. Their laughter suggests that they are having difficulty in climbing the stairs, probably falling against the wall in hysterics. Finally they appear, their laughter subsiding somewhat.* CHUCH *lags behind.* MOTHER *and* APPLES *walk directly to the door but* CHUCH *starts up the ladder.* MOTHER *turns and calls to him as he knocks on the door.*

MOTHER. Where are you going, dummy? Come here . . .

CHUCH. I tole ya I'm not hittin' Johnny.

MOTHER [*calling*]. Heh, Johnny . . . it's your old Mother.

CHUCH. You said I don't have to hit him . . .

MOTHER [*knocking*]. Will you shut up . . . !

APPLES. He ain't home.

CHUCH. Come on, let's go.

MOTHER. Cross the roof . . . come in the fire escape, Chuchie . . . and open the door.

CHUCH. All right. . . . [*He scurries up the fire escape.*]

APPLES. You gonna sweat him out? Huh, Mother . . . ?

MOTHER. We gonna sweat him out.

APPLES. You know what I like about you, Mother?

MOTHER. What do you like about me?

APPLES. I'm gonna tell you what I like about you.

MOTHER. What?

APPLES. No matter what the band plays . . . you hear your own music.

MOTHER. That stuff was a hundred per cent pure. Man, I feel like King Kong ridin' a cloud . . . [MOTHER *opens the door and they both enter.*]

CHUCH [*coming from the other side*]. That door was open there all the time!

MOTHER. Chuch, I goofed. What are you doing?

CHUCH. I'm sitting down.

MOTHER. I know you're sitting down. Go down to the car and keep an eye on that whacky broad . . .

CHUCH. Make Apples go down. I don't want to go near that whacky broad. She's always trying to grab me . . .

MOTHER. Well, let her grab you, but keep an eye on her . . .

CHUCH. I always get the short end . . . [CHUCH *goes out. The phone rings,* APPLES *picks it up.*]

APPLES. Hold on a minute, willya . . . It's Ginnino . . . No, nothing happened. No, I'm not laughin' at you, Mother's startin' to float. Yeh . . . huh, yeh. Man, we almost got arrested four times today, and the day's not over yet. Mother's floatin' away, and he ain't coming back. . . .

MOTHER. Lay down the red carpet for our man.

APPLES. Heh, little Jim . . . Mother and me and that whacky broad, the one with all the money. We're going up to Connecticut . . . Her family went to Europe. She's out in the car now . . . with no clothes on. They raided the hotel she's at . . . and she had to run . . . she got no clothes on. Man, are you crazy? She got a coat on . . .

PUTSKI [*enters hurriedly,* CHUCH *following her*]. Don't touch me . . . He tried to touch me . . . I was sitting lighting a cigarette and he grabbed the inside of my leg and I won't stand for it. After all, it's my car.

CHUCH. I didn't try to touch her. She grabbed me. . . .

PUTSKI. I don't want to go down to the car . . . I'll just sit here like the Queen Mother and not say a word.

APPLES. Where's your place in Connecticut . . . ?

PUTSKI. Just outside of Greenwich . . . and it's not my place, it's Lester's place, Lester's the man Mummy married since Daddy disappeared. . . .

APPLES. There's five bathrooms in the house. One for everybody . . . No, man, we're looking to collect some money. Right, Mother.

MOTHER. Right. Money or the lumps.

APPLES. Little Jim wants to know if we pick him up on the way.

MOTHER. He's with us.

APPLES. As soon as we can, man . . . sit tight and hold right . . . right? And there you go, Jim!

MOTHER. What time is it, Apples . . . ?

APPLES. My clock says eleven o'clock . . .

MOTHER. That's a nice clock you got there . . .

APPLES. I mean watcht. I allus say clock . . .

MOTHER. Yeh, an you *allus* say *axt.* It's *ask* with a K, not axt, you silly bastard . . .

APPLES. Wait a minute, teacher. I'll ring the bell and get the rest of the kids in. . . .

[*Everything becomes unusually silent for a good minute.* PUTSKI *is back in a chair, staring dreamily at the ceiling.* APPLES *hums, "like a saxophone";* MOTHER *stands doing absolutely nothing. Only* CHUCH *looks about wondering why a silence has descended . . . all being addicted and under the influence of drugs, their sense of time becomes peculiar, not noticeable to themselves, but to an onlooker they appear to be either in slow motion or hopped. There is a sense of a vacuum . . . and then, coming from nowhere a sense of chaos and speed.* MOTHER *sits, takes out a book and reads as though he were in the public library.*]

CHUCH. What are we doin'?

APPLES. We're waitin' . . .

CHUCH. What are we waitin' for?

APPLES. The money—we're waitin' for the money.

CHUCH. Oh. . . .

PUTSKI. I can't stand people who feel a compulsion to talk endlessly . . .

APPLES. What are you reading? You're allus readin' . . . He allus reading, Chuch. You remember what happened to Crazy Stanley.

CHUCH. Yeh . . . Crazy Stanley was allus readin'. I saw him flip. He never read comic books. Always readin' about the planets, rocket ships.

APPLES. You hear that, Mother?

MOTHER. Yeh . . .

APPLES. Keep on readin'. Just keep on readin' . . .

MOTHER. You ever thought about committing suicide, Apples?

APPLES. No, man, I'm young yet. I'm only nineteen . . .

CHUCH. Will you guys shut up!

APPLES. You know something, Chuch? You ugly.

MOTHER. Apples is right, Chuch. You're ugly . . .

APPLES. You can't help it if you're ugly, Chuch. Mother's ugly too, but it doesn't bother him. . . .

MOTHER. You know something, Apples, you're getting

disrespectful just because we're friends, and you
know something else, you'd better have eyes in the
back of your head when you start getting disrespectful. . . .

APPLES. Take it easy, Brother Mother.

MOTHER. Don't butter me, Apples. Get your hands out
of your pockets. And don't turn your back because
I'll punch you right in the back.

CHUCH. Go ahead, kill each other. Go ahead. There's
seven million people in this city, and we have to
fight each other. Go ahead, I don't know whose side
I'm going to be on, start punching I'll pick a side.

MOTHER. Chuch, do yourself a favor.

CHUCH. Mother, do me a favor? Just do me a favor.
Don't start puttin' ideas in my head.

APPLES. Take it easy, Chuch, we ain't gonna steal
nothin'. We're going to Connecticut . . .

CHUCH. He sees an ole lady pushin' a baby carriage
around at night collecting newspapers . . . an' a bell
goes off. Some people got water on the knee, and he's
got hermits on the brain. . . .

MOTHER. What are you talking about, Chuch?

CHUCH. You told me I can't keep chasin' the tiger's tail.
I got to lock horns if I want to get my fix! You told
me where she kept the money . . . out of the frying
pan and into the gold-plated casserole. I could sleep
tight if I had a bundle of thousands under my pillow . . . huh?

MOTHER. We're gonna go to Connecticut. They got an
A.S.P.C.A. in Connecticut.

CHUCH. Go by the A.S.P.C.A.? The cops come two hours
after he died . . . and then the A.S.P.C.A. truck come
too. The cop says the dog is dead. He died in my
arms and he tells me the dog is dead. . . . I says to
the guy from the A.S.P.C.A.— What'll I do with
him? Throw him in the garbage, he says, we don't
take the dead ones . . . that's for the sanitation department.

MOTHER. Huh, Chuchie Duchie . . . you can buy a cocker spaniel for ten bucks . . . !

CHUCH. Three dollars and sixteen cents . . . three dollars and sixteen cents! That's all. . . . God punished me.

[JOHNNY *bursts in the door. A* MAN *slides down the ladder and plants himself in the hallway.*]

MAN. Back up, Johnny . . . back up like a mule.

CHUCH. I killed the old lady, Johnny. I didn't mean to kill her. He wouldn't give me no more credit. Three dollars and sixteen cents!

MOTHER. You got the eight hundred . . . ?

JOHNNY. Where's my wife . . . ?

MOTHER. Button up your buttons, honey, we're getting out of here. . . .

CHUCH. Johnny, you look bad. . . .

JOHNNY. I'll be all right. . . .

CHUCH. Yeh, sure, but three dollars and sixteen cents. I didn't mean to do it. [*Goes off, mumbling.*]

MOTHER. Button 'em up.

PUTSKI. I had the most wonderful dream. . . .

MOTHER. Get her down to the car. I'll take care of Johnny. . . .

PUTSKI. I'm not moving until it's perfectly understood that everyone will have their own room . . . and there'll be no going from one room to another . . . I hope no one here had any ideas about me . . . because they're completely mistaken. . . .

APPLES. Come on, nobody's got any ideas about you. . . .

MOTHER. Get her down to the car. . . .

PUTSKI [*going out*]. It has to be perfectly understood that the run of the premises are yours—you can eat until your hearts are content . . . but there'll be no fooling around, no voyages from one room to another. Hey, who's that guy?

MOTHER. Come here, Junkey— I'm not going to hurt you. I'm not greedy. Come here, I want to give you something . . . honest. You're sick, Junkey . . . can you see me way over here? I'm smiling.

JOHNNY. You'll get your eight hundred . . . every lousy cent of it.

MOTHER. Your word is your bond, my man—you know how to use that thing you've got in your hand— Hey, can you see me over here? Look, pure white—a free ride on the midnight carousel, tax free, on the house.

JOHNNY. I'm through!

MOTHER. No more trying to get the things you wanted all your life . . . and you fly, Johnny, like a bird.

JOHNNY. I'm through, Mother, I'm quitting.

[POLO *enters.*]

POLO. Heh, Mother . . . There's eight hundred . . . Count it downstairs, will you?

MOTHER. He'll crawl . . . [*He goes out.*]

JOHNNY. Where's Celia . . . ?

POLO. She'll be here . . .

JOHNNY. Did you put the old man on his plane . . . ?

POLO. Where you going?

JOHNNY. I'm a half-hour from hell, Polo. I'm going up to the St. Nicholas and get myself a room. I'm going to kick it. . . .

POLO. I was in that room with you once before, Johnny . . .

JOHNNY. I lock myself up for three days . . . and I won't touch a thing. When I come out, I'll be straight again . . .

POLO. You won't last a day in that room . . .

JOHNNY. Come with me. You come with me . . . you watch me. You can keep me locked up for three days . . . That's all it takes, Polo. Three lousy days . . .

POLO. Johnny, I can't watch you go through that again . . .

JOHNNY. I did it once before—and I'll do it again.

POLO. Listen, Johnny—I held you down on that bed for three days! Maybe you can go through that hell again, but I can't watch you again . . . Johnny, sit down, willya . . . ?

JOHNNY. Polo, my time's running out . . .

POLO. Listen to me . . . Celia almost lost the baby. She's all right . . . take it easy. We left her at the doctor's . . . He wanted her to lay down for an hour. She knows you don't have to run any more . . .

JOHNNY. She's all right . . . ? Don't lie to me, Polo . . .

POLO. I just called the doctor's—she's on her way home.

JOHNNY. And the old man . . . ?

POLO. I told him I paid for it, Johnny—in the doctor's office. And I left him sitting there . . . saying, no, no, no, no, Polo, you couldn't do that to your brother . . .

JOHNNY. They'll be coming here . . .

POLO. You couldn't walk one block.

JOHNNY. Polo, I got to get out of here. I can't let them see me like this . . . Polo, I'm quitting, don't you believe me?

POLO. For the first time, I do. I know you can do it . . .

JOHNNY. Then for the last time, Polo, help me. Get a cab. Get me out of here. Polo, I don't want them to see me!

POLO. All right, Johnny, I'll go with you. I'll do what I have to do.

JOHNNY. It's starting, Polo . . . it's starting. Oh God . . .

FATHER [*knocks on door*]. Polo? Polo? Open the door . . .

POLO. Go in the back room and be quiet . . .

[JOHNNY *goes into the bedroom.*]

FATHER. Polo . . . !

POLO [*going to door*]. I'm sorry, Pop, I . . .

FATHER. Did you find him? Did you find your brother Johnny?

POLO. No, Pop—did you go to all the places I told you to go?

FATHER. Nobody's seen him . . .

POLO. Celia'll be right home—I called her.

FATHER. It's a good thing that was a false alarm, Polo.

POLO. She's all right. She's on her way home.

FATHER. Where are you going?

POLO. Pop, your plane leaves in an hour.

FATHER. Planes fly every day. Where are you going? You want to get out of here now, huh? That's all you want. Three thousand dollars' worth of poison in your brother's arm and you paid for it!

POLO. Twenty-five hundred.

FATHER. That was the right thing to do? Help your brother kill himself. You have an alibi . . . What have you got to say for yourself?

POLO. Nothing.

FATHER. What have you got to say to me?

POLO. Get on your plane and go back to Palm Beach where everything is nice and quiet. Come on, Pop— I want you to get out of here.

FATHER. Get away from that bag, and don't call me Pop. Let's just be two men talking. Talk to me like I'm your brother. You'll get out of here, maybe not on your own two feet, but you'll get out of here.

POLO. Take it easy, Pop.

FATHER. I'm getting red in the face, huh? Maybe I'd better sit down. I'm not as young as I used to be. I'm soft, not hard enough for you.

POLO. Now, look, Pop, you don't know what you're doing.

FATHER. Where's your brother? You're not your brother's keeper. Are you going to shut up on me again? You're forgetting I'm your father!

POLO. Well, for crissakes look at you. You don't even know what's happened and you're trying to put the blame somewhere.

FATHER. My son, if you knew how ashamed I was to admit that you're my son. Am I a child? Are you my father? You know what I'm going to do . . . ? You remember once how Pete the big bay horse kicked me and put me in the hospital . . . and when I came out I turned that bastard loose in the barn and locked the doors . . . that ungrateful sonofabitch that I slept in the straw with when he was sick. I fought that horse with my bare hands . . . and you and Johnny were up in the hayloft, yelling, "Look out, Pop . . . that horse is going to kill you!" I'm going to beat you, Polo! And you can punch back, like he kicked back. You fight back. Take your coat off.

POLO. No, I'm not going to take my coat off. You couldn't hurt me any more if you killed me. Listen. You were two thousand miles away but I was here. You told me a hundred times in every letter you ever wrote that I should fall on my hands and knees and light twenty candles a day because my brother had taken me in.

FATHER. You couldn't write to me and tell me?

POLO. Write to you and tell you what? That your favorite son was a goddamned junkey? You going to swing. Swing! Take your failures out on me . . . and when you finish I'm going to tell you where your son is . . . I took care of him . . . I'm my brother's keeper more than you know. [*The* FATHER *swings and hits* POLO *soundly across the face with an open hand.*] You poor old man. What are you hitting me for? What have I done? You walk around with your head in the clouds. Why don't you stand still for a minute and try to find something out?

FATHER. Dope? Junkey? And you paid for it? [*The kitchen door opens and* CELIA *enters.*]

CELIA. Johnny— Johnny— Where's Johnny?

POLO. He's not here. We looked all over, we couldn't find him. Isn't that right, Pop?

CELIA. I don't know who his friends are, Polo. You'd know that. There were two men here last night. What were their names?

FATHER. I don't know. One of them had on glasses.

POLO. Are you all right?

CELIA. I won't be all right until I see Johnny.

FATHER. He knows where he is . . .

POLO. What did the doctor say?

CELIA. My baby is all right.

POLO. This isn't the place to be. All you have to do is get out of here for a few—

CELIA. I live here and I'm staying here. I'm all right and I won't scream or cry, but are you all right, Polo? Are you?

POLO. You're going to miss your plane, Pop.

FATHER. I told you before, planes fly every day.

CELIA. Where is my husband?

POLO. He's waiting for me. He asked me to keep you and the old man away from him. Don't push me. He'd die of shame if you saw him now, and you'd get sick. I'll be running out in the street looking for a taxi again. I tell you, I know what I'm doing.

CELIA. You don't know what you're doing and don't know what you've done, Polo. I just keep thinking that you hate him—that you hate your brother!

POLO. You know I love him . . .

CELIA. You just don't love. When you love you have to be responsible to what you love.

POLO. He'll help himself—he wants to quit.

CELIA. He'll never do it by himself and you *know* that.

POLO. I don't know that.

CELIA. Polo, don't turn your back, you can look at me. I know you meant well, and that you mean well now, but I talked to my doctor, Polo, there is little any of us can do . . . There is little that all the doctors in the world can do right now but try to help him, and you *know* that. There's a slight chance . . . only a slight one—and don't tell me that you've been feeding him money all this time and that you don't know. You're afraid to admit that. . . .

POLO. Don't you see, as long as he gets it, he's all right. You'd never know he was any different.

CELIA. Polo! You're not two little kids huddled in a

dark room any more. I should be angry at you, but I'm not.

POLO. I'm not afraid of anything . . . and I didn't do any wrong. When you have your baby—and if you can imagine for one minute your child writhing in *pain*—and all you have to do is reach out and hand—

CELIA. I'd reach out and stop its crying . . . I'd give it anything it needed but I wouldn't stop there, I'd try to find out what caused the pain—I love your brother Johnny, I have faith in that love. He is a perfect human being, and I'm proud of him, not ashamed of him, and I don't pity him, and I'm not afraid of him . . . and the more I see you now, the more I realize that your love is irresponsible. Now you tell me where he is, Polo, or I'll call the police and have them find him . . .

FATHER. You'd call the police, you're so proud of him . . .

CELIA. I'm not a member of your vacuum age, Mr. Pope. And I'm sorry I cannot regard you as his father at this moment; unfortunately you are just another man . . .

FATHER. No. No police. We'll get a doctor . . .

CELIA. They'd only have to call the police. Isn't that right, Polo?

FATHER. But we can take care of him together. I don't have to go back to Palm Beach, I can get a good job up here. We can all take care of him together. You don't have to call the police . . .

CELIA. There's a place in Kentucky that takes care of people like Johnny.

FATHER. What people like Johnny? Who do you think you're talking about? There's nothing wrong with him! What the hell—people drink, don't they? So he takes a little something once in a while, what are you running to the police for . . . ?

JOHNNY [*off*]. Polo! [*Comes in.*] Get them out of here,

get them out of here. I don't want them to see me like this.

FATHER. Johnny...

JOHNNY. Pop. Watch over me—watch over me. Don't let them come near me again. Don't let me go, willya, Pop.

FATHER. For crissakes, Polo, he's dying. He's freezing—what do we do?

POLO. Hold on, for the love of God, hold on. We're all here...

FATHER. Easy, Johnny, easy... Polo, what do I do?

POLO. Rock him—rock him like a baby in your arms. Hold him, hold him tight and never let him go. Rock him, you rock him, Pop, I rocked him long enough, you watch over him!

JOHNNY. Celia, Celia, Celia. I didn't want you to see this. I didn't want anybody to see this.

CELIA. Well, we've seen it, Johnny, and we can't just make believe we didn't, can we?

JOHNNY. Pop, I'm sorry about all that ... all that—you know. Next time I open my mouth ... you just haul off and give me a belt.

FATHER. Okay, kid.

JOHNNY. Pop, will you please go; I want to be alone with my wife.

FATHER. Yeh— You want to walk me over to the hotel, Polo?

POLO. Yeh, come on ... [*Polo starts to leave.*]

FATHER. Good night, honey ... [*Goes out.*]

CELIA. Good night, Pop. Come over for breakfast, please.

POLO [*from the doorway*]. You'll be all right, Johnny. [*He leaves with* FATHER.]

JOHNNY. Hey—Pop—hey—if you drop your hat crossing the— Celia, I'm sorry, you don't know how sorry I am ...

CELIA. I don't care how sorry you are, Johnny. I want

to call the police and I want you to go into a hospital. I'm going to call them, no matter what you say, darling. We can't live like this, can we? You can live or die ...

JOHNNY. I'm all right. It's so unbelievable. To know everything that's right. Thou shalt not kill or walk on the grass; I've been taught everything good ... Make the phone call ...

CELIA. Give me the police ... I'd like to report a drug addict. My husband. Yes, he's here now. Would you send over whoever you send in a case like this—and try to hurry, please. Thank you. Mrs. Celia Pope, 967 Rivington Street ... fourth flight up. And would you hurry, please ... Thank you.

CURTAIN

THE ZOO STORY

A PLAY IN ONE SCENE

by Edward Albee
for William Flanagan

The Zoo Story © 1959 by Edward Albee
Reprinted by permission of
Coward-McCann, Inc.
All rights reserved.

This play is the sole property of the author and is fully protected by copyright. It may not be acted by professionals or by amateurs without written consent. Public readings and radio or television broadcasts are likewise forbidden. All inquiries concerning rights should be addressed to the author's agent, the William Morris Agency, 1740 Broadway, New York 19, N. Y.

First performance: September 28, 1959,
Berlin, Germany, Schiller Theater Werkstatt,

First American performance: January 14, 1960,
New York City, The Provincetown Playhouse.

THE PLAYERS:

PETER: *A man in his early forties, neither fat nor gaunt, neither handsome nor homely. He wears tweeds, smokes a pipe, carries horn-rimmed glasses. Although he is moving into middle age, his dress and his manner would suggest a man younger.*

JERRY: *A man in his late thirties, not poorly dressed, but carelessly. What was once a trim and lightly muscled body has begun to go to fat; and while he is no longer handsome, it is evident that he once was. His fall from physical grace should not suggest debauchery; he has, to come closest to it, a great weariness.*

THE SCENE:

It is Central Park; a Sunday afternoon in summer; the present. There are two park benches, one toward either side of the stage; they both face the audience. Behind them: foliage, trees, sky. At the beginning, Peter is seated on one of the benches.

STAGE DIRECTIONS: *As the curtain rises,* PETER *is seated on the bench stage-right. He is reading a book. He stops reading, cleans his glasses, goes back to reading.* JERRY *enters.*

JERRY. I've been to the zoo. [PETER *doesn't notice.*] I said, I've been to the zoo. MISTER, I'VE BEEN TO THE ZOO!

PETER. Hm? . . . What? . . . I'm sorry, were you talking to me?

JERRY. I went to the zoo, and then I walked until I came here. Have I been walking north?

PETER [*puzzled*]. North? Why . . . I . . . I think so. Let me see.

JERRY [*pointing past the audience*]. Is that Fifth Avenue?

PETER. Why yes; yes, it is.

JERRY. And what is that cross street there; that one, to the right?

PETER. That? Oh, that's Seventy-fourth Street.

JERRY. And the zoo is around Sixty-fifth Street; so, I've been walking north.

PETER [*anxious to get back to his reading*]. Yes; it would seem so.

JERRY. Good old north.

PETER [*lightly, by reflex*]. Ha, ha.

JERRY [*after a slight pause*]. But not due north.

PETER. I . . . well, no, not due north; but, we . . .
call it north. It's northerly.

JERRY [*watches as* PETER, *anxious to dismiss him, prepares his pipe*]. Well, boy; *you're* not going to get
lung cancer, are you?

PETER [*looks up, a little annoyed, then smiles*]. No, sir.
Not from this.

JERRY. No, sir. What you'll probably get is cancer of
the mouth, and then you'll have to wear one of
those things Freud wore after they took one whole
side of his jaw away. What do they call those things?

PETER [*uncomfortable*]. A prosthesis?

JERRY. The very thing! A prosthesis. You're an educated man, aren't you? Are you a doctor?

PETER. Oh, no; no. I read about it somewhere; *Time*
magazine, I think. [*He turns to his book.*]

JERRY. Well, *Time* magazine isn't for blockheads.

PETER. No, I suppose not.

JERRY. [*after a pause*]. Boy, I'm glad that's Fifth Avenue there.

PETER [*vaguely*]. Yes.

JERRY. I don't like the west side of the park much.

PETER. Oh? [*Then, slightly wary, but interested.*] Why?

JERRY [*offhand*]. I don't know.

PETER. Oh. [*He returns to his book.*]

JERRY [*he stands for a few seconds, looking at* PETER,
who finally looks up again, puzzled]. Do you mind if
we talk?

PETER [*obviously minding*]. Why ... no, no.

JERRY. Yes you do; you do.

PETER [*puts his book down, his pipe out and away, smiling*]. No, really; I don't mind.

JERRY. Yes you do.

PETER [*finally decided*]. No; I don't mind at all, really.

JERRY. It's ... it's a nice day.

PETER [*stares unnecessarily at the sky*]. Yes. Yes, it is;
lovely.

JERRY. I've been to the zoo.

PETER. Yes, I think you said so ... didn't you?

JERRY. You'll read about it in the papers tomorrow, if you don't see it on your TV tonight. You have TV, haven't you?

PETER. Why yes, we have two; one for the children.

JERRY. You're married!

PETER [*with pleased emphasis*]. Why, certainly.

JERRY. It isn't a law, for God's sake.

PETER. No ... no, of course not.

JERRY. And you have a wife.

PETER [*bewildered by the seeming lack of communication*]. Yes!

JERRY. And you have children.

PETER. Yes; two.

JERRY. Boys?

PETER. No, girls ... both girls.

JERRY. But you wanted boys.

PETER. Well ... naturally, every man wants a son, but ...

JERRY [*lightly mocking*]. But that's the way the cookie crumbles?

PETER [*annoyed*]. I wasn't going to say that.

JERRY. And you're not going to have any more kids, are you?

PETER [*a bit distantly*]. No. No more. [*Then back, and irksome.*] Why did you say that? How would you know about that?

JERRY. The way you cross your legs, perhaps; something in the voice. Or maybe I'm just guessing. Is it your wife?

PETER [*furious*]. That's none of your business! [*A silence.*] Do you understand? [JERRY *nods.* PETER *is quiet now.*] Well, you're right. We'll have no more children.

JERRY [*softly*]. That *is* the way the cookie crumbles.

PETER [*forgiving*]. Yes ... I guess so.

JERRY. Well, now; what else?

PETER. What were you saying about the zoo . . . that I'd read about it, or see . . . ?

JERRY. I'll tell you about it, soon. Do you mind if I ask you questions?

PETER. Oh, not really.

JERRY. I'll tell you why I do it; I don't talk to many people—except to say like: give me a beer, or where's the john, or what time does the feature go on, or keep your hands to yourself, buddy. You know— things like that.

PETER. I must say I don't . . .

JERRY. But every once in a while I like to talk to some-body, really *talk*; like to get to know somebody, know all about him.

PETER [*lightly laughing, still a little uncomfortable*]. And am I the guinea pig for today?

JERRY. On a sun-drenched Sunday afternoon like this? Who better than a nice married man with two daughters and . . . uh . . . a dog? [PETER *shakes his head.*] No? Two dogs. [PETER *shakes his head again.*] Hm. No dogs? [PETER *shakes his head, sadly.*] Oh, that's a shame. But you look like an animal man. CATS? [PETER *nods his head, ruefully.*] Cats! But, that can't be your idea. No, sir. Your wife and daughters? [PETER *nods his head.*] Is there anything else I should know?

PETER [*he has to clear his throat*]. There are . . . there are two parakeets. One . . . uh . . . one for each of my daughters.

JERRY. Birds.

PETER. My daughters keep them in a cage in their bed-room.

JERRY. Do they carry disease? The birds.

PETER. I don't believe so.

JERRY. That's too bad. If they did you could set them loose in the house and the cats could eat them and die, maybe. [PETER *looks blank for a moment, then laughs.*] And what else? What do you do to support your enormous household?

PETER. I ... uh ... I have an executive position with a ... a small publishing house. We ... uh ... we publish textbooks.

JERRY. That sounds 'nice; very nice. What do you make?

PETER [*still cheerful*]. Now look here!

JERRY. Oh, come on.

PETER. Well, I make around eighteen thousand a year, but I don't carry more than forty dollars at any one time ... in case you're a ... a holdup man ... ha, ha, ha.

JERRY [*ignoring the above*]. Where do you live? [PETER *is reluctant.*] Oh, look; I'm not going to rob you, and I'm not going to kidnap your parakeets, your cats, or your daughters.

PETER [*too loud*]. I live between Lexington and Third Avenue, on Seventy-fourth Street.

JERRY. That wasn't so hard, was it?

PETER. I didn't mean to seem ... ah ... it's that you don't really carry on a conversation; you just ask questions. And I'm ... I'm normally ... uh ... reticent. Why do you just stand there?

JERRY. I'll start walking around in a little while, and eventually I'll sit down. [*Recalling.*] Wait until you see the expression on his face.

PETER. What? Whose face? Look here; is this something about the zoo?

JERRY [*distantly*]. The what?

PETER. The zoo; the zoo. Something about the zoo.

JERRY. The zoo?

PETER. You've mentioned it several times.

JERRY [*still distant, but returning abruptly*]. The zoo? Oh, yes; the zoo. I was there before I came here. I told you that. Say, what's the dividing line between upper-middle-middle-class and lower-upper-middle-class?

PETER. My dear fellow, I . . .

JERRY. Don't my dear fellow me.

PETER [*unhappily*]. Was I patronizing? I believe I was; I'm sorry. But, you see, your question about the classes bewildered me.

JERRY. And when you're bewildered you become patronizing?

PETER. I . . . I don't express myself too well, sometimes. [*He attempts a joke on himself.*] I'm in publishing, not writing.

JERRY [*amused, but not at the humor*]. So be it. The truth *is: I* was being patronizing.

PETER. Oh, now; you needn't say that.

[*It is at this point that* JERRY *may begin to move about the stage with slowly increasing determination and authority, but pacing himself, so that the long speech about the dog comes at the high point of the arc.*]

JERRY. All right. Who are your favorite writers? Baudelaire and J. P. Marquand?

PETER [*wary*]. Well, I like a great many writers; I have a considerable . . . catholicity of taste, if I may say so. Those two men are fine, each in his way. [*Warming up.*] Baudelaire, of course . . . uh . . . is by far the finer of the two, but Marquand has a place . . . in our . . . uh . . . national . . .

JERRY. Skip it.

PETER. I . . . sorry.

JERRY. Do you know what I did before I went to the zoo today? I walked all the way up Fifth Avenue from Washington Square; all the way.

PETER. Oh; you live in the Village! [*This seems to enlighten* PETER.]

JERRY. No, I don't. I took the subway down to the Village so I could walk all the way up Fifth Avenue to the zoo. It's one of those things a person has to do; sometimes a person has to go a very long distance out of his way to come back a short distance correctly.

PETER [*almost pouting*]. Oh, I thought you lived in the Village.

JERRY. What were you trying to do? Make sense out of things? Bring order? The old pigeonhole bit? Well, that's easy; I'll tell you. I live in a four-story brownstone roominghouse on the upper West Side between Columbus Avenue and Central Park West. I live on the top floor; rear; west. It's a laughably small room, and one of my walls is made of beaverboard; this beaverboard separates my room from another laughably small room, so I assume that the two rooms were once one room, a small room, but not necessarily laughable. The room beyond my beaverboard wall is occupied by a colored queen who always keeps his door open; well, not always but *always* when he's plucking his eyebrows, which he does with Buddhist concentration. This colored queen has rotten teeth, which is rare, and he has a Japanese kimono, which is also pretty rare; and he wears this kimono to and from the john in the hall, which is pretty frequent. I mean, he goes to the john a lot. He never bothers me, and he never brings anyone up to his room. All he does is pluck his eyebrows, wear his kimono and go to the john. Now, the two front rooms on my floor are a little larger, I guess; but they're pretty small, too. There's a Puerto Rican family in one of them, a husband, a wife, and some kids; I don't know how many. These people entertain a lot. And in the other front room, there's somebody living there, but I don't know who it is. I've never seen who it is. Never. Never ever.

PETER [*embarrassed*]. Why . . . why do you live there?

JERRY [*from a distance again*]. I don't know.

PETER. It doesn't sound like a very nice place . . . where you live.

JERRY. Well, no; it isn't an apartment in the East Seventies. But, then again, I don't have one wife, two daughters, two cats and two parakeets. What I do

have, I have toilet articles, a few clothes, a hot plate
that I'm not supposed to have, a can opener, one
that works with a key, you know; a knife, two forks,
and two spoons, one small, one large; three plates, a
cup, a saucer, a drinking glass, two picture frames,
both empty, eight or nine books, a pack of pornographic playing cards, regular deck, an old Western
Union typewriter that prints nothing but capital
letters, and a small strongbox without a lock which
has in it . . . what? Rocks! Some rocks . . . sea-
rounded rocks I picked up on the beach when I was
a kid. Under which . . . weighed down . . . are some
letters . . . please letters . . . please why don't you do
this, and please when will you do that letters. And
when letters, too. When will you write? When will
you come? When? These letters are from more recent
years.

PETER [*stares glumly at his shoes, then*]. About those
two empty picture frames . . . ?

JERRY. I don't see why they need any explanation at all.
Isn't it clear? I don't have pictures of anyone to put
in them.

PETER. Your parents . . . perhaps . . . a girl friend . . .

JERRY. You're a very sweet man, and you're possessed
of a truly enviable innocence. But good old Mom
and good old Pop are dead . . . you know? . . . I'm
broken up about it, too . . . I mean really. BUT.
That particular vaudeville act is playing the cloud
circuit now, so I don't see how I can look at them,
all neat and framed. Besides, or, rather, to be
pointed about it, good old Mom walked out on good
old Pop when I was ten and a half years old; she
embarked on an adulterous turn of our southern
states . . . a journey of a year's duration . . . and her
most constant companion . . . among others, among
many others . . . was a Mr. Barleycorn. At least,
that's what good old Pop told me after he went
down . . . came back . . . brought her body north.

We'd received the news between Christmas and New Year's, you see, that good old Mom had parted with the ghost in some dump in Alabama. And, without the ghost . . . she was less welcome. I mean, what was she? A stiff . . . a northern stiff. At any rate, good old Pop celebrated the New Year for an even two weeks and then slapped into the front of a somewhat moving city omnibus, which sort of cleaned things out family-wise. Well no; then there was Mom's sister, who was given neither to sin nor the consolations of the bottle. I moved in on her, and my memory of her is slight excepting I remember still that she did all things dourly: sleeping, eating, working, praying. She dropped dead on the stairs to her apartment, my apartment then, too, on the afternoon of my high school graduation. A terribly middle-European joke, if you ask me.

PETER. Oh, my; oh, my.

JERRY. Oh, your what? But that was a long time ago, and I have no feeling about any of it that I care to admit to myself. Perhaps you can see, though, why good old Mom and good old Pop are frameless. What's your name? Your first name?

PETER. I'm Peter.

JERRY. I'd forgotten to ask you. I'm Jerry.

PETER [*with a slight, nervous laugh*]. Hello, Jerry.

JERRY. [*nods his hello*]. And let's see now; what's the point of having a girl's picture, especially in two frames? I have two picture frames, you remember. I never see the pretty ladies more than once, and most of them wouldn't be caught in the same room with a camera. It's odd, and I wonder if it's sad.

PETER. The girls?

JERRY. No. I wonder if it's sad that I never see the little ladies more than once. I've never been able to have sex with, or, how is it put? . . . make love to anybody more than once. Once; that's it. . . . Oh, wait; for a week and a half, when I was fifteen . . .

and I hang my head in shame that puberty was late . . . I was a h-o-m-o-s-e-x-u-a-l. I mean, I was queer . . . [*Very fast.*] . . . queer, queer, queer . . . with bells ringing, banners snapping in the wind. And for those eleven days, I met at least twice a day with the park superintendent's son . . . a Greek boy, whose birthday was the same as mine, except he was a year older. I think I was very much in love . . . maybe just with sex. But that was the jazz of a very special hotel, wasn't it? And now; oh, do I love the little ladies; really, I love them. For about an hour.

PETER. Well, it seems perfectly simple to me. . . .

JERRY [*angry*]. Look! Are you going to tell me to get married and have parakeets?

PETER [*angry himself*]. Forget the parakeets! And stay single if you want to. It's no business of mine. I didn't start this conversation in the . . .

JERRY. All right, all right. I'm sorry. All right? You're not angry?

PETER [*laughing*]. No, I'm not angry.

JERRY [*relieved*]. Good. [*Now back to his previous tone.*] Interesting that you asked me about the picture frames. I would have thought that you would have asked me about the pornographic playing cards.

PETER [*with a knowing smile*]. Oh, I've seen those cards.

JERRY. That's not the point. [*Laughs.*] I suppose when you were a kid you and your pals passed them around, or you had a pack of your own.

PETER. Well, I guess a lot of us did.

JERRY. And you threw them away just before you got married.

PETER. Oh, now; look here. I didn't *need* anything like that when I got older.

JERRY. No?

PETER [*embarrassed*]. I'd rather not talk about these things.

JERRY. So? Don't. Besides, I wasn't trying to plumb

your post-adolescent sexual life and hard times; what I wanted to get at is the value difference between pornographic playing cards when you're a kid, and pornographic playing cards when you're older. It's that when you're a kid you use the cards as a substitute for a real experience, and when you're older you use real experience as a substitute for the fantasy. But I imagine you'd rather hear about what happened at the zoo.

PETER [*enthusiastic*]. Oh, yes; the zoo. [*Then, awkward:*] That is ... if you....

JERRY. Let me tell you about why I went ... well, let me tell you some things. I've told you about the fourth floor of the roominghouse where I live. I think the rooms are better as you go down, floor by floor. I guess they are; I don't know. I don't know any of the people on the third and second floors. Oh, wait! I do know that there's a lady living on the third floor, in the front. I know because she cries all the time. Whenever I go out or come back in, whenever I pass her door, I always hear her crying, muffled, but ... very determined. Very determined indeed. But the one I'm getting to, and all about the dog, is the landlady. I don't like to use words that are too harsh in describing people. I don't like to. But the landlady is a fat, ugly, mean, stupid, unwashed, misanthropic, cheap, drunken bag of garbage. And you may have noticed that I very seldom use profanity, so I can't describe her as well as I might.

PETER. You describe her ... vividly.

JERRY. Well, thanks. Anyway, she has a dog, and I will tell you about the dog, and she and her dog are the gatekeepers of my dwelling. The woman is bad enough; she leans around in the entrance hall, spying to see that I don't bring in things or people, and when she's had her midafternoon pint of lemon-flavored gin she always stops me in the hall, and grabs ahold of my coat or my arm, and she presses her disgusting body up against me to keep me in a corner so she can talk to me. The smell of her body and her breath . . . you can't imagine it . . . and somewhere, somewhere in the back of that pea-size brain of hers, an organ developed just enough to let her eat, drink, and emit, she has some foul parody of sexual desire. And I, Peter, I am the object of her sweaty lust.

PETER. That's disgusting. That's . . . horrible.

JERRY. But I have found a way to keep her off. When she talks to me, when she presses herself to my body and mumbles about her room and how I should come there, I merely say: but, Love; wasn't yesterday enough for you, and the day before? Then she puzzles, she makes slits of her tiny eyes, she sways a little, and then, Peter . . . and it is at this moment that I think I might be doing some good in that tormented house . . . a simple-minded smile begins to form on her unthinkable face, and she giggles and groans as she thinks about yesterday and the day before; as she believes and relives what never happened. Then, she motions to that black monster of a dog she has, and she goes back to her room. And I am safe until our next meeting.

PETER. It's so . . . unthinkable. I find it hard to believe that people such as that really *are*.

JERRY [*lightly mocking*]. It's for reading about, isn't it?

PETER [*seriously*]. Yes.

JERRY. And fact is better left to fiction. You're right, Peter. Well, what I have been meaning to tell you about is the dog; I shall, now.

PETER [*nervously*]. Oh, yes; the dog.

JERRY. Don't go. You're not thinking of going, are you?

PETER. Well . . . no, I don't think so.

JERRY [*as if to a child*]. Because after I tell you about the dog, do you know what then? Then . . . then I'll tell you about what happened at the zoo.

PETER [*laughing faintly*]. You're . . . you're full of stories, aren't you?

JERRY. You don't *have* to listen. Nobody is holding you here; remember that. Keep that in your mind.

PETER [*irritably*]. I know that.

JERRY. You do? Good.

[*The following long speech, it seems to me, should be done with a great deal of action, to achieve a hypnotic effect on* PETER, *and on the audience, too. Some specific actions have been suggested, but the director and the actor playing* JERRY *might best work it out for themselves.*]

ALL RIGHT. [*As if reading from a huge billboard.*] THE STORY OF JERRY AND THE DOG! [*Natural again.*] What I am going to tell you has something to do with how sometimes it's necessary to go a long distance out of the way in order to come back a short distance correctly; or, maybe I only think that it has something to do with that. But, it's why I went to the zoo today, and why I walked north . . . northerly, rather . . . until I came here. All right. The dog, I think I told you, is a black monster of a beast: an oversized head, tiny, tiny ears, and eyes . . . bloodshot, infected, maybe; and a body you can see the ribs through the skin. The dog is black, all black; all black except for the bloodshot eyes, and . . . yes . . . and an open sore on its . . . *right* forepaw; that is red, too. And, oh yes; the poor monster, and I do believe it's an old dog . . . it's certainly a misused one . . . almost always has an erection . . . of sorts. That's red, too. And . . . what else? . . . oh, yes; there's a gray-yellow-white color, too, when he bares his fangs. Like this: Grrrrrr! Which is what he did when he saw me for the first time . . . the day I moved in. I worried about that animal the very first minute I met him. Now, animals don't take to me like Saint Francis had birds hanging off him all the time. What I mean is: animals are indifferent to

me . . . like people [*He smiles slightly.*] . . . most of
the time. But this dog wasn't indifferent. From the
very beginning he'd snarl and then go for me, to get
one of my legs. Not like he was rabid, you know; he
was sort of a stumbly dog, but he wasn't half-assed,
either. It was a good, stumbly run; but I always got
away. He got a piece of my trouser leg, look, you can
see right here, where it's mended; he got that the
second day I lived there; but, I kicked free and got
upstairs fast, so that was that. [*Puzzles.*] I still don't
know to this day how the other roomers manage it,
but you know what I *think:* I think it had to do
only with me. Cozy. So. Anyway, this went on for
over a week, whenever I came in; but never when I
went out. That's funny. Or, it *was* funny. I could
pack up and live in the street for all the dog cared.
Well, I thought about it up in my room one day,
one of the times after I'd bolted upstairs, and I made
up my mind. I decided: First, I'll kill the dog with
kindness, and if that doesn't work . . . I'll just kill
him. [PETER *winces.*] Don't react, Peter; just listen.
So, the next day I went out and bought a bag of
hamburgers, medium rare, no catsup, no onion; and
on the way home I threw away all the rolls and kept
just the meat.

[*Action for the following, perhaps.*]

When I got back to the roominghouse the dog was
waiting for me. I half opened the door that led into
the entrance hall, and there he was; waiting for me.
It figured. I went in, very cautiously, and I had the
hamburgers, you remember; I opened the bag, and I
set the meat down about twelve feet from where the
dog was snarling at me. Like so! He snarled; stopped
snarling; sniffed; moved slowly; then faster; then
faster toward the meat. Well, when he got to it he
stopped, and he looked at me. I smiled; but tenta-
tively, you understand. He turned his face back to
the hamburgers, smelled, sniffed some more, and

then ... RRRAAAAGGGGGHHHH, like that ...
he tore into them. It was as if he had never eaten
anything in his life before, except like garbage.
Which might very well have been the truth. I don't
think the landlady ever eats anything but garbage.
But. He ate all the hamburgers, almost all at once,
making sounds in his throat like a woman. *Then,*
when he'd finished the meat, the hamburger, and
tried to eat the paper, too, he sat down and smiled. I
think he smiled; I know cats do. It was a very grati-
fying few moments. Then, BAM, he snarled and
made for me again. He didn't get me this time,
either. So, I got upstairs, and I lay down on my bed
and started to think about the dog again. To be
truthful, I was offended, and I was damn mad, too.
It was six perfectly good hamburgers with not
enough pork in them to make it disgusting. I was offended. But, after a while, I decided to try it for a
few more days. If you think about it, this dog had
what amounted to an antipathy toward me; really.
And, I wondered if I mightn't overcome this antipathy. So, I tried it for five more days, but it was always
the same: snarl, sniff; move; faster; stare; gobble;
RAAGGGHHH; smile; snarl; BAM. Well, now; by
this time Columbus Avenue was strewn with hamburger rolls and I was less offended than disgusted.
So, I decided to kill the dog.

[PETER *raises a hand in protest.*]

Oh, don't be so alarmed, Peter; I didn't succeed.
The day I tried to kill the dog I bought only one
hamburger and what I thought was a murderous
portion of rat poison. When I bought the hamburger I asked the man not to bother with the roll,
all I wanted was the meat. I expected some reaction
from him, like: we don't sell no hamburgers without rolls; or, wha' d'ya wanna do, eat it out'a ya
han's? But no; he smiled benignly, wrapped up the
hamburger in waxed paper, and said: A bite for ya

pussy-cat? I wanted to say: No, not really; it's part of a plan to poison a dog I know. But, you can't say "a dog I know" without sounding funny; so I said, a little too loud, I'm afraid, and too formally: YES, A BITE FOR MY PUSSY-CAT. People looked up. It always happens when I try to simplify things; people look up. But that's neither hither nor thither. So. On my way back to the roominghouse, I kneaded the hamburger and the rat poison together between my hands, at that point feeling as much sadness as disgust. I opened the door to the entrance hall, and there the monster was, waiting to take the offering and then jump me. Poor bastard; he never learned that the moment he took to smile before he went for me gave me time enough to get out of range. BUT, there he was; malevolence with an erection, waiting. I put the poison patty down, moved toward the stairs and watched. The poor animal gobbled the food down as usual, smiled, which made me almost sick, and then, BAM. But, I sprinted up the stairs, as usual, and the dog didn't get me, as usual. AND IT CAME TO PASS THAT THE BEAST WAS DEATHLY ILL. I knew this because he no longer attended me, and because the landlady sobered up. She stopped me in the hall the same evening of the attempted murder and confided the information that God had struck her puppy-dog a surely fatal blow. She had forgotten her bewildered lust, and her eyes were wide open for the first time. They looked like the dog's eyes. She sniveled and implored me to pray for the animal. I wanted to say to her: Madam, I have myself to pray for, the colored queen, the Puerto Rican family, the person in the front room whom I've never seen, the woman who cries deliberately behind her closed door, and the rest of the people in all roominghouses, everywhere; besides, Madam, I don't understand how to pray. But . . . to simplify things . . . I told her I would pray. She looked up. She said that I was a liar, and that I probably wanted the dog to die. I told her, and there was so much truth here, that I didn't want the dog to die. I didn't, and not just because I'd poisoned him. I'm afraid that I must tell you I wanted the dog to live so that I could see what our new relationship might come to.

[PETER *indicates his increasing displeasure and slowly growing antagonism.*]

Please understand, Peter; that sort of thing is important. You must believe me; it *is* important. We have to know the effect of our actions. [*Another deep sigh.*] Well, anyway; the dog recovered. I have no idea why, unless he was a descendant of the puppy that guarded the gates of hell or some such resort. I'm not up on my mythology. [*He pronounces the word myth-o-*logy.] Are you?

[PETER *sets to thinking, but* JERRY *goes on.*]

At any rate, and you've missed the eight-thousand-dollar question, Peter; at any rate, the dog recovered his health and the landlady recovered her thirst, in no way altered by the bow-wow's deliverance. When I came home from a movie that was playing on Forty-second Street, a movie I'd seen, or one that was very much like one or several I'd seen, after the landlady told me puppykins was better, I was so hoping for the dog to be waiting for me. I was . . . well, how would you put it . . . enticed? . . . fascinated? . . . no, I don't think so . . . heart-shatteringly anxious, that's it; I was heart-shatteringly anxious to confront my friend again.

[PETER *reacts scoffingly.*]

Yes, Peter; friend. That's the only word for it. I was heart-shatteringly et cetera to confront my doggy friend again. I came in the door and advanced, unafraid, to the center of the entrance hall. The beast was there . . . looking at me. And, you know, he looked better for his scrape with the nevermind. I

stopped; I looked at him; he looked at me. I think
. . . I think we stayed a long time that way . . . still,
stone-statue . . . just looking at one another. I looked
more into his face than he looked into mine. I mean,
I can concentrate longer at looking into a dog's face
than a dog can concentrate at looking into mine, or
into anybody else's face, for that matter. But during
that twenty seconds or two hours that we looked into
each other's face, we made contact. Now, here is what
I had wanted to happen: I loved the dog now, and I
wanted him to love me. I had tried to love, and I had
tried to kill, and both had been unsuccessful by
themselves. I hoped . . . and I don't really know why
I expected the dog to understand anything, much
less my motivations . . . I hoped that the dog would
understand.

[PETER *seems to be hypnotized.*]

It's just . . . it's just that . . . [JERRY *is abnormally
tense, now.*] . . . it's just that if you can't deal with
people, you have to make a start somewhere. WITH
ANIMALS! [*Much faster now, and like a conspira-
tor.*] Don't you see? A person has to have some way of
dealing with SOMETHING. If not with people . . .
if not with people . . . SOMETHING. With a bed,
with a cockroach, with a mirror . . . no, that's too
hard, that's one of the last steps. With a cockroach,
with a . . . with a . . . with a carpet, a roll of toilet paper . . . no, not that, either . . . that's a mirror, too; always check bleeding. You see how hard it is to find
things? With a street corner, and too many lights, all
colors reflecting on the oily-wet streets . . . with a
wisp of smoke, a wisp . . . of smoke . . . with . . .
with pornographic playing cards, with a strongbox
. . . WITHOUT A LOCK . . . with love, with vom-
iting, with crying, with fury because the pretty little
ladies aren't pretty little ladies, with making money
with your body which is an act of love and I could
prove it, with howling because you're alive; with

God. How about that? WITH GOD WHO IS A COLORED QUEEN WHO WEARS A KIMONO AND PLUCKS HIS EYEBROWS, WHO IS A WOMAN WHO CRIES WITH DETERMINATION BEHIND HER CLOSED DOOR . . . with God who, I'm told, turned his back on the whole thing some time ago . . . with . . . some day, with people. [JERRY *sighs the next word heavily.*] People. With an idea; a concept. And where better, where ever better in this humiliating excuse for a jail, where better to communicate one single, simpleminded idea than in an entrance hall? Where? It would be A START! Where better to make a beginning . . . to understand and just possibly be understood . . . a beginning of an understanding, than with . . .

[*Here* JERRY *seems to fall into almost grotesque fatigue.*]

. . . than with A DOG. Just that; a dog.

[*Here there is a silence that might be prolonged for a moment or so; then* JERRY *wearily finishes his story.*]

A dog. It seemed like a perfectly sensible idea. Man is a dog's best friend, remember. So: the dog and I looked at each other. I longer than the dog. And what I saw then has been the same ever since. Whenever the dog and I see each other we both stop where we are. We regard each other with a mixture of sadness and suspicion, and then we feign indifference. We walk past each other safely; we have an understanding. It's very sad, but you'll have to admit that it is an understanding. We had made many attempts at contact, and we had failed. The dog has returned to garbage, and I to solitary but free passage. I have not returned. I mean to say, I have *gained* solitary free passage, if that much further loss can be said to be gain. I have learned that neither kindness nor cruelty by themselves, independent of each other, creates any effect beyond themselves; and I have learned that the two combined, together, at the same time, are the teaching emotion. And what is gained is loss. And what has been the result: the dog and I have attained a compromise; more of a bargain, really. We neither love nor hurt because we do not try to reach each other. And, *was* trying to feed the dog an act of love? And, perhaps, was the dog's attempt to bite me *not* an act of love? If we can so misunderstand, well then, why have we invented the word love in the first place?

[*There is silence.* JERRY *moves to* PETER's *bench and sits down beside him. This is the first time* JERRY *has sat down during the play.*]

The Story of Jerry and the Dog: the end.

[PETER *is silent.*]

Well, Peter? [JERRY *is suddenly cheerful.*] Well, Peter? Do you think I could sell that story to the *Reader's Digest* and make a couple of hundred bucks for *The Most Unforgettable Character I've Ever Met?* Huh?

[JERRY *is animated, but* PETER *is disturbed.*]

Oh, come on now, Peter; tell me what you think.

PETER [*numb*]. I . . . I don't understand what . . . I don't think I . . . [*Now, almost tearfully.*] Why did you tell me all of this?

JERRY. Why not?

PETER. I DON'T UNDERSTAND!

JERRY [*furious, but whispering*]. That's a lie.

PETER. No. No, it's not.

JERRY [*quietly*]. I tried to explain it to you as I went along. I went slowly; it all has to do with . . .

PETER. I DON'T WANT TO HEAR ANY MORE. I don't understand you, or your landlady, or her dog. . . .

JERRY. *Her* dog! I thought it was my . . . No. No, you're right. It *is* her dog. [*Looks at* PETER *intently, shaking his head.*] I don't know what I was thinking about;

of course you don't understand. [*In a monotone, wearily.*] I don't live in your block; I'm not married to two parakeets, or whatever your setup is. I am a *permanent transient,* and my home is the sickening roominghouses on the West Side of New York City, which is the greatest city in the world. Amen.

PETER. I'm . . . I'm sorry; I didn't mean to . . .

JERRY. Forget it. I suppose you don't quite know what to make of me, eh?

PETER [*a joke*]. We get all kinds in publishing. [*Chuckles.*]

JERRY. You're a funny man. [*He forces a laugh.*] You know that? You're a very . . . a richly comic person.

PETER [*modestly, but amused*]. Oh, now, not really. [*Still chuckling.*]

JERRY. Peter, do I annoy you, or confuse you?

PETER [*lightly*]. Well, I must confess that this wasn't the kind of afternoon I'd anticipated.

JERRY. You mean, I'm not the gentleman you were expecting.

PETER. I wasn't expecting anybody.

JERRY. No, I don't imagine you were. But I'm here, and I'm not leaving.

PETER [*consulting his watch*]. Well, you may not be, but I must be getting home soon.

JERRY. Oh, come on; stay a while longer.

PETER. I really should get home; you see . . .

JERRY [*tickles* PETER'S *ribs with his fingers*]. Oh, come on.

PETER [*he is very ticklish; as* JERRY *continues to tickle him his voice becomes falsetto*]. No, I . . . OHHHH! Don't do that. Stop, Stop. Ohhh, no, no.

JERRY. Oh, come on.

PETER [*as* JERRY *tickles*]. Oh, hee, hee, hee. I must go. I . . . hee, hee, hee. After all, stop, stop, hee, hee, hee, after all, the parakeets will be getting dinner ready soon. Hee, hee. And the cats are setting the table.

Stop, stop, and, and . . . [PETER *is beside himself now.*] . . . and we're having . . . hee, hee . . . uh . . . ho, ho, ho.

[JERRY *stops tickling* PETER, *but the combination of the tickling and his own mad whimsy has* PETER *laughing almost hysterically. As his laughter continues, then subsides,* JERRY *watches him, with a curious fixed smile.*]

JERRY. Peter?

PETER. Oh, ha, ha, ha, ha, ha. What? What?

JERRY. Listen, now.

PETER. Oh, ho, ho. What . . . what is it, Jerry? Oh, my.

JERRY [*mysteriously*]. Peter, do you want to know what happened at the zoo?

PETER. Ah, ha, ha. The what? Oh, yes; the zoo. Oh, ho, ho. Well, I had my own zoo there for a moment with . . . hee, hee, the parakeets getting dinner ready, and the . . . ha, ha, whatever it was, the . . .

JERRY [*calmly*]. Yes, that was very funny, Peter. I wouldn't have expected it. But do you want to hear about what happened at the zoo, or not?

PETER. Yes. Yes, by all means; tell me what happened at the zoo. Oh, my. I don't know what happened to me.

JERRY. Now I'll let you in on what happened at the zoo; but first, I should tell you why I went to the zoo. I went to the zoo to find out more about the way people exist with animals, and the way animals exist with each other, and with people too. It probably wasn't a fair test, what with everyone separated by bars from everyone else, the animals for the most part from each other, and always the people from the animals. But, if it's a zoo, that's the way it is. [*He pokes* PETER *on the arm.*] Move over.

PETER [*friendly*]. I'm sorry, haven't you enough room? [*He shifts a little.*]

JERRY [*smiling slightly*]. Well, all the animals are

there, and all the people are there, and it's Sunday and all the children are there. [*He pokes* PETER *again.*] Move over.

PETER [*patiently, still friendly*]. All right. [*He moves some more, and* JERRY *has all the room he might need.*]

JERRY. And it's a hot day, so all the stench is there, too, and all the balloon sellers, and all the ice cream sellers, and all the seals are barking, and all the birds are screaming. [*Pokes* PETER *harder.*] Move over!

PETER [*beginning to be annoyed*]. Look here, you have more than enough room! [*But he moves more, and is now fairly cramped at one end of the bench.*]

JERRY. And I am there, and it's feeding time at the lions' house, and the lion keeper comes into the lion cage, one of the lion cages, to feed one of the lions. [*Punches* PETER *on the arm, hard.*] MOVE OVER!

PETER [*very annoyed*]. I can't move over any more, and stop hitting me. What's the matter with you?

JERRY. Do you want to hear the story? [*Punches* PETER'S *arm again.*]

PETER [*flabbergasted*]. I'm not so sure! I certainly don't want to be punched in the arm.

JERRY [*punches* PETER'S *arm again*]. Like that?

PETER. Stop it! What's the matter with you?

JERRY. I'm crazy, you bastard.

PETER. That isn't funny.

JERRY. Listen to me, Peter. I want this bench. You go sit on the bench over there, and if you're good I'll tell you the rest of the story.

PETER [*flustered*]. But . . . whatever for? What *is* the matter with you? Besides, I see no reason why I should give up this bench. I sit on this bench almost every Sunday afternoon, in good weather. It's secluded here; there's never anyone sitting here, so I have it all to myself.

JERRY [*softly*]. Get off this bench, Peter; I want it.

PETER [*almost whining*]. No.

JERRY. I said I want this bench, and I'm going to have it. Now get over there.

PETER. People can't have everything they want. You should know that; it's a rule; people can have some of the things they want, but they can't have everything.

JERRY [*laughs*]. Imbecile! You're slow-witted!

PETER. Stop that!

JERRY. You're a vegetable! Go lie down on the ground.

PETER [*intense*]. Now *you* listen to me. I've put up with you all afternoon.

JERRY. Not really.

PETER. LONG ENOUGH. I've put up with you long enough. I've listened to you because you seemed . . . well, because I thought you wanted to talk to somebody.

JERRY. You put things well; economically, and, yet . . . oh, what is the word I want to put justice to your . . . JESUS, you make me sick . . . get off here and give me my bench.

PETER. MY BENCH!

JERRY [*pushes* PETER *almost, but not quite, off the bench*]. Get out of my sight.

PETER [*regaining his position*]. God da . . . mn you. That's enough! I've had enough of you. I will not give up this bench; you can't have it, and that's that. Now, go away. [JERRY *snorts but does not move.*] Go away, I said. [JERRY *does not move.*] Get away from here. If you don't move on . . . you're a bum . . . that's what you are. . . . If you don't move on, I'll get a policeman here and make you go. [JERRY *laughs, stays.*] I warn you, I'll call a policeman.

JERRY [*softly*]. You won't find a policeman around here; they're all over on the west side of the park chasing fairies down from trees or out of the bushes.

That's all they do. That's their function. So scream your head off; it won't do you any good.

PETER. POLICE! I warn you, I'll have you arrested. POLICE! [*Pause.*] I said POLICE! [*Pause.*] I feel ridiculous.

JERRY. You look ridiculous: a grown man screaming for the police on a bright Sunday afternoon in the park with nobody harming you. If a policeman *did* fill his quota and come sludging over this way he'd probably take you in as a nut.

PETER [*with disgust and impotence*]. Great God, I just came here to read, and now you want me to give up the bench. You're mad.

JERRY. Hey, I got news for you, as they say. I'm on your precious bench, and you're never going to have it for yourself again.

PETER [*furious*]. Look, you; get off my bench. I don't care if it makes any sense or not. I want this bench to myself; I want you OFF IT!

JERRY [*mocking*]. Aw . . . look who's mad.

PETER. GET OUT!

JERRY. No.

PETER. I WARN YOU!

JERRY. Do you know how ridiculous you look *now?*

PETER [*his fury and self-consciousness have possessed him*]. It doesn't matter. [*He is almost crying.*] GET AWAY FROM MY BENCH!

JERRY. Why? You have everything in the world you want; you've told me about your home, and your family, and *your own* little zoo. You have everything, and now you want this bench. Are these the things men fight for? Tell me, Peter, is this bench, this iron and this wood, is this your honor? Is this the thing in the world you'd fight for? Can you think of anything more absurd?

PETER. Absurd? Look, I'm not going to talk to you about honor, or even try to explain it to you. Besides, it isn't a question of honor; but even if it were, you wouldn't understand.

JERRY [*contemptuously*]. You don't even know what you're saying, do you? This is probably the first time in your life you've had anything more trying to face than changing your cats' toilet box. Stupid! Don't you have any idea, not even the slightest, what other people *need?*

PETER. Oh, boy, listen to you; well, you don't need this bench. That's for sure.

JERRY. Yes; yes, I do.

PETER [*quivering*]. I've come here for years; I have hours of great pleasure, great satisfaction, right here. And that's important to a man. I'm a responsible person, and I'm a GROWNUP. This is my bench, and you have no right to take it away from me.

JERRY. Fight for it, then. Defend yourself; defend your bench.

PETER. You've *pushed* me to it. Get up and fight.

JERRY. Like a man?

PETER [*still angry*]. Yes, like a man, if you insist on mocking me even further.

JERRY. I'll have to give you credit for one thing: you *are* a vegetable, and a slightly nearsighted one, I think . . .

PETER. THAT'S ENOUGH. . . .

JERRY. . . . but, you know, as they say on TV all the time—you know—and I mean this, Peter, you have a certain dignity; it surprises me. . . .

PETER. STOP!

JERRY [*rises lazily*]. Very well, Peter, we'll battle for the bench, but we're not evenly matched. [*He takes out and clicks open an ugly-looking knife.*]

PETER [*suddenly awakening to the reality of the situation*]. You *are* mad! You're stark raving mad! YOU'RE GOING TO KILL ME!

[*But before* PETER *has time to think what to do,* JERRY *tosses the knife at* PETER'S *feet.*]

JERRY. There you go. Pick it up. You have the knife and we'll be more evenly matched.

PETER [*horrified*]. No!

JERRY [*rushes over to* PETER, *grabs him by the collar;* PETER *rises; their faces almost touch*]. Now you pick up that knife and you fight with me. You fight for your self-respect; you fight for that goddamned bench.

PETER [*struggling*]. No! Let . . . let go of me! He . . . Help!

JERRY [*slaps* PETER *on each "fight"*]. You fight, you miserable bastard; fight for that bench; fight for your parakeets; fight for your cats, fight for your two daughters; fight for your wife; fight for your manhood, you pathetic little vegetable. [*Spits in* PETER'S *face.*] You couldn't even get your wife with a male child.

PETER [*breaks away, enraged*]. It's a matter of genetics, not manhood, you . . . you monster. [*He darts down, picks up the knife and backs off a little; he is breathing heavily.*] I'll give you one last chance; get out of here and leave me alone! [*He holds the knife with a firm arm, but far in front of him, not to attack, but to defend.*]

JERRY [*sighs heavily*]. So be it!

[*With a rush he charges* PETER *and impales himself on the knife. Tableau: For just a moment, complete silence,* JERRY *impaled on the knife at the end of* PETER'S *still firm arm. Then* PETER *screams, pulls away, leaving the knife in* JERRY. JERRY *is motionless, on point. Then he, too, screams, and it must be the sound of an infuriated and fatally wounded animal. With the knife in him, he stumbles back to the bench that* PETER *had vacated. He crumbles there, sitting, facing* PETER, *his eyes wide in agony, his mouth open.*]

PETER [*whispering*]. Oh my God, oh my God, oh my

God. . . . [*He repeats these words many times, very rapidly.*]

JERRY [JERRY *is dying; but now his expression seems to change. His features relax, and while his voice varies, sometimes wrenched with pain, for the most part he seems removed from his dying. He smiles*]. Thank you, Peter. I mean that, now; thank you very much. [PETER'S *mouth drops open. He cannot move; he is transfixed.*] Oh, Peter, I was so afraid I'd drive you away. [*He laughs as best he can.*] You don't know how afraid I was you'd go away and leave me. And now I'll tell you what happened at the zoo. I think . . . I think this is what happened at the zoo . . . I think. I think that while I was at the zoo I decided that I would walk north . . . northerly, rather . . . until I found you . . . or somebody . . . and I decided that I would talk to you . . . I would tell you things . . . and things that I would tell you would . . . Well, here we are. You see? Here we *are*. But . . . I don't . . . could I have planned all this? No . . . no, I couldn't have. But I think I did. And now I've told you what you wanted to know, haven't I? And now you know all about what happened at the zoo. And now you know what you'll see in your TV, and the face I told you about . . . you remember . . . the face I told you about . . . my face, the face you see right now. Peter . . . Peter? . . . Peter . . . thank you. I came unto you [*He laughs, so faintly.*] and you have comforted me. Dear Peter.

PETER [*almost fainting*]. Oh my God!

JERRY. You'd better go now. Somebody might come by, and you don't want to be here when anyone comes.

PETER [*does not move, but begins to weep*]. Oh my God, oh my God.

JERRY [*most faintly, now; he is very near death*]. You won't be coming back here any more, Peter; you've been dispossessed. You've lost your bench, but you've defended your honor. And Peter, I'll tell you something now; you're not really a vegetable; it's all right, you're an animal. You're an animal, too. But you'd better hurry now, Peter. Hurry, you'd better go . . . see? [JERRY *takes a handkerchief and with great effort and pain wipes the knife handle clean of fingerprints.*] Hurry away, Peter. [PETER *begins to stagger away.*] Wait . . . wait, Peter. Take your book . . . book. Right here . . . beside me . . . on your bench . . . my bench, rather. Come . . . take your book. [PETER *starts for the book, but retreats.*] Hurry . . . Peter. [PETER *rushes to the bench, grabs the book, retreats.*] Very good, Peter . . . very good. Now . . . hurry away. [PETER *hesitates for a moment, then flees, stage-left.*] Hurry away. . . . [*His eyes are closed now.*] Hurry away, your parakeets are making the dinner . . . the cats . . . are setting the table . . .

PETER [*off stage, a pitiful howl*]. OH MY GOD!

JERRY [*his eyes still closed, he shakes his head and speaks; a combination of scornful mimicry and supplication*]. Oh . . . my . . . God.

[*He is dead.*]

CURTAIN